A Multilateral Tax Treaty

Series on International Taxation

VOLUME 64

Series Editors

Prof. Ruth Mason, University of Virginia School of Law
Prof. Dr Ekkehart Reimer, University of Heidelberg

Introduction & Contents

The Series on International Taxation deals with a wide variety of topics in the global tax arena. The authors include many of the field's leading experts as well as talented newcomers. Their expert views and incisive commentary have proven highly useful to practitioners and academics alike.

Objective

The volumes published in this series are aimed at offering high-quality analytical information and practical solutions to international tax practitioners.

Readership

Practitioners, academics and policy makers in international tax law.

Frequency of Publication

2-3 new volumes published each year.

The titles published in this series are listed at the end of this volume.

A Multilateral Tax Treaty

Designing an Instrument to Modernise International Tax Law

D.M. Broekhuijsen

 Wolters Kluwer

Published by:
Kluwer Law International B.V.
PO Box 316
2400 AH Alphen aan den Rijn
The Netherlands
E-mail: international-sales@wolterskluwer.com
Website: lrus.wolterskluwer.com

Sold and distributed in North, Central and South America by:
Wolters Kluwer Legal & Regulatory U.S.
7201 McKinney Circle
Frederick, MD 21704
United States of America
Email: customer.service@wolterskluwer.com

Sold and distributed in all other countries by:
Air Business Subscriptions
Rockwood House
Haywards Heath
West Sussex
RH16 3DH
United Kingdom
Email: international-customerservice@wolterskluwer.com

ISBN 978-90-411-9872-3

e-Book: ISBN 978-90-411-9873-0
web-PDF: ISBN 978-90-411-9848-8

Table of Contents

Preface

When I started writing this book, which is based on my PhD thesis, I did not think that a multilateral tax treaty would ever be achievable. I set out in 2011 with the firm belief my research would involve a utopia, a pie in the sky. Luckily, recent developments proved me wrong. In fact, the OECD's Base Erosion and Profit Shifting (BEPS) Project got so much traction that the text of the Multilateral Instrument, used to implement the BEPS Project's outcomes in the bilateral tax treaty network, was released several hours after I submitted my manuscript for review.

This development, fortunately, presented opportunities rather than challenges. The book's core arguments have become increasingly relevant in the light of the recent signature of the Multilateral Instrument. A lot can be said about the Multilateral Instrument's operation, its complex flexibility system and the way its 'compatibility clauses' work. I did not avoid addressing these issues. However, I have always found the more fundamental questions more intriguing. What may be expected of current (and future) multilateral tax agreements? What should multilateral tax cooperation bring? Now it is clear that that multilateral agreement is possible in the area of international taxation, such questions have only become more compelling. I hope this book provides a good first attempt to answer these, and similar, queries.

Writing about a utopia turned reality necessitates an inspiring working atmosphere and scrupulous yet supportive colleagues. In this respect, I am greatly indebted to my colleagues at Leiden University's Institute for Tax Law and Economics. Specifically, I would like to thank my supervisors, Prof. Frank Engelen and Prof. Sjoerd Douma, as well as my former 'bosses', Prof. Allard Lubbers and Prof. Koos Boer. In addition, I would like to thank Prof. Henk Vording and Dr Jan Vleggeert for their ceaseless feedback and suggestions. My thanks also go to Prof. Allison Christians, Prof. Ekkehart Reimer, Prof. Frank Pötgens, Dr Niels van Willigen and Prof. Tanja Bender for reviewing and discussing my work. I would also like to thank the faculty and staff of the Institute for Austrian and International Tax Law of the Wirtschaftsuniverstät Wien for my inspiring research stay there. Finally, my thanks go to my roommates, Koen and Netty, for working in my presence, and to my paranymphs, Tirza and Sean, for being present when I was working.

Most essential, however, have been my dear friends and my family. My special thanks go to my parents, sister and two brothers, and, most especially, to you, Yvette.

D.M. Broekhuijsen
February 2018

List of Abbreviations

ACE	Allowance for Corporate Equity
BC	BEPS Convention
BEPS	Base Erosion and Profit Shifting
BEPS Convention or BC	Multilateral Convention to Implement Tax Treaty Related Measures to Prevent Base Erosion and Profit Shifting
BRICS	Brazil, Russia, India, China, South Africa
CCCTB	Common Consolidated Corporate Tax Base
CFA	Committee on Fiscal Affairs (of the OECD)
Ch.	Chapter
COP	Conference of the Parties
CPB	Centraal Planburea (Netherlands Bureau for Economic Policy Analysis)
EBITDA	Earnings Before Interest, Taxes, Depreciation and Amortization
ECHR	European Convention on Human Rights
ECJ	European Court of Justice
ECtHR	European Court of Human Rights
EU	European Union
FDI	Foreign Direct Investment
GAAR	General Anti-avoidance Rule
GATT	General Agreement on Tariffs and Trade
IAEA	International Atomic Energy Agency
IBFD	International Bureau for Fiscal Documentation
ICAO	International Civil Aviation Organization
ICJ	International Court of Justice

ICRW	International Convention for the Regulation of Whaling
ILC	International Law Commission
IMF	International Monetary Fund
IMO	International Maritime Organization
IO	International Organisation
IPCC	International Panel on Climate Change
ITC	International Tax Center Leiden
IWC	International Whaling Commission
LOB	Limitation on Benefits
MNE	Multinational Enterprise
NAFO	Northwest Atlantic Fisheries Organization
NAFTA	North American Free Trade Agreement
NATO Treaty	North Atlantic Treaty
NGO	Non-governmental Organisation
OECD	Organization for Economic Co-operation and Development
OECD MTC	OECD Model Tax Convention
OEEC	Organization for European Economic Cooperation
OUP	Oxford University Press
para.	Paragraph
PCIJ	Permanent Court of International Justice
PE	Permanent Establishment
PPT	Principal Purpose Test
Sec.	Section
SSRN	Social Science Research Network
TFEU	Treaty on the Functioning of the European Union
UN	United Nations
UNFCCC	UN Framework Convention on Climate Change
UNHCR	UN High Commissioner for Refugees
UNTS	United Nations Treaty Service
VCLT	Vienna Convention on the Law of Treaties
WHO	World Health Organization
WTO	World Trade Organization

CHAPTER 1
Introduction

Globalisation has changed the way businesses do business. The importance of electronic commerce and intangibles has risen, and non-governmental organisations (NGOs) are underscoring that the current international tax regime works to the detriment of developing countries. Low effective tax burdens on multinationals' profits make for newspaper headlines.

Generally, the globalisation hypothesis runs thus. Capital is global, but governments are local and divided. Absent a level playing field or further integrative cooperation, governments have no other choice but to compete to attract investors, for example, by lowering corporate tax burdens or by relaxing regulation. The globalising nature of the economy constrains the ability of governments to pursue preferred social policies. So:

> while cooperative action is collectively rational, in the absence of a coordinating coercive authority, and in the absence of trust between jurisdictional units (which would enable them to coordinate their actions), there is a temptation to engage in individually rational competition, to protect one's national producers. But the end result of that 'game' is a collectively irrational, non-optimal state of affairs where people in society experience fewer (labour, safety, and environmental) protections and lower wages; and the state as a whole finds its capacity to raise revenue, through taxing multinational corporations, much reduced.[1]

Where circumstances have indeed been changing, the norms of the international tax system itself have not. The network of bilateral tax treaties is extensive and hard to adjust to changing circumstances. Under the influence of globalisation, international tax law has become a series of unrelieved collective action problems related to the

---

1. M. Moore, *Globalization and Democratization: Institutional Design for Global Institutions*, 37 Journal of Social Philosophy 21 (2006).

issues of tax competition and tax arbitrage, particular in respect of the taxation of multinational enterprises (MNEs).[2] It has, in simple terms, become outdated.[3]

For this reason, many states have set out to develop a multilateral instrument with the purpose of amending bilateral treaties in a quicker and more comprehensive fashion. Indeed, as much as 100 jurisdictions have participated in the ad-hoc group on the implementation of the Base Erosion and Profit Shifting (BEPS) Project,[4] leading to the recent adoption of the text of the Multilateral Convention to Implement Tax Treaty Related Measures to Prevent Base Erosion and Profit Shifting (hereinafter: 'BEPS Convention').[5]

First and foremost, the main purpose of this instrument is the coordinated and consistent implementation of the output of the BEPS Project. Indeed, the BEPS Project requires a number of changes to the bilateral tax treaty network. Amendments are needed on points such as hybrid mismatch arrangements (Action 2), treaty shopping (Action 6), the permanent establishment (PE) threshold (Action 7) and dispute resolution (Action 14). As renegotiating each and every bilateral tax treaty would take decades, this could jeopardise the Project: political momentum might be lost. The multilateral agreement could provide a solution: it would 'modify a limited number of provisions common to most existing bilateral treaties, and would, for those treaties that do not already have such provisions, add new provisions specifically designed to counter BEPS'.[6]

Second, under the current loose type of coordination by means of the OECD Model Tax Convention (hereinafter: OECD MTC) and its Commentaries, states are free to modify on or to postpone the implementation of new standards in their bilateral treaty relations. By agreeing with new guidelines, states show a basic willingness to move in the same direction. But many, if not all, of the current solutions needed to tackle BEPS require coordinated responses. A country will only move if the others do too. Again, the multilateral agreement is key: a level playing field established by a multilateral agreement enables parties to coordinate on their policy directions.

That the text of the multilateral convention to implement the BEPS outcomes has been agreed upon, can be called an impressive achievement. But zooming out from the efforts of the BEPS Project, reactions to collective action problems are also likely to be necessary in the future, stressing the need for a structural, rather than an ad-hoc, multilateral solution for international tax. The BEPS Project has, so to speak, merely

---

2. *See*, for this term, A. Christians et al., *Taxation as a Global Socio-Legal Phenomenon*, 14 ILSA Journal of International and Comparative Law 304 (2007), available at SSRN: http://papers.ssrn.com/sol3/papers.cfm?abstract_id = 1088455, p. 304.
3. OECD, *Action Plan on Base Erosion and Profit Shifting* (2013) OECD Publishing, http://www.oecd.org/ctp/BEPSActionPlan.pdf, p. 73; C. Peters, *On the Legitimacy of International Tax Law* (IBFD 2014).
4. At http://www.oecd.org/tax/treaties/work-underway-for-the-development-of-the-beps-multilateral-instrument.htm.
5. *Multilateral Convention to Implement Tax Treaty Related Measures to Prevent Base Erosion and Profit Shifting*, OECD, available at http://www.oecd.org/tax/treaties/multilateral-convention-to-implement-tax-treaty-related-measures-to-prevent-BEPS.pdf.
6. OECD, *Developing a Multilateral Instrument to Modify Bilateral Tax Treaties* (2014) OECD/G20 Base Erosion and Profit Shifting Project, http://dx.doi.org/10.1787/9789264219250-en pp. 17–18.

unveiled the problems related to amending and coordinating on bilateral tax relationships. A more fundamental reconsideration is, in the words of the Organization for
Economic Co-operation and Development (OECD), 'necessary not only to tackle BEPS,
but also to ensure the sustainability of the consensual framework to eliminate double
taxation'.[7] The benefits of a structural multilateral solution would allow policy makers
to continuously adapt and respond to the 'rapidly evolving nature of the global
economy'.[8]

Yet, the outlook for full-fledged universal multilateralism is bleak: international
law is often no panacea, as it is, at the end of the day, characterised by anarchy and
without higher authority. Ultimately, the enactment of international rules depends on
the joint consent of sovereign states, which are materially different from one another.
In fact, there are only a few multilateral treaties that enjoy widespread (if not universal)
ratification; most multilateral treaties fail to attract universal support,[9] and big contemporary problems of international cooperation, like global warming, prove very hard
to solve.[10] In addition, states almost never agree to centralised international enforcement mechanisms, and rely on self-enforcement instead.[11] What actually can be
achieved in international cooperation is, in other words, limited.

Hence, the question arises: *how to design a multilateral agreement for international taxation that fundamentally transforms the way states cooperate in the field of
international tax* (hereinafter: 'the multilateral agreement for international taxation' or
'the multilateral agreement')? The answer to this question is relevant: it helps us
understand what international policy makers need to work towards. What may be
expected of a multilateral agreement? In this regard, the purpose of this research
transcends the matter of implementing the outcomes of the BEPS Project. Implementing the BEPS Project is important, but unlikely the last international tax policy project
for which changes to bilateral tax treaties will be required. Nevertheless, the BEPS
Convention does provide a great acid test for the research's outcomes.

---

7. *Id.*, at p. 9; OECD, *Developing a Multilateral Instrument to Modify Bilateral Tax Treaties, Action
   15: 2015 Final Report* (2015) OECD/G20 Base Erosion and Profit Shifting Project, OECD
   Publishing, Paris. http://dx.doi.org/10.1787/9789264241688-en, p. 9 (emphasis added).
8. OECD, *BEPS Action Plan (2013)* p. 24.
9. *See* G. Blum, *Bilateralism, Multilateralism, and the Architecture of International Law*, 49
   Harvard International Law Journal 323, 335 (2008).
10. *See*, for such scepticism, J.L. Goldsmith and E.A. Posner, *The Limits of International Law* (OUP
    2005).
11. From a political perspective: R.O. Keohane and J.S.J. Nye, *Power and Interdependence*
    (Longman 3d ed., 1989) p. 295: 'Centralized enforcement of rules in international regimes
    through hierarchical arrangement is normally out of the question: There is no police force and
    only a tiny international bureaucracy. If states are to comply with regime rules, they must do
    so on the basis of long-term self-interest.' And a lawyers' perspective: F. Mégret, *International
    Law as Law*, in: The Cambridge Companion to International Law (J. Crawford and M.
    Koskenniemi eds, Cambridge University Press 2012) p. 71: 'The international legal system has
    traditionally had little enforcement capability in the form, for example, of an international
    executive. This fundamental weakness of international law is all too well known.'

So, the research questions addressed in this book are:

(I) What are the problems related to the non-binding and loose form of multilateral tax cooperation practiced by the OECD (Chapter 3)?

(II) What should multilateral tax cooperation ideally look like (Chapter 4)?

(III) What can realistically be achieved in multilateral tax cooperation (Chapter 5)?

(IV) What strategy should be employed to design a multilateral agreement for international taxation that fundamentally and structurally transforms the way states coordinate their international tax relations (Chapter 6)?

(V) How should a multilateral agreement for international taxation be designed (Chapter 7)?

(VI) How should, in the light of the answers to questions IV and V, the Multilateral Convention to Implement Tax Treaty Related Measures to Prevent Base Erosion and Profit Shifting be evaluated (Chapter 8)?

Chapters 2 and 3 introduce the thinking about the type of multilateral agreement discussed in this book. First, Chapter 2 analyses earlier efforts for multilateral international tax rules in the period of about 1920 until 1992. Chapter 3 assesses current multilateral coordination in international tax law, which takes place in the form of the OECD MTC and its Commentaries. What follows from the analysis in both chapters, is that a multilateral agreement for international taxation should not completely replace the bilateral tax treaty network currently in force. Rather, the potential of a multilateral agreement is to solve the issues related to the implementation of new norms in the network of bilateral tax treaties, and to create a level playing field, so that cooperation between states can converge on solutions for collective action problems.

But this understanding provides little insight in what a multilateral agreement *can and should look like*. For this reason, Chapters 4 and 5 build two views on multilateral cooperation in international taxation, providing the footing for a design strategy for a multilateral agreement set forth in Chapter 6. The first view, set forth in Chapter 4, uses political philosophy to construct a normative view on how states can ensure that international tax law is 'fair' and sustainable in the future. Chapter 5, on the other hand, explores the limits of multilateral cooperation in the area of international taxation from a 'realistic' perspective. A multilateral agreement is not easily agreed upon. Indeed, what a multilateral agreement would do, is shift the balance between multilateral agreement and national autonomy, and upset the equilibria struck in tax treaties. To get some grip on this matter, Chapter 5 explains international cooperation in international tax matters through the lens of liberal thought, regarding states as self-interested, rational and calculating actors, that enter into either multilateral or bilateral structures depending on expected gains. From this point of view, cooperation is seen as 'instrumental', in that international rules perform valuable functions for states that are looking to maximise (or protect) their interests. States accept rules that they favour, and free ride or renege when rules diverge from their needs. Chapter 6 then combines the normative and instrumental optics of Chapters 4 and 5 into a design strategy for a multilateral agreement for international taxation by means of which states can structurally address collective action problems of international taxation as well as swiftly implement cooperation outcomes in their bilateral relations.

Chapter 7 then offers a number of international public law mechanisms by means of which the multilateral agreement for international taxation should be designed, illustrating the book's core arguments.

Chapters 1–7 were – ostensibly – finished on 24 November 2016, three hours before the text of the BEPS Convention was released by the OECD. Nevertheless, an additional chapter was added, in which the BEPS Convention was evaluated against the findings presented in the book. This evaluation, set forth in Chapter 8, does however not engage in any 'new' research on the topic nor deals with questions not previously covered by Chapters 1–7. In adding Chapter 8 to this book, Chapters 1–7 were largely left unaltered.

As follows from this short overview, the book's core arguments are indebted to viewpoints from the fields of international relations and political science. As an international tax lawyer, the author has drawn inspiration from these fields in drafting the two main criteria – principled and pragmatic – of the framework set forth in Chapters 4–6. In this regard, the approach taken is fundamentally different from that of the 'traditional' legal scholar, whose research activities relate to positive (international tax) law and its sources. To him or her, international tax law's legal sources are a given.[12] When this work was started in 2011, however, the OECD BEPS Project had not yet begun. It was therefore necessary to use an external perspective to explain and envisage the problem structure and possible objectives of a multilateral agreement for international taxation.

The book's normative framework therefore reflects a central concern: it seeks to confront multilateral cooperation in international taxation without losing touch with reality. For this reason, the normative framework includes a normative or 'idealist' (Chapter 4) as well as a pragmatic or 'realist' (Chapter 5) view on multilateral cooperation in international taxation, ultimately resulting in the position taken in Chapter 6.[13] Perhaps as a result of the central concern, the author has continuously had the feeling of moving in parallel with the cooperative outcomes of the BEPS Project (*see* further Chapter 8).

Chapter 4's normative view is important: it should not be forgotten that international law, created *for* and *by* states, can allow and legitimise *any* type of state behaviour – i.e., of any state (or group of states) that finds itself in a position of power.

---

12. S.C.W. Douma, *Legal Research in International and EU Tax Law* (Kluwer 2014) p. 18.
13. For the different perspectives of Chs 4 and 5, the author was inspired by the distinction between international law and international relations set out by R.O. Keohane, *International Relations and International Law: Two Optics*, in: Power and Governance in a Partially Globalized World (R.O. Keohane ed., Routledge 2002). Keohane argues that international law provides a 'normative' optic, which is about the legitimacy and fairness of the way international law is created, whereas international relations perspective provides an 'instrumentalist' optic, which explains state cooperation on the basis of self-interests.

Consequently, Chapter 4's analytical starting point is a cosmopolitan take on procedural fairness, permitting a normative consideration of multilateralism in an anarchical world. But a normative view on cooperation in international taxation *alone* would potentially overestimate what multilateral agreements can realistically do. This would have made the view vulnerable to the critique that it fails to reflect actual cooperative outcomes. Hence Chapter 5's focus on states' self-interests, which attempts to explain – and predict – 'realistic' outcomes of multilateral cooperation in the field of international taxation.[14]

The decision to use an external perspective helped shape other methodological choices as well. First of all, to achieve a higher degree of abstraction, it has sometimes been necessary to depart from existing paradigms, such as the idea that bilateral tax treaties only *allocate* taxing rights between jurisdictions. Moreover, considerations about amendments to (domestic) tax systems could not be fully avoided. The OECD in the BEPS Project clearly distinguishes between multilateral measures that will require tax treaty amendments and multilateral measures that require amendments to domestic law.[15] The same distinction is not meticulously observed in this book. Chapter 5's view on multilateral cooperation, for instance, which explains as much as possible with as little as possible, may also be applied to policy considerations concerning domestic law.[16] Furthermore, the relationship between a worldwide multilateral agreement and the efforts of harmonising corporate income taxation within the European Union (EU) has not been considered.[17] Finally, the author has been inspired

---

14. Presenting the 'idealist' and 'realist' perspectives of Chs 4 and 5 as direct opposites is, strictly speaking, not accurate. The 'idealist' view presented in Ch. 4 relies on some 'realism' to show it is not too far removed from what actually exists in the real world (for instance, reference is made to states' intentions underlying the BEPS Project). Vice versa, the 'realist' view of Ch. 5 is rooted in 'idealist' conceptions of social reality (it, for instance, builds on assumptions related to contracting under uncertainty). Nevertheless, Chs 4 and 5 have different analytical points of departure ('fairness' versus 'state interests') and even though more fluid than presented, both positions serve to end up in Ch. 6's intermediate position, anyway. In any case, the inevitable reliance of 'idealist' views on 'realist' arguments, and vice versa, is structural to international legal scholarship, as M. Koskenniemi, *From Apology to Utopia: the Structure of International Legal Argument* (Cambridge University Press Reissued ed., 2005) has argued.

15. Domestic law changes are, for example, needed in relation to BEPS Actions 2–5. The OECD aims to proceed on the basis of an 'implementation framework' to implement the Project's outcomes.

16. The author does recognise that explaining necessary amendments to domestic law might require a more complex political view on state cooperation than the one build up in Ch. 5. In Ch. 5, the author conceives states to interact as unitary actors, i.e., as 'black boxes'. A more complex, two-level model would have the benefit to 'open up the black box', i.e., to take into account domestic politics too. *See, e.g.*, R.D. Putnam, *Diplomacy and Domestic Politics: The Logic of Two-Level Games*, 42 International Organization 427 (1988). *See* further for a discussion, D. Beach, *Analyzing Foreign Policy* (Palgrave Macmillan 2012) pp. 47–57.

17. The competence on direct taxation is with the EU Member States: the EU Treaties hence do not prevent Member States to conclude an external multilateral tax treaty (*see* Art. 216 of the Treaty on the Functioning of the EU), as long as norms concluded are consistent with EU law.
    Nevertheless, the implementation of an anti-avoidance directive (which concerns amendments to domestic law) might have legal consequences as regards the possibility of Member States to enter into a worldwide agreement on the same issues individually. Art. 216 TFEU holds that 'the Union may conclude an agreement with one or more third countries where (...) the conclusion of an agreement (...) is likely to affect common rules or alter their scope'. This rule codifies the ERTA doctrine (as in ECJ, *Commission v. Council*, 31 Mar. 1971, C 33/70 (ERTA)), in which the ECJ held in paras 17 and 18: 'each time the Community, with a view to

by the BEPS Project in providing examples and points for discussion; hence the emphasis on collective action problems of corporate income tax. The book's conclusions, however, also hold for collective action problems of international tax law, unrelated to the BEPS Project.

implementing a common policy envisaged by the Treaty, adopts provisions laying down common rules, whatever form these may take, the Member States no longer have the right, acting individually or even collectively, to undertake obligations with third countries which affect those rules (...). As and when such common rules come into being, the Community alone is in a position to assume and carry out contractual obligations towards third countries affecting the whole sphere of application of the Community legal system.' As the worldwide multilateral implementation of the BEPS Project could undermine the collective efforts within the EU, the ERTA doctrine may be applicable in relation to the issues that the anti-abuse directive covers.

CHAPTER 2

Efforts for Multilateral International Tax Rules: 1920–1992

2.1 INTRODUCTION

It is not the first time that the aspiration for a multilateral agreement for international taxation has arisen. There were efforts for what used to be called a 'multilateral tax treaty' in the period preceding the 1963 OECD MTC: that of 1920–1960, and in particular in the interwar period of 1920–1939.[18] Also, an effort was made in the late 1950s. This 'old' or 'comprehensive' style multilateral tax treaty would have included substantive international tax rules and would be able to completely replace or supplant the bilateral tax treaty network,[19] solving the issue of double taxation in a

---

18. Today's system is 'largely a creature' of the interwar period of 1920–1939: M.J. Graetz, *The David R. Tillinghast Lecture: Taxing International Income – Inadequate Principles, Outdated Concepts, and Unsatisfactory Policy*, 54 Tax Law Review 261 (2001). *See also* M.J. Graetz and M.M. O'Hear, *The 'Original Intent' of U.S. International Taxation*, 51 Duke Law Journal 1021, 1023 (1997).

19. K. Brooks, *The Potential of Multilateral Tax Treaties*, in: Tax Treaties: Building Bridges between Law and Economics (M. Lang et al., eds, IBFD 2010) provides a synopsis of the different uses of the 'comprehensive' multilateral tax convention; *see* especially the footnote 25 at p. 219. A thorough evaluation of the concept is provided by M. Lang ed., *Multilateral Tax Treaties: New Developments in International Tax Law* (Kluwer Law International 1998). Also of interest is V. Thuronyi, *International Tax Cooperation and a Multilateral Treaty*, 26 Brooklyn Journal of International Law 1641, 1675–1680 (2000), who further develops and refines the approach of a comprehensive multilateral tax treaty, considering that it would require the constitution of an international organisation to be administered. The bilateral tax treaty network could simply 'phase out' during a transition period.

   A comprehensive multilateral agreement would have many benefits. Apart from the advantage that it would facilitate the amendment of international tax rules, the agreement would also be able to deal with triangular cases, facilitate treaty interpretation and improve legal certainty. H. Loukota, *Multilateral Tax Treaty Versus Bilateral Tax Treaty Network*, in: Multilateral Tax Treaties (M. Lang ed., Kluwer Law International 1998) pp. 90–91.

comprehensive, multilateral way. It would have had the benefits of providing uniform interpretations of tax treaty law, solving triangular cases, deal with problems such as set out in the partnership report,[20] etc.[21]

But what in fact developed over the course of the twentieth century was a sort of second-best solution to solving double taxation: a system of bilateral tax treaties, loosely coordinated on by a non-binding multilateral instrument: the OECD MTC and its Commentary. Where only in the 1990s the OECD explicitly abandoned the goal of concluding a 'comprehensive' multilateral tax treaty, the bilateral tax treaty, patterned on a non-binding model tax convention, became increasingly successful and popular.

Why did the efforts for an 'old' style multilateral tax treaty fail, and did the network of bilateral tax treaties develop in its stead? As we will see, the question sets the stage for all further discussions about a multilateral agreement for international taxation in the rest of the book.

2.2 AN ANALYSIS OF EARLIER EFFORTS FOR MULTILATERAL AGREEMENT IN THE AREA OF INTERNATIONAL TAXATION

2.2.1 1920–1943: The Founding Period of International Tax Law

At the start of the work of the League of Nations on the avoidance of double taxation in the beginning of 1920, the idea was to come to a coordinated multilateral solution to double taxation. Indeed, the League of Nations Fiscal Committee's initial objective was to draft a multilateral tax treaty by which tax jurisdiction would be allocated.[22] Although the efforts were aimed at concluding a 'comprehensive' multilateral tax treaty, and not at a multilateral tax treaty to amend bilateral tax treaties, it is worth examining these efforts here.

The efforts to conclude a multilateral tax treaty were dropped primarily due to disagreements on the formulation of a general principle to allocate tax jurisdiction, i.e., on the primacy of source or residence, which determined obvious winners and losers particularly for the division of tax jurisdiction over mobile capital, such as interests and dividends. In the words of Carroll:

> [T]he discussions had revealed that [the adoption of a plurilateral convention] was hardly tenable in regard to certain classes of income, notably interest and dividends, because of the conflicts in opinions and methods of taxation.[23]

---

20. OECD, *The Application of the OECD Model Tax Convention to Partnerships* (1999) OECD, Issues in International Taxation No. 6.
21. *See, e.g.*, H. Loukota (1998); V. Thuronyi (2000) and a reaction to that work by D.M. Ring, *Prospects for a Multilateral Tax Treaty*, 26 Brooklyn Journal of International Law 1699 (2000).
22. T. Rixen, *Bilateralism or Multilateralism? The Political Economy of Avoiding International Double Taxation*, 16 European Journal of International Relations 589, 591 (2010).
23. M.B. Carroll, *Prevention of International Double Taxation and Fiscal Evasion: Two Decades of Progress under the League of Nations* (League of Nations 1939) p. 33.

And according to T.S. Adams, the key US Treasury tax advisor at that time, the different opinions regarding the taxation of interest and dividends prevented the adoption of a multilateral, uniform solution:

> Now, here is the point which interests me profoundly: on practically every subject except the taxation of bond interests and dividends from shares, they [the governmental experts] have come to a virtual unanimity of opinion. Income arises in hundreds of forms; compensation for personal service, rent of all types; interest of all kinds, annuities; royalties; pensions; gains and profits from hundreds of distinct trades, professions and businesses. The treatment of all these classes of income has been discussed and debated at length, from the standpoints of a score of different countries with divergent interests and different methods of administering the income tax. And as I have said, the experts have ended by endorsing three model conventions which in form and appearance are very different. But in substance they differ, practically, on nothing except the taxation of income from transferable securities. This agreement has been reached unconsciously almost.[24]

Graetz and O'Hear describe the actions of Adams as follows:

> [A]fter the League process generated substantial consensus on allocation rules except for those governing interest and dividends, Adams urged the nations of the world to sign a multilateral agreement institutionalizing all of the consensus rules, but leaving interest and dividends for another day.[25]

Being unable to unite the source-residence differences among states in relation to dividends and interests in a multilateral convention, bilateral treaties were therefore the only outcome by which the different opinions regarding source and residence could be reconciled.[26] Indeed, in 1927, the impasse led to a conclusion of the League of Nations Committee of Technical Experts, which is worth reproducing here in full:

> It would certainly be desirable that the States should conclude collective conventions, or even a single convention embodying all the others. Nevertheless, the Committee did not feel justified in recommending the adoption of this course. In the matter of double taxation in particular, the fiscal systems of the various countries are so fundamentally different that it seems at present practically impossible to draft a collective convention, unless it were worded in such general terms as to be of no practical value. In the matter of tax evasion also, although

---

24. T.S. Adams, *International and Interstate Aspects of Double Taxation*, 22 National Tax Association Proceedings 193, 196 (1929).

25. M.J. Graetz and M.M. O'Hear (1997) pp. 1096–1097.

26. M.B. Carroll (1939) p. 35. It is noteworthy that one multilateral treaty, the 1922 Treaty of Rome, was signed by multiple states but was eventually only ratified by Italy and Austria. *See* O. Bühler, *Prinzipien des internationalen Steuerrechts IStR: ein systematischer Versuch* (IBFD 1964) p. 50: 'Bemerkenswert ist hier u.a. der Anlauf zu einem Kollektivabkommen über die direkten Steuern zwischen den Nachfolgestaaten der österreichisch-ungarischen Doppelmonarchie (Österreich, Ungarn, Italien, Polen, Rumänien, Jugoslawien von 1922, das aber in der Durchführung scheiterte. Das DBAbk Deutschland-italien von 1925 brachten als erstes eine systematische Durcharbeitung des Typs eines Abkommens mit *Freistellungs- und Aufteilungsprinzip* namentlich für die gewerblichen Einkünfte; nach dem Modell dieses Vertrages wurden in den folgenden 13 Jahren der Zwischenkriegszeit etwa 30 Verträge zwischen kontinental-europäischen Staaten abgeschlossen.' Also, P. Verloren Van Themaat, *Internationaal belastingrecht: Een studie naar aanleiding van literatuur en verdragen over de uitschakeling van dubbele belasting* (H.J. Paris Amsterdam 1946) p. 41.

unanimity would not seem to be unattainable, there is no doubt that the accession of all countries to a single Convention could only be obtained as the result of prolonged and delicate negotiations, while there is no reason to delay the putting into force of bilateral conventions which would immediately satisfy the legitimate interests of the tax-payers as well as those of the Contracting States.

For this reason, the Committee preferred to draw up standard bilateral conventions. If these texts are used by Governments in concluding such conventions, a certain measure of uniformity will be introduced in international fiscal law and, at a later stage of that law, a system of general conventions may be established which will make possible the unification and codification of the rules previously laid down.[27]

Despite the fact that the Technical Experts had concluded in 1927 that adopting a multilateral convention was hardly tenable due to differences between source and residence states, the aim to achieving a multilateral tax convention within the League of Nations was not dropped.

Between 1929–1935, again efforts were made to draft multilateral tax conventions. However, these efforts were undertaken at a time when the bilateral tax convention became increasingly popular in solving the problem of double taxation in Europe, whilst political tension was on the rise or already existed.

Indeed, between 1929 and 1935, the League of Nations Fiscal Committee, urged by the resolution taken by the International Chamber of Commerce at its 1929 Amsterdam Congress,[28] again undertook an endeavour to conclude a collective tax convention. In its first three meetings, it looked into the possibility of 'framing plurilateral conventions for the Avoidance of Double Taxation of Certain Categories of Income'. To this end, a subcommittee was formed, which was instructed to submit a draft plurilateral convention based on four proposals by the Fiscal Committee. Each of these proposals dealt with very specific items of income, such as authors' royalties or rights, interest on public debt, annuities (proposal 1), the salaries of officials and public employees (proposal 2), immovable property (proposal 3), and, interestingly, the profits of an enterprise with a PE (proposal 4).[29] The Fiscal Committee considered that proposals on these items might be adopted by a considerable number of states, if carefully formulated.

---

27. League of Nations, *Double Taxation and Tax Evasion. Report Presented by the Committee of Technical Experts on Double Taxation and Tax Evasion* (1927) C. 216. M 85. 1927 II, p. 8. The same ideas can be found in the League of Nations, *Double Taxation and Tax Evasion: Report by the General Meeting of Governmental Experts on Double Taxation and Fiscal Evasion* (1928) C.562.M.178. 1928 II, at p. 5: 'The Meeting declared in particular that it agreed with the technical experts in recognizing that, although it would be desirable for States to conclude collective conventions, or even a single general convention embodying all the others, the extreme diversity of existing fiscal systems made it impossible at the present time to recommend a convention which could be unanimously accepted, unless the text were worded in such general terms as to be devoid of any practical value.'
28. League of Nations, *Fiscal Committee: Report to the Council on the Work of the First Session of the Committe* (1929) C.516.M.175.1929.II, p. 6.
29. League of Nations, *Fiscal Committee: Report to the Council on the Work of the Second Session of the Committe* (1930) C.340.M.140.1930.II pp. 8–9.

Clearly, the proposals were on items of immobile income, and hence without many distributive concerns. Public employees, interest on public debt and immovable property were considered, particularly at the time the report was drafted, to be closely economically related to the territory or sovereignty of the source of income. Such sources of income could, after all, best be taxed in the jurisdiction where taxation could best be administratively enforced. Perhaps multilateral agreement on these items was possible. However, the problem was that the classes of income were not all-inclusive: articles on items of mobile capital (dividends, interest) were absent from the work of the Fiscal Committee. Double taxation would, even if a plurilateral convention was signed, not be fully prevented.

At the third session of the League of Nations Fiscal Committee, the subcommittee presented its draft ('Draft A') to the Fiscal Committee. The draft included articles on immovable property, profits of an enterprise with a PE, (the seat of management of) maritime and air navigation enterprises, public loans, frontier workers, authors' rights, life annuities, salaries of public servants, and public pensions.[30] But the Fiscal Committee, even after making some amendments, was not very enthusiastic about the proposed draft convention:

> these proposals could not at present be accepted by other countries because the clauses of Draft A settled the position of both residents and non-residents, with the object of entirely preventing double taxation for both, so far as concerns the classes of income contemplated in the draft – an arrangement which would impose upon Governments, in respect of their own residents, obligations which they are not prepared to assume.[31]

The Fiscal Committee itself therefore attempted to provide another solution, which it set out in 'Draft B', which would settle the issue of double taxation for non-residents ('natural and juristic persons not domiciled in [the High Contracting Parties'] territory') only. Articles 2 and 3 of Draft B set out that each state could tax the income of non-residents, except in relation to certain classes of income (i.e., maritime or air navigation, business income not derived from a PE, public loans, frontier workers, author's rights and life annuities).[32] But discussing both drafts, the Committee:

> does not feel that it can reach a final decision at present. It seems necessary to reconsider whether there is any real possibility of an adequate number of accessions to either or both of these two types of convention.[33]

In order to see whether either of the two conventions would be feasible, the Fiscal Committee considered to forward both drafts to the members of the League of Nations,

---

30. *See* Appendix I to League of Nations, *Fiscal Committee: Report to the Council on the Work of the Third Session of the Committe* (1931) C.415.M.171.1931.II.A.
31. *Id.*, at p. 3.
32. *Id.*, at Appendix III.
33. *Id.*, at p. 4.

requesting whether they could accept one of the drafts, and if not, to offer observations on them.[34] In the subsequent session of the Committee, however, no further mention was made of either of the proposals.[35]

Why did the members of the Committee feel unfavourable towards both proposals? An educated guess: both Draft A and B, relating to certain items of income only, lacked practical relevance, particularly given the political climate at the time. From the time the Committee began its work to the end of 1939, the number of general (and mostly bilateral) tax treaties increased from about thirty to sixty.[36] The drafts, however, left much of the double taxation problem intact.[37] Draft B, in particular, related to non-residents only. Moreover, Draft A required states not to tax their residents on their worldwide income in relation to the classes of income identified, which prevented states to take a taxpayer's full income into account (e.g., for the purposes of progressive income tax rates). And as the drafts were proposed at the end of the 1930s, political tensions in Europe were rising. As pointed out by Picciotto, Britain in particular proved to be an obstacle in this regard:

> The British Treasury took the firm view that it could see no reason to sacrifice a penny of revenue in order to stimulate British and German firms to set up business in each other's countries, or to encourage individuals to speculate in buying foreign shares. On the contrary, double taxation was a welcome deterrent to such activities.[38]

2.2.2 1943–1946: Emerging Consensus under Model Bilateral Tax Conventions, a Comparison of the London and Mexico Drafts

To achieve uniformity among states in an area where no generally accepted rules existed, and where a comprehensive multilateral tax convention seemed unachievable, the international community set out to develop non-binding model bilateral tax agreements. Three non-binding model treaties, those spoken of by T.S. Adams, (*see* section 2.2.1) were adopted by a 1928 League of Nations meeting of government experts.[39] These models in turn formed the basis for the 1943–1946 Mexico and London

---

34. *Id.*, at p. 5.
35. League of Nations, *Fiscal Committee: Report to the Council on the Work of the Fourth Session of the Committe* (1933) C.399.M.204.1933.II.A.
36. M.B. Carroll (1939), Appendix II; at the end of 1939, there were 60.
37. This was already pointed out by the Fiscal Committee when the work on the plurilateral convention was initiated. League of Nations, *Fiscal Committee: Report to the Council on the Work of the Second Session of the Committe* (1930).
38. S. Picciotto, *International Business Taxation: A Study in the Internationalization of Business Regulation* (Cambridge University Press Electronic ed., 1992) pp. 25–26.
39. League of Nations, *1928 Report by the General Meeting of Governmental Experts on Double Taxation and Fiscal Evasion* (1928).

Model Bilateral Tax Conventions (the 'London and Mexico Drafts').[40] The 1963 OECD MTC is considered 'a modern version of the models of Mexico and London'.[41]

The Mexico and London Drafts originated from the work of the League of Nations that continued during the Second World War. A meeting was organised in Mexico, where the Latin American (capital-importing) countries, Canada and the US were represented. The resulting draft predicated almost entirely on the principle of taxation at source.[42] Shortly after the Second World War in 1946, however, the texts were re-examined by the full League of Nations Fiscal Committee, which primarily consisted of capital-exporting countries.[43] This led to the London Draft, which reasserted the principles developed in the pre-war League models, and was grounded on the principle of residence.

Now, it is worth examining these Mexico and London Drafts, primarily because they reiterated the conflict between source and residence states hinted at in the previous section, but also contained some overlapping principles. Where did these conventions fundamentally differ and overlap? How close were states on agreeing on a multilateral treaty, as argued by Adams (*see* section 2.2.1)? As we will see, the main differences between the drafts, and therefore between the capital-importing and capital-exporting countries of the post-war world, existed on items of mobile income. The following Table 1 summarises the results.

Table 1   A Comparison Between the Mexico and London Drafts[44]

Item of Income	Mexico Draft	London Draft	Observations
Interest	Source[45]	Residence[46]	No overlap
Dividends	Source[47]	Residence (unless 'dominant participation')[48]	No overlap
Royalties	Source[49]	Residence (unless affiliated companies)[50]	No overlap

40. League of Nations, *Fiscal Committee: London and Mexico Model Tax Conventions Commentary and Text* (1946) C.88.M.88.1946.II.A, discussed in S. Picciotto (1992) pp. 49–53.
41. A.J. Van Den Tempel, *Relief from Double Taxation: A Comparison of the Work of the League of Nations and of the Organisation for Economic Cooperation and Development* (IBFD 1967) p. 45.
42. M.B. Carroll, *International Tax Law*, 2 The International Lawyer 692, 708 (1968).
43. M. Kobetsky, *International Taxation of Permanent Establishments: Principles and Policy* (Cambridge University Press 2011) p. 143.
44. The comparison is based on League of Nations, *London and Mexico Model Tax Conventions Commentary and Text (1946)* (1946), and draws from M.B. Carroll (1968) (which contains such a comparison) and A.J. Van Den Tempel (1967).
45. Article IX of the Mexico Draft.
46. Article IX of the London Draft.
47. Article IX of the Mexico Draft.
48. Article VI of the London Draft.
49. Article X of the Mexico Draft.
50. Article X of the London Draft.

Item of Income	Mexico Draft	London Draft	Observations
Capital gains – real property	Source[51]	Source[52]	Overlap
Other capital gains	No rule	Residence, unless 'appertaining to enterprise'[53]	N.A.
Business income	'Where the business or activity is carried out'; in the case of isolated or occasional transactions and no PE: residence.[54]	If PE: location of PE; if no PE: residence.[55]	Overlap to a remarkably high degree
Real Property (and mining royalties)	Source[56]	Source[57]	Overlap
Employment	Working state, but in residence state when employment does not exceed 183 days in working state.[58]	Working state, but in residence state when employment does not exceed 183 days in working state.[59]	Overlap
Pensions	Residence[60]	Residence[61]	Overlap
Provisions on the allocation of business income	Similar[62]	Similar[63]	Overlap

As the table shows, overlap existed for almost all types of active income of individuals, as well as for income from real estate. Taxing real property in the source state is practical, as real estate is immobile: hence the overlap. It can only be guessed at why little distributive concerns existed on the other points: perhaps the presence of convincing pragmatic as well as theoretical arguments pointed at an existing preference for residence taxation. Residence taxation for the active income of individuals makes sense: an individual's place of residence is relatively easy to define, and it enables the taking into account of an individual's 'ability to pay' under a worldwide tax system. Moreover, taxation at residence overlaps with political allegiance, therefore

---

51. Article XII of the Mexico Draft.
52. Article XII of the London Draft.
53. Article XII of the London Draft.
54. Article IV of the Mexico Draft.
55. Article IV of the London Draft.
56. Article II and Art. X of the Mexico Draft.
57. Articles II and X of the London Draft.
58. Article VII of the Mexico Draft.
59. Article VI of the London Draft.
60. Article XI of the Mexico Draft.
61. Article XI of the London Draft.
62. Article VI of the Protocol to the Mexico Draft.
63. Article VI of the Protocol to the London Draft.

functioning as a proxy for the maxim 'no taxation without representation'.[64] Finally, and perhaps most importantly, the residence state is best placed to enforce taxation, as it has the best means to administer taxes.

Rules for the allocation of active business income, as embodied by the PE concept and the arm's length standard, presumably had no obvious winners and losers, given the broad terms used for of both notions. The relevance of this observation will be explained in Chapter 5. But the point is that the comparison between the London and Mexico Drafts suggests that a compromise between creditor and debtor countries was not far off, even though the Mexico draft employed a lower threshold for the source country to tax business income.[65] Under both conventions, residence countries were given the right to tax residents on their worldwide income, whilst the concept of a PE or 'business activity' triggered taxation at source, provided this was limited to the profits of the establishment.[66] The PE concept, perhaps due to the pressure placed on the capital-importing states by the big capital-exporting countries of the time such as the US,[67] ultimately survived in the later OECD Models. As Kobetsky notes, the Fiscal Committee in London rejected the capital-importing countries' arguments for a lower threshold,[68] and considered that the concept of the PE, which had also played a part in the Committee's earlier work on the 1928 Draft Models,[69] already featured in nearly all tax treaties on business income.[70]

Likewise, under both conventions, the method used to allocate business income between PEs[71] was considerably similar. It was primarily based on the rules set out in the 1935 Allocation Convention as developed by the League of Nations Fiscal

---

64. *See, e.g.,* R.S. Avi-Yonah, *International Tax as International Law: An Analysis of the International Tax Regime* (Cambridge University Press 2007) p. 11.
65. The Mexico Draft employed the concept of the place of the 'business activity' instead of the 'location of the permanent establishment'.
66. M. Kobetsky (2011) pp. 143–149.
67. *Id.,* at pp. 149–150.
68. Reasons can be found at pp. 13–14 of League of Nations, *London and Mexico Model Tax Conventions Commentary and Text (1946)* (1946).
69. M. Kobetsky (2011) p. 144. The permanent establishment concept was already established in the 1927 proposal of the Technical Experts to the Financial Committee: League of Nations, *1927 Report on Double Taxation* (1927). To this proposal, two conventions (Conventions 1b and 1c) were later added by the Meeting of Governmental Experts in: League of Nations, *1928 Report by the General Meeting of Governmental Experts on Double Taxation and Fiscal Evasion* (1928). All three proposed model conventions of 1927 (1a, 1b and 1c) contained the same concept of a permanent establishment, which consisted of a list of undertakings, that, for example, included 'real centres of management, branches, mines and oilfields, factories, workshops, agencies, warehouses, offices and depots'.
70. League of Nations, *London and Mexico Model Tax Conventions Commentary and Text (1946)* (1946) p. 14.
71. The problem of the profit allocation between affiliated companies (i.e., the setting of transfer prices between associated enterprises) was less well recognised, as each affiliate was recognised as a separate legal person, for which its accounts could 'simply' be used. *See* S. Picciotto (1992) p. 27 and also W. Schön, *International Tax Coordination for a Second-Best World (Part III),* 2 World Tax Journal 227, 231 (2010).

Committee between 1929 and 1935.[72] As the 1928 Models had left open the question how profits were to be allocated between PEs, the Fiscal Committee addressed this issue by means of a draft convention. Interestingly, this convention was multilateral and was surprisingly close to be readied by the Fiscal Committee for signature. The Fiscal Committee held that:

> in view of its limited scope, and of the intentional restriction of its provisions to the fundamental rules, this draft by itself might, in the Committee's opinion, form the basis of a multilateral Convention. The Committee therefore proposes to the Council that it should be transmitted to Governments, with a request that they express their opinion thereof.[73]

However, governments' responses were not that definitely in favour. Only a few states declared themselves ready to sign a multilateral convention. Consequently, the Committee considered that more progress would likely be achieved by means of bilateral agreements. This was considered not to be problematic, as most of the draft's core principles were generally approved, and a model convention, insofar as it constituted the basis for bilateral agreements:

> creates automatically a uniformity of practice and legislation, while, on the other hand, inasmuch as it may be modified in any bilateral agreement reached, it is sufficiently elastic to be adapted to the different conditions obtaining in different countries or pairs of countries.[74]

In this regard, the Committee was undeniably right: the arm's length standard has featured in the London and Mexico Drafts as well as in all later OECD Models. Hence, it seems that substantial multilateral consensus on the arm's length principle as well as on the PE standards existed.

So, the comparison shows that there are many rules of international tax law that were (and are) de facto multilateral. The similarities between the London and Mexico Models suggest that multilateral consensus existed, at least for compromises on most immobile items of income. And it goes without saying that the allocation rules on which overlap existed under the London and Mexico drafts, continue to be used in a similar form worldwide in both bilateral tax treaties as well as in the OECD and United Nations (UN) Models,[75] with the arm's length standard and the PE concept as the most

---

72. League of Nations, 1935 Revised Draft Convention for the Allocation of Business Income between States for the Purposes of Taxation, printed in: League of Nations, *Fiscal Committee: Report to the Council on the Fifth Session of the Committee* (1935) C.252.M.124.1935.II.A, Annex I.
73. League of Nations, *Fiscal Committee: Report to the Council on the Work of the Fourth Session of the Committe* (1933) p. 2.
74. League of Nations, *Fiscal Committee: Report to the Council on the Fifth Session of the Committee* (1935) pp. 3–4.
75. Y. Brauner, *An International Tax Regime in Crystallization*, 56 Tax Law Review 259 (2003) sec. 2 ('Rules that are more purely international, like the source rules and the transfer pricing rules, seem to be closest to harmonization already.').

obvious demonstrations. It has even been argued that such concepts are part of an 'international tax language'[76] that practitioners all over the world recognise and apply.

2.2.3 1946–1992: Impracticalities of Further Efforts for a Comprehensive Multilateral Tax Treaty

There was another effort for a comprehensive multilateral solution to the avoidance of double taxation in the period after the Second World War, i.e., in the Cold War and the decolonisation period. But again, it proved difficult to achieve multilateral consensus on important tax policy issues among a greater group of states.[77] In 1958, but this time by the OEEC's (Organization for European Economic Cooperation, the OECD's predecessor) Fiscal Committee, another effort was made to draft a multilateral convention.[78] The International Chamber of Commerce, by means of its 1955 Tokyo congress, urged the international experts of the OEEC Fiscal Committee to consider drafting a multilateral tax treaty.[79] This multilateral treaty 'would have the great advantage of securing uniformity of principles and practice in double taxation matters in a vast area of world trade'.[80] The suggestion seemed welcome: all of the OEEC's member countries wanted to 'prevent further disintegration of international fiscal law and come to a greater measure of uniformity in its structure, rules and concepts'.[81]

But again, practical arguments prevented the formulation of a comprehensive multilateral convention. Around the time the Tokyo congress tried to intervene, the number of bilateral tax conventions concluded had risen rapidly (to about 130 in 1956).[82] Perhaps because of this, the Fiscal Committee proposed that it would first consider the drafting of a model bilateral tax convention, which could then function as a basis for proceeding towards harmonisation by a multilateral convention. This seems a logical step: a model bilateral tax treaty was achievable, whereas, in the words of the Committee, it was impossible to envisage how long it would take to implement a multilateral convention.[83]

---

76. K. Vogel, *The Influence of the OECD Commentaries on Treaty Interpretation*, 54 Bulletin for International Fiscal Documentation 612, 616 (2000): 'If a term – by which I mean not only individual words, but also coherent expressions or sentences – was already used by the Draft Convention of 1963 and explained by its Commentaries, I suggest that this term be considered to have become in the course of time part of the "international tax language".'
77. Also within the UN, the UN's Fiscal Committee, working under the UN's Economic and Social Council, was unable to achieve agreement. S. Picciotto (1992) 48.
78. According to van den Tempel, the League of Nations was in fact 'hardly less western in character than the OECD'. *See* A.J. Van Den Tempel (1967) p. 9.
79. OEEC, *Report by the Fiscal Committee on Its Activities* (1958) C(58) 118, Part I, para. 16.
80. A.J. Van Den Tempel (1967) p. 10.
81. *Id.*, at p. 13.
82. *See* OEEC, *1958 Report by the Fiscal Committee on its Activities (I)* (1958) (the figure in par. 7) as well as Appendix A (*see* on this Ch. 3.2), which can be found online at DANS. http://dx.doi .org/10.17026/dans-x22-k8wh.
83. *Id.*, at para. 14.

It was not until 1992 that the OECD Committee on Fiscal Affairs (CFA), in the introduction to the OECD MTC, finally abandoned the efforts for a multilateral convention.[84] A multilateral agreement was, given the success of the OECD MTC, no longer considered practicable. It held:

> Despite these two conventions [the Nordic Convention and the Convention on Mutual Administrative Assistance in Tax Matters], there are no reasons to believe that the elaboration and conclusion of a multilateral tax convention involving all Member countries could now be considered a practicable solution.[85]

2.3 CONCLUSION

From the start, the goal of the negotiators of the current system for the avoidance of double taxation has been to achieve a comprehensive multilateral tax treaty. But despite such efforts, states failed to reach agreement.

Reasons for the failure of reaching agreement on a comprehensive multilateral tax treaty were likely a deadly mix of strongly diverging interests, bad timing and the increasingly reducing relevance of the multilateral tax treaty. Indeed, whilst the Chamber of Commerce kept urging negotiators to adopt a multilateral treaty for international tax matters, bilateralism flourished. In the light of the quickly expanding network of bilateral tax treaties, an 'old' style multilateral tax treaty became increasingly unfeasible and impracticable.

So, the system of bilateral treaties that emerged was considered a kind of second-best solution to the comprehensive multilateral tax treaty that might one day prove feasible. It is in this light that an effort for a new multilateral treaty in the area of international taxation has to be understood.

On the one hand, any effort for a multilateral agreement for international taxation has to take the bilateral tax treaty network as a given. As Schön phrases it: 'any new move in tax coordination should take the existence of the current network of double taxation treaties as a proof of procedural success of the bilateral concept'.[86] And indeed, this might mean that full comprehensive multilateralism in the field of international taxation might never be achieved. For instance, according to Vann, it is not possible for the bilateral network simply to evolve into a multilateral treaty.[87] He says:

---

84. In the 1963 report of the Fiscal Committee on the Draft Convention for the avoidance of double taxation, the ambition to draft a multilateral convention was reiterated, but it seems that no further action was taken. OECD, *OECD, Report of the Fiscal Committee on the Draft Convention for the Avoidance of Double Taxation with respect to Taxes on Income and Capital Among the Member Countries of the O.E.C.D.* (1963) C(63) 87, Part I, p. 6.
85. OECD, *Introduction*, in: Model Tax Convention on Income and on Capital: Condensed Version (2014) para. 40 (emphasis added).
86. W. Schön, *International Tax Coordination for a Second-Best World (Part I)*, 1 World Tax Journal 67, 86 (2009).
87. R.J. Vann, *A Model Tax Treaty for the Asian-Pacific Region? (Part I)*, 45 Bulletin for International Fiscal Documentation 99, 100 (1991).

[A]lthough it is possible to refine the actual terms of the OECD Model and to elaborate the Commentary so as to cover new cases as they arise, the time has passed for radical revision within the current bilateral framework (...) In other words, the OECD Model is the culmination of 50 years of development.[88]

On the other hand, loosely coordinated on by non-binding bilateral tax treaty models such as the OECD MTC, multilateral consensus has not been absent from the system of bilateral tax treaties. Indeed, history shows that disagreement between states existed primarily in relation to items of mobile income. On source rules distributing items of income that could be considered immobile in the pre- and interwar economies, such as interest on public loans, public pensions, frontier workers and immovable property (e.g., in the proposals discussed in section 2.2.1) and later on employment and pensions (*see*, *e.g.*, the Table 1 in 2.2.2), a form of multilateral consensus seemed to exist. And even today, multilateral consensus, expressed in model tax conventions, has been particularly strong in the field of concepts. The PE concept and the principle to price transactions at arm's length can be called part of the 'international tax language' that practitioners all over the world recognise and apply.

This finding implies that a distinction between bilateralism and multilateralism in the area of international tax cooperation should not necessarily be sharp. It has been argued that the 'weak' multilateralism of Action 15's BEPS Convention will, in the long run, end up in a full multilateral tax treaty to replace all bilateral treaties.[89] That is, perhaps, a premature conclusion. On the other hand, Avery Jones has argued that 'what countries really do is to sign up to variations on the Model Treaty. Practitioners would save a lot of time if treaties were presented as variations to the Model Treaty; we would not need to read the rest to see whether it has been changed.'[90] It follows that the existing network of bilateral treaties can be interpreted as a (long) list of reservations on the OECD MTC – from this perspective, the existing system can be seen as essentially multilateral in the 'strong' sense. In any case, this dichotomy of 'weak' and 'strong' forms of multilateralism in the field of international tax law is a theme to which we will return.

---

88. *Id.*, at p. 103. Likewise, Graetz has argued that it has become 'extremely difficult to move in the tax area toward the kind of multilateral negotiating practice that, for example, occurs through the General Agreement on Tariffs and Trade (GATT) in the international trade arena'. M.J. Graetz and M.M. O'Hear (1997) p. 1107.
89. A. Miller and A. Kirkpatrick, *The Use of Multilateral Instruments to Achieve the BEPS Action Plan Agenda*, [2013] British Tax Review 682, 686 (2013).
90. J.F. Avery Jones, *The David R. Tillinghast Lecture: Are Tax Treaties Necessary?*, 53 Tax Law Review 1, 6 (1999).

CHAPTER 3

The Prospects of a Multilateral Agreement for International Taxation

3.1 INTRODUCTION

Without a doubt, the OECD has had, through its Model and Commentary, an enormous impact on international tax norms. By means of soft-law governance through the OECD MTC and Commentaries, the OECD has created consensus in the interpretation and application of tax treaties of its members.[91] The OECD MTC has influenced many of the tax treaties currently in force,[92] and that the OECD has played a very important role in developing international tax policy is almost an understatement.[93] In fact, as Christians notes, the OECD has been so successful with its multilateral soft law that a debate has ensued on whether its Commentary on the OECD MTC can arise to become legally binding on the parties to a tax treaty patterned on the OECD MTC, even for non-OECD Members.[94]

---

91. OECD, *International Regulatory Co-operation: Case Studies, Vol. 1: Chemicals, Consumer Products, Tax and Competition* (2013) OECD Publishing, http://dx.doi.org/10.1787/978926420048 7-en ('This type of flexible co-ordination has clear advantages. It greatly facilitates the relations between tax administrations involved in the negotiation, application and interpretation of bilateral tax treaties, whilst preserving the tax sovereignty of countries involved.'), at p. 55.
92. M. Lang et al., eds, *The Impact of the OECD and UN Model Conventions on Bilateral Tax Treaties* (Cambridge University Press 2012).
93. As Avi-Yonah, for instance, says, 'the freedom of most countries to adopt international tax rules is severely constrained, even before entering into any tax treaties, by the need to adapt to generally accepted principles of international taxation'. R.S. Avi-Yonah (2007) pp. 3–4.
94. A. Christians, *How Nations Share*, 87 Indiana Law Journal 1407, 48 (2012). She obviously refers to S.C.W. Douma and F.A. Engelen eds, *The Legal Status of the OECD Commentaries* (IBFD 2008), and in particular to the work by Engelen in that book F.A. Engelen, *How Acquiescence and Estoppel Can Operate to the Effect that the States Parties to a Tax Treaty are Legally Bound to Interpret the Treaty in Accordance with the Commentaries on the OECD Model Tax Convention*, in: The Legal Status of the OECD Commentaries (S. Douma and F.A. Engelen eds, IBFD 2008).

But there are limits to the type of cooperation that currently takes place. By amending the OECD MTC, the OECD has hoped that its member countries conform to the latest MTC when concluding or revising their bilateral tax treaties. And when applying and interpreting the provisions of bilateral tax conventions based on the OECD MTC, the OECD has hoped that countries 'follow the Commentaries on the Articles of the Model Tax Convention, as modified from time to time'.[95] But the OECD MTC and its Commentaries, used by the OECD to influence and update the contents of the network of bilateral tax treaties, are not legally binding.[96] This means that they are not enforceable on the international (inter-nation) and domestic (taxpayers and judges) levels, preventing the international tax system to quickly adapt to changing circumstances. Moreover, because states can depart from the OECD's models if they wish, they have been prevented from reacting in a coordinated way to address collective action problems that are now materialising under the BEPS Project. As a result, the international tax system has become outdated and unresponsive to present-day needs.

As to amendments to the OECD MTC: states are not committed to actually update their treaties to conform to the latest version of the OECD MTC. Indeed, as shown in section 3.2, implementing the changes to the OECD MTC in bilateral tax treaties takes a generation, as each and every one of the bilateral tax treaties needs to be revised. And as shown in section 3.3: unfortunately, 'rule-stretching', i.e., changing the interpretation of tax treaty terms by means of amending the OECD Commentary proves hardly effective either a method to modernise the international tax system, as courts disregard such efforts when applying and interpreting tax treaty rules to cases brought before

---

95. *OECD Council Recommendation (23 October 1997) C(97)195/FINAL*, OECD. The text of the recommendation (emphasis added) holds:

> THE COUNCIL, (...)
> TAKING NOTE of the Model Tax Convention and the Commentaries thereon (...),
> *which may be amended from time to time hereafter;*
> I. RECOMMENDS the Governments of Member countries:
>
> 1. To pursue their efforts to conclude bilateral tax conventions on income and on capital with those Member countries, and where appropriate with non-member countries, with which they have not yet entered into such conventions, *and to revise those of the existing conventions that may no longer reflect present-day needs;*
> 2. When concluding new bilateral conventions or revising existing bilateral conventions *to conform to the Model Tax Convention, as interpreted by the Commentaries thereon;*
> 3. That their tax administrations *follow the Commentaries* on the Articles of the Model Tax Convention, *as modified from time to time*, when applying and interpreting the provisions of their bilateral tax conventions that are based on these Articles (emphasis added).

96. Most tax scholars agree on this. *See, e.g.*, K. Vogel (2000), F. Van Brunschot, *The Judiciary and the OECD Model Tax Convention and Its Commentaries*, 59 Bulletin for International Fiscal Documentation 5 (2005) D.A. Ward et al., *The Interpretation of Income Tax Treaties with Particular Reference to the Commentaries on the OECD Model* (International Fiscal Association 2005); H. Pijl, *The OECD Commentary as a Source of International Law and the Role of the Judiciary*, 46 European Taxation 216, 224 (2006); J.M. Mössner, *Klaus Vogel Lecture 2009 – Comments*, 64 Bulletin for International Taxation 16, 17 (2010); D.M. Broekhuijsen, *A Modern Understanding of Article 31(3)(c) of the Vienna Convention (1969): A New Haunt for the Commentaries to the OECD Model?*, 67 Bulletin for International Taxation September (2013).

them. Indeed, the willingness of domestic courts of OECD Member countries to dynamically apply the OECD Commentary when interpreting a tax treaty varies greatly.

The loose form of coordination under the OECD MTC and Commentaries causes another problem (section 3.4). Given that states are free to modify and postpone on implementing changes to the OECD MTC in their bilateral tax treaties, and that not all judges dynamically apply the OECD Commentary when interpreting bilateral tax treaties, a level playing field is absent in coordinating on the rules required to address the collective action problems, such as those related to tax competition and tax arbitrage. This makes coordinated action difficult if not impossible to organise, as states have an incentive to enjoy the benefits of non-cooperation ('free ride') where others agree to restrict their rules.

Hence, the OECD has a reason to be worried. It has largely exercised its influence on the rules of bilateral tax treaties by amending the OECD MTC and Commentaries to the OECD MTC. As to the short run: the implementation of some of the Project's most important outcomes depends on states to agree to the BEPS Convention, as implementing the outcomes through the OECD MTC will take decades. Also, it depends on judges to apply the Commentaries (and transfer pricing guidelines) related to the Project's outcomes when interpreting tax treaties. But particularly in the long run, the outlook is unforgiving: the unsuitability of using the OECD MTC and its Commentaries to update the bilateral tax treaty system jeopardises the sustainability of the international tax system as a whole. A fundamental reconsideration of multilateral cooperation in international tax law is clearly necessary.

3.2 THE RELEVANCE OF THE OECD MTC IN MODERNISING THE TAX TREATY NETWORK

Tax treaties are rigid tools. Vann, for instance, argued in 1991 that the framework of bilateral tax treaties based on the OECD MTC had become irrelevant, as many of the pressing issues at the time were not dealt with by the tax treaties then in force.[97] Indeed, tax treaty negotiations can be lengthy, as they require friendly political relationships and the commitment of not one but two states. That makes it likely that a considerable amount of time – decades, not years – is required before new norms set out in an OECD MTC are incorporated into tax treaties.

Although the OECD MTC and the Commentary have proven to be quite successful,[98] as they have provided states with negotiation flexibility and have greatly uniformised and influenced the existing rules of international tax, governments do not have to follow the OECD MTC when (re)negotiate tax treaties. Instead, member countries can amend their bilateral tax treaties if they consider this 'opportune'.[99]

---

97. R.J. Vann (1991).
98. *See, e.g.,* M. Lang et al., (2012).
99. OECD, *Rules of Procedure of the Organisation* (2013) Art. 18(b).

Data from the International Bureau for Fiscal Documentation (IBFD's) tax treaty database on tax treaties, in force on 1 January 2013,[100] shows that the average time (i.e., the 'estimated mean') it takes before an OECD Member country's tax treaty[101] is updated is about seventeen years (the data and calculations are taken up in *Appendix A*, which can be accessed online).[102] And this figure only takes into account the time between subsequent treaty updates of treaties that were *actually* amended. In other words: this figure excludes treaties that were never amended, as such treaties lack two subsequent amendment moments. Putting 1 January 2013 as a fictional amendment date on these treaties, the result would be eighteen years.[103]

More specifically, the data shows that the content of tax treaties severely lags behind the content of the latest OECD MTC update. And every time the OECD introduces a new version of the OECD MTC, the gap widens.[104] Figure 1 below expresses this point. How many of the tax treaties in force before the introduction of a new OECD MTC version were actually amended or renegotiated in or after the year in which a new version of the OECD MTC was published? Surely, if a tax treaty has, since its conclusion, never been amended or renegotiated (i.e., by means of a new treaty or protocol), it is impossible that such a treaty could include any of the provisions of the OECD MTC adopted posterior to that treaty's conclusion.

Each of the three bars represents the total number of treaties in force anterior to the 1977, 1992 or 2003 versions of the OECD MTC, respectively. Only those treaties have been taken into account that were still in force on 1 January 2013 (i.e., treaties that were terminated before 2013 are not included in the figure). The number of treaties that have, as of those years, not been updated, have been depicted in white. Note also

---

100. The Tax Treaty Database can be found in the Tax Research Platform of the International Bureau of Fiscal Documentation (website: www.ibfd.org). The IBFD keeps records of the date of the conclusion of treaties and their protocols.
101. Only the treaties of the founding states of the OECD were taken into account. These are: the Republic of Austria, the Kingdom of Belgium, the Dominion of Canada, the Kingdom of Denmark, the French Republic, the Federal Republic of Germany, the Kingdom of Greece, the Republic of Iceland, the Republic of Ireland, the Italian Republic, the Grand Duchy of Luxembourg, the Kingdom of the Netherlands, the Kingdom of Norway, the Portuguese Republic, the Kingdom of Spain, the Kingdom of Sweden, the Swiss Confederation, the Turkish Republic, the United Kingdom of Great Britain and Northern Ireland, and the United States of America. The count includes tax treaties of these countries with non-OECD Member countries.
102. *Appendix A* can be found online at DANS, the Netherlands Institute for Permanent Access to Digital Research Resources: D.M. Broekhuijsen, *A Multilateral Agreement for International Taxation: Designing an Instrument to Modernise International Tax Law.* DANS, http://dx.doi.org/10.17026/dans-x22-k8wh.
103. In counting the amendments to tax treaties in force, terminated treaties which have not been followed up by a new treaty, abandoned treaties as well as treaties that were not ratified before 1 Jan. 2013, were excluded. Moreover, all pre-war (1940) treaties were not considered.
    A treaty was considered to be 'updated' if, within the same bilateral treaty party relationship: (1) a new bilateral treaty was concluded; (2) a protocol to a treaty was concluded; or (3) when the exchange of notes, the records of discussions between parties, or a mutual agreement changed the wording of the tax convention in question.
104. This is also recognised by the OECD: OECD, *Developing a Multilateral Instrument to Modify Bilateral Tax Treaties, Action 15: 2015 Final Report* (2015) p. 9.

that the total amount of tax treaties increases over time (the reason is, simply, that countries have expanded their tax treaty networks over the second half of the twentieth century).

Figure 1   Have Tax Treaties of OECD Founding Members Been Updated since the Introduction of the OECD MTCs of 1977, 1992 and 2000? Measured on 1 January 2013

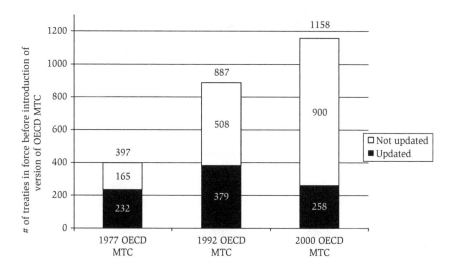

Figure 1 shows that, on 1 January 2013, 41% of the tax treaties in force before the 1977 version of the OECD MTC were not amended between 1977 and 2013. This signifies that many of the OECD founding members' pre-1977 tax treaties currently in force do not even reflect the standards set out in 1977 Model. Similarly, 57% of the treaties in force before 1992 and 77% of the treaties in force before 2000 have not been changed since the years 1992 and 2000, respectively. Consequently, updates to the OECD MTC are barely reflected in tax treaties of the OECD Member countries. This clearly compels a reconsideration of the way tax treaties are amended. And note: in practice, the influence of the OECD MTC on bilateral tax treaties might be even worse, as changes to the contents/texts of tax treaties, effectuated, for example, by protocols or by renegotiations, were not considered. The author has merely reasoned that a tax treaty, unaltered after the introduction of a new version of the OECD MTC, can in no way include the rules of that OECD MTC.

3.3   THE RELEVANCE OF THE OECD COMMENTARIES IN MODERNISING THE TAX TREATY NETWORK

3.3.1   Introduction

What about the OECD Commentaries? Can they be used to 'update' the bilateral tax treaty network? After all, they are guidelines that may be used by courts, taxpayers and tax authorities in interpreting and applying tax treaties based on the OECD MTC. And whoever controls the interpretation of tax treaties, also controls their contents.

Nevertheless, the updates to the OECD Commentary are neither binding on the domestic judiciary nor enforceable by taxpayers or tax authorities before a court. Instead, the availability of multiple 'OECD-endorsed' interpretations of a tax treaty term brings up the question which meaning takes precedence: the 'old' interpretation, prevalent before the date of conclusion of a tax treaty, or the 'new' interpretation, introduced in the OECD Commentaries after a tax treaty's conclusion? The main argument to apply a 'newer' version of the OECD Commentary to interpret an older tax treaty depends on the degree to which it can be argued that states intended to give a tax treaty term the meaning that was set out in the OECD Commentaries that existed when the tax treaty was concluded.[105] Hence, the practice of using the OECD Commentaries to influence (or even alter) the contents of tax treaty terms may prove a quagmire.[106]

An analysis of relevant case law decided by courts in OECD Member countries provides some (factual) insight in the way the OECD Commentary is used to 'modernise' the terms of a tax treaty through interpretative rule-stretching. The practice of international tax law is of course not limited to judicial decision-making; the OECD Commentary's role in influencing non-judicial (administrative) decisions should not be ignored. Nevertheless, for practical purposes, the analysis is limited to case law of courts only, distilling a general picture from a practice of tax law that is transparent and well-documented and, due to precedential effects awarded to court decisions, influential. The analysis is included in *Appendix B*, which can be found online.[107]

To circumvent discussions about the 'status' of the OECD Commentary under international law and in the process of tax treaty interpretation – this issue is still under debate in tax law doctrine – the reasoning of the courts as to the interpretative relevance of the OECD Commentary was not considered in the analysis. Instead, it focuses on the Commentary's *effects* under five different groups of circumstances.

The general impression left by this outcome-oriented analysis is that courts of OECD Member countries, as between themselves, do not coherently deal with treaty-posterior versions of the OECD Commentary. Indeed, the analysis confirms that if the Commentary introduces a meaning that is of a 'gap-filling' or 'contradictory' nature in relation to the version existing at the time a specific bilateral tax treaty was concluded,

---

105. M. Lang and F. Brugger, *The Role of the OECD Commentary in Tax Treaty Interpretation*, 23 Australian Tax Forum 95, 108 (2008)., *also* the work of Hans Pijl, who sets out the dilemma of dynamically using the OECD Commentary in examples from practice, e.g., H. Pijl, *Interpretation of Article 7 of the OECD Model, Permanent Establishment Financing and Other Dealings*, 65 Bulletin for International Taxation 294 (2011).

106. The occasional explicit reference to the OECD Commentary in the text or protocol of a tax treaty does not seem to change this conclusion. *See* C. West, *References to the OECD Commentaries in Tax Treaties: A Steady March from 'Soft' Law to 'Hard' Law?*, 9 World Tax Journal 117, 159 (2017): 'Hard law reference to the OECD or UN Commentaries in the treaty or protocol to the treaty has, at best, ensured that the courts must consult the Commentaries, but use of the Commentaries by the judiciary will continue to vary.'

107. *Appendix B* can be found online at DANS, the Netherlands Institute for Permanent Access to Digital Research Resources: D.M. Broekhuijsen, *A Multilateral Agreement for International Taxation: Designing an Instrument to Modernise International Tax Law*. DANS, http://dx.doi.org/10.17026/dans-x22-k8wh. It consists of a case law code book and a database.

its effect in courts of the OECD Member countries varies greatly. This suggests that the dynamic application of the OECD Commentary is far from limitless,[108] and that ultimately, amendments to bilateral tax treaties cannot be effectively introduced by stretching the interpretation of the terms of the OECD MTC. Using the OECD Commentary to influence the contents of tax treaties is, in other words, problematic.

The methodology used in the research set forth in *Appendix B* was as follows.

3.3.2 Case Selection

First, a group of relevant cases, all settled within the jurisdiction of OECD Member countries, was selected by using a specific search query within the database of the International Tax Law Reports.[109] The search function was applied on 1 January 2013 and brought up about 150 judgments in which the word 'interpretation' was found within the same paragraph[110] as the words 'tax treaty', 'tax agreement' or 'tax convention'.[111]

If a case included more than one interpretative issue, each issue was assessed as if it were an individual case. This was, for instance, the case when a judge clearly interpreted two distinct treaty terms, or when a judgment dealt with the application of more than one tax treaty.

From these 'cases', an additional selection excluded those which clearly fell outside the ambit of this research. Cases deselected were those in which the Commentary could clearly not have played a role, i.e.: (1) those that dealt with the interpretation of domestic tax law rather than the term of a tax treaty; (2) those not related to a tax treaty on income and capital, but, for example, to inheritance tax treaties; (3) those that dealt with tax treaty provisions that were clearly not in conformity with the OECD MTC;[112] and (4) those that dealt with the interpretation of treaty terms such as

---

108. The issue can be further complicated by the question of the retroactive effect of the OECD Commentary. To what extent can taxpayers rely on the expectation that an 'old' construction of a treaty provision would apply in the future? Indeed, the question comes up whether significant amendments to the OECD Commentary may be applied with retroactive effect to pre-existing ('old') facts or circumstances (i.e., in relation to situations that have their origin under an 'old' construction of a treaty provision, but continue to exist under a 'new' construction of a treaty provision, as is, for example, the case with the profits of a PE, capital gains, and interest). As Van der Velde and the author have argued elsewhere, the retroactive application of OECD Commentary under circumstance 5b (*see* Table 2 below) could harm a taxpayer's legitimate expectations, provided that the OECD Commentary is not introduced to counter an 'evident' lacuna in tax treaty law. *See* D.M. Broekhuijsen and K.M. Van Der Velde, *The Retroactive Effects of Changes to the Commentaries on the OECD Model*, 69 Bulletin for International Taxation 623 (2015).

109. These are available through Lexis Nexis Academic. *See* http://www.lexisnexis.co.uk/store/uk /International-Tax-Law-Reports/product.

110. And not, for example, in the editor's note to the case or in the case's summary.

111. The search function, which works on the basis of Boolean search logic, reads as follows: 'Interpretation W/p tax treaty OR tax agreement OR tax convention.' The search function has been applied in the Lexis Nexis database on the International Tax Law Reports on 1 Jan. 2013.

112. Here the author has followed the approach of P. Baker, *Double Taxation Conventions, a Manual on the OECD Model Tax Convention on Income and on Capital* (Sweet and Maxwell 3d

'profits',[113] 'income' or 'gains', which require domestic law rules to be calculated or determined, rather than the interpretative rules of the OECD Commentary.[114]

The use of the search function, in combination with the additional selection, resulted in a sample of 'neutral' cases (i.e., cases on tax treaty interpretation in which the Commentary could have been, but also in which it could *not* have been, of relevance). This allowed for the generalisation of the Commentary's relevance under a set of varying circumstances.

3.3.3 Coding and Grouping

In accordance with the facts of a case, each case was first coded on and then grouped within five categories of circumstances. The circumstances, here formulated in the form of questions, are:[115]

---

ed., 2001) at para. E-16 (a case-by-case interpretation is required to determine whether the difference in wording between treaty and OECD MTC also results in a different meaning between the two texts).

113. It has to be noted that the term 'profits' *strictu sensu* does not encompass the discussion on the *attribution* of profits (e.g., to a PE). Terms such as 'remuneration' also fit in this category.

114. Tax treaties merely allocate taxable income but do not regulate the calculation or determination of that income. For instance, in the proceedings of a seminar documented in B.J. Arnold, J. Sasseville and E.M. Zolt, *Summary of the Proceedings of an Invitational Seminar on Tax Treaties in the 21st Century*, 56 Bulletin for International Taxation 233, 243–244 (2002), participants observed 'that the tension between seeking a common interpretation of a treaty and referring to domestic law is not restricted to Art. 3(2). For example, determining the profits attributable to a permanent establishment requires reliance on the domestic law of each country; otherwise, treaties would have to contain detailed computational rules providing each and every detail (e.g., depreciation rates and rules) for determining taxable profits. Therefore, it was argued, recourse to domestic law is necessary wherever the treaty is silent or unclear, irrespective of whether or not Art. 3(2) is included in the treaty. It was argued that, in the absence of reliance on domestic law, tax treaties or the Commentary to the OECD Model would have to be transformed into a complete tax code.' Closely related is the issue that Martin points out: domestic law is to be applied before a tax treaty can restrict the application of that domestic law, named the 'subsidiarity of tax treaties': *see* P. Martin, *Interaction Between Tax Treaties and Domestic Law*, 65 Bulletin for International Taxation 205, 206 (2011).

115. These circumstances are generally considered relevant in the literature on the interpretation of tax treaties. They also follow from the position of the OECD's Committee on Fiscal Affairs as set out in the Introduction to the Commentary. Literature from which these circumstances follow is: K. Vogel, *Double Tax Treaties and their Interpretation*, 4 International Tax and Business Lawyer 1 (1986); H.J. Ault, *The Role of the OECD Commentaries in the Interpretation of Tax Treaties*, 22 Intertax 144 (1994); M. Edwards-Ker, *Tax Treaty Interpretation* (In-Depth 1994); E. Reimer, *Interpretation of Tax Treaties*, 39 European Taxation 458 (1999); E. Van Der Bruggen, *Unless the Vienna Convention Otherwise Requires: Notes on the Relationship Between Article 3(2) of the OECD Model Tax Convention and Articles 31 and 32 of the Vienna Convention on the Law of Treaties*, 43 European Taxation 142 (2003); F.A. Engelen, *Interpretation of Tax Treaties under International Law: A Study of Articles 31, 32 and 33 of the Vienna Convention on the Law of Treaties and their Application to Tax Treaties* (IBFD 2004); G. Maisto, *The Observations on the OECD Commentaries in the Interpretation of Tax Treaties*, in: A Tax Globalist, Essays in Honour of Maarten J. Ellis (H. Arendonk, F.A. Engelen and S. Jansen eds, IBFD 2005); M. Waters, *The Relevance of the OECD Commentaries in the Interpretation of Tax Treaties*, in: Praxis des Internationalen Steuerrechts, Festschrift für Helmut Loukota zum 65. Geburtstag (M. Lang and H. Jirousek eds, Linde Verlag Wien 2005); D.A. Ward et al., (2005) H. Pijl (2011).

(1) Was a reservation on the provisions of the OECD MTC or an observation on the Commentary submitted?

(2) Was the relevant treaty term *not* defined in the treaty?

(3) Was one of the treaty parties *not* a member of the OECD?

(4) Did the Commentary exist before the conclusion of the relevant bilateral tax treaty?[116]

(5) If question 4 was answered with **no** (i.e., the Commentary was adopted *after* the conclusion of the relevant bilateral tax treaty), was that Commentary:

    (a) similar to;

    (b) expounding on;

    (c) gap-filling in relation to;

    (d) or contradictory to Commentary existing at the time of conclusion of a treaty?[117]

For each case, questions 1–4 were answered with either 'yes' or 'no', question 5 with 'a'; 'b'; 'c' and 'd'. The answers were coded per case in a codebook and its related Excel database, which can be found in *Appendix B*. If a question could be answered with 'yes', that case was placed in that group. If a case could be placed in more than one group, it was.

3.3.4 Analysis

Subsequently, the influence of the Commentaries in all of the cases selected was determined, distinguishing between three possible entries: either the Commentary was used by the court, and therefore of relevance, or it was not used or disregarded by the court, and therefore not of relevance. In some cases, the Commentary's influence could not be determined or established. These cases were coded 'N.A. ("not applicable"). For each circumstance, this then resulted in a list of cases in which the Commentary was of relevance, a list of cases in which the Commentary was not of relevance, and a list of cases in which the relevance of the Commentary could not be determined.

---

116. But what if the Court itself did not explicitly refer to the OECD Commentary? To answer question 4, the author looked not only at the text of the judgement itself, but also at the arguments of parties. Coding rules were thus: if a court explicitly referred or cited a version of Commentary, the author coded the year of that version. Where the court referred to two versions, the author coded the version that has been published latest in time. Where a court did not explicitly refer to the Commentary, the author coded the year of adoption of the version referred to by one of the parties to the dispute. Where neither the Court nor the parties referred to the OECD Commentary, the author coded the year of the version to which an advocate general referred (if there was any). Where nothing in the judgement pointed at a Court's consideration of the Commentary, the author answered this question with N.A.

117. In this regard, the author followed M. Waters (2005). As to the issue of anti-abuse rules, the author followed the approach of B.J. Arnold and S. Van Weeghel, *The Relationship between Tax Treaties and Domestic Anti-Abuse Measures*, in: Tax Treaties and Domestic Law (G. Maisto ed., IBFD 2006).

The gradual normative influence of the Commentary on each decision (e.g., decisive, supplementary, etc.) was not considered: coding the relative influence of the Commentary proved too problematic (one of the problems was that in most decisions, courts do not give explicit reasons for their use of the Commentary).

3.3.5 Outcomes

The outcome of the analysis is expressed in the following table. For each circumstance, the table shows the number of cases in which courts have, and have not, used the OECD Commentary.

Table 2   The Relevance of the OECD Commentary under Varying Circumstances in Courts of OECD Member Countries

Circumstance	Total Number of Case Issues in Group	The Commentary Was Relevant	The Commentary Was Not Relevant	N.A. (Unable to Determine)	% of Cases in Which OECD Commentary Was Irrelevant
1. An observation or reservation has been submitted	8	4	4	0	50%
2. The relevant treaty term is not defined in the treaty	26	15	10	1	38%
3. One of the parties is not a member of the OECD	14	12	2	0	14%
4. The Commentary existed before the conclusion of the relevant treaty	11	9	2	0	18%
5a. The Commentary was adopted after the conclusion of a treaty, and that commentary was similar to (a) or expounding on (b) the version existing at the time the treaty was concluded	40	35	5	0	12%

Circumstance	Total Number of Case Issues in Group	The Commentary Was Relevant	The Commentary Was Not Relevant	N.A. (Unable to Determine)	% of Cases in Which OECD Commentary Was Irrelevant
5b. The Commentary was adopted after the conclusion of a treaty, and that Commentary was gap-filling in relation to (c) or contradictory to (d) the version existing at the time the treaty was concluded	20	12	8	0	40%
Total number of case issues selected	84	57	26	1	31%

From the analysis follows that the Commentary is generally complied with by courts when it does not introduce significant changes to the versions that existed at the time the relevant treaty was concluded. Indeed, the general picture is that the OECD Commentary is followed and used by courts in circumstances 4 and 5a in 82% and 88% of the cases considered, respectively.

But courts of OECD Member countries are more careful in applying Commentary that contains gap-filling or contradictory guidance in comparison to versions existing at the time the relevant treaty was concluded. Indeed, under circumstance 5b, courts disregard the OECD Commentary in 40% of the cases. This figure deviates significantly from the Commentary's record under the other circumstances. For instance, the situation that one of the treaty parties is not an OECD Member country seems to be of limited relevance in courts' considerations to use the Commentary: it was still used in 86% of the cases, despite the fact that non-OECD Member countries have had no or little influence in drafting the Commentary.

In the light of the current need for coherent action in the international tax field, the figure of 40% compels a reconsideration of the way the OECD seeks to dynamically influence the application and interpretation of bilateral tax treaties. This figure expresses that newly drafted OECD Commentary, for example, following from the BEPS Reports, may only have a moderate effect in practice. If the OECD Commentary on BEPS is disregarded in 40% of all cases brought to court in OECD Member countries' jurisdictions, that would make the implementation of the OECD's work in addressing BEPS vulnerable. After all, absent an international adjudicator, domestic courts have the 'final say' on the contents of tax treaty law in each jurisdiction.

What are the consequences? First of all, there is the problem of implementation effectiveness. Should the latest transfer pricing guidelines (i.e., the outcomes of BEPS

Actions 8–10) not be applied in OECD jurisdictions, the effect of changes to the transfer pricing guidelines would be severely limited. Moreover, the analysis above includes cases decided by courts of OECD Member countries only. The question therefore arises: what about the effect of the OECD Commentary in courts of non-OECD Member countries? Literature suggests a lower level of compliance in court decisions in these jurisdictions, as non-OECD Member countries have not had a similar degree of influence in formulating the OECD Commentary (and OECD MTC).[118]

Second, the reluctance of one court to apply the latest version of the OECD Commentary could jeopardize the BEPS Project as a whole (the importance of a level playing field, *see also* section 3.4).

So, in terms of effectiveness, amending the OECD Commentary so as to influence the contents of bilateral tax treaties may be questioned. But that is not all: the practice of influencing the contents of bilateral tax treaties in this deficient way is not without costs. The uncertain relevance of the OECD Commentary in courts of OECD Member countries under circumstance 5b negatively impacts the ability of taxpayers to know their obligations under tax treaty law. Indeed, the uncertainty introduced by substantial OECD Commentary amendments leaves practitioners clueless on whether the latest version of compels them to enter into costly restructurings. An indication of the relevance of this observation is that taxpayers' legitimate expectations may be harmed when OECD Commentary of type '5b' (*see* the Table 2 above) is applied with retroactive effect to facts and circumstances predating an update to the OECD Commentary.[119]

Hence, the problems of 'modernising' the tax treaty network by means of the OECD Commentary are numerous. The case law analysis clearly shows that the current 'system' to influence the contents of bilateral tax treaties is not without limits. A multilateral agreement has the potential to address these concerns. Indeed, Parliaments, not judges or a creative executive, are best placed to implement new norms in tax treaties.[120]

3.4   A LEVEL PLAYING FIELD

The loose form of coordination under the OECD MTC and Commentaries creates another problem: it does not allow states to coordinate on the parallel amendment of

---

118. D.A. Ward et al., (2005) pp. 35–36: 'the presumption that the [Non-OECD member] parties have a common intention is (...) much weaker, as the non-OECD member country would not have had the opportunity to participate in the discussions and the drafting of the relevant Commentary.' From the extensive study by M. Lang et al., (2012) follows that this position is (often implicitly) taken in, for example, Brazil (*see* pp. 172–173); China (p. 262); Colombia (p. 295); India (pp. 552–554); Peru (p. 798); Russia (p. 919). It goes without saying that if the relevant tax treaty is not based on the OECD Model, the question is irrelevant.
119. D.M. Broekhuijsen and K.M. Van Der Velde (2015).
120. *See also* E. Kemmeren, *De rol van het OESO-Commentaar bij de uitleg van belastingverdragen en het Europese recht: Trias politica onder toenemende druk?*, in: Principieel belastingrecht: Liber Amicorum Richard Happé (H. Gribnau ed., Wolf Legal Publishers 2011), who argues that the dynamic application of changes to the OECD MTC not supported by the text of a tax treaty, upsets the balance between lawmaker, judge and executive.

bilateral tax treaties. This greatly reduces the ability of international tax policy makers to coordinate on international tax rules in an integrative way. Because states coordinate on the avoidance of double taxation by means of soft law, they are free to modify, disregard or postpone on implementing that soft law when negotiating or amending their bilateral tax treaty relations. Indeed, the loose type of coordination has not been able to prevent the many collective action problems now addressed in the BEPS Project. Tax competition is, in other words, structurally 'built in' in the method by means of which states cooperate in international tax law. This prevents states to reach common, more optimal and fairer solutions than those currently reached. In sum: under the current coordination system, every single nation, or group of nations, has the dominant strategy to compete with others to attract investors. Without a level playing field, collective action problems like BEPS will just shift to the countries ('free riders') that have not accepted certain treaty amendments.[121] This incentive exists, as some countries may foresee a larger inflow of foreign direct investment (FDI) if others restrict their rules.

This is also recognised by the OECD in its report on drafting a multilateral instrument. The OECD considers that 'some provisions of the treaty-based portion of the BEPS Project require broad state participation in order to successfully address BEPS concerns'.[122] And the explanatory statement to the final BEPS package states that some minimum standards were agreed upon 'in particular to tackle issues in cases where no action by some countries would have created negative spill overs (including adverse impacts of competitiveness) on other countries'.[123] Countries have recognised the need to level the playing field in the areas of preventing treaty shopping, country-by-country reporting, fighting harmful tax competition and improving dispute resolution.[124] And indeed, some of these areas are reflected in the BEPS Convention, in which the parties announce they are 'conscious of the need to ensure swift, co-ordinated and consistent implementation of the treaty-related BEPS measures in a multilateral context'.[125]

What is at stake? The lack of a level playing field may cause participating states to take unilateral action (for instance, by means of unilateral anti-abuse or CFC rules),[126] or lead them to continue relaxing their tax rules and engage in further tax competition, undermining common, multilateral solutions. Neither of these two alternatives are more attractive in the long run. Increased and enduring tax competition may mean that tax systems will become increasingly redundant. Alternatively, international tax law may end up as a 'global tax chaos' due to the uncontrolled growth of domestic anti-abuse rules. A level playing field created by a multilateral agreement may therefore be perceived as an attractive solution in between these two extremes.

---

121. F.A. Engelen and A.F. Gunn, *Het BEPS-project: een inleiding*, WFR 2013/1413 para. 4.2.
122. OECD, *Developing a Multilateral Instrument to Modify Bilateral Tax Treaties* (2014) p. 17.
123. OECD, *Developing a Multilateral Instrument to Modify Bilateral Tax Treaties, Action 15: 2015 Final Report* (2015) p. 6.
124. OECD, *Preventing the Granting of Treaty Benefits in Inappropriate Circumstances, Action 6: 2015 Final Report* (2015) OECD/G20 Base Erosion and Profit Shifting Project, OECD Publishing, Paris, http://dx.doi.org/10.1787/9789264241688-en., p. 6.
125. Preamble to the BEPS Convention.
126. H. Loukota (1998) p. 88.

3.5 CONCLUSION: THE PROSPECTS OF A MULTILATERAL AGREEMENT FOR INTERNATIONAL TAXATION

From the previous chapter follows that agreement on a 'comprehensive' multilateral tax treaty might never be achieved, and that any effort for multilateral agreement has to take the bilateral tax treaty system as a given.

At the same time, a 'new move in tax coordination' is becoming increasingly urgent and necessary for international tax law. The collective action problems of tax avoidance and tax evasion are high on the political agenda, yet, as follows from this chapter, the loose type of coordination currently practiced by the OECD is lacking in terms of its ability to dynamically influence and modernise the bilateral tax treaty network in line with present-day needs. Indeed, amending the OECD MTC so as to influence the norms of bilateral tax treaties is unsuited as a way to modernise international tax law: states rarely amend their tax treaties, and if they do, they are not compelled to conform to the most recent version of the OECD MTC. Likewise, stretching the interpretation of a tax treaty rule by amending the OECD Commentary is not very effective either, as courts of varying OECD Member countries are reluctant to apply new interpretative rules to older tax treaties.

Moreover, the loose type of coordination provided by the OECD MTC fails at addressing collective action problems that relate to the interests of the international community as a whole.[127] Although essentially a multilateral structure from which states deviate in their bilateral tax treaty relations, the OECD MTC does not compel states to undertake coordinated action. States can, after all, decide to postpone the implementation of the latest version of the OECD MTC in their treaties, or disregard updates to the OECD MTC completely.

For these reasons alone, thinking about a 'new' style multilateral agreement for international taxation is a necessary step in addressing common action problems such as those related to tax arbitrage and tax competition. First of all, the binding nature of a multilateral agreement would take care of amending bilateral tax treaties in one go.[128] In the words of the OECD:

---

127. *See* A. Christians et al., (2007). For the argument that a comparable shift has taken place in in relation to international law in general: B. Simma, *From Bilateralism to Community Interest in International Law*, in: Recueil des Cours: Collected Courses of The Hague Academy of International Law 1994 IV (Martinus Nijhoff 1995).

128. There is however a very important underlying assumption in the OECD's rhetoric. The OECD considers that a multilateral agreement to amend bilateral tax treaties is able to 'overcome the hurdle of cumbersome bilateral negotiations and produce important efficiency gains'. The assumption, in other words, seems to be that a decrease in procedural hurdles will quicken tax treaty amendments. OECD, *Action 15: A Mandate for the Development of a Multilateral Instrument on Tax Treaty Measures to Tackle BEPS* (2015) OECD/G20 Base Erosion and Profit Shifting Project, http://www.oecd.org/ctp/beps-action-15-mandate-for-development-of-multi lateral-instrument.pdf, p. 15. On the question whether a multilateral negotiation *will* actually be quicker than all those bilateral negotiations, *see* further Chs 5 and 6.

> If undertaken on a purely treaty-by-treaty basis, the sheer number of treaties in effect may make such a process very lengthy, the more so where countries embark on comprehensive renegotiations of their bilateral tax treaties.[129]

> the simple reality [is] that only a multilateral instrument can overcome the practical difficulties associated with trying to rapidly modify the 3000 + bilateral treaty network.[130]

Second, a multilateral agreement has the potential to provide a level playing field, which enables states to coordinate on common policy goals. In the words of the Action 15 – Final Report:

> to ensure a level playing field and fairly shared tax burdens, flexibility and respect for bilateral relations will need to be balanced against core commitments that reflect new international standards that countries are urged to meet and for which the multilateral instrument is a facilitative tool.[131]

So, there is a need for a legal instrument that fundamentally increases the role of multilateralism in swiftly adapting or changing the rules contained in bilateral treaties in a binding manner. And introducing these adaptations and changes in a coordinated way will create a level playing field in which states can reach collective outcomes on collective action problems. In this regard, the multilateral agreement built upon in this book should be seen as a method:

(I) to make (OECD) coordination outcomes binding, so that they have direct impact on the texts and/or the interpretation of bilateral treaties, potentially providing for a more expeditious tax treaty amendment process;

(II) that assists states in agreeing to tax treaty amendments in a more structural, complete and uniform manner.[132]

The BEPS Convention, evaluated in Chapter 8, is a good first step. Yet, as we will see, a more fundamental multilateral solution for international taxation will be necessary to address the collective action problems of today as well as those of tomorrow.

---

129. OECD, *BEPS Action Plan (2013)* pp. 23–24.
130. OECD, *Developing a Multilateral Instrument to Modify Bilateral Tax Treaties,* Action 15: 2015 Final Report (2015) para. 12.
131. *Id.,* at para. 17.
132. Inspired on: A. Miller and A. Kirkpatrick (2013) p. 685.

In a Perfect World: A Normative View on Multilateral Cooperation in International Taxation

4.1 INTRODUCTION

The previous chapter has shown that what the multilateral treaty should, most importantly, do, is solve the issues related to the implementation of new norms in the network of bilateral tax treaties, and create a level playing field, so that cooperation between states can converge on the necessary solutions for collective action problems. But these objectives do not provide any insight in what the multilateral agreement can and should look like. Questions are, for example: how can and should international tax law of the future be made? Who can and should participate? What types of norms can multilaterally be achieved and should be aimed for?

This chapter will set forth a normative view on multilateral cooperation in the area of international taxation. In this chapter, the aim is to construct an 'ideal' model of international tax cooperation by considering how states could enhance the 'fairness' of international tax law, addressing the 'should' part of the questions above. The chapter provides, in other words, the compass on which the designers of a multilateral solution for international tax should navigate. The next chapter moderates this ideal by providing a 'realistic' or 'instrumental' perspective on multilateral cooperation in international taxation. The aim of Chapter 5 is, in other words, to explore what is, in fact, politically feasible in the international tax arena (the 'can' part of the questions above). In the considerations of states whether to enter into a multilateral agreement, 'achieving fairness' is unlikely to be the dominant determinant: defending the national interests is a more likely motive. Chapter 6 brings the outcomes of Chapters 4 and 5 together by formulating a design strategy for a multilateral agreement for international taxation.

Why consider the 'fairness' of international tax rules as a compass to guide the design of a multilateral agreement for international taxation? It goes without saying that 'norms' and 'values' have increasingly come to matter in international tax. The idea that MNEs should pay a 'fair share' is on the rise.[133] And indeed, concepts of 'fairness' have likely been the catalyst for state cooperation on the BEPS Project. After all, the BEPS Project aims to 'restore the trust of ordinary people in the fairness of their tax systems';[134] as 'governments are harmed (…) individual taxpayers are harmed (…) businesses are harmed.'[135] A multilateral agreement for international taxation provides an exciting opportunity in this regard: it enables states to articulate and promote emerging ideas of 'fair' international tax rules. A multilateral tax deal can, in other words, be seen as a launching pad for coherent action to make international tax law, which has been eroded by the effects of globalisation, 'fair' again.[136]

But what does 'fairness' mean in international tax law? The answer proves elusive. First of all, the world has evolved through globalisation (i.e., states engage in tax competition for mobile capital), whereas the existing norms of 'fairness' are based on a concept of international tax rules that stems from the 1960s, where states, and not taxpayers, were the most relevant actors in international law. Bilateral tax treaties were, after all, designed to coordinate the issue of jurisdictional overlap for the matter of direct taxation. As a consequence, traditional theories on fairness of international tax rules[137] do not address the fact that enterprises operating in a cross-border context are

---

133. *See*, for a Dutch pioneer in this regard, R.H. Happé, *Belastingethiek: een kwestie van fair share*, in: Belastingen en ethiek, geschriften van de Vereniging voor Belastingwetenschap No. 243 (Kluwer 2011) and R.H. Happé, *Fiscale ethiek voor multinationals*, WFR 2015/938.
134. OECD, *Developing a Multilateral Instrument to Modify Bilateral Tax Treaties, Action 15: 2015 Final Report* (2015) p. 4.
135. OECD, *BEPS Action Plan (2013)* p. 8.
136. *See*, for this point generally, R. García Antón, *The 21st Century Multilateralism on International Taxation: The Emperor's New Clothes?*, 8 World Tax Journal 147 (2016), who wants to use a multilateral treaty to replace the benefits principle with 'tax fairness' and 'solidarity'. These terms comprise a solution for the source-residence dichotomy, and may accordingly also require a redistribution of tax revenue between rich and poor. 'Stamping out global inequalities and poverty constitutes enough member surplus to justify the leap to a worldwide multilateral framework, but within a different, truly universal, platform, such as the United Nations.'
137. In the traditional conception of international tax, bilateral tax treaties were designed to coordinate the issue of jurisdictional overlap, and to reduce barriers to international trade. The related concepts of 'fairness' of this traditional understanding of international tax law are that of inter-nation equity, which concerns the fair allocation of tax in the relationships between sovereign states, and that of inter-individual equity, which concerns the fair distribution of tax burdens among taxpayers. *See, e.g.*, M.J. Graetz (2001) 294–297. The concept of inter-individual equity most of all relates to the division of tax burdens *within* the state, and the inter-nation equity concept, first and most famously set out by the Musgraves, relates to the division of taxing rights *between* states. In both concepts, state borders are, hence, important. R.A. Musgrave and P.B. Musgrave, *Inter-nation Equity*, in: Modern Fiscal Issues: Essays in Honor of Carl S. Shoup (R.M. Bird and J.G. Head eds, University of Toronto Press 1972); also: C. Peters (2014).
    For those interested in 'fair' international tax rules, the work of the Musgraves provides a first foothold. Their point of departure was 'national neutrality': cross-border investments should at least generate the same before-tax return as domestic investments, and to the excess, the source state has a claim which may be stronger as the residence state is richer and the source state is poorer. The Musgraves hence departed from the commonly accepted bases for the taxation of international income: source and residence. *See* N.H. Kaufman, *Fairness and the*

treated differently from those who do not. In other words, in the globalised world, state borders have become increasingly immaterial in international economic society,[138] and consequently, fairness theory based on the existence of state borders, has become outdated. Second, it proves very difficult to isolate a concept of 'distributive fairness' – i.e., 'the degree to which the rules satisfy the participants' expectations of justifiable distribution of costs and benefits' –[139] from notions of economic neutrality.[140] Yet, the question of the 'fair' distribution of the tax burden is not only an economic one, but also one that is philosophical and, ultimately, political.[141]

Taxation of International Income, 29 Law and Policy in International Business 145 (1998). In their view, the residence state had the strongest claim to tax. The reason for this stronger claim, the Musgraves suggested, is first that taxpayers owe their tax allegiance to their country of residence for the rights and privileges that adhere to them as residents. Second, inclusion of the foreign source income in the resident country is necessary to achieve equity (i.e., inter-individual equity) among resident taxpayers. After all, the collection of the necessary information (including that on the personal circumstances) of the taxpayer is most easily to administer in the residence state. Third, the resident country has tax sovereignty over the property of residents that is part of that country's natural resources. Finally, the resident claim 'may be justified in benefit terms, as a payment for productivity-enhancing benefits provided by the country of residence to its own factors of production prior to transfer abroad'. P.B. Musgrave, *Consumption Tax Proposals in an International Setting*, 54 Tax Law Review 77, 79 (2000). The view that the resident state has a stronger claim seems to have stuck in international tax law. The fact that a taxpayer is a resident of a particular country makes that taxpayer different from non-resident taxpayers, justifying a different tax treatment of residents and non-residents. *See, e.g.*, K. Brooks, *Inter-nation Equity: The Development of an Important but Underappreciated International Tax Policy Objective*, in: Tax Reform in the 21st Century: A Volume in Memory of Richard Musgrave (J.G. Head and R. Krever eds, Kluwer Law International 2009).

138. C. Peters (2014) p. 105. As M.F. De Wilde, *'Sharing the Pie': Taxing Multinationals in a Global Market* (Erasmus University Rotterdam 2015) p. 47 expresses this: 'I fail to see why a taxpayer's tax residence would constitute a different circumstance and therefore justifies this different tax treatment [depending on where the taxpayer has its tax residence]. In today's reality where economic operators move increasingly effortlessly across tax-borders in an emerging global market place, the tax residence is economically immaterial.' *Id.*, at p. 47.

139. T.M. Franck, *Fairness in International Law and Institutions* (Clarendon Press 1995) p. 7.

140. *See, e.g.*, the recent work of M.F. De Wilde (2015a) pp. 59–60: 'It is argued that the notion of fairness in corporate taxation is founded on the equality principle, thereby conforming to the historically widely acknowledged notion of equal treatment before the law. Economic equal circumstances should be treated equally for tax purposes. Unequal economic circumstances should be treated unequally for tax purposes insofar as the circumstances are unequal. From the equality postulate it can be deduced that everyone in an economic relationship with a taxing state has the obligation to contribute to the financing of public goods from which one benefits in accordance with one's means – "equity". And production factors should be distributed on the basis of market mechanisms without, or at least with as little as possible, public interference – "economic efficiency". Taxation should be in line with economic reality; it should not affect business decisions – tax neutrality, including the neutrality of legal form. Income should be taxed once, as close as possible to its source.' Also: A.H. Rosenzweig, *Defining a Country's 'Fair Share' of Taxes*, 42 Florida State University Law Review 373 (2015), who advocates that the residence state has a claim to some minimum return, to be calculated at arm's length; any MNE profits in excess of this normal return should be divided among all states involved, using formulary apportionment. This, he considers, would truly maximise the efficiency of the international tax regime. *See also* D.M. Broekhuijsen and H. Vording, *Multilaterale samenwerking ten aanzien van het BEPS-Project: een prognose*, WFR 2016/53.

141. That tax theory should not exclusively be approached by economic thought was, as Gribnau shows, already recognised by Nicolaas Gerard Pierson (1838–1909), who had an important role in formulating tax theory in the Netherlands. *See* H. Gribnau, *Tweehonderd jaar belasting-wetenschap*, in: Tweehonderd jaar Rijksbelastingen (H. Vording ed., SDU 2015) p. 208. The

So, absent an easy (re)definition of distributive fairness, it makes sense, for the purposes of the design of a multilateral agreement that aims to create international legal obligation, to emphasise 'the extent to which the rules are made and applied in accordance with what the participants perceive as right process'[142] instead.[143]

But more importantly, the question what a fair distribution entails in international tax law will be heavily debated or contested in practice (*see* further sections 5.4.3 and 5.4.4), emphasising the relevance of procedural fairness in international cooperation.[144] After all, where establishing a justifiable and fair distribution of costs and benefits proves difficult, it makes sense that actors enter into norm-generating discourse and partake in interstate discussions. The point is, of course, that if such discourse and discussions are perceived as unfair, as actors are prevented to voice their opinions and interests, outcomes will also be perceived as biased or unfair. Hence, 'correct' procedure is indispensable to ensure that all relevant political, moral and social factors can be integrated in actual legal outcomes, making those outcomes 'neutral' or 'fair' in the eyes of all actors.[145]

To construct an outline of what is required by a 'correct' decision-making process for international tax law, let us take two cosmopolitan views on procedural fairness. The cosmopolitan viewpoint provides a move away from the state-centred, traditional

---

importance of a philosophical perspective on distributive justice has also been stressed by, among others, the founder of the academic study of tax law in Leiden: H.J. Hofstra, *Over belastingbeginselen*, WFR 1979/1212 ('De belastingheffing vormt enerzijds een juridisch, rechtsfilosofisch, staatkundig probleem, maar heeft anderzijds ingrijpende economische en sociale gevolgen. Historisch hebben de juristen de fiscale problematiek grotendeels verwaarloosd (...) Het gevolg is geweest dat de theoretische beschouwingen in hoofdzaak aan de economen werden overgelaten. Hun benadering is echter een geheel andere dan die van de jurist.') But, as Vording notes, it has proven difficult to 'translate' political philosophy to substantive tax principles, as 'using' such principles to 'test' a substantive tax rule is contingent on what society aims to achieve with that rule. It therefore makes sense to turn to a 'procedural' concept of fairness instead. H. Vording, *Vooruitgang in de fiscale rechtswetenschap*, in: Vooruit met het recht (J.H. Nieuwenhuis and C.J.J.M. Stolker eds, Boom Juridische Uitgevers 2006) p. 104.

142. T.M. Franck (1995) p. 7.
143. Indeed, as Tsilly Dagan points out, 'Since the normative goals of international taxation are unclear, one could point to procedure as an answer. Perhaps – it may be argued – including all the potential stakeholders in the design of multilateral accords would lead to better results in terms of promoting the interests of the entire international community. Indeed, if actual voice and genuine input for all the actors on the international scene is attained, such a procedure may yield results that actually promote the collective good. The decision making process that is required in order to achieve such results must be carefully designed. Such a procedure should carefully identify the stakeholders involved and find paths to allow for an open deliberative process where the variety of normative considerations can be honestly discussed and seriously considered. It may even be the case that making decisions on international taxation requires a full-blown political institution.' T. Dagan, *Community Obligations in International Taxation*, Global Trust Working Paper Series 01/2016 (2016), available at SSRN: http://papers.ssrn.com/sol3/papers.cfm?abstract_id = 2736923.
144. Indeed, as one author generally phrases it: international law 'gives states the tools to achieve certain outcomes, rather than telling them what outcomes they should reach'. F. Mégret (2012) p. 67.
145. Such principles are of course relevant at all levels. *See, e.g.,* H. Gribnau, *Belastingen als moreel fenomeen: vertrouwen en legitimiteit in de praktijk* (Boom fiscale uitgevers 2013), who stresses the importance of legitimacy and trust in relation to domestic tax law.

concept of state relations in the world (i.e., a world in which borders between states are material and important), and leads to a worldview which centralises on the individual. Cosmopolitanism encompasses 'the idea that all human beings, regardless of their political affiliation, are (or can and should be) citizens in a single community'.[146] The concept is said to relate to Diogenes of Sinope, who had a reputation of sleeping and eating wherever he chose to and defecating in public. When asked where he came from, he declared himself a citizen of the world,[147] presumably because he hoped this would disqualify the local authorities to fine him for his behaviour. At the core of (modern) cosmopolitanism lies, as Brock says, 'the view that every human being has standing as an ultimate unit of moral concern and is entitled to equal consideration of her interests no matter what other affiliations, especially national affiliations, she might have'.[148] The attractiveness of the cosmopolitan view is hence that it seeks to provide solutions for the erosive effects of globalisation by recasting the state-border oriented international system. By centring on the individual as a citizen of the world, the cosmopolitan view is able to provide 'ideal' solutions for countering the temptation of states to engage in individually rational but collectively irrational behaviour, of which tax arbitrage and tax competition are the effects.[149] It places international political processes as well as the market forces under greater political control.[150] Therefore, the cosmopolitan view is relevant in addressing the problem of BEPS. After all, the BEPS Project seeks to resolve the issues caused by the inability of governments to collectively deal with the mobility of capital and the increased interconnectedness of their economies.

The two views on procedural fairness that guide and inform the design of a multilateral agreement for international taxation are Jürgen Habermas' concept of legitimate law (section 4.2.1) and Martha Nussbaum's social contract (section 4.2.2).

---

146. P. Kleingeld and E. Brown, *Cosmopolitanism*, in: Stanford Encyclopedia of Philosophy (E.N. Zalta ed., Stanford University Fall 2014 ed., 2014).

147. Diogenes Laertius, *Lives of Eminent Philosophers, Volume II: Books 6-10* (R.D. Hicks *trans.*, Loeb Classical Library 2015, Harvard University Press 1925), book VI, p. 65.

148. G. Brock, *Global Justice*, in: Stanford Encyclopedia of Philosophy (E.N. Zalta ed., Stanford University Spring 2015 ed., 2015) sec. 2.3.

149. *See also* Ring on the value of cosmopolitan views on tax competition: D.M. Ring, *Democracy, Sovereignty and Tax Competition: The Role of Tax Sovereignty in Shaping Tax Cooperation*, 9 Florida Tax Review 555, 589 (2009): 'perhaps we can find room for a moderate variant of cosmopolitan theory which grants a special, and possibly dominant, obligation to fellow citizens but maintains a heightened set of duties to all persons. (...) If the currently incomplete cosmopolitan theories could develop a framework for the stable world order that would implement their vision of global justice, the sovereign state system might be flexible enough to accommodate it.'

150. For instance, a cosmopolitan idea of democracy, for example, that of David Held, requires democracy on all levels, so that 'globalised' issues can be placed under an overarching form of democratic control. It requires in the short run, for example, the strengthening of the UN, compulsory jurisdiction before the International Court of Justice and an enhanced engagement of civil society, and in the long run, for example, a global parliament. D. Held, *Democracy and the Global Order: From the Modern State to Cosmopolitan Governance* (Polity 1995).

Both perspectives, further developed for the area of international taxation by Peters[151] and Christians,[152] lead to similar models of procedural fairness in international taxation (section 4.2.3).

4.2 TWO COSMOPOLITAN VIEWS ON PROCEDURAL FAIRNESS

4.2.1 Habermas' Concept of Legitimate Law

The work of Habermas, in particular his *Between Facts and Norms*,[153] provides fertile ground to consider the fairness of international tax law. The legitimacy viewpoint matters, as societies are stable and fair over the long run only when they are perceived as legitimate by their members.

In *Between Facts and Norms*, Habermas seeks to provide a normative account of legitimate law. Ultimately, Habermas' point is that that the quality of procedures and public participation in these procedures is of importance to guarantee that the law created is perceived as 'fair' by its addressees. In particular, Habermas advances the need for fair process in the form of 'deliberative democracy', in which participants are treated equally and discussions take place on the basis of rational argument. This guarantees that law is legitimate, i.e., that it includes all relevant moral, social and economic perspectives.[154]

Some writers, and particularly Cees Peters, have applied Habermas' work to assess current international tax lawmaking, as well as to construct an exemplary type of legitimate governance structure for the future of international tax law.[155] Since Peters summarises the complex work of Habermas adequately for the purposes of international tax law,[156] the author will only briefly reflect on Habermas' work here (doing some damage, obviously, to his extensive theory).

4.2.1.1 *Social and System Integration*

Habermas argues how societies have evolved through globalisation, whereas the existing norms and lawmaking processes of these societies have not been able to accommodate this evolution. As we will see, this view can be applied to the area of international tax law to show that international tax lawmaking taking place within the OECD as well as within domestic settings is flawed.

---

151. C. Peters (2014).
152. A. Christians, *Sovereignty, Taxation and Social Contract*, 18 Minnesota Journal of International Law 99 (2009).
153. J. Habermas, *Between Facts and Norms: Contributions to a Discourse Theory of Law and Democracy* (W. Rehg trans. Polity 1996).
154. For a further exploration on these types of issues in relation to EU and OECD soft law: H. Gribnau, *Soft Law and Taxation: EU and International Aspects*, 2 Legisprudence 67 (2008).
155. *See* C. Peters (2014) and P. Essers, *International Tax Justice between Machiavelli and Habermas*, 68 Bulletin for International Taxation 54 (2014).
156. C. Peters (2014) Ch. 6.

Central to applying the Habermasian argument to international taxation is the claim that state borders prevent states to act coherently on globalised issues: it is 'no longer appropriate to identify "society" with the state and to regard this society as an association of individuals only'.[157] The point is that where state borders have become increasingly immaterial for the economic world,[158] they have not become irrelevant for the world of lawmakers. Tax systems differ from one state to the other and are used by states to attract investment. Cooperation on the international level functions on the basis of competition rather than collaboration. The work of Habermas, when applied to the area of international taxation, can be used to better understand this situation.

To further understand Habermas' argument, it is relevant that he distinguishes between two opposing forces that make up society: 'social integration', the result of intended actions of individuals, which are brought about by 'a normatively secured or communicatively achieved consensus', and 'system integration', a structural effect, which relates to a mechanism that coordinates individual decisions by means of consequences that extend beyond the actors' consciousness.[159] As Peters expresses it: on the one hand, there are ways in which we can take control of our lives ('agency'), but on the other hand, we are being directed by society (the 'system'), such as the market.[160] Habermas' claim in this regard is that systems, such as the market, are 'increasingly removing the possibilities of society to get organised on the basis of communicative processes in the lifeworld'.[161]

4.2.1.2   Deliberative Democracy

What is needed, according to Habermas, is to react to this situation, so that the influence of social and communicative processes in society is restored. First of all, this requires democratic self-determination: legal persons can be autonomous only when they understand themselves as the authors of the law, i.e., of the legal order ('*public autonomy*').[162] In the words of Habermas:

> the principle of democracy should establish a procedure of legitimate law-making. Specifically, the democratic principle states that only those statutes may claim legitimacy that can meet with the assent (Zustimmung) of all citizens in a discursive process of legislation that in turn has been legally constituted.[163]

But at the same time, the law thus created must secure a space of *private autonomy* of those subject to it, i.e., it must secure a space for individual freedom

---

157. *Id.*, at p. 175.
158. *Id.*, at p. 25.
159. J. Habermas, *The Theory of Communicative Action, Volume 2: Lifeworld and System: A Critique of Functionalist Reason* (Polity Press 1987) p. 117.
160. C. Peters (2014) p. 178.
161. J. Bohman and W. Rehg, *Jürgen Habermas*, in: Stanford Encyclopedia of Philosophy (E.N. Zalta ed., Stanford University Fall 2014 ed., 2014) p. 3.1; C. Peters (2014) pp. 178–179. This reflects Habermas' colonisation thesis.
162. J. Habermas (1996) sec. 9.2.2. J. Bohman and W. Rehg (2014) sec. 3.4.
163. J. Habermas (1996) sec. 3.2.1.

(including equality before the law, negative human rights and the right of political participation). State power, in other words, has to be restricted or restrained by law.

Each of these two concepts, i.e., public and private autonomy, is 'equiprimordial', which means that each can only be fully realised if the other is fully realised and vice versa. Habermas therefore has very influentially struck a middle ground in between the liberal tradition (i.e., citizens must be protected from arbitrary governmental influence by basic rights) and the republican tradition (i.e., popular sovereignty leads citizens to agree on the common good). In the words of Bohman and Rehg:

> the exercise of public autonomy in its full sense presupposes participants who understand themselves as individually free (privately autonomous), which in turn presupposes that they can shape their individual freedoms through the exercise of public autonomy.[164]

In simple terms, legitimate lawmaking requires that certain civil rights are recognised, so that citizens can live free of government bounds. At the same time, drafting these rules requires that all those interested have the possibility to participate in the lawmaking process, so that it may be presumed that all citizens in society can assent to the law thus created. This is what 'deliberative democracy' favoured by Habermas requires.

The point seems to be then, that both public and private autonomy are required for 'legitimate law'. And indeed, specifically in relation to tax law, this point is shared by others. Gribnau, albeit on the basis of different theory,[165] comes to a similar conclusion: legitimation through 'correct' legal procedure is necessary but not sufficient for legitimate tax law. Law cannot be separated from the needs and interests of the society that it means to affect. This means that tax law needs to be constructed in accordance with 'correct' process, but also that it must protect those it addresses by reflecting basic principles and values such as legal certainty, equality before the law and proportionality.[166]

Not only Peters, but also Essers[167] have applied the idea of Habermas' deliberative democracy to international tax law. Applying the idea of 'deliberative democracy' to international tax law exposes a gap in respect of where the norms of international taxation are generated. Either they are created domestically, under the influence of the 'tax law market',[168] and are lacking because they are purely driven by 'systemic' and uncommunicative forces of tax competition, or they are created within the current framework of the OECD, which suffers from being exclusive and non-transparent.[169] As Peters notices, this tension features in the acts of domestic policy makers. On the

---

164. J. Bohman and W. Rehg (2014) sec. 3.4.
165. Gribnau centralises the citizen rather than the state, leading him to consider thinkers such as Spinoza and Sloterdijk.
166. H. Gribnau, *Soevereiniteit en legitimiteit: Grenzen aan (fiscale regelgeving)* (SDU Uitgevers 2008). He applies his perspective to lawmaking and law-application in The Netherlands in H. Gribnau (2013a).
167. P. Essers (2014).
168. *See* C. Peters (2014).
169. *Id.*, at p. 212.

one hand, governments claim to seek international cooperation on international tax issues, whilst on the other hand, they praise the competitive strength of their domestic tax systems.[170]

That a pure domestic lawmaking setting, influenced by the 'tax law marketplace', does not present the ideal location for the formulation of legitimate norms of international taxation makes sense from a Habermasian viewpoint: absent a level playing field or further integrative cooperation, governments have been given no other choice but to compete to attract investors. Some of the tax rules created under the influence of the 'marketplace' have in fact been invented primarily for that purpose. At the same time, taxpayers have had the utmost freedom to benefit from the rules thus put in place, necessitating governments to shift the tax burden to those who cannot take advantage of cross-border activity. It is therefore no wonder that tax rules are increasingly considered to operate unequally,[171] and have consequently led to public outrage and calls for MNEs to 'do more than the law requires'.[172]

The other place where international tax norms are created inadequately is within the institutional framework of the OECD. According to Essers, what is especially lacking in this regard is the participation and influence of national parliaments, citizens and taxpayers in the OECD. 'Parliaments can only discuss the results of the OECD meetings with the ministers of the national government; citizens can only hold their national parliamentarians accountable in the elections every four years.'[173] Therefore, from the Habermasian perspective, 'it is essential that national parliaments and citizens are truly involved in the process of achieving international tax justice'.[174] Likewise, in Peters' view, the legitimacy of the lawmaking framework of the OECD falters in two respects: it falters in terms of the inclusiveness of the deliberations, and in terms of the transparency and openness of the lawmaking procedures.[175] Peters points, for instance, at the use of public discussion drafts. These, in the absence of empirical research on the diversity of responses to these discussion drafts and on the relationship between responses and decisions eventually made, run the risk of turning into a wildcard for the international business community to 'steer' deliberations towards its particular interests, at the expense of other ideas.[176] As a consequence of this, Peters argues, the quality of the decision-making processes (i.e., 'input legitimacy') is lacking.[177] Tax measures should be the result of true and inclusive democratic deliberation between and within countries.[178]

---

170. *Id.*, at p. 213.
171. *See, e.g.,* M.F. De Wilde (2015a).
172. For example, R.H. Happé (2015).
173. P. Essers (2014) p. 57.
174. *Id.*, at p. 57.
175. C. Peters (2014) sec. 6.6.2.3.
176. *Id.*, at sec. 6.6.2.3.
177. *Id.*, at p. 341. This term derives from the work of F.W. Scharpf, *Governing in Europe: Effective and Democratic?* (OUP 1999).
178. P. Essers (2014) p. 65.

4.2.1.3 Deliberative International Tax Law

On this basis, it is then possible to develop the characteristics of a framework that would ensure the legitimacy of international tax law in the long run. Indeed, Peters extends the Habermasian national model of legitimate law to the level of international tax law (note that Habermas himself has not yet fully applied his theory to the international level). This leads Peters to consider a set of cosmopolitan procedures called 'deliberative international tax law'.[179] Ultimately, he says, 'it is completely up to the taxpayers themselves – in their capacity as citizens – to formulate the normative content of international tax law'.[180] Therefore, according to Peters, legitimate international tax law 'requires a never-ending rational discussion – i.e., an exchange of arguments – about the norms of national and international tax law'.[181] Ideally, the main characteristic of this set of procedures is that it should allow 'taxpayers the possibility to express their disagreement about the existing set of norms and to be actively – and on equal terms – part of the deliberations'.[182] This requires:

> procedures that are at the basis of the deliberations about the (normative) meaning of law. These procedures should ensure a free and continuous discussion about which laws should prevail.[183] (...) Taxes need to originate from a political and legal system that has its roots in the communicative processes of society. The members of a society need to recognise themselves in their taxing system and in the norms that are at the basis of this system. This implies in the first place that there needs to be a never-ending rational discussion – i.e. an exchange of arguments – about the norms of national and international tax law.[184]

This cosmopolitan 'deliberative international tax law' framework should eventually replace the state consent model of legitimacy that is currently applied.[185] But Peters recognises that in the short run, for example, for the design of the multilateral instrument,[186] this would be a bridge too far. As state consent is still the basis for public international law,[187] he proposes a more moderate form of his 'deliberative international tax law', in which states and stakeholders (e.g., business communities and networks such as Tax Justice), on the basis of equality, rationality, openness and

---

179. C. Peters (2014) sec. 8.4.
180. *Id.*, at p. 307. Another way to extend Habermas' work to the international level could have been the centralisation of the self-determination of the democratic nation state rather than the individual. This would not have led to a model in which taxpayer involvement would be increased, but would have emphasised the bargaining between democratic *states*. As Bohman notes, the Habermasian 'idea of a self-legislating *demos* of citizens ruling and being ruled in return, requires a delimited political community of citizens, consisting of all those and *only* those who are full citizens and thus *both* authors and subjects of the law'. But international rule-making includes not *demos* but *demoi*. See J. Bohman, *From Demos to Demoi: Democracy across Borders*, 18 Ratio Juris 293 (2005).
181. C. Peters (2014) p. 386.
182. *Id.*, at p. 308.
183. *Id.*, at p. 196.
184. *Id.*, at p. 200.
185. *Id.*, at p. 308.
186. *Id.*, at sec. 8.6.1.3.
187. Peters' view could therefore be in line with what Buchanan and Keohane suggest: state consent should be taken into account as a *necessary*, but not as a *sufficient* condition for legitimate

transparency, discuss the shared problems of international taxation.[188] So, in sum, 'more Habermas' would be required when considering reforms of international tax law.[189] This suggestion emphasises the need for transparent and inclusive deliberation.

4.2.2 Nussbaum's Social Contract

The work of Martha Nussbaum, who makes the social contract the focus of her book *Frontiers of Justice*, may also be used to develop a cosmopolitan normative framework for international tax law.[190] Nussbaum's approach is helpful because it provides a different normative framework for achieving a 'correct' level playing field. Unlike Rawls and Habermas, who work from fair procedure to just rules (which is called 'the procedural model' of fair societies), Nussbaum works backwards: from outcomes (she calls these 'capabilities') to process. This allows her to take into account the asymmetries of power and capacity that exist in the world, for which she believes the traditional social contractarian approaches provide unsatisfactory answers.[191] If, in other words, we know what the basic capabilities of human dignity are, Nussbaum's reverse approach enables us to make normative claims on how to make sure that the entitlement to these capabilities can be exercised by people everywhere.

4.2.2.1 The Sovereign Duty

The author who has 'translated' this approach to the area of international taxation is Allison Christians,[192] one of the rising stars of international tax academia and recently named one of the most influential tax leaders worldwide.[193] To apply Nussbaum's approach to international tax law, Christians first needs some evidence of outcomes ('entitlements') in international tax law that, in order to be effectuated, need to be protected by others. For this, she uses the OECD's project on harmful tax competition as evidence of the fact that states have come to 'consider the impact of national tax policy decisions on the revenue policies of other states'.[194] She terms this 'the sovereign duty'. The sovereign duty encompasses the paradox that in order to protect their tax sovereignty, states have no choice but to cooperate and respect the tax systems of other

---

international rules. A. Buchanan and R.O. Keohane, *The Legitimacy of Global Governance Institutions*, in: Legitimacy, Justice and Public International Law (L.H. Meyer ed., Cambridge University Press 2009) p. 40.

188. C. Peters (2014) sec. 8.4.3.
189. P. Essers (2014).
190. M.C. Nussbaum, *Frontiers of Justice* (Harvard University Press 2006), as applied to international tax by A. Christians (2009).
191. M.C. Nussbaum (2006) pp. 18–22. *See also* A. Christians (2009) pp. 132–137.
192. A. Christians (2009). *See also* A. Christians et al., (2007) p. 311: 'Interpreting the work of the OECD on harmful tax competition as a forging, or defining, of a social contract is one way to frame the issues [on tax cooperation] for debate on both substantive merits (which rules, standards, and principles are being chosen) and instrumental ones (how the goals are being developed, implemented and monitored).'
193. *See* http://www.internationaltaxreview.com/Article/3525537/The-Global-Tax-50-2015-The-leaders-creating-an-impact-around-the-world.html.
194. A. Christians (2009) p. 147.

states.[195] Where traditionally the concept of sovereignty was equated to the ultimate and complete autonomy over tax matters,[196] the sovereign duty resembles the idea that states cannot do as they please, but rather, that they have the duty to adhere to some baselines in tax system design.[197] Christians says that the rhetoric found in the OECD's work on harmful tax practices evidences that such a duty has come to exist:

> By means of the harmful tax practices project, the OECD shifted its emphasis from a principal concern for protecting the tax base of OECD countries toward a principal goal of creating a level playing field for all countries. This shift demonstrates a deliberate effort to resolve practical issues but it also reflects the unresolved tension of simultaneously trying to cement the sovereign right to tax and identify the contours of a positive sovereign duty to protect that right.[198]

It is important to realise that Christians wrote her article before the BEPS Project was launched. At that time, the concept of the sovereign duty was perhaps still implicit in the OECD's work on harmful tax practices. However, it barely needs explaining that Christians' concept of 'sovereign duty' can be even more clearly recognised in relation to the OECD's work on BEPS:

> When designing their domestic tax rules, sovereign states may not sufficiently take into account the effect of other countries' rules (...). The global economy requires countries to collaborate on tax matters in order to be able to protect their tax sovereignty.[199]

Indeed, a core concept of the BEPS report is that cooperative action is necessary, on the one hand, to prevent the erosion of the domestic tax base, and, on the other hand, to prevent an international tax chaos caused by unilateral anti-abuse rules:

> These weaknesses put the existing consensus-based framework at risk, and a bold move by policy makers is necessary to present worsening problems. Inaction in this area would likely result in some governments losing corporate tax revenue, the emergence of competing sets of international standards, and the replacement of the current consensus-based framework by unilateral measures, which could lead to global tax chaos (...).[200]

---

195. For the term 'sovereignty paradox', *see* H.G. Schermers and N.M. Blokker, *International Institutional Law: Unity Within Diversity* (Martinus Nijhoff 5th rev ed., 2011) para. 1887.
196. A. Christians (2009) p. 101.
197. Christians' work resembles that of P. Dietsch, *Rethinking Sovereignty in International Fiscal Policy*, 37 Review of International Studies 2107 (2011), who argues that 'sovereignty' in international tax theory may also be seen as responsibility, i.e., consisting of both duties as well as obligations of states. At p. 2115: 'Not only may the recognition and legal international sovereignty of states depend on their fulfilling certain standards with respect to the treatment of their own citizens, but states also have obligations to take into account the effects of their policies on the citizens of other states.' Deutsch breaks this responsibility down into three 'increasingly demanding duties', namely: (1) Transparency of income and tax information; (2) Respect for the fiscal choices of others; and (3) Distributive justice.
198. A. Christians (2009) p. 127. She, for instance, quotes the OECD: '[a]ll countries, regardless of their tax systems, should meet [certain] standards so that competition takes place on the basis of legitimate commercial considerations rather than on the basis of lack of transparency (...)', citing OECD, *A Process for Achieving a Global Level Playing Field* (OECD Global Forum on Taxation June 2004). Further examples can be found *id.*, at pp. 120–129.
199. OECD, *BEPS Action Plan (2013)* p. 9.
200. *Id.*, at p. 10.

50

So, a 'sovereign duty' can be recognised in the OECD's harmful tax competition project as well as in the OECD's BEPS Project. The bottom line is, then, that the 'sovereign duty' is a sign of a changed attitude of governments towards international tax: in order to exercise their tax sovereignty, governments must take into account the effect of their tax systems on that of others. This provides the basis for Christians to introduce Nussbaum's work on the social contract in the area of international tax law. And this, in turn, allows her to make some normative claims as to the scope and contents of the 'sovereign duty'.

4.2.2.2 Interpreting the Sovereign Duty as a Social Contract

Indeed, Christians turns to Nussbaum to 'provide a structure for thinking about duty in tax system design that is already implicitly at play in the attempts of OECD officials to create an international consciousness regarding tax policy'.[201] Remember that Nussbaum's approach is outcome rather than procedural-driven: her argument works backwards. Before the duties under a social contract may be assigned to those under the social contract, one must first turn to the question what people need and are entitled to. Or as Christians explains it: 'to the extent that all people have certain basic entitlements, we must believe that all people similarly have the duty to promote and preserve these entitlements in others'.[202] For Nussbaum, in other words, establishing the contents of the social contract is to construct entitlements of individuals first, and duties afterwards. Nussbaum expresses this as follows:

> I would argue, indeed, that so far as definiteness goes, the shoe is squarely on the other foot: we can give a pretty clear and definite account of what all world citizens should have, what their human dignity entitles them to, prior to and to some extent independently of solving the difficult problem of assigning the duties (...). The list of capabilities, deriving from the concept of a life worthy of human dignity, is much easier to draw up and justify than any particular assignment of the correlative duties (...). But if human beings have such entitlements, then we are all under a collective obligation to provide the people of the world with what they need.[203]

As people acting individually may neglect or overlap in exercising such duties, Nussbaum argues that people must turn to institutions, such as the state. States can be assigned the task of seeing that duties are met collectively.[204] So, states are the institutions to which these duties are delegated, and they consequently have the duty of ensuring that capabilities, which society wishes to protect, may be exercised by others. Thus, the outcome-oriented approach enables a consideration of fairness in relation to those outside the state (it is, therefore, cosmopolitan). This subsequently

---

201. A. Christians (2009) p. 130. She does not use the work of Rawls as, in line with what Nussbaum argues, this approach is not coherent when applied to states instead of people. *See id.*, at p. 138.
202. *Id.*, at p. 140.
203. These quotes can be found on pp. 277–280 of M.C. Nussbaum (2006).
204. A. Christians (2009) p. 140.

enables Christians to normatively assess the work of the OECD on tax competition, in which the OECD has strived for a global level playing field:

> The explanation might be that, at least among many of the most powerful actors on the international tax stage, the belief is growing that the sovereign right to tax is a liberty that cannot be enjoyed by any one state without a single, global social contract under which every person in the world agrees to vest in their states a duty to protect that right, by preventing individuals from engaging in behaviour that, while potentially advantageous to the individual, and even to the state, may cause others in the world to be worse off.[205]

4.2.2.3 Mutual Advantage

A first insight that Christians provides by applying Nussbaum's inverse social contract to international tax, is that a social contract for mutual advantage can only be identified when there is mutual advantage to be gained. In other words: only after economic opportunities ('entitlements') can be identified, can a sovereign duty (i.e., fiscal responsibility) under an implicit social contract be recognised.

In other words, for those who benefit from cooperation rather than competition, a social contract, that ultimately protects the sovereign right to tax, can be identified. Membership in the social contract's group of participants may imply that unilateral, isolated action in tax system design is neither possible nor desirable.[206] For states with large budgets and large internal markets, for instance, advantages can easily be recognised. Such states are potentially disadvantaged, in a Hobbesian state of nature, by 'poaching by tax havens via predatory practices such as bank secrecy'.[207] A similar account would seem to hold for the states actively participating in the BEPS Project, as in the state of nature, states compete for mobile capital, eroding such budgets. It might be in the interests of such states to seek cooperation for mutual advantage. What Nussbaum's account in relation to those states teaches us, therefore, is that cooperation between those 'within' the contract should be based on a mutual respect for each other's sovereignty. For Nussbaum, sovereignty 'has moral importance, as a way people have of asserting their autonomy, their right to give themselves laws of their own making'.[208]

However, for those that do not expect to be advantaged by entering a contract, the identification of such a contract, and the duties connected to it, is problematic.[209] And perhaps, a Hobbesian state of nature has more to offer certain states than cooperation, even in the face of development aid[210] and technical assistance in tax

---

205. *Id.*, at p. 143.
206. *Id.*, at p. 145.
207. *Id.*, at p. 138.
208. M.C. Nussbaum (2006) p. 314.
209. A. Christians (2009) p. 145.
210. Christians suggests that in the project on Harmful Tax Competition, one of the potential benefits of cooperation for tax havens could be the promise of continued financial assistance from OECD Countries. *See id.*, at p. 138.

cooperation[211] that cooperation with other states might bring. Consequently, for some states, engaging in tax competition might remain more beneficial than tax cooperation would.[212] Indeed, what Christians, by means of the work of Nussbaum, teaches us in relation to such states, is that a social contract only exists when opportunities can be identified. But the consequences for states 'outside' the social contract could be severe. Following the theory of the social contract, states outside of the group of the social contract are:

> at least in the realm of taxation, in a Hobbesian-style state of nature with respect to all other states, engaged in perpetual conflict, capable of cooperation for mutual advantage where it exists, but not required to cooperate and therefore subject to perpetual uncertainty regarding how other states may act and what possible reactions may be pursued without resorting to violence.[213]

Being outside the social contract means being in a Hobbesian state of nature. Hence, states are free to use whatever fiscal policy is necessary to protect their tax bases, subject only to the limits of self-interest. Coercion is, in these situations, allowed.

4.2.2.4 An Open Debate about the Scope and Content of the Social Contract

A second insight relates to the content and scope of the social contract's sovereign duty, and to the way this content is established. Christians suggests that the implicit social contract 'appears to involve a basic list of economic rights and obligations owing to all persons, regardless of their affiliation with any one particular country, region or locale'.[214] For tax, this might imply that:

> if every person is in fact entitled to be spared an inequitable tax burden, then every person must have a duty to every other person to be honest and pay a 'fair share' of taxation. Since that concept is then and, even if definable, difficult (perhaps impossible) to implement, we may come back to the state as a logical institution in

---

211. The OECD suggests in the progress report on the multilateral instrument that for developing states the 'practical problems that are encountered in trying to address BEPS from within the bilateral tax treaty system alone are even more relevant than for developed countries Developing countries find it more difficult than other countries both to conclude double tax treaties, and to interest other countries in tax treaty (re)negotiation, and their tax treaty negotiation expertise is often more limited than in the governments of developed economies. A multilateral instrument therefore offers the best opportunity to ensure that developing countries reap the benefits of multilateral efforts to tackle BEPS.' OECD, *Developing a Multilateral Instrument to Modify Bilateral Tax Treaties* (2014) p. 16. However, the claim that such states might benefit from the BEPS Project is not free of criticism. Dagan, for instance, points out that the anti-tax competition rhetoric found in the OECD's BEPS Action plan does not fundamentally depart from the source-residence 'distributive baseline' found in current tax treaties, which is tilted in favour of residence states. T. Dagan, *BRICS: Theoretical Framework and the Potential of Cooperation*, in: BRICS and the Emergence of International Tax Coordination (Y. Brauner and P. Pistone eds, IBFD 2015). Also, but specifically in relation to the LOB/PPT clauses: L. Wagenaar, *The Effect of the OECD Base Erosion and Profit Shifting Action Plan on Developing Countries*, 69 Bulletin for International Taxation 84, 89–90 (2015).
212. T. Dagan (2015) p. 21.
213. A. Christians (2009) p. 150.
214. *Id.*, at p. 149.

which to rest the power to determine what constitutes fairness and then to figure out how to compel everyone – associated with whatever particular state – to comply with that determination.[215]

This, in turn, requires a reassessment of the concept of equity or fairness.[216] Christians considers:

> it is no longer coherent for states to adhere to tax policy assessment tools that rely for their implementation on the concept of the state as a closed system. (...) We cannot rationally talk about fairness, or what equity means, by looking only at persons within a given territory or subject to a given sovereign authority – we can only hope to determine whether a given system approaches equity by examining how a given rule impacts every person, both within and without the system.[217]

A consideration of what the sovereign duty entails requires some 'guiding principles' to 'connect ideas about sovereignty to what people owe and are owed as taxpayers in an increasingly open global economic system'.[218] These procedures 'deserve to be explicitly stated and subjected to rigorous analysis. Defining what sovereignty requires for tax system design necessitates an inclusive dialogue'.[219] And indeed, Nussbaum herself proposes, in order to implement her capabilities approach, a 'thin, decentralized, and yet forceful global public sphere': a world state is not an appropriate aspiration.[220] Christians' conclusion is similarly modest: 'reassessment should open up a discussion about how ideas about sovereignty, taxation and social contract emerge, are shaped and ultimately impact people around the world'.[221]

This brings us closer to the normative development of a level playing field, by means of which the exercise of entitlements, by people everywhere, can be assured. Christians' work demonstrates that fair consideration should be given to the impact of one tax system's design on other tax systems. The principles that guide such design need to be drafted in an inclusive and open manner.

4.2.3 Continuous, Inclusive and Transparent Deliberation on Tax Rules

From the two views considered above, two conclusions can be drawn. First, procedurally 'fair' international tax lawmaking should be approached from a perspective of the influence of lawmaking on citizens, and, vice versa, of citizens on lawmaking. Following Habermas, as explained by Peters: tax lawmaking should be inclusive, in that citizens (in the form of civil society, taxpayer communities and states) should be able to have a real and tangible opportunity to influence tax lawmaking. Norms are only legitimised by means of free and continuous deliberation by the members of a society. Likewise, from Christians' and Nussbaum's work, it follows that states 'inside'

---

215. *Id.*, at p. 147.
216. *Id.*, at p. 145.
217. *Id.*, at p. 147.
218. *Id.*, at p. 152.
219. *Id.*, at p. 152.
220. M.C. Nussbaum (2006) Ch. 6 sec. IX.
221. A. Christians (2009) p. 153.

the social contract should take account of the impact of their tax system design on that of others. By implication, this means that deliberation on the principles that guide this design should take place in an inclusive manner. But what also follows from Christians is that a social contract can only be constructed when there is mutual advantage to be gained. For those 'outside' the group of the social contract, i.e., in relation to those who gain no economic opportunities from cooperating, a Hobbesian state of nature exists. This suggests that nothing would prevent countries to act out of their pure self-interests, in which states may strategise on the basis of power and coercion, rather than principle.

Second, an analysis of the work of Habermas and Nussbaum leads to the conclusion that transparency of the lawmaking deliberations is essential for fair international tax norms. Absent a 'global democracy' – which is unlikely and in today's world hard to conceive[222] – it is important that the procedures establishing international tax rules should promote every taxpayer being able to follow the lawmaking processes and scrutinise the tax laws that are proposed. Transparency enables taxpayers to hold lawmakers accountable, for instance, through actions of a domestic democratic nature or the media. Or in Christians' terms: to connect ideas about sovereignty to what people owe and are owed in a global society, all those involved should in openness discuss the nature and the scope of the 'sovereign duty'. Only when lawmaking is both transparent and inclusive can it be guaranteed that the rules resulting from such process are 'neutral' and hence 'fair'.

It might seem that this account on procedural fairness is quite static and promotes stability rather than change. But the cosmopolitan concepts of procedural fairness discussed above appear to attach important consequences to the passing of time. Correct procedures can also ensure that *outcomes* are considered fair *in the future*. Let us suppose that at a particular moment in time, the international community shares a common understanding of what 'fairness' entails in international taxation. The point of the discussion above is that continuous fair deliberation can also ensure that the norms of today remain in line with social criteria of the future. As soon as a norm of appropriate behaviour is contested, deliberation allows actors to try to figure out and justify whether the norm still applies under changed circumstances.

From this follows that current tax lawmaking suffers from some procedural fairness issues. International tax policy is currently set by the OECD, a 'club' like organisation.[223] This 'club' underperforms in truly involving citizens in its lawmaking processes. Moreover, non-member (particularly developing) countries have, thus far, within the existing lawmaking processes, mostly been included in the 'endorsement

---

222. The sheer size of such an enterprise would make a global democracy unlikely. Think of cultural barriers, the amount of citizens that would have to be involved, different languages, etc. The communicative process would hence be difficult. Moreover, even if states would function as 'federal entities' in such a system, the system itself would lack legitimacy as many states themselves are undemocratic. *See* M.C. Nussbaum (2006) pp. 313–314 and e.g., A. Buchanan and R.O. Keohane (2009).

223. For this type of terminology: R.O. Keohane and J.S.J. Nye, *The Club Model of Multilateral Cooperation and Problems of Democratic Legitimacy*, in: Power and Governance in a Partially Globalized World (R.O. Keohane ed., Routledge 2002). Also called 'closed' organisations by H.G. Schermers and N.M. Blokker (2011) paras 53–57.

phase of policymaking rather than in the vital stage of idea development and negotiation'.[224] Non-member countries are unrepresented in OECD working groups,[225] may have little influence in setting the agenda of the work undertaken by the CFA,[226] and have a more limited ability to file observations of and reservations to the texts of the OECD Model and Commentaries than OECD Members do.[227] But most importantly, non-members have no vote in the OECD Council, the OECD's most important legislative body. This means that, even if non-members are granted the role of observer, their formal status and influence in the organisation remains diffuse.

A multilateral agreement for international taxation may alleviate these issues. The multilateral agreement can enable states to enter into a continuous and inclusive norm-generating discourse, where they search for the best arguments. Moreover, the multilateral agreement should promote transparency. This would allow state parties and other citizen-led groups such as NGOs and businesses to continuously check and evaluate norms. A tentative conclusion is, therefore, that the multilateral agreement should establish a recurring forum that facilitates such elements.

4.3 CONCLUSIONS

Two cosmopolitan accounts of procedural fairness were helpful in providing a normative framework for a multilateral agreement for international taxation. Both emphasise the position of the taxpayer rather than the state and can be used to guide the conscious design of this agreement in a globalising world.

The work of Nussbaum (represented by Christians) and Habermas (represented by Peters) aims to show how societies can create rules that are 'fair' in a procedural sense. To achieve substantively fair (tax) rules in the long run, Habermas argues, law must be legitimate. For this, it is important that laws, that protect a space of individual

---

224. A. Christians, *Taxation in a Time of Crisis: Policy Leadership from the OECD to the G20*, 5 Northwestern Journal of Law & Social Policy 19, 36 (2010).
225. There are some major non-member economies that have 'observer status' in the CFA: Argentina, Chili, China, Russia, South Africa and India. *See* http://www.oecd.org/ctp/oecdinvitesindiatoparticipateinitscommitteeonfiscalaffairs.htm. As to the work on the BEPS Project, a number of non-member countries from a cross-section of regions have participated directly in the CFA's work on the project, such as Albania, Bangladesh, Kenya, Tunisia and Vietnam. *See* http://www.oecd.org/tax/developing-countries-and-beps.htm#participation, last accessed 22 Oct. 2015. Obviously, it is clear that such influence does not include all countries affected.
226. Ault says that the agenda is set by the CFA Bureau, an 'executive committee that meets periodically between CFA Meetings'. H.J. Ault, *Reflections on the Role of the OECD in Developing International Tax Norms*, 34 Brooklyn Journal of International Law 757, 760 (2008). The public servants that influence such processes do not formally belong to any country, but are drafted from OECD Member countries, bringing with them prior experiences and ways of thinking. For example: 'For official positions in the OECD, you will be recruited as an international civil servant and you are required to hold the nationality of an OECD member country.' *See* http://www.oecd.org/careers/whatwelookfor.htm. The agenda is important as it 'is one of the most important structural aspects of any negotiation as well as a significant determinant of negotiating power and influence'. W.R. Pendergast, *Managing the Negotiation Agenda*, 6 Negotiation Journal 135 (1990).
227. The positions of some non-member economies are taken into account under the heading 'positions of non-member countries' in the respective sections of the OECD Commentary.

freedom, are the result of a process of self-determination: only if the members of a society perceive themselves as the authors of the laws of that society, can law be seen as legitimate. This requires procedures in which the members of a society deliberate, on the basis openness, inclusivity and transparency, on the formation of that law. Nussbaum works backwards: from 'capabilities' to procedure. In order to be entitled to certain capabilities, we must protect and guarantee the same entitlements of others. Interpreting the work of the OECD on harmful tax competition as evidence of Nussbaum's 'reverse' social contract, allows Christians to argue that in designing tax systems, those 'inside' the social contract may be expected to act responsible, i.e., to take into account the impact of their tax systems on that of others (the 'sovereign duty'). Consequently, what is required, is an open and inclusive discussion between actors on this 'sovereign duty'. In this regard, a multilateral agreement could provide a promising platform for the future creation of 'fairer' international tax rules.

CHAPTER 5

In a Less than Perfect World: A Realistic View on Multilateral Cooperation in International Taxation

5.1 INTRODUCTION

Now that a normative view on multilateral cooperation in international tax law has been constructed in the previous chapter, let us examine what is actually feasible in the international tax arena.[228] The purpose of this chapter is to put the normative claims of the previous chapter in a practical perspective, drafting a 'realistic' or 'instrumental' view on international tax cooperation.

Suppose, for example, that it is proposed that the P.E. concept is, in some way, broadened to include non-physical forms of local 'presence' (e.g., digital local presence). What will influence states to enter into either bilateral or multilateral tax relations on such a proposal? A state's decision to cooperate in either bilateral or multilateral relations reflects its rational perceptions of the economic gain of either course of action. These perceptions of gains typically have two dimensions: size and uncertainty. 'Size' reflects a state's perception of the gains to be had from cooperation with (an)other state(s); the larger the perceived gain (the 'size of the pie'), the more the negotiations will tend to focus on the distribution of the gain over participating states. 'Uncertainty' reflects a negotiating state's lack of knowledge on the future impact of alternative courses of action on its own position (whatever the 'size of the pie'). The larger this uncertainty, the less 'distributive' the negotiations will tend to be, as it incentivises states to agree on broadly acceptable, or 'central', substantive arrangements.

---

228. The chapter is largely based on D.M. Broekhuijsen and H. Vording, *The Multilateral Tax Instrument: How to Avoid a Stalemate on Distributional Issues?*, British Tax Review 39 (2016). The text has been partly rewritten and some sections have been added, deleted or moved to different sections of the book.

If the economic gains of cooperation are perceived to be large and certain, states will be inclined to distribute the gains in bilateral agreements. If gains are expected to be small and uncertain, states will tend to focus on general multilateral principles of cooperation rather than agreement on specific rules. In between these extreme positions, multilateral agreement is easier to achieve on matters of design and concept ('rules of the road'), than on specific rules which have obvious distributive implications on states' economic positions. As we will see, the commitments set out in the BEPS Convention generally fit into this pattern, at least to the extent that distributive issues are avoided. But looking forward, this also means that binding multilateral agreement on rules that strike at the heart of tax competition and tax arbitrage is very unlikely. Indeed, from this chapter follows that achieving multilateral cooperation on rules of a formulary apportionment-type of nature (i.e., what are the baselines for dividing the tax pie? Sales, labour, or assets?) may be very problematic.

In this chapter, theory stemming from the field of international relations is used to construct an analytical framework for analysing international tax relations. In section 5.2, the assumption of the rational, self-interested, welfare-maximising state is selected as the most useful point of departure for analysing states' 'behaviour' in concluding tax treaties. Some recent economic contributions to the tax treaties literature that generally fit this assumption will be discussed in section 5.3, explaining states' choices between bilateral and multilateral forms of cooperation in terms of distribution of economic gain. External (spill-over) effects turn out to be an important challenge to that analysis. In section 5.4, the discussions turn to the impact of a multilateral agreement on bilateral tax treaty relations. The existence of a 'veil of uncertainty' is added, showing how negotiating states' decisions may be affected by uncertainty regarding the impact of (new) rules on their economic positions. The resulting analytical framework, summarised in section 5.4.3, is used to discuss the feasibility of a multilateral approach in regard of several potential tax policy changes, and to suggest a direction for a design strategy for a multilateral agreement for international taxation. Also, the mitigating effect of two procedural elements of multilateral cooperation – transparency and the number of participants – is considered in section 5.4.7. In the face of distributive conflict, inconsiderate action on such procedural elements can make matters worse. Procedural design choices in this regard therefore soften the risk of negotiation breakdown on widely acceptable compromises. Section 5.5 concludes.

5.2 SELECTING THE MOST PROMISING INTERNATIONAL RELATIONS PERSPECTIVE FOR ANALYSING INTERNATIONAL TAX RELATIONS

Adding a multilateral agreement to the existing patchwork of bilateral treaties could qualify as a 'regime' change in international relations between states. An international regime is a set of principles, norms, rules and decision-making procedures that guides states' actions in any specific field of international cooperation. Regimes must be distinguished from international agreements: the purpose of regimes is to facilitate agreements.[229] Applied to the field of taxation, the regime's relevant principles could be, for example, national tax sovereignty, an idea of states' 'fair shares' based on concepts like source and residence, a perception of the international tax environment as a competitive 'market' for FDI. The relevant norms can be found in the various MTCs, with the OECD MTC and its Commentary as the dominant one. The 'rules' are the terms of bilateral treaties. Moreover, decision-making procedures are predominantly national (tax administration and tax courts), and are added to by mutual agreement procedures. Regime change would imply that the set of decision-making procedures is expanded with a multilateral agreement that not only generates new norms but also new rules. It could also imply changes in underlying principles: a reduced role of national tax sovereignty, a changing perception of 'fair shares', and/or a more cooperative idea of the international tax environment.

Literature on international relations has developed along several lines, based on different and often competing views on states, politics and the role of academic analysis. Following Ring, three perspectives that seem particularly relevant to international taxation can be sorted out.[230] These three perspectives are used as pragmatic analytical tools: their purpose is to understand, explain and predict the very complex reality of cooperation by oversimplifying that reality.[231]

One is (neo)realism. In this perspective, states are rational self-interested actors in an anarchic world, sceptical to sacrifice their own self-interest to adhere to normative notions of 'ethical' conduct. It is about survival: leading notions of (neo)realism are power politics, groupism (i.e., states, clans, clubs, etc.), egoism and anarchy.[232] The keys to understanding the world from a realist view are the distribution of power in the system, and a state's relative position to others.[233] For international regimes to develop in such a world, dominant states have to take the lead. But given a 'survival of the fittest'-mentality, states may reject a regime that 'coordinates action and generates gains for all players if that regime allows another state to achieve relative gains'.[234] The inference would be that shifts in dominance could be regarded as triggering regime change. The existing regime, loosely based on the OECD consensus, may be seen as reflecting US dominance. The Brazil, Russia, India, China, South Africa (BRICS) nations challenge this consensus – and the relative weight of the EU in international taxation has a tendency to increase. Non-OECD Members cooperate in the forum of the OECD because this at least provides them with the ability to voice their

---

229. S.D. Krasner, *Structural Causes and Regime Consequences: Regimes as Intervening Variables*, in: International Regimes (S.D. Krasner ed., Cornell University Press 1983) 186–187. He notes at 187: 'regime-governed behaviour must not be based solely on short-term calculations of interest. Since regimes encompass principles and norms, the utility function that is being maximized must embody some sense of general obligation.'
230. D.M. Ring, International Tax Relations: Theory and Implications, 60 Tax Law Review 83 (2007), offers an excellent overview of the international relations literature from the perspective of international taxation.
231. *See*, on the role of political theory, D. Beach (2012) p. 9.
232. W.C. Wohlforth, *Realism*, in: The Oxford Handbook of International Relations (C. Reus-Smit and D. Snidal eds, OUP 2009) pp. 132–133.
233. D. Beach (2012) p. 35.
234. D.M. Ring (2007) p. 102.

concerns. Given their weaker power positions, this is an opportunity they may not have been able to secure absent cooperation in the regime.[235]

A second perspective is 'neoliberal institutionalism' (not to be confused with the neoliberal policies associated with Thatcher and Reagan). Like (neo)realists, neoliberal institutionalists start from the analytical starting point that international cooperation takes place in an anarchical system in which states are the relevant actors, with the distribution of power and wealth as the most important factors defining state behaviour. States enter into cooperative regimes if there are gains to be had from cooperation. Yet, the core conception of neoliberal institutionalism is a 'market' idea of economic rationality: states can use cooperative regimes to overcome suboptimal outcomes caused by individualistic, uncoordinated behaviour,[236] provided that states have a common interest in cooperating.

The basis for this argument, set out by Keohane, is the analogy with the prisoners' dilemma. It runs thus: two prisoners are locked up for having committed a crime and are questioned separately by the public prosecutor (the DA):

> Each prisoner knows that if neither confesses, the DA will only have sufficient evidence to convict them to misdemeanours, leading to thirty day prison terms for each. If both confess, however, they will each be sentenced to a year in the penitentiary. This prospect might seem to give both an incentive not to confess, except that the clever DA has promised that if either confesses while the other refuses, the confessor will not be prosecuted at all, while his recalcitrant partner is punished severely with a five-year sentence.[237]

On the basis of narrow self-interest, prisoner A knows that he should confess, whatever his partner, prisoner B, does. If B refuses to confess, A's confession will let him go free. If B confesses, A's own confession will at least save him from the severe five-year sentence. However, the walls between the two prison rooms prevent the prisoners from communicating, and there is only one game played. Therefore, both A and B's preferred course of action, if they are self-interested and rational individuals, is to confess, as they expect the other to do the same. They hence receive prison sentences that they could have avoided.

Keohane argues that many of the cooperative structures in international relations resemble prisoners' dilemmas. In that light, he argues, international regimes are of value to states: regimes can prevent market failure (i.e., prevent larger prison sentences for the prisoners) by taking care of communication (i.e., by making transparent the walls that separate the two prisoners from one another). Freed from these walls, the prisoners 'can learn about each other's intentions and actions, agree on standards of behaviour, and learn about the relationship between their actions and outcomes'.[238] By providing actors with information, by enabling states to make credible commitments,

---

235. *Id.*, at p. 104.
236. R.O. Keohane, *After Hegemony: Cooperation and Discord in the World Political Economy* (Princeton University Press 1984) Ch. 6. For a discussion: D. Beach (2012) pp. 53–56.
237. R.O. Keohane (1984) pp. 68–69.
238. L.L. Martin, *The Political Economy of International Cooperation*, in: Global Public Goods: International Cooperation in the 21st Century (I. Kaul, I. Grunberg and M.A. Stern eds, OUP 1999) p. 55.

and by making long-term cooperative outcomes more beneficial than short-term defection,[239] regimes, in other words, prevent states from 'cheating'.

The prisoners' dilemma analogy teaches us that the neoliberal institutionalist's analysis focuses on the size and distribution of the *absolute* rather than *relative* gains of cooperation,[240] and on transaction costs, which are also related to the number of participating states. Moreover, in extending the prisoners' dilemma to international relations, neoliberal institutionalists are concerned with *durable* cooperation, as is often the case in economically interdependent relationships between states. Provided that states have a common, albeit conflicting, interest on an issue, regimes are helpful.[241] So, cooperation could be opted for to deal with 'club' goods (such as joint defence or free trade) where non-participants can be excluded from the benefits of cooperation. But even with public goods (such as reduction of pollution) where exclusion is more difficult, cooperation is possible, provided that disagreements are not impossible to deal with through bargaining. Within a regime, for instance, initially uncooperative states can be compensated by means of side-payments. Also, linkages can be created among issues.[242] Applied to the area of international taxation, the feasibility of a shift from the existing international tax regime to a more committing multilateral regime must be analysed by comparing net gains or losses for each participating state. Assuming that states maximise national welfare, the impact of alternative regimes on national GDPs is a relevant measure.

A third perspective is constructivism. This approach centres on the ways in which our views on international relations are framed by (implicit) principles and by the analytical tools used.[243] The approach is driven by the role of beliefs and ideas in conceptualising issues of international cooperation. As Ring says, in the constructivist view: (1) states' interests are contingent on their understanding of the world because these interests are not a given; (2) states rely on experts due to the technical nature of many of the international issues; and (3) some degree of intersubjective, shared understandings about the subject at hand are required before states can engage in cooperation.[244] Hence, constructivists depart from fundamentally different assumptions than neoliberal institutionalists and (neo)realists do.[245] Neoliberal institutionalists and (neo)realists, with their 'consequentialist' focus on material factors (i.e., costs and benefits), treat identities and interests as exogenous and given. Just like economic analysis does not explain the origin and constitutive rules of the market itself, neoliberal institutionalist and neorealist analysis, which are imported from

---

239. D. Beach (2012) pp. 54–55.
240. (Neo)realists are interested in the *relative* gains of cooperation: How do I fare in relation to my competitors? *See, e.g.*, R. Jarvis, *Realism, Neoliberalism, and Cooperation: Understanding the Debate*, 24 International Security 42 (1999).
241. R.O. Keohane (1984) p. 97.
242. *Id.*, at p. 90.
243. D. Beach (2012) pp. 57–61; I. Hurd, *Constructivism*, in: The Oxford Handbook of International Relations (C. Reus-Smit and D. Snidal eds, OUP 2009).
244. D.M. Ring (2007) pp. 110–112.
245. The two logics are distinguished as 'the logic of consequences' and 'the logic of appropriateness' by J.G. March and J.P. Olsen, *The Institutional Dynamics of International Political Orders*, 52 International Organization 943 (1998).

economics,[246] tell us little about the social order or 'structure' that defines who actors are and what they want. Constructivists, on the other hand, *are* interested in the origins and significance of these identities and interests. So, while material factors are important, ideas and values matter too. In the words of Wendt: constructivists accept 'that the structures of human association are determined primarily by shared ideas rather than material forces, and that the identities and interests of purposive actors are constructed by these shared ideas rather than given by nature'.[247]

Given that specific identities of specific states may shape their interests, this may also help explain international outcomes. Examples are numerous. Finnemore, for instance, uses constructivist analysis to explain why states have intervened to provide humanitarian relief in countries and areas of negligible geostrategic and/or economic interest.[248] Sikkink argues that 'values' explain the emergence of human rights after the Second World War in Europe and the United States.[249] Peter Haas uses constructivist theory for an institutional account of gradual accommodation of governments to environmental problems via social learning.[250] And applied to the field of international taxation, Webb uses constructivist insights to show how norms of 'liberal economic ideology' as well as fiscal sovereignty helped shape the debate on harmful tax competition.[251] Constructivism thus emphasises the role of social debate in international taxation, which may relate to (re)defining the boundary between 'acceptable' and 'unacceptable' tax incentives and tax planning behaviour, as well as to an emerging concept of 'fair shares'. Regime change would come about as a result of gradually changing views on the interests at stake in international taxation: from preventing double taxation to combating tax avoidance.

As this brief outline shows, each of these three perspectives may have relevance in understanding the prospects of multilateralism in international tax law. This chapter will, however, focus on the neoliberal institutionalist tradition, for several reasons. First, institutional neoliberalism is arguably better at explaining issues related to political economy, such as trade, than neorealist models, which are better at explaining security-related issues, particularly between powerful states.[252] In fact, most literature in the field of tax cooperation and coordination fits in the neoliberal institutionalist

246. J.G. Ruggie, *What Makes the World Hang Together? Neo-Utilitarianism and the Social Constructivist Challenge*, 52 International Organization 855, 871–872 (1998).
247. A. Wendt, *Social Theory of International Politics* (Cambridge University Press 1999) p. 1.
248. M. Finnemore, *Constructing Norms of Humanitarian Intervention*, in: The Culture of National Security: Norms and Identity in World Politics (P.J. Katzenstein ed., Columbia University Press 1996).
249. K. Sikkink, *The Power of Principled Ideas: Human Rights Policies in the United States and Western Europe*, in: Ideas and Foreign Policy (J. Goldstein and R. Keohane eds, Cornell University Press 1993).
250. P.M. Haas, *Epistemic Communities, Constructivism, and International Environmental Politics* (Routledge 2015). *See*, for an overview of important constructivist contributions, E. Adler, *Constructivism in International Relations: Sources, Contributions, and Debates*, in: Handbook of International Relations (W. Carlsnaes, T. Risse and B. Simmons eds, SAGE 2nd ed., 2013).
251. M. Webb, *Defining the Boundaries of Legitimate State Practice: Norms, Transnational Actors and the OECD's Project on Harmful Tax Competition*, 11 Review of International Political Economy 787 (2004).
252. D. Beach (2012) pp. 31–61. Nevertheless, realists will of course claim that all important foreign policy issues are, in the end, related to security. And institutionalists will argue that their

tradition, as it employs a model of self-interested players in a 'game' played in a world characterised by high levels of economic interdependence. Ring, for instance, shows that the neoliberal institutionalist tradition more accurately reflects the experience of the double taxation regime than realist models of regime formation do.[253] Generally speaking, her argument is that the neoliberal institutionalist model is best fit to the idea that tax treaty relationships are entered into by governments because they enhance durable trade relationships (i.e., they encourage investment). Realist models cannot, for instance, convincingly explain why developing countries, in their relations with other developing countries, participate in bilateral tax treaties patterned on a model that favours residence taxation.[254] To be sure, there is literature that explores the relevance of leadership in the making of the international tax order – usually with the US as the 'Stackelberg' leader.[255] This literature suggests, for example, that states can play the 'tax game' cooperatively, when a large capital-exporting state unilaterally adopts the full residence principle. Under the umbrella of that principle, smaller states will have no incentive to reduce their source state tax rates. From this line of reasoning follows that the chances of achieving multilateral agreement will depend on the participation of large players (which is plausible enough without taking recourse to game theory).

Second, the constructivist approach can, for the purposes of analysing international tax relations, best be seen as complementary to the neoliberal institutionalist one.[256] As Ring notes, constructivism:

> proposes a model of how states may come to adopt new positions and how purveyors of knowledge can under certain circumstances shape the direction of new policy. Despite a major role of cognitivists [that is, constructivists] as sceptics and critics, cognitive theories frequently are understood (even by advocates) as being 'complementary' to realism and neoliberalism.[257]

Indeed, the reality of international tax affairs is most comfortably reflected when assuming that major decisions in international tax are fundamentally constrained by egocentrism and economic rationality.[258] Bilateral tax agreements are entered into by

---

models are relevant for security issues too, as they are about providing information (misperceptions, simply put, may lead to war). *See id.*, at pp. 31–61.

253. D.M. Ring (2007) p. 147.

254. *Id.*, at pp. 128–129. *See* further on this (the footnotes in), sec. 5.3.4.

255. R.H. Gordon, *Can Capital Income Taxes Survive in Open Economies?*, 47 The Journal of Finance 1159 (1992); R. Altshuler, R. Altshuler and T.J. Goodspeed, *Follow the Leader? Evidence on European and US Tax Competition*, 43 Public Finance Review 485 (2015). Stackelberg leadership (named after the German economist Heinrich von Stackelberg) is a specific game with two unequal participants, in which the smaller participant adapts to the choices made by the stronger one.

256. I. Hurd (2009) sec. 3.2.

257. D.M. Ring (2007) p. 112.

258. Four methods to integrate the constructivist with the rationalist perspective can generally be identified: competition (both are checked against reality and one is excluded for being inferior/unclear); by distinguishing 'domains of application' (e.g., differentiating high stake decisions from low stake ones); by sequencing (each approach depends on the other temporally) and by incorporation (one theory can be logically derived from the other). *See* J.G. March and J.P. Olsen (1998) pp. 952–953. *See also* J. Jupille, J.A. Caporaso and J.T. Checkel,

states, first and foremost, for their economic gains.[259] Consequently, state decisions to alter tax relationships are likely to be constrained by the extent to which such decisions increase/decrease such gains. This is in keeping with neoliberal institutionalism. Yet, this does not mean that 'ideas' and 'values' play no role in international tax, even if, in a multilateral negotiation, protecting national economic interests is a more likely determinant of state behaviour than 'achieving tax fairness'. Since the launch of the BEPS Project, the idea of achieving a 'fair' international tax system has clearly become of relevance to international outcomes, and, as such, the emerging idea of 'tax fairness' has most likely been the catalyst that has spurred cooperation on the BEPS Project.[260] If public opinion will indeed continue to ask for 'fairer' or more effective taxation of international capital flows, the constructivist perspective to international tax relations may prove of relevance to refine neoliberal institutionalist explanations of international tax cooperation.[261] State preferences in international taxation, are, in other words, unlikely to be fixed and given. They may, over time, and spurred on by normative forces related to 'tax fairness', be subject to (modest) change. How such change occurs and can be facilitated, is however the subject of Chapter 6.

By focusing on the neoliberal institutionalist interpretation of states' 'behaviour' in concluding tax treaties, one implicitly accepts a number of assumptions. A recent review of literature on 'rational design' of international cooperative regimes[262] lists four assumptions that fit in with the (neo)liberal institutionalist approach to treaty negotiations. These are: (1) rationality: states develop cooperative regimes to serve their interests; (2) the expected gains are sufficiently large to enhance cooperation; (3) establishing forms of cooperation is costly; (4) states are risk-averse, i.e., they try to reduce the eventuality of outcomes which negatively impact their future positions.

Under these assumptions, it is not necessary to presume that states' behaviour in concluding tax treaties is unboundedly rational. The intuitions underlying tax treaty negotiations (reduction of both tax frontiers and avoidance options) may be plausible enough and may mean that the requirements of assumptions (1) and (2) are met. But the fundamental question: 'what do states gain by concluding tax treaties?' has only recently been explored empirically;[263] and it may be assumed that states conclude tax

---

Integrating Institutions: Rationalism, Constructivism, and the Study of the European Union, 36 Comparative Political Studies 7, 19-24 (2003). In this book, *see also* Ch. 6, a sequential approach is used, problematising state preferences rather than taking them as fixed and given.

259. *See, e.g.*, A. Pickering, *Why Negotiate Tax Treaties*, in: Papers on Selected Topics in Negotiation of Tax Treaties for Developing Countries (A. Trepelkov, H. Tonino and D. Halka eds, UN 2014).

260. *See* I. Grinberg, *The New International Tax Diplomacy*, 104 Georgetown Law Journal 1137, 1169 (2016).

261. Likewise, D.M. Ring (2007) p. 148, argues that 'neoliberalist regime theory alone cannot adequately account for the double taxation regime. The "epistemically informed bargaining" model [which includes constructivist theory] more fully captures the factors crucial to regime formation. (…) its sustained importance in the process is powerfully demonstrated over the decades.'

262. B. Koremenos, *Loosening the Ties That Bind: A Learning Model of Agreement Flexibility*, 55 International Organization 289 (2001) 781-782.

263. A. Lejour, *The Foreign Investment Effects of Tax Treaties* (2013) CPB Netherlands Bureau for Economic Policy Analysis: CPB Discussion Paper 265 finds that the level of a state's participation in the tax treaty network has a significant positive impact on its FDI stock, while noting that previous empirical studies found little (or even a negative) effect.

treaties under conditions of uncertainty regarding the size (and their own share) of economic gains – which means that assumption 4 is critical. 'Rationality', in other words, does not mean access to full information, or the ability to calculate perfectly. Rationality is 'bounded'.[264] And indeed, in the upcoming discussion, the potential impact of uncertainty on the feasibility of a multilateral tax deal plays an important role.

Finally, the analysis starts from the idea that states are the key actors in the international area. In this regard, the neoliberal institutionalist perspective presumes states to have fixed rather than dynamic interests,[265] and to function like 'black boxes', in which the influence of domestic politics and pressure groups on international cooperation is marginalised.[266]

5.3 THE NEOLIBERAL INSTITUTIONALIST VIEW ON BILATERAL TAX RELATIONS

5.3.1 Introduction

The arguments recently developed by Rixen,[267] and by Thompson and Verdier[268] function as good neoliberal institutionalist starting points to explain the choice of states to enter either in bilateral or multilateral tax agreements. But it should be noted that both contributions are best understood as addressing negotiations on withholding tax rates. Issues of double income taxation can be resolved unilaterally: from any state's perspective, it is optimal to offer either a foreign tax credit or full exemption to its resident investors[269] (even when tax treaties will still be useful to coordinate source rules, the definition of residency, exchange of information, etc.). The mutual reduction of withholding taxes, on the other hand, is a game that includes important distributional issues in terms of treaty partners' tax revenues.

5.3.2 Bilateralism as a Response to Asymmetric Interests

Rixen presents the tax treaty negotiation game as focused on withholding taxes. He does argue, however, that bilateral tax treaties are settled upon by states because they provide a better solution for reducing double taxation than when a state offers unilateral relief for foreign taxation of residents. That is, he believes, because a

---

264. The concept of 'bounded rationality' stems from the work of Herbert Simon, e.g. H. Simon, *The Sciences of the Artificial* (MIT Press 1981).
265. But *see* the discussion in Ch. 6 and above.
266. This means that the role of domestic politics on state behaviour is not accounted for. *See*, for the influence of domestic politics on (neo)liberal theory, R.D. Putnam (1988).
267. T. Rixen (2010).
268. A. Thompson and D. Verdier, *Multilateralism, Bilateralism, and Regime Design*, 58 International Studies Quarterly 15 (2014).
269. A. Easson, *Do We Still Need Tax Treaties*, 54 Bulletin for International Taxation 619 (2000); T. Dagan, *The Tax Treaties Myth*, 32 New York University Journal of International Law and Politics 939 (2000).

reduction of tax levied at source reduces the cost of relief. It would seem that this reasoning is based on a very specific assumption: that withholding taxes are creditable under home state tax rules. Under exemption systems, this is not typically the case (as the foreign income is exempted, the tax burdens on that income are ignored).

But he does not need that assumption: his basic argument is that states have asymmetric (source or residence) interests in setting withholding tax rates. For each bilateral negotiation, a state has a (net) source or residence interest. Net importers (of capital, labour, etc.) favour taxation at source. Alternatively, net export states want to protect their resident investors' interests and thus seek to lower taxation at source. However, in reality, states have interests that differ from one interstate relationship to another, as economic flows between states are not reciprocal. As Rixen points out:

> [B]eing a net exporter or net importer is a relational attribute that can vary with respect to different countries. Country A could have source interests in relation to country B, if A is a net capital importer from B. At the same time, A might have residence interests in relation to country C, exporting capital to C. In relation to country D, there might not be any distributive conflict, if capital flows between A and D are symmetric.[270]

Rixen therefore rationalises the dominance of bilateral agreements in the tax field as a coordination game driven by distributive concerns. He argues that a full multilateral approach (as in the 'old' idea of a multilateral treaty) would only be needed when bilateral treaties had sizeable external effects. He believes that this is not the case. The only justification for a multilateral initiative is reduction of transaction costs by disseminating information and shared practices in the form of a model convention that provides a focal point for bilateral negotiations. This, of course, neatly describes the status quo.

It should be added that there is a dynamic side to the distributive concerns that drive bilateral coordination. When states set withholding taxes optimally, by implication they must have taken into account the impact of relevant tax base elasticities to maximise overall welfare. Reducing those tax rates in bilateral treaties will cause market responses in terms of mobility and economic growth, and have an impact on overall welfare as well. Assuming (as the neoliberal tradition does) that states enter a contract because of some net advantage, it follows that state A will be prepared to reduce its withholding tax rates (and accept a loss in tax revenue) vis-à-vis state B, if and only if it expects a gain that exceeds the tax revenue loss. The same applies to state B's position. The contracting parties' games may therefore be more complicated than assumed by the simple term 'distribution' – there will usually be a longer-term positive sum to be distributed, depending on expected market responses.

5.3.3   Bilateralism as a Means to Maximise Membership Surplus

Thompson and Verdier offer a slightly different approach – or at least, different analytical tools. They argue that the driving force behind concluding treaties is

---

270. T. Rixen (2010) p. 597.

'membership surplus': the gains that each party draws from participation (the concept is, probably, not very different from Rixen's distributive gains). Bilateral approaches allow for tailor-made negotiation on the distribution of the surplus. Multilateral treaties save on negotiation costs, but are feasible only if the membership surplus can be distributed with sufficient precision. Their conclusion is that multilateralism is most attractive when (a) transaction costs for the bilateral alternative are high while (b) the membership surplus of cooperation is low. The latter may mean that members' costs of complying with the treaty are low and/or that externalities for non-participants are high (i.e., much of the gains of an agreement would leak away to non-participants). Vice versa, bilateralism is most attractive when (a) the transaction costs of a bilateral deal are low while (b) the membership surplus of cooperation is high (i.e., parties are able to exclude non-participants from the benefits of their agreement).

The point made by Thompson and Verdier can be illustrated by an example, to show that their approach is able to explain the institutional setup of withholding tax reductions. Assume for simplicity that the only issue in concluding tax treaties was the rate of national withholding taxes on dividends. Now states A and B can create 'membership surplus' by concluding a bilateral treaty reducing those tax rates. Their expected gains in national welfare depend on the existing stocks of investment by A in B, and by B in A (which determine the initial loss in withholding tax revenue) and by expected changes in future flows of those investments (which predict gains in national welfare). As withholding taxes are typically inefficient disincentives to FDI, it may be expected that mutual reduction of such taxes is a positive sum game. That is, there is membership surplus to be divided. And the division of the surplus is typically determined by negotiating tax rate reductions. The outcome may well be that state A reduces its withholding tax rate to 15%, while state B is prepared to settle for 5%. The reason may be that state A has a higher statutory rate to start with; that it has much higher stocks of 'state B' investments than vice versa; or that it expects a smaller inflow of new investments (hence, smaller gains) compared to state B's expectations.

As to the transaction costs of forging bilateral treaties to reduce withholding taxes, these can safely be assumed to be relatively low. Unlike, for instance, negotiations on human rights which require agreement on more principled ('constitutional') matters that surpass deep ideological rifts,[271] reduction of withholding taxes is simply a matter of money. It is in essence a reciprocal exchange of commitments ('I reduce my tax rate if you reduce yours'). Moreover, the OECD MTC and Commentary have further reduced transaction costs by providing focal points for negotiations and by creating a high degree of uniformity in the interpretation and application of bilateral tax treaties based on the OECD MTC. Indeed, most existing bilateral tax treaties are based on the OECD MTC; and the Commentaries are widely used in their interpretation.[272]

Now compare this, still following Thompson and Verdier, with the alternative states A and B have of concluding a multilateral treaty with states C–Z. Assume that this treaty fixes the withholding tax rate on dividends at 10% for all participants. The

---

271. For example, M. Craven, *Legal Differentiation and the Concept of the Human Rights Treaty in International Law*, 11 European Journal of International Law 489 (2000).
272. M. Lang et al., (2012).

'membership surplus' will still be positive. It will also be much larger than the surplus of the bilateral A-B treaty, as the entire world is now involved. But the relevant benchmark is rather the joint surplus of *all* bilateral A–Z treaties. Then obviously, the positions of many states will be harmed by the inflexibility of the 10% tax rate. Considering their stocks of FDI and their expectations of future investment flows, states will actually prefer a zero rate in some bilateral relations while preferring 15% in other cases. Their acceptance of a general 10% rate implies a sacrifice – and if the sacrifice is too big compared to the gains of increased FDI, a state will not participate in the multilateral treaty and rather prefer bilateral solutions.

5.3.4 The Substance of Tax Treaties: Distributive Issues and 'Rules of the Road'

Ultimately, the analysis by Thompson and Verdier leads to the same conclusion as Rixen's: a bilateral setting allows states to optimally benefit from negotiating a reduction of withholding taxes. In Rixen's case, the reason is asymmetry in investment relations; with Thompson & Verdier, the reason may also be differences in (initial) tax rates and in tax revenue requirements that reflect differences in underlying attitudes towards the role of government in the national economy.

It must be stressed that both analyses apply specifically to the setting of withholding tax rates and treat bilateral and multilateral agreements as alternative approaches. Of course, tax treaties typically do much more than reducing withholding tax rates. For one thing, they define concepts, such as resident, dividend, etc. – concepts that can be labelled 'rules of the road'.

The typical prisoners' dilemma game (*see* section 5.2) is based on the assumption that there is just one Pareto-optimal outcome, which can only be obtained when parties are able to commit credibly to cooperation. But there are games with more than one Pareto-optimal outcome. Brennan and Buchanan label these 'rules of the road',[273] as they literally include the driving left/right choice. The classic example: two cars arrive at an intersection simultaneously.[274] One car, a Volkswagen, is northbound. The other car, a Volvo, is eastbound. There are two ways for them to cross the intersection safely: either the Volvo goes first, or the Volkswagen does. But: neither of the two car drivers wants to wait. There are two possible solution rules. A first option is a coordination rule that is based on the specific characteristics of either of the two actors. For instance, such a rule could hold: all Volvos drive on and all Volkswagens wait. As the *same* actor will always get the outcome he prefers, such a coordination rule is likely to have distributional implications, which makes cooperative solutions hard to achieve. Another option is that the actors adopt a rule in which the context determines who gets his most preferred outcome. Ideally, such a 'fairness' rule would ensure that all actors get

---

273. G. Brennan and J. M. Buchanan, *The Reason of Rules* (Cambridge University Press 1985).
274. A.A. Stein, *Why Nations Cooperate: Circumstance and Choice in International Relations* (Cornell University Press 1990) p. 38. This been called a 'dilemma of common aversions and divergent interests' by Stein, which occurs when actors do not prefer the same outcome, but do agree that there is one outcome they want to avoid at all costs.

their preferred outcome half the time. Both 'right gives way' and 'right has precedence' meet this requirement: sometimes, the Volvo comes from the right, sometimes the Volkswagen. Once an equilibrium is set, no driver would gain from deviating from the preferred outcome, as he would only hurt himself.[275]

More generally, one can think of the choice of technical standards, units of measurement, and a forum language for international communication.[276] When first making the choice, states will prefer one option over another. But as soon as an international consensus starts to emerge, individual states have little incentive to defect.[277] On the contrary: changing 'rules of the road' (i.e., changing 'right gives way' to 'left gives way') is costly. Once a specific 'rule of the road' is agreed upon and in force, a change to an alternative rule will have economic implications.

To some extent, choosing common definitions will even have network effects. As the number of states that apply a common concept or standard increases, so does the incentive for other states to join in.[278] This could then explain that the OECD has never had a concern to increase the amount of participating states when formulating its soft standards, even though these have also influenced non-members.[279] The concepts of the OECD MTC have 'provide[d] benefits that the market has failed to provide – coordination of the tax rules between nations'.[280]

---

275. L.L. Martin, *Interests, Power, and Multilateralism*, 46 International Organization 765, 775 (1992).
276. As Rixen notes, the OECD MTC can also be considered to provide 'constructed focal points', which is a concept that was introduced by G. Garrett and B. Weingast, *Ideas, Interests, and Institutions: Constructing the EC's Internal Market*, in: Ideas and Foreign Policy (J. Goldstein and R. Keohane eds, Cornell University Press 1993). *See* further sec. 6.3.3.
277. A car driver could of course threaten to defect, but this is not cheating: it is a public attempt to force the other actors to accept different equilibrium outcomes. A.A. Stein (1990) p. 42.
278. L.L. Martin (1992) p. 777.
279. Non-members have voluntarily taken up the OECD's standards in their tax conventions – between themselves too, *see* the introduction to M. Lang et al., (2012).
280. D.M. Ring (2007) p. 128. As to the contents of the treaties between OECD and Non-OECD states, research in the field of bilateral investment treaties, which countries use to compete for capital as well, suggests that source countries (called 'host' countries in the respective literature) compete with other hosts, and therefore cannot demand changes to the core provisions of BITs used by 'home' (resident) countries. Z. Elkins, A.T. Guzman and B. Simmons, *Competing for Capital: The Diffusion of Bilateral Investment Treaties, 1960-2000*, 60 International Organization 811 (2006). However, this may also be explained by a neorealist (state power-oriented) view. For a neorealist view, reference can be made to Krasner. In an article on the international distribution of the spectrums of telecommunication, he notes that in a distribution, the problem is not 'how to get to the Pareto frontier' (i.e., both state A and B have an incentive to enter into a bilateral treaty) 'but which point along the frontier will be chosen' (i.e., how the distribution between A and B works out). The exercise of state power is important in this regard: it may be used to dictate the rules of the game. It is a matter of who moves first. First movers can dictate the outcome of the distribution, 'provided that the other player is convinced that the first player's strategy is irrevocable'. S.D. Krasner, *Global Communications and National Power: Life on the Pareto Frontier*, 43 World Politics 336 (1991). So, non-OECD Member countries have maybe had no option but to accept OECD standards in bilateral tax treaty negotiations between them and OECD Members, even though this meant that they had to accept some component of coercion in doing so. As Ring notes, the fact that source (non-OECD Member) states, absent direct access to the lawmaking activities of the OECD, worked through the UN to produce a draft more geared towards their interests, could be evidence of this. Participation 'inside the regime with the potential for some influence is preferential to sitting outside the regime entirely'. D.M. Ring (2007) p. 128. And indeed, a

But it should be kept in mind that the first stage of the process ('we need a definition of residency, but which one?') may be a sensitive one as divergent interests may be at stake.[281] Nevertheless, when looking at tax treaty practice, it is evident that multilateralism has been strongest in the field of concepts. There is simply no point in renegotiating concepts like 'dividend' in every bilateral treaty relation.

5.3.5 Introducing External Effects

The previous section has shown that the reduction of withholding tax rates through bilateral tax treaties can be adequately explained by Rixen's and Thompson and Verdier's work. However, these analyses do not take into account external effects (spill-overs), which are indeed at the core of international tax law's collective action problems (i.e., the BEPS Project). These effects have been studied in BEPS Action 11; the overall estimate is that BEPS accounts for a worldwide reduction in corporate tax revenues of between 4% and 10%.[282]

It should be noted that much of this tax revenue loss cannot be dealt with by amending tax treaties. Especially differences in corporate income tax rates remain a major source of external effects (each state's tax rate choice depending on the choices made by others).

The spill-over effects of tax treaties are labelled 'network externalities': 'if country A, having a treaty with country B, signs a treaty with country C, it may in effect create a treaty between B and C'.[283] These externalities are created by some familiar traits of the international tax order, such as the concept of residence and the separate entity approach. Returning to the analyses of Rixen, and Thompson and Verdier: if two states conclude an agreement to reduce their withholding tax rates, a resident of a third state can get access to those reduced rates, depending on the residence criteria used by state A and/or state B. The size of this externality is significant though hard to calculate. One sign is that nearly 40% of worldwide FDI stocks is located in just ten countries representing 3% of worldwide GDP. Of these countries, the Netherlands, Switzerland and Belgium are the largest – and interestingly, seven out of ten are EU Member countries.[284] Another indication is that especially the tax revenue loss of developing countries may well run into the billions.[285]

The existence of sizeable external effects of bilateral tax treaty provisions reduces the rationale for concluding bilateral treaties – or, as a recent International Monetary

neorealist would argue in this regard that this is an example of how weaker states have used a regime to achieve a result slightly better than their initial power positions would have secured. *Id.*, at pp. 127–128.

281. It is not surprising that the OECD MTC is much less precise when it comes to concepts referring to factual situations, especially residency.

282. OECD (2015), Measuring and Monitoring BEPS, Action 11 – 2015 Final Report, OECD/G20 Base Erosion and Profit Shifting Project, OECD Publishing, Paris.

283. IMF, *Spillovers in International Corporate Taxation* (2014) IMF Policy Paper, 9 May 2014 at 14, and further discussion at 25–28.

284. *Id.*, at 6; OECD, *Measuring and Monitoring BEPS*, at 49–51, offers comparable figures without specifying the states involved.

285. *Id.*, at p. 27.

Fund (IMF) paper summarises in bold: 'considerable caution is needed in entering into any bilateral tax treaty'.[286] The only way to 'repair' the treaty network, the IMF suggests, is general adoption of Limitation on Benefits (LOB) clauses (as suggested in OECD BEPS Action 6).[287]

The presence of external effects may also underscore the relevance of a multilateral approach in reducing externalities, which is what the BEPS Project is about. In contrast to the reduction of double taxation, the point is now to address collective action problems – public good issues – of which BEPS is the prime example.[288] 'Solving' BEPS requires wide or even global participation to be effective, while to any state, free riding (defecting) is an attractive option. For example, for many states the adoption of LOB clauses is typically a collective-decision-making problem. Addressing the collective action problems of international tax law might hence intuitively be better served by a multilateral agreement.

5.4 THE NEOLIBERAL INSTITUTIONALIST VIEW ON MULTILATERAL TAX RELATIONS

5.4.1 The Substance of a Multilateral Agreement for International Taxation

A response to the externalities pointed out above would be to move from coordination (as in sections 5.3.2 and 5.3.3) to cooperation in the arena of international taxation, where common goals get precedence over national goals.

However, the gains of cooperation in the international tax area (the 'size of the pie') are not that clear. As we have seen, for a multilateral agreement to be viable, states must be able to foresee net benefits (the multilateral deal should be a 'positive sum game'). These benefits could be measured by means of the membership surplus. As set forth in section 5.3.3, there are two sides to this surplus: it has to be significant, and it must be possible to limit free riding.

There is indeed significant surplus to be gained by a multilateral treaty. This is also reflected in the BEPS Action plan. Indeed, one of its fundamental conceptions is that in order to *remain* sovereign in the international tax area, states must cooperate, as:

> Inaction in this area would likely result in some governments losing corporate tax revenue, the emergence of competing sets of international standards and the replacement of the current consensus-based framework by unilateral measures, which could lead to a global tax chaos.[289]

Just how significant the surplus is, that is where uncertainty begins. As regards the BEPS Project, three types of uncertainties can be discerned. There are uncertainties

---

286. *Id.*, at p. 27.
287. OECD, *Preventing the Granting of Treaty Benefits in Inappropriate Circumstances, Action 6: 2015 Final Report* (2015) 5.
288. On public goods and private goods in general: R. Comes and T. Sandler, *The Theory of Externalities, Public Goods, and Club Goods* (Cambridge University Press 1986).
289. OECD, *BEPS Action Plan (2013)* 10–11.

about: (1) the severity of BEPS activities; (2) the regional/ national impact of BEPS activities on revenues and on wealth in general; and (3) the national economic implications of different policy responses in tackling BEPS. Especially the second and third sources of uncertainty might prove to be of relevance to signing a multilateral agreement, as these make the distributive implications of action (a multilateral agreement) and inaction (no multilateral agreement) hard to predict.

As regards (1), although there is abundant evidence of sizeable profit shifting, it remains difficult to distinguish 'acceptable' from unacceptable profit shifting behaviour,[290] the more so as the distinction itself is part of the BEPS Project. Consequently, it is difficult for states to estimate how much tax revenue they lose on BEPS behaviour (point 2). It is the explicit aim of BEPS Action 11 to improve the quality and availability of relevant data – but evidently, much work still needs to be done.

Moreover, even *if* the loss of tax revenue due to BEPS behaviour could be calculated, this figure would not directly inform us about the loss of welfare (e.g., a low MNE tax burden must, in the end, benefit individuals, be it shareholders, employees or customers). Some caution is therefore warranted as regards the overall welfare benefits of tackling BEPS.[291] As to prevention of free riding, much will depend on the substantive steps taken. If these steps do not include rules that strengthen the tie between the state where tax is paid and the taxpayer's 'economic reality', free riding is a persistent threat to the goals of the BEPS Project. Anyway, the gains to be had from the BEPS Project may not, in themselves, be so evident that they could operate as a 'game changer'.

And as for point 3: assuming that a multilateral tax agreement allows for the rapid implementation of new or altered concepts in the tax treaties of all participating states, how can states be sure what the impact on their own position would be? And how would that affect their willingness to 'sign in'?

5.4.2 The Veil of Uncertainty

Literature on the impact of uncertainty on negotiations is fairly unanimous in its conclusions: when parties are uncertain how the choice between alternative rules will affect their own future positions, negotiations will tend to be successful in terms of establishing principles and concepts, rather than specific rules.

---

290. C. Fuest et al., *Profit Shifting and 'Aggressive' Tax Planning by Multinational Firms: Issues and Options for Reform*, 5 World Tax Journal (2013); D. Dharmapala, *What Do We Know about Base Erosion and Profit Shifting? A Review of the Empirical Literature*, 35 Fiscal Studies 421 (2014) makes no such estimates but discusses the empirical evidence on MNE tax planning behaviour. A fairly low 'consensus' value seems to be in sight for the impact of changes in relative tax rates on MNEs tax planning activity. Dharmapala notes on p. 444 that 'in the more recent empirical literature, the estimated magnitude of BEPS is typically much smaller than that found in earlier studies'.

291. Remember that the official economic impact assessment of the CCCTB concluded that its adoption would not increase overall welfare in the EU. Cpb Netherlands for Economic Policy Analysis, *The Economic Effects of EU-Reforms in Corporate Income Tax Systems: Study for the European Commission Directorate General for Taxation and Customs Union* (2009) TAXUD/2007/DE/324.

Evidently, there is John Rawls' veil of ignorance to start with. In his Theory of Justice,[292] he develops a contractarian approach to the construction of a fair constitution (i.e., the basic rules and institutions of a society). Rawls' conception of fairness is that an outcome is fair whenever the procedure generating that outcome was fair. Hence his veil of ignorance: to make sure that people make no judgments based on short-sighted self-interest, they should be deprived of information regarding their own positions under alternative constitutional rules and institutions. As a result, they will agree upon a constitution that is fair towards any member of society.

Ignorance is a strong assumption, and Brennan and Buchanan, in their *Reason of Rules*,[293] have coined the concept of a 'veil of uncertainty'. Their setting is comparable to Rawls': people participate in decision-making on the rules and institutions of their society-to-be. But even without assuming ignorance, participants will find it difficult to estimate the impact of general rules and principles on their own positions and economic interests in the future. They face an uncertainty which:

> serves the salutary function of making potential agreement more rather than less likely. Faced with genuine uncertainty about how his position will be affected by the operation of a particular rule, the individual is led by his self-interest calculus to concentrate on choice options that eliminate or minimize prospects for potentially disastrous results.[294]

Here, the assumption of risk-aversion turns up again:[295] when faced with uncertainty, negotiators will try to avert outcomes that may be harmful to their future positions. And the result, as Brennan and Buchanan claim, is that each participant 'will tend to agree on arrangements that might be called "fair" in the sense that patterns of outcomes generated under such arrangements will be broadly acceptable, regardless of where the participant might be located in such outcomes'. That is to say, the risk-averse participant will prefer a multilateral agreement that produces reasonable or 'centralized' outcomes for a broad range of future states-of-the-world.[296]

This line of reasoning can be applied to the position of states in negotiating rules for international taxation, i.e., in choosing between alternative basic rules and

---

292. J. Rawls, *A Theory of Justice* (Harvard University Press 1971).
293. G. Brennan and J.M. Buchanan, *The Reason of Rules: Constitutional Political Economy*, in: The Collected Works of James M. Buchanan (Liberty Fund 1985).
294. *Id.*, at Ch. 2 sec. VII, 19–23.
295. *See* B. Koremenos (2001) on the assumptions underlying rational design of international institutions.
296. The same argument has been used in other areas of international law too, *see, e.g.,* J. Goldstein and L.L. Martin, *Legalization, Trade Liberalization, and Domestic Politics: A Cautionary Note*, 54 International Organization 603 (2000) (precise rules and 'legalisation' may be counterproductive to trade liberalisation within the WTO, as legalisation leads to more and better information about the distributional effects of proposed agreements, deterring the conclusion of cooperative deals) and O.R. Young, *The Politics of International Regime Formation: Managing Natural Resources and the Environment*, 43 International Organization 349–375 (1989) (in environmental distributive bargaining problems, a 'veil of uncertainty' may explain why actors have reached agreement in some environmental areas, such as in relation to arrangements governing the Mediterranean Basin and the transboundary flow of radioactive fallout, and not in areas of acid precipitation and biological diversity. 'Why is there a robust international regime for polar bears but not for other marine mammals such as walruses, sea lions, and sea otters?', *id.*, at p. 350). *See* further sec. 7.11.2 and footnotes therein.

institutions in this field. As the impact of these alternatives on national GDP, FDI, tax revenues, etc., becomes more difficult to estimate, discussions will move away from quarrels over distribution, towards finding rules that can be considered 'fair'. Ring makes a similar observation; she notes that uncertainty will lead states to integrative rather than distributive bargaining.[297] That is to say: absent a clear and quantifiable goal in terms of economic gains, the focus of negotiations moves towards more general aims such as fair rules.

The conclusion follows that binding multilateral agreement will be more easily obtainable for general principles and concepts than for specific separate issues. For example, a general reconsideration of the concept of treaty abuse will be easier to achieve than a rule against a specific form of abuse. Quoting Brennan and Buchanan once more:

> As an example, consider the position of a dairy farmer (...) He might strongly oppose a specific reduction in milk price supports, since such action will almost surely reduce his net wealth. At the same time, however, he might support a generalized rule that would eliminate political interference with any and all prices for services or goods. The effect of such a rule change or institutional reform on his own net wealth is less determinate in the latter case than in the former.[298]

5.4.3 A Synthesis: Uncertainty on Distributional Issues

To sum up: when states face a choice between bilateral and multilateral approaches, they may prefer the bilateral instrument when there are economic benefits that the contracting parties can divide between them; they will be more inclined to multilateral agreement when the distributional aspect is absent or very uncertain ('rules of the road', *see* section 5.3.4). To make the point more clear, two types of tax policy changes can be distinguished.[299]

On one side of the spectrum there are policy options that generate clear economic benefits. These options involve the (re)distribution of the 'pie'. In the (generally not too likely) case that there are *obvious* winners and losers, reaching multilateral agreement will be difficult.[300] Support for this argument can be found in the founding period of the OECD MTC. As follows from Chapter 2, the efforts to conclude a multilateral treaty were dropped primarily due to disagreements on the formulation of a general principle to allocate tax jurisdiction, i.e., source or residence, which determined obvious winners and losers for the allocation of tax jurisdiction over interests and dividends.[301] Bilateral agreements were needed to tailor the withholding tax rates to each reciprocal tax treaty relationship.

---

297. D.M. Ring (2007) p. 109.
298. G. Brennan and J.M. Buchanan (1985), Ch. 2 sec. VII, p. 34.
299. The same point is made by T. Rixen (2010) pp. 601–603.
300. Grinberg reaches the same conclusion on the basis of an analysis of the OECD's work on CFC rules. *See* I. Grinberg (2016) pp. 1170–1174.
301. *See* Ch. 2. The taxation of interest and dividends prevented the adoption of a multilateral, uniform solution.

On the other side of the spectrum are hypothetical tax policy changes that provide completely new techniques or terminologies for solving a *new* problem. It may concern 'rules of the road' for taxing new economic phenomena, or an amendment of existing rules without obvious distributive aspects. In these cases, multilateral agreement can be reached more easily. Again, support for this argument can be found in the founding period of the OECD MTC. Even when it proved impossible to reach multilateral agreement on the precedence of either residence or source states, concepts such as 'PE' and 'arm's length' were established multilaterally, as the definition of these notions had no *obvious* distributive aspects.[302] Likewise, little distributive concerns seemed to exist as regards the allocation of taxation on, for example, employment and pensions (*see* Chapter 2.2: it makes sense to, in principle, allocate these items to the residence state). What mattered was that states selected the same 'fair' standard and did not end up with different solutions on these matters. And indeed, the distributive 'rules of the road' set forth in later OECD MTCs are part of an 'international tax language'[303] and may even be called 'multilateral' in a strong sense, as they are recognised by practitioners all over the world. So, the element of 'uncertainty' may help explain the overlap between the Mexico and London draft models, set out in Table 1 of section 2.2.2.

5.4.4 Some Illustrations: The Feasibility of a Multilateral Approach in Some Tax Policy Changes

To illustrate the relevance of these observations, let us now turn to various examples of tax policy changes. Some may serve to understand and/or predict negotiation outcomes of a number of the proposals of the BEPS Project (e.g., those on treaty abuse and interest deductions). But the point is more far-reaching than that. Literature argues that the BEPS Project deals with the symptoms but not the causes of the malfunctioning of the international tax system. Indeed, the inadequacy of the BEPS outcomes to 'remedy' corporate income taxation has been widely discussed,[304] and the Project has

---

302. S. Picciotto (1992) p. 23.
303. K. Vogel (2000) p. 616.
304. *See, e.g.*, M.P. Devereux and J. Vella, *Are We Heading Towards a Corporate Tax System Fit for the 21st Century?*, 35 Fiscal Studies 449 (2014); Y. Brauner, *BEPS: An Interim Evaluation*, 6 World Tax Journal 10 (2014); R. Tomazela, *A Critical Evaluation of the OECD's BEPS Project*, 79 Tax Notes International 239 (2015). It also convincingly follows from M.F. De Wilde (2015a) and A.C.G.a.C. De Graaf, P. De Haan and M.F. De Wilde, *Fundamental Change in Countries' Corporate Tax Framework Needed to Properly Address BEPS*, 42 Intertax 306 (2014) and R.S. Avi-Yonah and H. Xu, *Global Taxation after the Crisis: Why BEPS and MAATM Are Indadequate Responses, and What Can Be Done about It*, University of Michigan Public Law Research Paper No. 494 (2016), available at SSRN: http://papers.ssrn.com/sol3/papers.cfm?abstract_id = 271 6124 and Y. Brauner, *Treaties in the Aftermath of BEPS*, University of Floriday Levin College of Law Research Paper Nos 16–18 (2016), available at SSRN: https://papers.ssrn.com/sol3/papers.cfm?abstract_id = 2744712. Moreover, this is also the image that follows from the special edition on BEPS of *Weekblad Fiscaal Recht*, introduced by J. Vleggeert, *De implementatie van de BEPS-acties door Nederland: Kroonjuwelen versus 'aggressive tax planning indicators'*, WFR 2016/47.

been criticised to 'fail to provide a coherent and comprehensive approach, and offer instead proposals for a patch-up of existing rules'.[305]

Assuming this is indeed the case, some of the examples below are therefore panoramic: what do the observations summarised in section 5.4.3 tell us about international corporate taxation policy debates of the next decade? Each of the following cases may lead countries to reflect on their willingness to participate in a multilateral arrangement that they would not have chosen in a bilateral setting:

(1) *LOB and Principal Purpose Test (PPT) rules.* Under current rules of international taxation, entities may get access to treaty benefits even when they do not perform a relevant economic function within the group. Stronger requirements (in terms of local economic activity) could well reduce treaty shopping in the economists' broad sense of that concept. How would states perceive their interests? This probably is a matter of many winners, a few losers. Presently, the Netherlands and Luxemburg together host 25% of worldwide FDI stock. Behind this figure are, of course, most if not all of the world's MNEs. But should it be multilaterally decided that 'withholding tax shopping' must end, the number of losers (including Switzerland and to some extent the UK), and their political weight should be manageable. A principled multilateral agreement on LOB clauses might hence work, provided that parties are given enough leeway for bilateral fine-tuning. LOB clauses create clear and obvious distributive conflicts.

A brighter outlook applies to the PPT rule, as the text indicates that it involves a 'rule of the road': the key terms are 'reasonable', 'principal purpose', and 'object and purpose'.[306] These generate uncertain outcomes, and an agreement along these lines is typically served by a multilateral approach. Evidently, it would be in the interest of residence states to reduce source states' incentives to broaden their tax jurisdiction (by procedural safeguards, i.e., dispute resolution and/or exchange of information commitments). But 'asymmetric interests' (each state is predominantly a source state in one bilateral relationship, and a residence state in another) suggest the presence of a 'veil of uncertainty', enhancing a multilateral approach. Indeed, countries have committed to including a minimum level of protection against treaty shopping in their treaties,[307] and the PPT is posed as one of the BEPS Convention's central commitments.[308]

(2) *Transfer pricing guidelines and formulary apportionment.* The focus of Actions 8–10 of the BEPS Project lies on refining the arm's length standard which has developed into the 'rule of the road' for transactions between associated

305. BEPS Monitoring Group, Overall Evaluation of the G20/OECD Base Erosion and Profit Shifting (BEPS) Project, https://bepsmonitoringgroup.files.wordpress.com/2015/10/general-evaluation.pdf, p. 3.
306. OECD, *Preventing the Granting of Treaty Benefits in Inappropriate Circumstances, Action 6: 2015 Final Report* (2015) 55.
307. *See* the BEPS Convention and the discussion in Ch. 8; also: *id.*, at 10.
308. *See* Art. 7 of the BEPS Convention, discussed in Ch. 8.

enterprises. Hence, it is likely that refining the standards will not be met with a lot of resistance in a multilateral negotiation, as they are of a technical nature and are cast in flexible, non-binding documents that provide governments with ways out. A different forecast however applies in relation to the more difficult issues for which binding formulary apportionment or unitary taxation-type of solutions might be unavoidable.[309] At the heart of BEPS lies the possibility to 'move' (hard-to-measure) intangibles out of the reach of a high-tax environment (particularly the United States) towards a low-tax state.[310] The establishment of baselines and allocation standards for a formulary approach (e.g., labour, assets, innovation), or in other words: the establishment of the size and the shares of the 'tax pie', inevitably involves a distributive problem that creates obvious (and foreseeable) winners and losers. Should, for example, innovation rather than labour be chosen as the formula's benchmark, the US would win and China and India would lose. This makes multilateral cooperation on formulary apportionment unlikely. It is therefore not surprising that the final BEPS reports lack formulary apportionment-type of solutions. Turning the point around: it may therefore be said that any rule that makes use of a formula to distribute tax among countries is politically unlikely. Hence, a Common Consolidated Corporate Tax Base (CCCTB) may also prove to be politically very difficult to achieve. The same considerations might affect proposals on country-by-country (CbC) reporting, to the extent that they could be considered a step in the direction of formulary apportionment. Or to put it differently: considering the broad support for CbC-reporting rules, this must mean CbC is *not* perceived as a credible step towards formulary apportionment.[311]

(3) *Interest deductions*. One of the strongest substantive recommendations of the BEPS Project is the general adoption of an earnings stripping rule.[312] It consists of two parts: a fixed ratio rule (with a bandwidth of 10–30% of earnings before interests, taxes, depreciation and amortization (EBITDA)) and a group ratio rule (that would allow additional deduction of third-party interest if interest payments of the worldwide group exceed the fixed ratio). This might be a 'veil of uncertainty' situation. Most, if not all, states will see their corporate tax bases broadened, though the effect will be more limited in states that already restrict interest deduction. There may be a negative impact on investments, as the cost of capital increases – but this impact typically gets

---

309. For example, R.S. Avi-Yonah and I. Benshalom, *Formulary Apportionment: Myths and Prospects*, 3 World Tax Journal 371, 380 (2011) and M. Kobetsky, *The Case for Unitary Taxation of International Enterprises*, 62 Bulletin for International Taxation 201 (2008).
310. Y. Brauner, *What the BEPS*, 16 Florida Tax Review 55, 96 (2014).
311. Instead, as I. Grinberg (2016) p. 1167 notes, transparency and information reporting requirements are not 'facially distributional'.
312. OECD, *Limiting Base Erosion Involving Interest Deductions and Other Financial Payments, Action 4: 2015 Final Report* (2015) OECD/G20 Base Erosion and Profit Shifting Project, OECD Publishing, Paris. http://dx.doi.org/10.1787/9789264241176-en.

smaller as more countries join in. The OECD proposal has much to going for it to make it the new 'rule of the road' for deductibility of interest.

What complicates the issue however is that Action 4 requires changes in domestic legislation. The explanatory statement to the 2015 final BEPS reports notes that countries have 'agreed a general policy direction' on the matter,[313] while the Action 4 Final Report announces a multilateral review process of implementation efforts and their impact on MNE behaviour.[314]

(4) *'Digital presence'*. Now that international trade in goods and especially services can increasingly do without a traditional PE, pressure has developed to widen the definition of local 'presence' in the source state. The OECD has suggested some options (Action 1), though the Final Report makes no specific recommendations. This is understandable, as any proposal on this issue would raise a clear distributive conflict. Assume there would be a proposal to replace Article 5 MTC with a sales criterion (e.g., local sales create tax liability when exceeding a fixed threshold amount), how would states assess their own position? In this case, the answer is reasonably clear: the US would lose, the rest of the world might well win (or expect to win). The role of tax havens as 'home state' to internet services is a (potential) game changer. And in the end, it would be hard to estimate what amount of tax money is involved (after all, Google and Microsoft do have PE's in Europe). The prediction would be: the level of uncertainty would not be enough to be able to hide a clear distributional conflict between the US and the rest of the world. The debate on 'digital presence' may lead nowhere.

(5) *Minimum withholding tax rates*. The BEPS Project is not aimed at rearranging the international allocation of taxing rights. But the pressure by NGOs to consider the interests of developing countries could lead to a focus on minimum withholding tax rates. As a UN report recently observed:

With the current international discussion about the need to ensure taxing rights over economic engagement in one's territory, and concern about profit shifting through 'off-shoring' intangible property (...) there is likely to be renewed interest in withholding taxes as an efficient, and relatively secure against avoidance, means of enforcing source State taxing rights.[315]

Within the OECD arena, the philosophy has always been that withholding taxes are hurdles to international investment and should be reduced to, preferably, zero. But developing countries have different interests. For them, withholding taxes are much easier to handle with limited

---

313. OECD, *Developing a Multilateral Instrument to Modify Bilateral Tax Treaties, Action 15: 2015 Final Report* (2015).
314. OECD, *Limiting Base Erosion Involving Interest Deductions and Other Financial Payments, Action 4: 2015 Final Report* (2015), 79–80.
315. UN Economic and Social Council, Further Progress in Strengthening the Work of the Committee of Experts on International Cooperation in Tax Matters: Report of the Secretary-General, 8 May 2013.

administrative capacity. Here again there is an obvious distributive issue, but one that can easily be politicised: it may be hijacked by public opinion. A multilateral tax agreement could provide for a targeted solution, for example, inserting 10% minimum withholding tax rates in all treaties with qualifying developing countries.

(6) Proposals for 'destination-based' corporate income tax systems. In international tax literature, some suggestions for a destination-based corporate income tax system have surfaced, which can be considered as the economist's answer for a 'fair'[316] and/or 'neutral'[317] corporate income tax system. What unites these proposals is that a move towards a destination-based corporate income tax system requires a switch to a different proxy as the basis for establishing taxing claims:[318] the relevant proxy would be the location of certain transactions, such as sales in the destination state, rather than the location of production factors.

From the simple starting point of equality (and hence economic neutrality) as fairness,[319] De Wilde, for instance, proposes establishing an unlimited tax liability in each tax jurisdiction in which the taxpayer has a nexus (i.e., the economic activity).[320] Moreover, he suggests that the multinational itself should constitute the taxable entity,[321] its economic rents the taxable

---

316. M.F. De Wilde (2015a).
317. The 'neutrality' question deals with the design of a corporate income tax systems which create minimum distortion to the economic behaviour of corporate taxpayers. The most extensive argument is that of the Oxford Centre for Business Taxation. For example, A. Auerbach and M.P. Devereux, *Consumption and Cash-flow Taxes in an International Setting*, Oxford University Centre for Business Taxation WP 13/11 (2013); M.P. Devereux and R. De La Feria, *Designing and Implementing a Destination-based corporate tax*, Oxford University Centre for Business Taxation WP 14/07 (2014); A. Auerbach and M.P. Devereux, *Cash Flow Taxes in an International Setting*, Said Business School RP 2015-3 (2015).
318. M.P. Devereux and R. De La Feria (2014) p. 15.
319. M.F. De Wilde (2015a) pp. 37 and 52. 'The basic argument made is that the notion of fairness in corporate taxation is founded on the equality principle, conforming to the historically widely acknowledged notion of equal treatment before the law.'
320. De Wilde proposes a system in which worldwide tax liability is established in the country closest to the 'source' or 'nexus' of the income. This would cause a tax system to be internally coherent, as it is irrelevant where the taxpayer's place of residence is located. As long as the economic operator is subjected to an unlimited tax liability in the nexus state, cross-border economic operations are not taxed differently from internal economic operations. Would all countries apply this system, they would effectively tax their fraction of the worldwide income to which they are entitled. *Id.*, at Ch. 3.
321. The advantage of a unitary taxation approach is that it counters the distortive effects caused by the separate entity approach. As De Wilde notes, the separate entity approach allows MNEs to influence taxation in different countries by choosing the place of incorporation (residence) and legal form. *Id.*, at p. 164. Taxing the enterprise as a unity, on the other hand, installs neutrality of legal form in corporate taxation. It has the effect that a group of affiliated entities is treated as a single entity for corporate tax purposes. Moreover, it resolves market distortions caused by the different tax treatment of financing instruments, i.e., debt and equity, within groups of affiliated companies. *See id.*, at Ch. 4.

base,[322] and the tax base would be assigned to the market jurisdiction on the basis of a sales factor.[323] Double taxation would be avoided by a Dutch-style relief system, that could be positioned somewhere in the middle of the spectrum between a credit and an exemption system.[324] What would remain is a disparity between tax rates.

Allocating the tax base by means of a destination-based attribution key (sales) removes the current incentive to shift taxable profit across borders. Indeed, the most important argument to turn to a destination-based tax base is that the consumer is immobile: 'a tax based solely on the revenue generated in each market cannot be avoided by switching factors of production (and trade flows) between countries'.[325] However, the switch from a source-based corporate income tax towards one in which the proxy for establishing tax claims is based on a sales factor would imply a switch from producing countries to consumption countries. This clearly introduces the problems identified under point 2. Individual action seems pointless, as a switch to a destination-based system by some countries and not by others would only result in significant double taxation and double non-taxation distortions.[326] Hence, despite its elegance, proposals for destination-based corporate income taxation are likely to remain, at least for the time being, as De Wilde phrases it, 'on the drawing board'.[327]

Summing up, rules that create obvious and foreseeable winners and losers in the international tax area, such as formulary apportionment-type of rules, are likely to be unfeasible in a multilateral setting. It is therefore not surprising that the OECD Final Reports and the BEPS Convention (*see* Chapter 8) avoid making proposals/rules with evident distributional impact, and make strong recommendations on typical 'rule of the road' issues, increasing the likelihood that a multilateral agreement for international taxation will gain widespread support.

---

322. Technically, this could be achieved by an allowance for corporate equity (ACE) as this system leads to a tax on economic rent. *Id.*, at Ch. 5. An ACE allows a deduction for the opportunity cost of equity capital. As the remuneration for both debt and equity capital are tax deductible, only the provision of production factors is taken into consideration for tax purposes. It hence leads to a system that does not affect financing decisions. M.F. De Wilde, *'Sharing the Pie': Taxing Multinationals in a Global Market*, 43 Intertax 438, 443 (2015).
323. *See* M.F. De Wilde (2015a) Ch. 6.
324. *Id.*, at Ch. 3.
325. A. Auerbach and M.P. Devereux (2013) p. 3.
326. R.J. Vann, *Policy Forum: The Policy Underpinnings of the BEPS Project: Preserving the International Corporate Income Tax?*, 62 Canadian Tax Journal 433 (2014).
327. M.F. De Wilde (2015a) p. 60.

5.4.5 Two Rational Design Presumptions Point Towards Using Flexibility Mechanisms

Thus far, it has been argued that the prospects of multilateral agreement depend on the absence of obvious economic gains (or losses) to be distributed over participating states, and/or on a high level of uncertainty regarding the size of those gains for participating states. Both considerations point into the direction of two 'standard' rational design hypotheses, based on the literature regarding the rational design of international agreements:[328]

- *Presumption 1. Actors have an incentive to design institutions with flexibility when they are faced with uncertainty about how the division of gains will work out in the future.*[329] By using flexibility arrangements, actors can 'insure' themselves against unanticipated negative consequences.[330] Moreover, more flexible arrangements can lead to a 'learning' process, in which states learn over the course of time about the costs and benefits of policy action, reducing uncertainties.[331] Such 'learning' agreements are not aimed at providing once-and-for all solutions, but are rather built to *manage* a problem in the future.
- *Presumption 2. States may reduce distributional problems by adopting a more flexible agreement structure.*[332] For international tax, this flexibility is reflected in the fact that the reduction of double taxation is organised bilaterally. Hence, this hypothesis does nothing more but reflect the conclusions of sections 5.3.2 and 5.3.3: bilateralism is favoured over multilateralism because it enables states to maximise the membership surplus (*see* Figure 2 below).

---

328. These presumptions are based on some of the conjectures presented by B. Koremenos (2001). The total number of conjectures adds up to sixteen, and covers, i.e., membership (inclusive or restrictive), issue scope (limited or broad), centralisation and flexibility. They have been empirically tested in B. Koremenos, *The Continent of International Law: Explaining Agreement Design* (Cambridge University Press 2016).
329. B. Koremenos (2001) 793.
330. B. Koremenos, *Contracting around International Uncertainty*, 99 American Political Science Review 549, 549 (2005).
331. B. Koremenos (2001).
332. *Id.*, at 794.

Figure 2   Design Strategy: The Argument

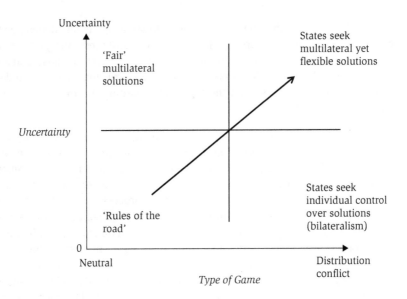

5.4.6   What Types of Flexibility Mechanisms?

Presumptions 1 and 2 hence will lead states to consider flexibility mechanisms when designing a multilateral agreement. The question then is: what *types* of flexibility mechanisms could be considered?

Generally speaking, literature on the rational design of international agreements distinguishes between three types of flexibility mechanisms: *transformative*, *adaptive* and *interpretative* flexibility.[333] *Transformative* flexibility allows the institution itself to be changed so that actors can respond as circumstances change; such mechanisms allow the development of substantive commitments over time. *Adaptive* flexibility allows actors to depart from institutional norms, for instance, due to a change in domestic circumstances, whilst the institution itself remains in place. The goal of this type of flexibility is to isolate external shocks, whilst the broader institution is insulated

---

333. *See id.*, at 773; A. Thompson, *Rational Design in Motion: Uncertainty and Flexibility in the Global Climate Regime*, 16 European Journal of International Relations 269, 270–271 (2010) (who first introduces 'interpretative' flexibility by the term 'means flexibility') and C. Marcoux, *Institutional Flexibility in the Design of Multilateral Environmental Agreements*, 26 Conflict Management and Peace Science 209 (2009). The latter two articles are about agreements in the area of the international environment. The agreements for the international environment are an ideal case for investigating uncertainty-flexibility designs, as political processes are transparent and outcomes distinct. As will be argued in Ch. 5, the problems underlying the environmental agreements are comparable to tackling BEPS. *See*, on flexibility more in general, L.R. Helfer, *Flexibility in International Agreements*, in: Interdisciplinary Perspectives on International Law and International Relations (J.L. Dunoff and M.A. Pollack eds, Cambridge University Press 2012).

from their impact. Examples of such rules are escape mechanisms and withdrawal clauses. Finally, *interpretative flexibility* has aspects of both other two types: it grants individual participants leeway in interpreting and applying agreed rules. The most common forms of this type of flexibility are the use of reservations, which ensure that states whose interests depart from the treaty's text are not forced to make an all-or-nothing choice, and the use of open norms or 'rules of the road'.[334] Nevertheless, the use of such norms is not without bounds: the more states are uncertain about the behaviour of others under such norms (does certain behaviour constitute cooperation or defection?), the more a need exists for information and dispute resolution mechanisms.[335] As Abbott and Snidal say, delegation, i.e., the delegation of authority to, for example, courts,[336] may particularly be used to deal with incomplete contracting problems.[337]

Be that as it may, the underlying problem structure of a multilateral agreement for international taxation points in the direction of using *interpretative* and *transformative* flexibility mechanisms. Indeed, hypothesis 1 points in the direction of using 'rules of the road', which contain interpretative flexibility by allowing states to 'insure' themselves against uncertain future outcomes of a multilateral agreement. This enables states to create solutions as they go along. Additionally, a transformative flexibility design allows states to tackle completely new problems as they come up. This reflects the wish of the OECD to create an 'innovative approach to international tax matters, reflecting the rapidly evolving nature of the global economy'.[338] More importantly, as argued in the next chapter, it allows states to 'learn', i.e., develop international rules over time. Once detailed commitments are under negotiation, presumption 2 points in the direction of a generous use of reservations. Reservations to multilateral norms create *inter se* (potentially bilateral) arrangements between parties within the multilateral regime, providing a flexible solution to the distribution problem. Although this strategy comes at the cost of uniformity and complexity, states individually remain in control over proposed solutions whilst not losing sight of the agreement's principal purpose (to amend the network of bilateral tax treaties and provide a level playing field).

---

334. C. Marcoux (2009) pp. 211–212.
335. J. Mccall Smith, *The Politics of Dispute Settlement Design: Explaining Legalism in Regional Trade Pacts*, 54 International Organization 137 (2000); B. Koremenos, *Centralization Increases with Uncertainty About Behaviour* (2001) pp. 27–28 and B. Koremenos, *If Only Half of International Agreements Have Dispute Resolution Provisions, Which Half Needs Explaining?*, 36 Journal of Legal Studies 189 (2007).
336. K.W. Abbott et al., *The Concept of Legalization*, 54 International Organization 401, 415 (2000).
337. K.W. Abbott and D. Snidal, *Hard and Soft Law in International Governance*, 54 International Organization 421–456, 433 (2000).
338. OECD, *BEPS Action Plan (2013)* p. 24.

5.4.7 Procedural Elements of a Multilateral Agreement for International Taxation

5.4.7.1 Participants

But especially in a multilateral agreement, the interests of states might be so different that negotiations could eventually end up in a choice between poor agreements (i.e., 'rules of the road' will not be further developed) and negotiation failure. Certainly, efforts should be made for the eventual universalisation of the regime, as is pointed out in Chapter 4. Moreover, there is an obvious logic to including more states in a multilateral agreement, as the current system's externalities can only be reduced when more (and the most economically relevant) states accept to sign a multilateral tax deal (*see* section 5.3.5). The point is that the membership parameter depends on the amount and type of actors needed to resolve a problem. But rational design theory suggests that as numbers increase in a multilateral negotiation, this may lead to broader-deeper trade-offs.[339]

Indeed, the need for flexibility mechanisms will make negotiations far more complex and therefore, in terms of transaction costs, more expensive. Yet without such mechanisms, a step towards broader membership diffuses the influence of the individual state on lawmaking (this point is, essentially, a central argument of the discussions above), making such a state likely to renege. Moreover, tax rules are already of a very technical (and hence often complex) nature.[340] Indeed, as Ault says:

> The OECD has been most successful where it works to establish principles of sufficient specificity to be helpful in channelling policy formulation, but not principles so detailed as to be too restrictive of the ways in which the countries can implement them.[341]

As Blum notes, 'the introduction of additional parties to treaty negotiations is hardly ever cost-free. It potentially increases barriers to efficient agreements and exacerbates problems of information asymmetry, strategic barriers, psychological barriers, and institutional constraints'.[342] Indeed, increased transaction costs 'may cause some states to remain outside an agreement even if their participation would increase the total surplus'.[343]

So, abruptly broadening state participation (e.g., by means of a switch to another established institution such as the UN) has the drawback that developed countries are

---

339. B. Koremenos (2001) p. 785; G.W. Downs, D.M. Rocke and P.N. Barsoom, *Managing the Evolution of Multilateralism*, 52 International Organization 397 (1998). *See also* G. Blum (2008) p. 351; A.T. Guzman, *How International Law Works: A Rational Choice Theory* (OUP 2008) pp. 170–176.
340. This also explains that countries have negotiated, in limited numbers only, on the development of the OECD MTC. More participants would have made 'the model no longer a model', and would have reduced the quality of the output that the OECD sought to achieve. H.J. Ault, *The Role of the OECD Commentaries in the Interpretation of Tax Treaties*, in: Essays on International Taxation (H.H. Alpert and K. van Raad eds, Kluwer Law and Taxation 1993).
341. H.J. Ault (2008) p. 780.
342. G. Blum (2008) p. 351.
343. A.T. Guzman (2008) p. 171.

likely to oppose such a move. During the Addis Ababa 2015 Financing for Development Conference, initiatives for an equal voice of developing countries in setting international tax policy, organised around the G77 and China, were blocked by developed states.[344] Would the locus of decision-making and policy setting in international tax be moved to the more diverse-member forum of the UN *in one go*, the current control of developed nations over international tax matters would become far more diffused.

Hence, a quick expansion of countries involved in decision-making would probably come at the cost of reaching consensus, or even worse, might prevent rational states to renegotiate at all.[345] Consequently, to mitigate some of these risks, it may be wise, when starting off, to limit decision-making to the countries whose shared interests are greater than their differences, so that the road towards further agreement can be paved.[346] Also, decision-making can be slowly expanded over time to a wider and more diverse group of participants.[347] So, the neoliberal viewpoint leaves some leeway as regards broadening participation to more and more diverse groups of states.

It is unlikely that a procedurally fair system, such as the one set out in Chapter 4, will be immediately accepted. Nevertheless, there are indications that the OECD is working towards a system in line with such a system, i.e., that includes all of those interested. That the final BEPS package has been presented as a *fait accompli* to the rest of the world, causing some writers to question the Project's legitimacy,[348] seems a necessary compromise not to expand decision-making too quickly. But it should be kept in mind that what needs to be worked towards to, is that the states participating in the ad-hoc group or 'implementation framework' are ultimately given a real, tangible and equal influence on lawmaking taking place, i.e., on the adoption of the texts, setting of the agenda, etc.

---

344. UN General Assembly, *Resolution adopted by the General Assembly on 27 July 2015: Addis Ababa Action Agenda of the Third International Conference on Financing for Development* (2015) UN A/RES/69/313, at paras 28 and 29, sets out that the financing for development initiative continues to work on the basis of already existing international consensus on international tax issues.
345. B. Koremenos (2001) pp. 794–795.
346. R.O. Keohane and J.S.J. Nye (1989) pp. 294–295.
347. G.W. Downs, D.M. Rocke and P.N. Barsoom (1998) (admitting potential members sequentially over time based on their preferences for cooperation produces a multilateral organisation that will often be deeper at every stage than the cooperative structure that would have been obtained by an inclusive strategy). And: M.J. Gilligan, *Is There a Broader-Deeper Trade-off in International Multilateral Agreements?*, 58 International Organization 459 (2004) (a more diverse group of states may be allowed to set their tax policies at different levels).
348. *See, e.g.*, I.J. Mosquera Valderrama, *Legitimacy and the Making of International Tax Law: The Challenges of Multilateralism*, 7 World Tax Journal 7 (2015): 'The risk may exist that countries fail to reach consensus on the provisions of the multilateral agreement and that such agreement will have several reservations or opting out provisions by countries that may result in a lack of commitment to the provisions of the agreement by the OECD and the non-OECD countries.'; and C. Peters (2014) p. 342: 'In the absence of appropriately institutionalized procedures, there is the fatal perception that the arguments and interests of the non-members are being heard, but that these do not find their way in the decisions that are being made.'

5.4.7.2 Transparency

The neoliberal institutionalist view on international tax relations also provides some insights into whether negotiations and deliberations should be transparent in a broad sense, i.e., to the public and to other actors. Following Finel and Lord, two 'logics' of transparency can be discerned: one positive and one negative.[349]

In a positive logic of transparency, transparency first of all increases the effectiveness of regimes by reliably projecting states' intentions. This can prevent conflicts from escalating.[350] Improving transparency is, by definition, a way to perfect markets. For instance, Keohane argued that international regimes may overcome market failure by helping to 'dissolve' the walls of the prisons in a classic prisoners' dilemma, as this improves information flows and decreases transaction costs.[351] More particular in relation to lawmaking, transparency ensures that 'rules of the road' are perceived as fair by all, in the sense that they can be scrutinised to incorporate all relevant interests. In this regard, as Keohane notes, 'outsiders' will be reluctant to make agreements with 'insiders', expecting that the resulting bargains are unfair. The problem is not one of insufficient information, but rather one of systematically biased patterns of information, which are recognised before any agreement is arrived at. 'Awareness that others have greater knowledge than oneself, and are therefore capable of manipulating a relationship or even engaging for successful deception and double-cross, is a barrier to making agreement', he says.[352] Second, transparency obviously promotes democratic values: the more citizens know about the actions of bureaucrats, the better they can hold them accountable. Indeed, a point of Chapter 4 in this regard, reiterated here, is that as tax lawmaking becomes more and more removed from its democratic basis of justification, and as international institutions gain greater authority to influence the lives of individuals, the direct influence of national legislatures on lawmaking is reduced. This underscores the need for transparent deliberations, which allows civil society to follow and influence lawmaking taking place.[353]

But transparency has its drawbacks too. Identifying these drawbacks does, however, require relaxing some of the presumptions of neoliberal institutionalism set forth in section 5.2. The point is that transparency is of little help to a negotiation when the public can 'measure' the bargaining success or failure of its representatives by means of a publicly known 'baseline' (such as the terms/equilibria of existing bilateral tax treaties). Such a baseline may be set, as we have seen in section 5.4.3, when departing from an existing bilateral tax treaty equilibrium cannot be concealed by a 'veil of uncertainty'.

---

349. B. Finel and K. Lord, *The Surprising Logic of Transparency*, 43 International Studies Quarterly 315 (1999).
350. *Id.*, at p. 319.
351. R.O. Keohane (1984); *see also* A.A. Stein (1990), Ch. 3.
352. R.O. Keohane (1984) p. 93.
353. M. Donaldson and B. Kingsbury, *Power and the Public: The Nature and Effects of Formal Transparency Policies in Global Governance Institutions*, in: Transparency in International Law (A. Bianchi and A. Peters eds, Cambridge University Press 2013) pp. 502–504.

A transparent negotiation may further complicate matters, as it provides an incentive for that party to 'posture', which relates to the effect that representatives become concerned with achieving bargaining success in the eyes of the electorate.[354] This concern then motivates representatives to adopt uncompromising positions during negotiations, so that they will not 'fail' in the eyes of the public. If the public indeed expects its representatives to pursue the national interests (i.e., increase or protect domestic welfare),[355] a public renegotiation can prevent parties from explore workable compromises, as negotiation efforts can be compared to publicly known baselines. In a closed-door environment, on the other hand, representatives can blame other states for the positions ultimately adopted.[356] In the event that the public can indeed 'measure' the success of a negotiation against publicly know tax treaty equilibria,[357] transparency may hence increase the risk of negotiation breakdown.

The point is that openness has obvious benefits, but has costs too. Transparency can however be achieved to varying degrees, as there are many techniques to enhance transparency without making *all* information immediately available.[358] For instance, decision-makers may provide a reasoned account on why an issue will not be discussed in public, placing the onus of proof on those that seek confidentiality.[359] Also, policy makers may set the time period after which the records of closed meetings are published: although deliberations may take place behind closed doors, policy makers may at least make sufficient information available so that the public can understand the law made by a body. Publishing the *travaux préparatoires* online, including

---

354. This has been argued by D. Stasavage, *Open-Door or Closed-Door? Transparency in Domestic and International Bargaining*, 58 International Organization 667 (2004).

355. T. Risse and M. Klein, *Deliberation in Negotiations*, 17 Journal of European Public Policy 708 (2010) argue that negotiations 'behind closed doors' are conductive to persuasion the more actors know about the preferences of audiences whose consent is required. Vice versa, a transparent negotiation setting is conductive to persuasion the more that actors are uncertain about the preferences of audiences whose consent is required.

356. S.J. Barkin, *When Institutions can Hurt You: Transparency, Domestic Politics, and International Cooperation*, 52 International Politics 349 (2015). *See also* D. Stasavage (2004).

357. Put differently: transparency may work when the public does not expect representatives to pursue the maximisation of domestic welfare, or when 'measuring' negotiation success is impossible because gains are uncertain.

358. *See*, in this regard, R.O. Keohane and J.S.J. Nye (2002) p. 239: 'As experiments continue with governance and trisectoral networks, it will be important to develop more modest normative principles and practices to enhance transparency and accountability – not only of IGOs but of corporations and NGOs that constitute global governance today. For example, increased transparency advances accountability, but transparency need not be instantaneous or complete. Consider the delayed release of Federal Reserve Board hearings or the details of Supreme Court deliberations.' Similarly, L.R. Helfer, *Constitutional Analogies in the International Legal System*, 37 Loyola of Los Angeles Law Review 193, 231–237 (2003) shows that international lawmakers make use of a wide range of transparency and accountability mechanisms, from soft to more radical.

359. A.E. Boyle and K. Mccall Smith, *Transparency in International Law-Making*, in: Transparency in International Law (A. Bianchi and A. Peters eds, Cambridge University Press 2013) refer to the *Convention on Access to Information, Public Participation in Decision-Making and Access to Justice in Environmental Matters* (adopted 25 Jun. 1998), 2161 UNTS 447 and the *Agreement for the Implementation of the Provisions of the United Nations Convention on the Law of the Sea of 10 December 1982 Relating to the Conservation and Management of Straddling Fish Stocks and Highly Migratory Fish Stocks* (adopted 4 Aug. 1995), 2167 UNTS 88 in this regard, *see* pp. 429–430.

preparatory documents, could help in this regard.[360] Policy makers can also resort to intensifying public consultation.[361] Alternatively, they can invite NGOs to participate as observers at the meetings of treaty parties.[362] In this regard, as noted by Schermers and Blokker, the importance of NGOs in the work of international organisations (IOs) has risen. Through their expertise, by mobilising public opinion and by linking 'the local and the global', IOs have been able to close in on social reality.[363]

The OECD works on the basis of a compromise. It has clearly put a lot of effort in being as transparent as possible. For instance, the OECD is transparent about the tax rules drafted and the technical aspects of those rules, and has systemically heard the voice of the public through public discussion drafts. As Mosquera Valderrama points out in relation to the BEPS Project: the key documents, the draft actions, the discussion drafts, they have all been published on the OECD website. So, the first impression is that the OECD meets the criteria of transparency.[364] Yet, the OECD only publishes what it wishes to publish, and probably not without a reason. Insufficient information is available on how decisions by the OECD are *actually* made.[365] Although the OECD claims to be transparent, little is revealed about how the OECD has adopted the BEPS proposals, how nations actually have 'used' the OECD in this regard.[366] But this protects negotiations on obvious distributive issues from being politicised against widely known preexisting baselines, for example, set by existing terms of bilateral tax treaties.

So, the question of transparency is a dilemma. On the one hand, the neoliberal institutionalist view strongly suggests that transparency increases the efficiency of a regime. Moreover, it increases the accountability of international lawmakers. But there are risks too. If the adoption of a multilateral agreement is interpreted as a 'negotiation

---

360. A.E. Boyle and K. Mccall Smith (2013) p. 432.
361. N.M.A. Kreveld, *Consultatie bij fiscale wetgeving* (SDU 2016) develops a practical decision-making model for domestic lawmakers to decide to use a particular type of consultation method, given the varying aims and purposes of the inquiry.
362. A.E. Boyle and K. Mccall Smith (2013) p. 426, includes references to conventions in this regard at footnote 36.
363. H.G. Schermers and N.M. Blokker (2011) para. 188–189. But *see* S. Charnovitz, *Nongovernmental Organizations and International Law*, 100 American Journal of International Law 348, 368 (2006), who says: 'of course, NGO participation does not necessarily improve the outputs from IOs or multilateral negotiations. Consultation with NGOs takes time, which can exact a cost. Moreover, while inviting the NGOs in makes the entire process more transparent to the public, such transparency can lead to different results than would ensue if governments arrived at agreements behind closed doors.'
364. I.J. Mosquera Valderrama (2015) sec. 6.2.1.
365. There is no detailed information available about the collaborative processes by means of which the rules of the BEPS Action items were established. It is not possible to learn what arguments played a role and what did not, who has set the agenda, who made what decisions and who had what influence, to what extent consensus has been reached on a particular action item, for example, why 'ad-hoc partial solutions' were chosen over the 'comprehensive and principled rethinking' of the challenges posed by BEPS. *See*, in this regard, the criticism of Y. Brauner (2014a). Mosquera Valderrama recognises that the deliberations taken place between states in the BEPS Project have not been published, which prevents any insights in how the interests of non-member countries were actually taken into account. I.J. Mosquera Valderrama (2015) sec. 6.2.1.
366. A. Christians, *Networks, Norms, and National Tax Policy*, 9 Washington University Global Studies Law Review 1, 15 (2010).

failure' by a state's public, for instance, when a flagrant loss of domestic welfare cannot be concealed by a 'veil of uncertainty', transparency can undermine rather than facilitate negotiation outcomes, as it prevents negotiators from blaming them on others. Transparency should be treated with care. But given the wide variety of transparency mechanisms at the disposal of lawmakers, there is no reason not to consider transparency as the appropriate standard for, rather than the exception to, international lawmaking. Deviations from the standard, if necessary, can be justified and explained.

5.5 CONCLUSIONS

In predicting how negotiations will turn out for a multilateral agreement for international taxation, the neoliberal institutionalist insights from the work of Rixen and Thompson and Verdier are useful. These explain why the reduction of withholding taxes is organised bilaterally: this provides states with the instrument to maximise their membership surplus (in the terms of Thompson and Verdier) or their gains in an asymmetrical distribution conflict (as reasoned by Rixen).

This line of thought does however not fully account for externalities of the tax treaties network, such as those caused by BEPS. Internalising these external effects requires collective action. But before states will agree to a multilateral arrangement, they must be able to foresee some gains in multilateral cooperation compared to likely alternatives (such as further loss of corporate income tax revenues, or increasing reliance on unilateral rules to protect the national tax base). Although some distributive benefits/membership surplus might be gained through multilateral cooperation in relation to tax avoidance and tax competition, there is a great deal of uncertainty about how significant these gains are. In the face of uncertainty, the risk-averse state will tend to agree on 'centralised' or 'fair' multilateral arrangements, i.e., arrangements that may be expected to generate acceptable outcomes for a broad range of future states-of-the-world. Hence, as the impact of different policy options is more difficult to measure, discussions will move away from quarrels over distribution, in which states will seek individual control over decision-making, towards finding principles and rules that can be considered 'fair'.

These two factors (the size of the gains to be distributed, and the level of uncertainty surrounding that size) provide us with an insight into the feasibility of different future policy actions, as well as the design of a multilateral agreement. The multilateral approach can be helpful in improving and reformulating 'rules of the road'. Remaining distribution problems and uncertainty concerns can be relaxed by flexible regime design options, such as reservations. Moreover, negotiation breakdown can be mitigated by only including like-minded parties in the deliberations, and by closing the doors of negotiations, so that compromises are not openly set off against publicly known baselines. Relaxing these procedural restrictions can be experimented with, however, as transparency can be realised in varying ways and to varying degrees, and inclusivity can be achieved gradually.

This does in no way guarantee success in the near or even remote future. Instead, this may mean that solving the fundamental problems underlying BEPS, for example, replacing the arm's length standard with formulary apportionment-type of rules, may prove very difficult. But focusing on 'rules of the road' and avoiding issues with clear distributional impact increases the chances of a multilateral agreement for international taxation gaining widespread support.

CHAPTER 6

A Design Strategy for a Multilateral Agreement for International Taxation

6.1 INTRODUCTION

So far, we have learned that in their cooperative efforts, states should aim at being 'procedurally fair' (Chapter 4). This requires that deliberations on international tax law are continuous, transparent and inclusive, which, in turn, allows the lawmaking process to include all relevant moral, social and political perspectives, leading to law that is 'neutral' and hence 'fair'. And indeed, provided that steps are taken one at a time and with care, the amount of participating states may be incrementally increased (*see* section 5.4.7.1). Moreover, although opening the doors to the negotiations can cause the public to 'measure' bargaining success by setting off negotiation outcomes against publicly known baselines, there is a strong suggestion that transparency enhances cooperation, and transparency may be achieved in varying ways and to varying degrees (*see* section 5.4.7.2).

We have also learned that there are limits to the substantive rules that can be agreed upon in a multilateral negotiation (Chapter 5). Multilateral agreement is discouraged by the presence of obvious distributive issues. A multilateral agreement for international taxation should therefore leave a good deal of room for accommodating divergent state interests, for example, by reservations and 'rules of the road'. Disagreement should, so to speak, not be emphasised by precise rules from which parties cannot deviate. But this means that some rules, such as those that make use of formulary apportionment mechanisms, may be politically unfeasible. Therefore, when state action in the tax field continues to be constrained by egocentric rationality and the need to protect the national economic interests, the development of distributive norms of international taxation, whatever their contents may be, is likely to be slow and indeterminate.

In the light of these outcomes, the aim of this chapter is to argue that achieving procedural fairness in international taxation is not only 'the right thing to do', but also indispensable for enabling the international tax regime to continuously adapt and evolve. This resonates well with the normative view set forth in Chapter 4 on 'fair' international tax rules. But it also matches Chapter 5's suggestion that cooperation in the international tax field requires transformative flexibility mechanisms. In the face of uncertainty, states may employ such mechanisms to ensure that the arrangement itself can be changed once further information becomes available. States can, over time, learn more about the effects and impacts of certain courses of action or inaction and act accordingly. Moreover, a flexibility design would provide states with the ability to tackle issues as they come up. It is, in this light, for instance, not unthinkable that emerging ideas on 'fair share' propel states into further cooperation on international tax matters in the future (i.e., BEPS 2.0, 3.0, 4.0, etc.), much like it did for the 2013 BEPS Project.[367]

So, the most promising strategy for designing a multilateral agreement for international taxation is one in which the multilateral agreement functions as a robust 'managerial' framework that facilitates interaction, enabling the system to progressively transform and develop *over time*.[368] This involves considering the two functions of the multilateral agreement for international taxation set forth in Chapter 3. As follows from Chapter 3, the potential of a multilateral agreement is to facilitate international tax cooperation by: (1) providing a structural solution to swiftly amend bilateral tax relationships; and (2) providing a structural level playing field, so that states can coordinate on addressing collective action problems:

(1) *A level playing field.* The multilateral agreement for international taxation requires a level playing field in which states can coordinate on tax policy options necessary to address the collective action problems, such as rule deficiencies associated with tax competition and tax arbitrage. In such terms, states, when entering into the agreement, perceive *ex ante* a management risk *ex post.* How can the multilateral agreement's designers ensure that substantive treaty commitments, over time, evolve and are maintained collectively?

(2) *A quicker tax treaty amendment process.* The multilateral agreement for international taxation must be able to enhance the implementation or renegotiation of new norms in bilateral tax treaties. How can this be achieved, given the restraints on cooperation posed by egocentric, rational states acting to protect their self-interests?

---

367. Indeed, ideas on fairness can have a strong influence on cooperative outcomes, *see* the discussion in sec. 5.2. *See also* Keohane, who notes that 'perceptions of self-interest depend both on actors' expectations of the likely consequences that will follow from particular actions and on their fundamental values'. R.O. Keohane (1984) p. 63.

368. *See,* for this approach generally, J. Brunnée and S.J. Toope, *Environmental Security and Freshwater Resources: Ecosystem Regime Building,* 91 American Journal of International Law 26 (1997) and M.P. Cottrell and D.M. Trubek, *Law as Problem Solving: Standards, Networks, Experimentation, and Deliberation in Global Space,* 21 Transnational Law and Contemporary Problems 359 (2012).

Section 6.2 paves the way for the 'managerial' design strategy to international tax cooperation. Section 6.3 then builds up the 'managerial' design strategy using three elements borrowed from neoliberal institutional theory supplemented with constructivist viewpoints.[369] These are: (1) continuous interaction; (2) building on shared understandings; and (3) the role of legal norms. The combination of these three elements can cause international tax cooperation to deepen over time. By facilitating states to gather expertise and knowledge, by building trust and confidence amongst parties, by providing a forum for continuous interaction, and by streamlining the tax treaty amendment process, states can strengthen initially weak commitments by means of further (bilateral or multilateral) interaction. Section 6.4 illustrates the managerial design strategy by referring to the regime on the very complex, uncertain and as such comparable issue of global warming. Although this regime is not considered very effective, the fact is that an agreement is in place and that progress, albeit slowly, is made.[370] Conclusions are drawn in section 6.5.

6.2 A FORUM FOR DISCUSSIONS

6.2.1 The Level Playing Field

Multilateral agreements are often non-committal when it comes to setting binding rules. Such agreements are best regarded as forums for further bargaining on issues collectively accepted as relevant,[371] rather than as systems that punish violations and mandate rules.[372] Indeed, Goldsmith and Posner have argued that:

> most multilateral treaties that are not purely hortatory are based on some form of embedded bilateral cooperation. What little genuine multilateral cooperation we might see is thin, in the sense that it does not require nations to depart much, if at all, from what they would have done in the absence of the treaty.[373]

---

369. As argued in sec. 5.2, the constructivist perspective is seen as complementary to the neoliberal institutional one.

370. The main instrument in this regard is the *United Nations Framework Convention on Climate Change* (adopted 9 May 1992), 1771 UNTS 107. The instrument does not contain binding restrictions on greenhouse gas emissions but rather sets commitments for further cooperation. *See, e.g.,* M. Bothe, *The United Nations Framework Convention on Climate Change: An Unprecedented Multilevel Regulatory Challenge*, 63 Zeitschrift für ausländisches öffentliches Recht und Völkerrecht 239 (2003); J.K. Sebenius, *Designing Negotiations Toward a New Regime: The Case of Global Warming*, 15 International Security 110 (1991).

371. J.D. Fearon, *Bargaining, Enforcement, and International Cooperation*, 52 International Organization 269 (1998).

372. Some authors restrict the use of the term 'enforcement' only to situations of treaty breach or non-observance. *See* C.J. Tams, *Enforcement*, in: Making Treaties Work: Human Rights, Environment and Arms Control (G. Ulfstein ed., Cambridge University Press 2007) p. 393. Here, however, the term is used in a broader sense, and relate it to the upward delegation of adjudicative as well as (quasi)-legislative authority, by means of which, generally speaking, behaviour can be sanctioned and obligations mandated. *See* B. Koremenos (2016); A. Aust, *Modern Treaty Law and Practice* (Cambridge University Press 3d ed., 2013) p. 51.

373. J.L. Goldsmith and E.A. Posner, *International Agreements: A Rational Choice Approach*, 44 Virginia Journal of International Law 113, 138 (2003). *See also* J.L. Goldsmith and E.A. Posner (2005).

While this is a distinctly general kind of observation, the point is that by using multilateralism, states are often unable to achieve more than they would have under bilateral deals or even unilaterally.[374] Under the current system, the OECD produces soft law, which provides a state – member or not – with relative flexibility in reciprocally deciding on its commitments. A state is, at least in theory, relatively free to use or ignore OECD soft law when concluding a tax convention.[375] OECD soft law has, so to speak, influenced tax treaty negotiations 'from the bottom up'. There is little reason to regard a multilateral agreement for international taxation, that would lead states to collectively agree to binding rules, as a more deeply institutionalised system than the one currently in place.

In this light, the delegation of authority to, i.e., a legislative or adjudicative body, that can mandate state compliance with certain requirements (e.g., by means of binding resolutions or adjudicative decisions) or impose financial sanctions, is unlikely. The tax sovereignty costs of an upward shift of authority that such centralised institutional mechanisms would require are likely to be too high. They are in any case higher than in other, less politicized areas of international law, such as in the law on food standards or transportation, where delegation and institutionalisation are common. Taxation is, after all, tightly connected to the operation of the state and lies at the core of all state functions.[376] An indication of these costs is that government authority over direct taxation has not been delegated upward within the highly integrated EU.[377] 'Tax sovereignty' is, in other words, not merely a rhetorical resource to be bargained away for influence over tax policies of others, but, as Ring notes:

> (1) a loss of tax sovereignty can undermine both the significant functional roles played by a nation-state (revenue and fiscal policy) and important normative governance values (democratic accountability and legitimacy); (2) sovereignty rhetoric, though capable of being misused and of obscuring critical issues, nonetheless provides a valuable signalling benefit.[378]

Considering the highly politicised and 'core' role of taxation in state matters, the sovereignty costs of an upward shift of authority in the field of direct taxation may even be similar to those of upward power shifts in the area of national security, which encompasses issues related to the survival of the nation state. Unsurprisingly, delegation in the securities field is moderate or has severely lagged behind other institutional

---

374. *See also* G.W. Downs, D.M. Rocke and P.N. Barsoom, *Is the Good News About Compliance Good News About Cooperation?*, 50 International Organization 379 (1996).
375. This point is, in essence, also made in Ch. 3.
376. L. Murphy and T. Nagel, *The Myth of Ownership: Taxes and Justice* (OUP 2002) in their work on the 'fairness' of taxes are convinced that there are no property rights antecedent to tax structure. At p. 9: 'It is illegitimate to appeal to a baseline of property rights in, say pretax income, for the purpose of evaluating tax policies, when all such figures are the product of a system of which taxes are an inextricable part.'
377. The classic doctrine is established in ECJ, *Finanzamt Köln-Altstadt v. Schumacker*, 14 February 1995, C-279/93, para. 21: 'Although, as Community law stands at present, direct taxation does not as such fall within the purview of the Community, the powers retained by the Member States must nevertheless be exercised consistently with Community law.'
378. D.M. Ring, *What's at Stake in the Sovereignty Debate: International Tax and the Nation-State*, 49 Virginia Journal of International Law 155, 225 (2008).

developments.[379] Equally, the use of enforcement mechanisms to ensure the observance and developments of specific rules of international tax law might be very problematic.[380]

In addition to the argument that enforcement mechanisms may be unlikely, enforcement rules are generally *unnecessary* in international tax, i.e., as long as international tax remains ultimately based on bilateral arrangements. The current system of international tax law is self-enforcing; 'policing' capacities are not required. As Ring notes, avoiding double taxation is a transparent, reciprocal, iterated game. As a consequence, defections are not in a country's medium to long-term interest. If country A defects, this will immediately become clear for B, as B's residents, now facing double taxation, will start to complain about their tax treatment. This will trigger two responses. First, residents of B will hesitate to invest in A because country A cannot be relied on to provide relief on the basis of the tax convention. Second, B may seek to terminate the tax treaty, or engage in similar defections.[381] Neither option is desirable for A. In international tax, the best enforcement is self-enforcement.

In sum, a multilateral deal for international tax law can best be seen as a system that marginally influences bilateral negotiations 'from the top down', in which the relevant setting is one where states collectively negotiate on the basis of persuasion rather than enforcement and coercion. Starting off with general and unthreatening commitments, states may increase commitment and deepen cooperation, with the aim of converging on ideals over time.

6.2.2 A Quicker Tax Treaty Amendment Process

But there is another logic to using multilateralism as a forum for discussions. A multilateral treaty, when seen as a forum for discussions, has an implicit two-step rationality. In the first step, it has the benefit of solving a simple coordination problem: where and when will states meet, and what are the common value-maximising terms? It allows governments to take advantage of economies of scale, for example, by making

---

379. K.W. Abbott and D. Snidal (2000) pp. 440–441 distinguish by issue type in this respect. On the one end of their spectrum are issues of national security, in which sovereignty costs are high. Unsurprisingly, delegation is moderate in this field or has severely lagged behind other institutional developments. On the other end of their spectrum are 'technical matters' in which the incidence of legalised agreements and delegation is correspondingly high. Tax policy, they note, is sensitive and 'displays little overall institutionalization'. *See also* C.A. Bradley and J.G. Kelley, *The Concept of International Delegation*, 71 Law and Contemporary Problems 1, 30 (2008), who say that 'the costs of delegation are higher for subjects that have traditionally been regulated by the state, such as criminal law and punishment, family relationships, and religious freedom'.
380. This discussion of the issue of delegation is somewhat stylised. The costs of delegation also intensify with the independence of the international body and the legal effects (binding, non-binding) of the delegation, and may further depend on the type of delegation (adjudicative, regulatory, legislative, etc.). *See* C.A. Bradley and J.G. Kelley (2008). Moreover, as also noted in secs 5.4.6 and 7.10.3, the need for delegation may be inversely related to the degree of precision in an agreement. *See also* B. Koremenos, *When, What, and Why Do States Choose to Delegate?*, 71 Law and Contemporary Problems 151 (2008).
381. D.M. Ring (2007) p. 133.

all participants, at the same time, fly to New York. In the second step, states negotiate, in pairs if necessary, on the common value-maximising terms or principles hence identified.[382] In the second step, in other words, states may then engage in deeper forms of cooperation in line with common terms identified in step one.

To explore the relevance of this observation, it is wise to further investigate the different types of multilateralism. The backdrop of Chapter 5's analysis was the realisation of multilateral binding norms: *substantive* multilateralism. It goes without saying that if a multilateral norm *is* arrived at by participating states, this norm may influence the terms of their bilateral tax *in one go*. In this view, a multilateral agreement may be used to 'more expeditiously' amend bilateral tax treaties, provided that the time taken to agree upon the norm does not exceed eighteen years (*see* Chapter 3). Certainly, to surpass those eighteen years, the negotiation must be quite complex, and the question for the most part depends on the 'deepness' of the multilateral norm to be negotiated (i.e., obvious distributive problems may perhaps never be solved multilaterally).[383]

There is, however, another important aspect of multilateralism. Multilateralism may also be *formal*, when it is multilateral in name but ultimately bilateral in nature.[384] For instance, as Pauwelyn writes, as the World Trade Organization (WTO) treaty is about market access for goods or services from one state to another, WTO obligations are essentially bundles of bilateral relationships. 'Nor does the fact that an obligation is equally binding on all parties to a treaty make that obligation a collective obligation; it may consist of bundles of (the same) bilateral relationships,' Pauwelyn points out. A breach of WTO law can affect the rights of *only one* WTO Member.[385] Indeed, as Guzman writes, the WTO system works because states can selectively suspend their own compliance with portions of the agreement when another state violates WTO

---

382. J.L. Goldsmith and E.A. Posner (2005) p. 87; and R.O. Keohane (1984) pp. 89–92.
383. There is little research on the duration of international negotiations. But the literature (unsurprisingly) suggests that the aim to negotiate more substantial or deeper norms leads to lengthier negotiations. For example, J.D. Fearon (1998) and D.H. Bearce, C.D. Eldredge and B.J. Jolliff, *Do Finite Duration Provisions Reduce International Bargaining Delay?*, 69 International Organization 219 (2015) argue that a longer 'shadow of the future' (which reflects the future gains to be expected from cooperation) gives an incentive to states to bargain harder, delaying negotiations.
384. J.G. Ruggie, *Multilateralism: The Anatomy of an Institution*, 46 International Organization 561 (1992) argues what is distinctive about 'multilateralism' is that it not merely coordinates multilateral relations but also establishes multilateral principles. 'Let us examine next an institutional arrangement that is generally acknowledged to embody multilateralist principles: a collective security system. None has ever existed in pure form, but in principle the scheme is quite simple. It rests on the premise that peace is indivisible.' Also: R.O. Keohane, *Reciprocity in International Relations*, 40 International Organization 1 (1986), who distinguishes between 'specific' and 'diffuse' reciprocity.
385. J. Pauwelyn, *A Typology Of Multilateral Treaty Obligations: Are WTO Obligations Bilateral or Collective in Nature?*, 14 European Journal of International Law 907, 929–930 (2003).

law.[386] Likewise, the Vienna Convention on Diplomatic Relations is a multilateral treaty that imposes rights and obligations of states in relation to diplomats sent from *one* country to *another* country.[387]

The difference between multilateralism and bilateralism therefore need not necessarily be strict: formal multilateralism may be employed in step one so as to achieve bilateral negotiations in step two, at least in situations where arriving at substantive multilateralism proves impossible (*see* Chapter 5). Multilateralism in this 'formal' sense has the mundane benefit of reducing the transaction costs traditionally associated with bilateral treaty negotiations. The math is simple: it is cheaper to get together to negotiate bilateral agreements at one central place and time than to bilaterally negotiate at different places and times (i.e., the benefits of economies of scale); at the same time, the regime does not prevent states to continue bilateral negotiations outside the formal rounds. Further benefits can be achieved if states bargain in negotiating groups consisting of states with similar interests, rather than in pairs. Recognising this, the OECD organised a 'speed dating' session in relation to the BEPS Convention.[388] And indeed, a multilateral instrument:

> may overcome the hurdle of cumbersome bilateral negotiations and produce important efficiency gains (...).[389]

Moreover, transaction costs of negotiations in the second step can be further reduced by communal knowledge building, guiding principles and established proce-dure.[390] Establishing guiding principles at the outset 'makes it unnecessary to renego-tiate them each time a specific question arises'.[391] In addition, an independent secretariat and procedural structure may provide a degree of neutrality in managing interstate disputes and conflicts,[392] connect different rounds of bargaining, set the rules for negotiations and agreement, help states to draft negotiating texts,[393] and provide 'political leaders' who rely on negotiating skills to foster integrative bargaining.[394] Additionally, a multilateral forum that encourages the exchange and generation of

---

386. A.T. Guzman (2008) p. 66.
387. *Vienna Convention on Diplomatic Relations* (18 Apr. 1961), 500 UNTS 95. *See also* J. Pauwelyn (2003b) p. 911.
388. *See* K.A. Bell, *Multilateral Treaty Not Simple, But Clear: OECD's Saint-Amans*, Bloomberg BNA News, 30 Nov. 2016, https://www.bna.com/multilateral-treaty-not-n73014447884/.
389. OECD, *Developing a Multilateral Instrument to Modify Bilateral Tax Treaties* (2014) p. 15.
390. N.M. Simonelli, *Bargaining over International Multilateral Agreements: The Duration of Negotiations*, 37 International Interactions: Empirical and Theoretical Research in International Relations 147 (2011) shows that the involvement of international organisations in the negotiation of non-security related agreements reduces the length of the negotiations. The duration of multilateral negotiations is shorter when an international organisation makes a first proposal for non-security agreement negotiations, for example, related to the environment or commodities.
391. R.O. Keohane (1984) p. 90.
392. K.W. Abbott and D. Snidal, *Why States Act Through Formal International Organizations*, 42 The Journal of Conflict Resolution 3 (1998).
393. J.D. Fearon (1998).
394. O.R. Young, *Political Leadership and Regime Formation: On the Development of Institutions in International Society*, 45 International Organization 281, 293–294 (1991).

information among its members reduces transaction costs.[395] Hence, a robust multi-lateral framework may ensure that the marginal costs of dealing with each additional issue under the regime (even if these issues are ultimately fleshed out on a bilateral basis) may be lower than it would be without the regime (i.e., increasing returns to scale).[396]

In sum, it cannot be said for certain that this simple reduction of transaction costs may lead to a more expeditious bilateral tax treaty amendment process than that considered in Chapter 3. But even if it is assumed that states bilaterally negotiate in step 2 (i.e., that for some issues, 'substantive multilateralism' proves hardly possible), making it cheaper for governments to negotiate their bilateral agreements (i.e., by bringing representatives together at the same time and in the same place and by institutionalising negotiations), may prove sufficient to quicken the implementation of new norms in the bilateral tax treaty system. Doing nothing will in any case not quicken the implementation of new norms in bilateral tax treaties. In the words of the OECD:

> only a multilateral instrument can overcome the practical difficulties associated with trying to rapidly modify the 3000 + bilateral treaty network.[397]

6.2.3   Introducing the Managerial Approach to International Taxation

Based on these findings, perhaps the wisest thing to do is to 'manage' the development of matters that could be dealt with by multilateral agreement. Instead of enforcing and mandating further and deeper forms of cooperation, for which an upward shift of authority to administrative or judicial bodies would be required, it may be better to start off with achieving consensus on typical 'rules of the road' in a forum for discussions. Moreover, reducing the transaction costs traditionally associated with bilateral tax treaty negotiations may facilitate such negotiations.[398]

A multilateral agreement, built on this managerial approach to international cooperation, enables a regime to 'take on a momentum of its own, by providing a forum for discussions, serving as a focal point for international public opinion, and building trust among participants'.[399] Indeed, a robust multilateral institutional framework has the benefit of persisting over time, so that it can set gears in motion under which states' interests can slowly converge on certain ideals. Moreover, 'managing' the cooperation process may lead states to reconstruct, explore and redefine their self-interests, or 'learn'. This may, as is argued in the next section, allow the international

---

395. J.D. Morrow, *Modeling the Forms of International Cooperation: Distribution Versus Information*, 48 International Organization 387 (1994).
396. R.O. Keohane (1984) p. 90.
397. OECD, *Developing a Multilateral Instrument to Modify Bilateral Tax Treaties* (2014) pp. 15–16.
398. Hence the managerial approach to international cooperation: it is based on 'the finding that state compliance with international agreements is generally quite good and that enforcement has played little or no role in achieving and maintaining that record'. G.W. Downs, D.M. Rocke and P.N. Barsoom (1996) p. 380.
399. D. Bodansky, *WHO Technical Briefing Series: The Framework Convention/Protocol Approach* (1999) WHO/NCD/TFI/99.1.

tax system to progress towards substantive solutions for international tax's collective action problems, even if the scope and contents of such solutions are likely to be disputed or unclear in practice (*see* Figure 3 below).[400]

Figure 3   Regulatory Influence on Bilateral Tax Treaties

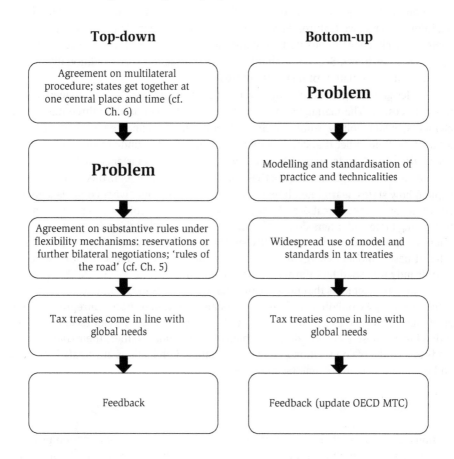

---

400. An argument to a similar effect is given by Schön in his seminal three-part articles on 'international tax coordination for a second-best world': W. Schön, *International Tax Coordination for a Second-Best World*: Part I (2009), Part II (2 World Tax Journal 65 (2010)) and Part III (2010b). He concludes that, given the point of departure that dramatic changes are unlikely, it is best to aim at creating rules that support 'continuity' among business options: basic choices made by (the owners of) a firm should not be distorted by sudden changes to tax treatment. From this view, rules too 'revolutionary' (e.g., formulary apportionment) should not be advocated.

6.3 THE DESIGN STRATEGY: 'MANAGING' INTERNATIONAL TAX MATTERS OVER TIME

6.3.1 Introduction

Based on the findings above, a multilateral treaty for international taxation should, at a minimum, have two features. First of all, it should make use of persuasive rather than coercive mechanisms to ensure that states tackle current and future collective action problems collectively. Second, it should reduce transaction costs traditionally associated with the negotiation of bilateral tax treaties.

A design strategy that resonates well with these outcomes is the managerial view to treaty design. The managerial view is generally characterised by three underlying elements, which follow from neoliberal literature, supplemented by constructivist arguments. Remember that constructivism can help further understand how rational, egocentric states' understandings of the world come into existence and change (*see* Chapter 5.2). Introducing constructivist arguments in neoliberal theory may hence explain how states 'learn', i.e., how regimes evolve over time, what compels actors to converge on certain ideals, and why some issues and solutions end up on the bargaining table and others do not.[401] Indeed, supplementing the neoliberal theory on international relations with constructivism leads, in the words of Ring, to 'a modified interest-based model where the institutional bargaining pursued by the states is significantly impacted by information or knowledge'.[402]

The three elements that underlie the managerial view are: continuous interaction (section 6.3.2), the building on shared understandings, i.e., by norm entrepreneurs and epistemic communities (section 6.3.3) and the use of legal norms (section 6.3.4). Individually, these elements do not enhance cooperation. Rather, their *combination* leads to a model of cooperation in which international obligations are created, evolved and are maintained over time (section 6.3.5).

6.3.2 Continuous Interaction

Section 6.2.2 showed that multilateral negotiation, by solving a coordination problem ('the first step' of multilateral cooperation), reduces the transaction costs of further

---

401. In constructivist literature, 'learning' is generally caused by the role of normative values and ideas, such as 'fairness'. The force of 'doing what is right' or 'doing what is fair' that compels states to enter into certain cooperative structures is captured by 'the logic of appropriateness'. March and Olsen describe the 'logic of appropriateness' to involve cognitive and ethical dimensions, targets, and aspirations. As an ethical matter, they say, appropriate action is action that is virtuous. J.G. March and J.P. Olsen (1998) pp. 951–952. *See also* more fundamentally: F.V. Kratochwil, *Rules, Norms, and Decisions: On the Conditions of Practical and Legal Reasoning in International Relations and Domestic Affairs* (Cambridge University Press 1989). And for discussions, e.g., T. Risse, *Let's Argue!: Communicative Action in World Politics*, 54 International Organization 1 (2000); H. Müller, *Arguing, Bargaining and All That: Communicative Action, Rationalist Theory and the Logic of Appropriateness in International Relations*, 10 European Journal of International Relations 395 (2004).
402. D.M. Ring (2007) p. 114.

(bilateral) interactions, as it takes benefit of economies of scale ('formal multilateralism'). This may allow states, in 'the second step' of multilateral cooperation, to more quickly negotiate bilateral treaties and therefore form deeper commitments over time.

Indeed, an important lesson of neoliberal theory is that cooperation amongst self-interested actors may emerge and then evolve on the deeper, second level of cooperation through initial weak forms of cooperation in step one, even when an enforcement system is not feasible. Provided that the cooperation game is iterated indefinitely, players can be expected to base their strategy on conditional, reciprocal cooperation called 'tit-for-tat'.[403] Under such form of interaction, one player repeats the previous action of the other player in a subsequent move. For instance, if player A cooperates in round one, player B cooperates in round two; if player A reneges in round one, player B reneges in round two. Knowing that actions are repeated by other players in subsequent moves, players may value future payoffs more than short-term gains. In the terms of international relations literature: when there is a large 'shadow of the future', cooperation will thrive.[404] The more important the outcomes of future plays are, the more sensible it is for actors to forego short-term payoffs.[405] A regime may therefore be used to repeatedly bring participants together, so as to instal infinite reciprocal iterations of the Prisoners' Dilemma game. This offsets the immediate costs of cooperation with long-term benefits.

For international lawyers, reciprocal interaction is a commonly used explanation for obligations in international law. Former President of the international Court of Justice (ICJ) Rosalyn Higgins, for instance, has argued that obligation in international law is essentially based on reciprocity, in which states trade self-interests:

> If consensus, often tacit and sometimes unenthusiastic, is the basis of international law, then that consensus comes about because states perceive a reciprocal advantage in cautioning self-restraint. It rarely is in the national interest to violate international law, even though there might be short-term advantages in doing so. For law as a process of decision-making this is enough.[406]

And in the view of Luis Henkin, almost all states observe international law almost all the time because of reciprocity: states observe those obligations they do not care about to maintain others they value, he says. To keep the system intact, a state observes law when it 'hurts' others, so that others will observe laws to that state's benefit.[407]

If regimes set standards of behaviour around which expectations of actors converge, then, by reducing the transaction costs of each iteration, repeated and reciprocal interaction is a necessary condition for the evolution of cooperation over

---

403. In this strategy, players cooperate on the first move, and in subsequent moves repeat what the other player did in the previous one. J.L. Goldsmith and E.A. Posner (2005) p. 87. *See also* R.O. Keohane (1986) p. 9.
404. This has been tested by R. Axelrod, *The Evolution of Cooperation* (Basic Books Inc. 1984).
405. R.O. Keohane (1986) p. 9.
406. R. Higgins, *Problems and Process: International Law and How We Use It* (OUP 1994) p. 16.
407. L. Henkin, *How Nations Behave: Law and Foreign Policy* (Columbia University Press 2nd ed., 1979) pp. 51–52.

time.[408] In fact, a minimum of two iterations is required for any form of cooperation to deepen: this logic already follows from agreeing to general value-maximising norms in the first step and engaging in deeper cooperation on these terms in a second step. For instance, the iteration perspective may explain why obligations under the law of treaties set out in the Vienna Convention on the Law of Treaties (VCLT)[409] deepen with each additional legal act. As to the conclusion of treaties, the VCLT expressly sets forth two iterations upon which obligations of states increase, namely during subsequent acts of signature and ratification. At each of these iterations 'a nation may formally cooperate with, or defect from, the efforts at cooperative action prescribed by the rules of the treaty at issue'.[410] Initially, a party can cooperate without undertaking any obligations. Upon signature, a party must refrain from taking action that goes against the object and purpose of the signed treaty. And upon entry into force, a party must comply with all the obligations imposed by the treaty. The deepness of obligations progressively increases with each iteration. The VCLT hence 'reflects a deep and pervasive concern with the promotion of iteration'.[411]

Of course, reciprocal iterations do not necessarily have to occur between pairs. Reciprocity may also take place if multilateral groups can be broken down into smaller clusters.[412] This means, in the words of Blum, that a multilateral negotiation is 'often essentially a series of bilateral negotiations evolving toward coalitions and broader consensus'.[413] For example, states may agree to restrict the concept of treaty residence by means of a general anti-avoidance rule (GAAR) to prevent unilateral action. Some players may, however, choose to defect under such a rule to attract short-term gains, such as an inflow of FDI. But knowing that other actors, under the reciprocal and conditional form of interaction of 'tit-for-tat', may then choose to defect as well, for example, by putting unilateral anti-abuse measures in place, the value of future interaction compels these players to cooperate. For both clusters of actors, neither a chaos of overlapping unilateral anti-abuse rules nor the complete redundancy of income tax systems due to increased tax competition is, in the long run, a more welcome alternative to multilateral cooperation. Hence, repeated reciprocity 'is an appropriate principle of behaviour when norms of obligations are weak – the usual case in world politics – but when the occurrence of mutually beneficial cooperation seems possible'.[414]

---

408. R. Axelrod (1984); building on this J. Brunnée and S.J. Toope (1997) pp. 32–37 and B. Frischmann, *A Dynamic Institutional Theory of International Law*, 51 Buffalo Law Review 679 (2004). *See also* R. Keohane, *The Demand for International Regimes*, 36 International Organization 325, 334 (1982): 'international regimes help to make governments' expectations consistent with one another. Regimes are developed in part because actors in world politics believe that with such arrangements they will be able to make mutually beneficial agreements that would otherwise be difficult or impossible to attain.'
409. *The Vienna Convention on the Law of Treaties* (adopted 23 May 1969), 1155 UNTS 331.
410. J.K. Setear, *An Iterative Perspective on Treaties: A Synthesis of International Relations Theory and International Law*, 37 Harvard International Law Journal 139, 191 (1996).
411. *Id.*, at p. 190.
412. R.O. Keohane (1986).
413. G. Blum (2008) p. 351.
414. R.O. Keohane (1986) p. 24.

In international tax law, like in other economic relationships, infinite reciprocal interaction is possible, as interstate relationships are lasting and interdependent: states in principle do not seek to eliminate each other by means of military retaliation (as is the case in security affairs).[415] An international regime can therefore facilitate iterated interaction by taking care of communication, so that actors 'can learn about each other's intentions and actions, agree on standards of behaviour, and learn about the relationship between their actions and outcomes'.[416] In sum, provided that states have an interest in the common, and that there is a 'shadow of the future', procedural arrangements that ensure that states keep playing the reciprocal cooperative game indefinitely can lead to more successful and deeper forms of cooperation over time.

6.3.3 Building on Shared Understandings

6.3.3.1 Introduction

Literature shows that states generally come to redefine an agreement by building on concepts that are already recognised by a wider public. On the basis of such recognised norms, states 'learn', i.e., develop interests and consequently develop new legal norms while old ones evolve. This argument is reflected in two main accounts on norm dynamics: on the role of norm entrepreneurs in developing norms (section 6.3.3.2) and on the role of epistemic communities (section 6.3.3.3). The central conviction is that, as Ernst Haas phrases it, 'change in human aspirations and human institutions over long periods is caused mostly by the way knowledge about nature and about society is married to political interests and objectives'.[417]

6.3.3.2 Norm Entrepreneurs

In an article about how norms come into existence, Finnemore and Sikkink point at the role of norm entrepreneurs. Norm entrepreneurs actively build norms, as 'norms do

---

415. R. Axelrod and R.O. Keohane, *Achieving Cooperation under Anarchy: Strategies and Institutions*, 38 World Politics 226, 232 (1985).
416. L.L. Martin (1999) p. 55.
417. E.B. Haas, *When Knowledge Is Power: Three Models of Change in International Organizations* (University of California Press 1990) p. 11. Haas argues that there are three models of organisational change: 'incremental growth', 'turbulent non-growth', and 'managed interdependence'. The latter (which he refers to as 'learning') is the ideal-type of change: 'learning should be seen as the actors' way of saying that life under conditions of turbulent nongrowth is not satisfactory, that something ought to be done to overcome turbulence. Learning could also represent a decision that incremental growth is simply not good enough because it is too slow and results in problem definitions that are excessively decomposable. (...) [M]y argument that institutions can be arenas for innovation in addition to being constraints on change clearly depends on the presumed capability of actors to use institutions to cope with problems never before experienced.' *Id.*, at p. 127.

not appear out of thin air'.[418] Norm entrepreneurs have strong notions about what is appropriate and desirable behaviour in their community.

The process of norm building, so Finnemore and Sikkink argue, can be understood to occur in three stages. The first stage is 'norm emergence', the second stage involves broad state acceptance which they call a 'norm cascade', in which some states persuade others to join, and the third stage involves norm internalisation where norms are 'taken for granted'. The first two stages are divided by a tipping point, at which 'a critical mass of relevant state actors adopt the norm'.[419] To reach the tipping point, it matters which states are 'in', as well as the amount of states that are persuaded. Once enough states are on board, i.e., when the crucial tipping point for a 'norm cascade' is reached, a different dynamic begins in which other countries adopt norms, even without being pressurised.[420]

In the most important first stage, norms are built by two main drivers: norm entrepreneurs and institutional platforms. But the norms that norm entrepreneurs create and name usually resonate within broader public understandings.[421] Actors are more likely to accept norms if these norms are similar to already accepted ideas. As Payne, for instance, says:

> actor A communicates to actors B, C and D that new normative concern Z should be embraced because Z is similar to already agreed norms X and Y.[422]

As regards the BEPS Project, for instance, the norms the OECD created resonated within wider public understandings, as most if not all of the outcomes of the BEPS Project proposed are based on existing notions familiar to those working in international taxation. For example, the idea of LOB rules, tweaking the PE concept, and alterations to the operation of the arm's length standard all functioned within frames already recognised by the wider public. In the same vein, the final BEPS reports do not contain any concepts that are completely new.

6.3.3.3   Epistemic Communities

Another account of the creation of shared understandings is one that centralises so-called epistemic communities and emphasises learning. First defined by Peter Haas, epistemic communities are networks of knowledge-based experts that work together

---

418. M. Finnemore and K. Sikkink, *International Norm Dynamics and Political Change*, 52 International Organization 887, 986 (1998). Also: E.A. Nadelmann, *Global Prohibition Regimes: The Evolution of Norms in International Society*, 44 International Organization 479, 482 (1990) to 'transnational moral entrepreneurs', which are groups that 'mobilize popular opinion and political support both within their host country and abroad; they stimulate and assist in the creation of like-minded organisations in other countries; and they play a significant role in elevating their objective beyond its identification with the national interests of their government'. Also: C.R. Sunstein, *Social Norms and Social Roles*, 96 Columbia Law Review 903 (1996).
419. M. Finnemore and K. Sikkink (1998) p. 895.
420. *Id.*, at p. 902.
421. *Id.*, at pp. 896–897.
422. R.A. Payne, *Persuasion, Frames and Norm Construction*, 7 European Journal of International Relations 37, 43 (2001).

on scientific, technical or economic matters. They often consist of experts with an authority claim within their domain of expertise, and for that reason enjoy social authority.[423] They help states identify their self-interests, frame issues for collective debate, and set policies and points for negotiation.[424] Lawmakers can collectively learn from epistemic communities, as they are persuaded by the virtue of new ideas,[425] which in turn leads to new shared understandings, by implication redefine interests, and therefore ultimately lead to new rules. In this regard, Haas says, 'we identify and interpret problems within existing frameworks and according to past protocols and then try to manage the problems according to the operating procedures that we have applied in the analogous cases'.[426] Epistemic communities, in other words, can help to create understandings that have some affiliation with previously existing ideas.[427]

From this perspective, for instance, Ring explains how the OECD has helped to form international tax policy. The influence and expertise of the OECD has changed the behaviour of actors. Tax rules are difficult. Because of their highly technical nature, 'the stories of international tax organisations and tax organisations and tax policy are likely intertwined with the story of knowledge and expertise'.[428] She therefore notes that the experts of the OECD, somewhat like an epistemic community, have helped states to understand the world as well as form their interests through, for example, the OECD MTC. Policymakers turn to experts to help them formulate policy, frame issues for debate and identify points for negotiation. This, she says, created a dynamic that:

> provided a setting in which many of the detailed issues of international taxation could be explored and elaborated by and among those with extensive knowledge. In addition, the momentum within these organizations to identify, enumerate, and solve the problems of double taxation propelled countries toward model treaties. The resulting model treaties themselves had an independent life of their own.[429]

Hence, the two above accounts, i.e., the first one on norm entrepreneurs and the other on epistemic communities, suggest that norm innovation takes place on the basis of beliefs that already exist. Epistemic communities help states, in a process of social learning, to identify their self-interests on the basis of new shared understandings. Norm entrepreneurs, likewise, name and create norms that resonate within broader public understandings.

---

423. P.M. Haas, *Epistemic Communities*, in: The Oxford Handbook of International Environmental Law (D. Bodansky, J. Brunnée and E. Hey eds, OUP 2012) p. 793.
424. P.M. Haas, *Introduction: Epistemic Communities and International Policy Coordination*, 46 International Organization 1, 2 (1992).
425. P.M. Haas (2012) p. 797.
426. P.M. Haas (1992) p. 28.
427. *Id.*, at pp. 28–29.
428. D.M. Ring, *Who Is Making International Tax Policy? International Organizations as Power Players in a High Stakes World*, 33 Fordham International Law Journal 649, 682 (2010).
429. D.M. Ring (2007) p. 145.

6.3.3.4 Transparency and Inclusivity

'Learning' by means of norm entrepreneurs and epistemic communities stresses the importance of transparency and inclusive deliberation.[430] What is needed, as pointed out above, is a mechanism in which knowledge can be gathered, in which problems can be solved, and in which states' interests can change. Hence, in the managerial design strategy, the idea of 'deliberation' (arguments and persuasion) plays a central role.

A more diverse and inclusive set of actors 'fosters exchange of policy knowledge and experience, promotes common understandings and purpose through continued interaction, contestation, and justification of action, and thus more likely leads to changes in legal norms'.[431] Or as Downs, Danish and Barsoom say:

> If collective deliberation and intraregime information can reliably transform state preferences so that even relatively regressive states find themselves increasingly committed to ever deeper levels of international cooperation, it makes good sense to be as inclusive as possible. membership restrictions would only lessen the aggregate amount of cooperation in the system with noncomitant advantage.[432]

Indeed, the argument for inclusiveness in the literature that deals with persuasion, rather than coercion, is that broad-based membership exerts a stronger and more authoritative 'community pressure' on reluctant states.[433]

Likewise, transparency, which has been discussed more extensively from the neoliberal institutionalist viewpoint in section 5.4.7.2, facilitates the exchange of information and hence enables states and non-state actors alike to take an active role in ongoing discussions, even if they have no formal status. Transparency may lubricate discussion, compromise and persuasion,[434] provided that the public does not 'measure' the success of its representatives against publicly known baselines. If understandings are to be shared, so that knowledge can be built, and if actors are to be persuaded rather than coerced into certain behaviour, transparency is indispensable. In the words of Ernst Haas, who writes about change in IOs:

> increasing the transparency of decision processes is a necessary, though far from sufficient, step in encouraging a transideological dialogue. Regimes and their organizations become less threatening to the outsiders when their inner workings are better understood. Once understood and subjected to knowledgeable critique,

---

430. See, for an explanation, from a rational perspective, of the importance of communication to solve dilemmas of the type that characterises negotiations in international tax law, i.e., 'games of common aversion': J.D. Morrow (1994).
431. M.P. Cottrell and D.M. Trubek (2012) p. 371.
432. G.W. Downs, K.W. Danish and P.N. Barsoom, The Transformational Model of International Regime Design: Triumph of Hope or Experience?, 38 Columbia Journal of Transnational Law 465, 507 (2000).
433. R. Goodman and D. Jinks, How to Influence States: Socialization and International Human Rights Law, 54 Duke Law Journal 621 (2004) describe this process as 'acculturation'. See pp. 667–673. See also T. Risse (2000) (open debate and constructive dialogue may construct common lifeworlds).
434. A.E. Boyle and K. Mccall Smith (2013) ('deliberation and transparency go together in most law-making processes').

the routines can then be revised to the satisfaction of the outsiders while accomplishing what the staff and the dominant coalition wish to do. Transparency does not guarantee successful and consensual redefinition of problems. But without it, no consensual redefinition seems possible.[435]

Important in this regard, and so far understated and only briefly discussed in section 4.2.3 ('continuous, inclusive and transparent deliberation on tax rules')[436] and section 5.4.7.2 ('transparency'),[437] is the role of non-state actors such as NGOs. The international theatre cannot be imagined without them, and NGOs have, as a matter of fact, grown in importance.[438] The point is that the involvement of NGOs may foster knowledge building. For instance, Koh emphasises their importance to the development of norms in the contemporary transnational stage:

> as governmental and nongovernmental transnational actors repeatedly interact within the transnational legal process, they generate and interpret international norms and then seek to internalize those norms domestically. To the extent that those norms are successfully internalized, they become future determinants of why nations obey.[439]

And indeed, the cooperative role of NGOs in propelling forward the international decision-making process is supported by the idea that NGOs can mobilise public opinion and defend viewpoints that are off-limits for governments.[440]

6.3.4 Legal Norms

According to the intuition of any lawyer, legal norms matter. The rules set out in the VCLT, for instance, hold that the existence of a legal obligation means this obligation is to be carried out in good faith: *pacta sunt servanda*.[441] The sense of duty, or of

---

435. E.B. Haas (1990) p. 219.
436. The point here is that the inclusion of non-state actors such as NGOs enhances the 'fairness' of international tax law.
437. The point here is that NGO inclusion should be seen in the light of the limitations posed by opening the doors to negotiations.
438. R. Thakur and T.G. Weiss, *Framing Global Governance, Five Gaps*, in: Thinking about Global Governance: Why People and Ideas Matter (T.G. Weiss ed., Routledge 2009) p. 147 ('The growing influence and power of civil society actors means that they have effectively entered the realm of policy-making.'). As regards tax, *see* A. Christians, *Tax Activists and the Global Movement for Development through Transparency*, in: Tax Law and Development (M. Stewart and Y. Brauner eds, Edward Elgar Publishing 2012), available at SSRN: http://ssrn.com/abstract = 1929055.
439. H.H. Koh, *Why Do Nations Obey International Law?*, 106 Yale Law Journal 2599, 2651 (1997). Also: H.H. Koh, *Transnational Legal Process*, 75 Nebraska Law Review 181 (1996).
440. *See, e.g.*, D.C. Esty, *Non-governmental Organizations at the World Trade Organization: Cooperation, Competition, or Exclusion*, 1 Journal of International Economic Law 123, 129 (1998): 'Non-governmental organizations can serve as service providers (either acting independently or as government subcontractors); mobilisers of public opinion, defenders of viewpoints that governments do not represent or under-represent; watchdogs or private enforcement agents; policy analysts and expert advisors to governments; and bridges between state and non-state actors connecting local and global politics.' Also: S. Charnovitz (2006); A.E. Boyle and C.M. Chinkin, *The Making of International Law* (OUP 2007) Ch. 2.
441. VCLT Art. 26.

obligation, that originates from legal norms almost speaks for itself. Yet, there are many authors who seek to explain why legal norms exert an influence on state behaviour. Let us look at some of them.

For Goldsmith and Posner, legal obligations are nothing but an extension of a state's self-interests. From this viewpoint, compliance with a legal norm can be explained by two reasons: retaliation and reputation. The element of retaliation that they describe is closely related to the importance of reciprocity, discussed in sections 6.2.2 and 6.3.2. Action leads to reaction: faced with uncertainty as regards the future reciprocal reactions of others, states choose to forego short-term gains for long-term cooperation. Reputation, on the other hand, refers to a state's beliefs about the likelihood that another state will comply with the treaty. When a state violates a treaty, that violation can be generalised to the state's reputational status under all treaties subject to international law, as well as to the quality of that state's institutions,[442] making violation costly.

But why would states use *legal* norms? After all, states can also decide to use soft law. Goldsmith and Posner give three arguments. First of all, legal norms require legislative consent, a process that conveys important information about a state's preferences for a norm. A parliamentary process reveals information to other treaty partners about the policy preferences of the state's legislature, and therefore of the state's public. It thus conveys information about the reliability of a state's commitment.[443] Second, legal norms take advantage of 'default rules' that apply to them. By entering into a legal norm, a state invokes the law of treaties, such as set out in the VCLT, on its interpretation, modification and application, etc. An incentive for states to enter into legal agreement, therefore, is to 'inform each other that the default rules set forth by the law of treaties will apply if a dispute arises'.[444] Lastly, the legal norm serves to signal the seriousness of a state's level of commitment. A legal obligation is, in other words, 'stronger' than a non-legal obligation.[445]

Unlike Goldsmith and Posner, who focus on rationality to explain state compliance, there are others who relate rule-following not to reputation and reciprocity, but to their duty-imposing character. This constructivist viewpoint tries to explain the role of legal norms beyond the fear of states for penalties or repercussions. Here, the role of traditions or rituals is emphasised, as is the relevance of identity, by means of which the individual identifies him or herself with the collective, as well as that of deliberation, that is seen as the basis for deciding moral questions.[446] As Chayes and Chayes note, what generally follows from the academic discussions in this regard is that actors follow norms because of the belief 'that social life would be impossible without some

---

442. J.L. Goldsmith and E.A. Posner (2005) p. 101. *See also* K.W. Abbott and D. Snidal (2000) p. 427 and A.T. Guzman, *A Compliance-Based Theory of International Law*, 90 California Law Review 1823 (2002).
443. J.L. Goldsmith and E.A. Posner (2005) pp. 91–95.
444. *Id.*, at pp. 95–98.
445. *Id.*, at pp. 98–99.
446. F.V. Kratochwil (1989) pp. 123–129. The author refers to Durkheim and Habermas for this.

kind of obligation to follow prescriptions'.[447] States who fail to comply, or, for instance, 'stretch' a legal interpretation – it is often possible to distinguish good legal argument from bad – have to justify or explain their deviant behaviour.[448] And as Braithwaite and Drahos show in their vast empirical study on international business regulation, for compliance, 'dialogue that redefines interests, delivers the discipline of complex interdependency and persuades to normative commitments is enough'.[449]

The point of both explanations is that legal norms matter in international cooperation, whether on the basis of fears for reputation and retaliation, or due to their duty-imposing character.

But what does this say about the *development* of legal rules? The point is made by Garrett and Weingast, in an influential article on the matter. Publicised legal norms can act as 'focal points' around which future negotiations can gravitate.[450] In their capacity to distinguish 'appropriate' behaviour from 'inappropriate' behaviour, legal norms serve as points of coordination, because they are the result of bargaining and argumentative processes that do not need to be repeated.[451] 'By embodying, selecting, and publicizing particular paths on which all actors are able to coordinate, institutions may (...) help construct a shared belief system that defines for the community what actions constitute cooperation and defection.'[452] Simply said, in a world where many solutions and alternatives exist for certain policy directions, legal norms can be used to give direction to further debate and negotiation, by distinguishing good from bad arguments, and by differentiating appropriate from inappropriate behaviour.

Garret and Weingast refer to the emergence of the EU internal market. The European Court of Justice (ECJ's) landmark *Cassis de Dijon* decision provided the first stepping stone in this regard by acknowledging the principle of mutual recognition: it 'acted as a focal point around which EC members could coordinate their bargaining'.[453] With mutual recognition established by the *Cassis de Dijon* decision acting as a focal point, the EU developed not in the direction of a heavily regulated internal market layered 'on top of' existing national regimes, but towards a successful 'constitutional'

---

447. A. Chayes and A.H. Chayes, *The New Sovereignty: Compliance with International Regulatory Agreements* (Harvard University Press 1995) pp. 116–117.
448. *Id.*, at pp. 118–123.
449. J. Braithwaite and P. Drahos, *Global Business Regulation* (Cambridge University Press 2000) pp. 553–559.
450. The logic of a focal point speaks of itself and is eloquently set out by Schelling. When a man loses his wife in the department store without any prior understanding of where to meet if the couple gets separated, the chances are good that they will think of some obvious place. Even if they both dislike walking, and an obvious meeting point would be a larger distance for the one than for the other (signalling an obvious conflicts of interest), 'the need for agreement overrules the potential disagreement, and each must concert with the other or lose altogether'. T.C. Schelling, *The Strategy of Conflict* (Harvard University Press New ed., 1980) Ch. 3.
451. The same argument, i.e., the coordinative function of law, is inherent to the work of G. Brennan and J.M. Buchanan (1985) Ch. 2 sec. VII, and is moreover made by made by J. Habermas (1996) in Ch. 3 of *Between Facts and Norms*, where he sets out that modern law solves a coordination problem between facticity and validity; between natural law and popular sovereignty.
452. G. Garrett and B. Weingast (1993) p. 176.
453. *Id.*, at p. 189.

system with only limited sanctioning powers.[454] Under this system, the benefits from cooperation were captured by the general idea of mutual recognition. This principle was then 'fairly' translated by the ECJ into acceptable and unacceptable standards of behaviour under the circumstances provided by specific cases.

But legal norms need not be precise to guide the development of rules. We have seen that precise rules can be counterproductive *ex ante*, as states might find that precise rules emphasise disagreement (*see* on this Chapter 5). Moreover, as Abbott and Snidal note, imprecise norms have benefits *ex post* too, as they may offer strategies for individual and collective learning. Such obligations 'offer flexibility and protection for states to work out problems over time through negotiation shaped by normative guidelines, rather than constrained by precise rules'.[455] And under such normative guidelines, new rules may be formulated once more information has become available,[456] such as the specific circumstances of a case decided on by the ECJ. Imprecise norms, in other words, can provide a normative template against which endless discussion of the scope of the norm and the appropriateness of behaviour can take place. The central constructivist argument here is that imprecise norms may come to be associated with the identity of the group. As it is status within the group that the actor seeks (i.e., isolation from the group would mean, for example, the loss of the opportunity for economic growth and political influence), imprecise rules may establish broad consensus which has institutionalising effects, and mobilise social pressure on states to adopt social norms. For instance, the adoption of a broad 'general anti-avoidance' norm might strengthen the rhetoric that aggressive tax planning is bad.[457] Over time, the strength of the norm and the stigma associated with its violation can create social pressure on actors to adopt anti-tax arbitrage policies.[458]

---

454. *Id.*, at pp. 196–197.
455. K.W. Abbott and D. Snidal (2000) p. 443.
456. *Id.*, at pp. 441–444.
457. As to BEPS, I. Grinberg (2016) p. 1178 writes that non-legal norms can have a similar same function: 'debates about international standards can act as a kind of focal point. Indeed, law firms and accounting firms around the world now routinely catalogue the various national proposals that are vaguely related to outcomes of the BEPS project, even as they depart from the details thereof. When a multilateral project is sufficiently politically salient, even an inconclusive part of the project may matter because it can act as a locus for subsequent domestic policy debates.'
458. For example, R.B. Mitchell, *Flexibility, Compliance and Norm Development in the Climate Regime*, in: Implementing the Climate Regime: International Compliance (O.S. Stokke, J. Hovi and G. Ulfstein eds, Earthscan Press 2005) pp. 79–80, in respect of the climate change regime: 'Perhaps the largest influence of the regime lies in its effect on how behaviours that contribute to climate change are framed (...) Although [the purpose of the Kyoto targets] is to create legal categories of compliant and non-compliant behaviours, their more important effect may be as foundations for social categories of identity. [The Kyoto targets] become the basis for a broader social definition (...).' Also: R. Goodman and D. Jinks (2004) pp. 680–685 and R.B. Mitchell, *International Control of Nuclear Proliferation: Beyond Carrots and Sticks*, 5 The Nonproliferation Review 40, 46 (1997). The counterargument is that explicit and precise international commitments create unequivocal social sanctions and mitigate holding-out behaviour (i.e., prevent actors from waiting and seeing who moves first). For example, C.R. Kelly, *Enmeshment as a Theory of Compliance*, 37 New York University Journal of International Law and Politics 303 (2005) ('Nations will self-enforce regime rules when: (i) those rule are precise, obligatory, can be objectively interpreted, and (ii) compliance is in their interest and within their capabilities.'). Also: A. Chayes and A.H. Chayes (1995) pp. 10–13.

6.3.5 Transforming International Tax Law over Time

The combination of the three elements, i.e., continuous interaction, legal norms and enabling actors to build on shared understandings, results in a theory about how international obligation is constituted, developed and maintained collectively over time.

One of the most important recent contributions to managerial theory has been that of Brunnée and Toope.[459] Brunnée and Toope provide a pragmatic view of how international obligation is created and maintained over time in their 'interactional' account of international law. They argue that international obligation is built and maintained by lining up prospective legal norms with their underlying shared understandings by means of an ongoing 'practice of legality'.

In particular, the authors focus on the work of Fuller to make their argument. Fuller has set out several 'desiderata' that are seen as the essential characteristics that embody the 'inner morality of law'.[460] They are: generality, promulgation, non-retroactivity, clarity, non-contradiction, not asking the impossible, constancy, and congruence between rules and official action.[461] Given that repeated interaction takes place on the basis of shared understandings, the point of Brunnée and Toope is that the adherence to these 'criteria of legality' creates a 'practice of legality'. This 'practice of legality' is crucial to international law's ability to promote adherence, to inspire the 'fidelity' of actors. It allows actors to 'pursue their purposes and organize their interactions through law'.[462] After all, states are both lawmakers as well as the subjects of international law; international law does not depend on hierarchy between lawgivers and subjects. Hence, their claim: international law 'can exist only when actors collaborate to build shared understandings and uphold a practice of legality'.[463] For them, consequently, international law is 'hard work'.[464]

Implicit in the interactional account of international law is also a claim of legitimacy.[465] If law is made on the basis of the three criteria of the interactional

---

459. J. Brunnée and S.J. Toope, *Legitimacy and Legality in International Law: An Interactional Account* (Cambridge University Press 2010).
460. L.L. Fuller, *The Morality of Law* (Yale University Press 1964).
461. J. Brunnée and S.J. Toope (2010) p. 7.
462. *Id.*, at p. 7.
463. *Id.*, at p. 7.
464. *Id.*, at pp. 5–9.
465. In this respect, the theory resembles that of T.M. Franck, *The Power of Legitimacy Among Nations* (OUP 1990) who argues that the legitimacy of international law is the factor that 'pulls' states into compliance. The qualities of law that make law 'legitimate' are: determinacy (i.e., clearness), symbolic validation, coherence (i.e., consistency of the rule itself and of its relation with other rules) and adherence (i.e., to a normative hierarchy). As Franck explains: 'each rule has an inherent pull power that is independent of the circumstances in which it is exerted, and that varies from rule to rule. This pull power is its index of legitimacy.' T.M. Franck, *Legitimacy in the International System*, 82 The American Journal of International Law 705 (1988). Nevertheless, Franck's theory has been criticised for being circular. As Keohane notes: 'Legitimacy is difficult to measure independent from the compliance that it is supposed to explain. For instance, Franck describes a rule's compliance "pull power" as "its index of legitimacy." Yet legitimacy is said to explain "compliance pull", making the argument circular.' R.O. Keohane (2002) p. 121; also A.T. Guzman (2002) pp. 1834–1835. Be that as it may, K.

framework, it can be said to be legitimate. Reciprocal interaction and building on shared understandings require broad participation by intergovernmental organisations, civil society organisations and other collective entities. This builds sustained relationships (which the authors name a 'deep sense of reciprocity'), which are created and maintained collectively.[466] Likewise, inclusive and transparent deliberations foster shared understandings, for instance, through epistemic communities or by the work of norm entrepreneurs. IOs, enterprises and NGOs are all important in the creation of such understandings.[467] In their discussions on the climate change regime, the authors, for instance, hold that the community of practice, created by the participation of many NGOs and business organisations, as either formal participants or as observants, is crucial for the working of the regime.[468] Hence, inherent to the theory is a strong claim that inclusive deliberations and transparency are important elements of successful international treaty regimes.

So, the managerial account of Brunnée and Toope integrates the three elements of the managerial approach. It shows that in the process of treaty negotiation, existing understandings (c.f. section 6.3.3: 'building on shared understandings') may be pushed or advanced modestly to allow for normative change, as long as this meets Fuller's 'criteria of legality' (c.f. section 6.3.4: 'legal norms') and becomes the object of a continuous practice (c.f. section 6.3.2: 'continuous interaction').[469] The three elements of the previous sections are, in other words, crucial for generation of effective legal obligation in the international setting.[470] For instance, the authors apply these criteria to explain the formation and development of obligation under the climate change regime. All three elements are there, as we will *see* in section 6.4: the climate change regime allows actors to build on shared understandings, has created a practice of interaction, and its procedural (and some of its substantive) elements meet Fuller's 'criteria of legality'.[471]

Another managerial account on international cooperation is that of the Chayes and Chayes, which also (but more implicitly) integrates the above three elements. Their argument is quite similar to that of Brunnée and Toope: states comply with (and hence develop)[472] international law because of 'continuous processes of argument and

---

Raustiala and A. Slaughter, *International Law, International Relations and Compliance*, in: The Handbook of International Relations (T.R. Carlnaes, T. Risse and B. Simmons eds, Sage Publications 2002) note that Franck's argument 'is quite consistent with many constructivist assumptions and insights. The theory of state behaviour embedded in legitimacy theory is non-instrumental: rather than game theory or bureaucratic politics, Franck invokes theories of legal process and obligation.'

466. J. Brunnée and S.J. Toope (2010) p. 40.
467. *Id.*, at p. 45.
468. *Id.*, at pp. 142–146.
469. J. Brunnée and S.J. Toope, *Interactional International Law: An Introduction*, 3 International Theory 307 (2011).
470. *Id.*, at p. 308.
471. J. Brunnée and S.J. Toope (2010) pp. 127–132.
472. The Chayes' work is primarily focused on compliance with international law, and not (also) on how international law is created and developed. Their theory simply departs from the presumption that international law exists (simply put: states consent to international law if it is in their self-interest to do so). Nevertheless, arguments about why states comply with international law are closely related to international law's development over time. After all: law

persuasion, "justificatory discourse" that ultimately "jawbones" states into compliance'.[473] International law is important in upholding such discourse.[474] And hence, the three elements of sections 6.3.2–6.3.4 are present.

But what really drives compliance in the view of the authors Chayes and Chayes is what they call 'the new sovereignty', which expresses the increasing interdependence of states in the international system. In this increasingly interdependent world, states have no choice but to cooperate to protect their interests. Indeed:

> sovereignty no longer consists in the freedom of states to act independently, in their perceived self-interests, but in membership in reasonably good standing in the regimes that make up the substance of international life. To be a player, a state must submit to the pressures that international regulations impose. Its behaviour in any single episode is likely to affect future relationships not only within the particular regime involved but in many others as well, and perhaps its position within the international system as a whole.[475]

In their book, the authors, Chayes and Chayes, first argue that coercive strategies are unsuitable to make states comply with international law. In sum, they argue that 'sanctioning authority is rarely granted by treaty, rarely used when granted, and likely to be ineffective when used'.[476] Instead, they argue, states comply on the basis of other reasons. Indeed, the authors, Chayes and Chayes, identify three elements under which there is an assumption that states have a propensity to comply. These are efficiency, interests and norms.[477]

As regards the first element, both the authors argue that governmental resources for policy analysis and decision-making are costly and in short supply. In simple terms: following an established treaty rule saves costs, as this makes a recalculation of each and every single decision unnecessary. As the authors point out: 'compliance is the normal organisational presumption'.[478] Following norms is, in other words, efficient. Second, the authors argue that it is a fair assumption that the parties' interests were served by entering into the treaty in the first place. And, they note, even if a state is unable to achieve all of its policy objectives:

> if the agreement is well designed – sensible, comprehensible, and with a practical eye to the probable patterns of conduct and interaction – compliance problems and

---

that is not complied with is either ineffective or a dead letter and hence becomes subject to scrutiny. In that case, it makes sense that a law is altered, scrapped or changed. As a consequence, the compliance perspective of the Chayes does not to touch on fundamentally different issues.

473. J. Brunnée and S.J. Toope, *Persuasion and Enforcement: Explaining Compliance with International Law*, 13 Finnish Yearbook of International Law 273, 281 (2002).

474. A. Chayes and A.H. Chayes (1995) pp. 115–124.

475. *Id.*, at pp. 26–27.

476. *Id.*, at pp. 32–33.

477. One of the elements that the authors, Chayes and Chayes, name that may induce non-compliance, however, is ambiguity. Yet, they say, detail also comes with difficulties and 'it may be wiser to indicate a general direction, to try to inform a process, rather than seeking to foresee in detail the circumstances in which the words will be brought to bear. If there is a degree of trust in those who are to apply the rules, a broader standard may be more effective in realizing the general policy behind the law than a series of detailed regulations.' *Id.*, at pp. 10–11.

478. *Id.*, at p. 4.

enforcement issues are likely to be manageable. If issues of noncompliance and enforcement are endemic, the real problem is likely to be that the negotiating process did not succeed in incorporating a broad enough range of the parties' interests, rather than wilful disobedience.[479]

Third, the authors argue that the existence of legal obligation translates into a presumption of compliance, in the absence of strong countervailing circumstances. The argument that law creates a duty of compliance is so familiar to many (i.e., *pacta sunt servanda*) that it is 'almost superfluous to adduce evidence or authority for a proposition that is so deeply ingrained in common understanding and so often reflected in the speech of national leaders'.[480]

Based on these assumptions, the authors argue that the principal sort of non-compliance is not wilful disobedience, but the lack of clarity or priority that states might have as regards the operation of an agreement. In the simplest form, this means that repeated interaction (i.e., participating in the regime, attending meetings, responding to requests and meeting deadlines), may set gears in motion that propel states to comply. This effect can be reinforced by, for instance, increased transparency, informal dispute settlement mechanisms, capacity building (the authors refer to the strengthening of technical and administrative means of participating states to comply with the treaty's rules) and the use of persuasion.[481] This, in sum, leads to a strategy that induces states to comply because:

> modern states are bound in a tightly woven fabric of international agreements, organizations, and institutions that shape their relations with each other and penetrated deeply into their internal economics and politics. The integrity and reliability of this system are of overriding importance for most states, most of the time. These considerations in turn reflect profound changes in the international system within which states must act and decide.[482]

To this they add that:

> Our experience as well as our research indicates that (...) the fundamental instrument for maintaining compliance with treaties at an acceptable level is an iterative process of discourse among the parties, the treaty organization, and the wider public. We propose that this process is usually viewed as management rather than enforcement. As in other managerial situations, the dominance atmosphere is one of actors engage in a cooperative venture, in which performance that seems for some reason unsatisfactory represents a problem to be solved by mutual consultation and analysis, rather than an offense to be punished. States are under the practical necessity to give reasons and justifications for suspect conduct. These are reviewed and critiqued not only informal dispute settlement processes but also in a variety of other venues, public and private, formal and informal, where they are addressed and evaluated.[483]

---

479. *Id.*, at p. 7.
480. *Id.*, at p. 8.
481. *Id.*, at pp. 22–28.
482. *Id.*, at p. 26.
483. *Id.*, at pp. 25–26.

So, in sum, the managerial design strategy to the multilateral agreement for international taxation integrates the three characteristics set forth above: continuous interaction (section 6.3.2), building on shared understandings (section 6.3.3) and legal norms (section 6.3.4). It is not characterised by enforcement mechanisms, but rather employs systems such as the continuous interaction between parties and other interested actors, legal norms as constructed focal points, and transparency and inclusivity to enhance learning. When combined with the need to use interpretative flexibility devices to achieve cooperative outcomes, as set forth in Chapter 5, this results in a regime in which parties are able to dynamically adjust commitment levels and alter their mutual expectations and actions over time.[484] In such a setting, for instance, parties' commitments can be discussed, increased or if necessary readjusted so that the likelihood of future compliance and continuing participation is maintained.

This managerial strategy to treaty design leads to the type of multilateral treaty that will be illustrated in the next section.

6.4   AN ILLUSTRATION: THE CLIMATE CHANGE REGIME

6.4.1   Introduction

The regime on climate change illustrates the above observations. The most important instrument of this regime is the 1992 UN Framework Convention on Climate Change (UNFCCC).[485] Its aim is to curb the emission of greenhouse gases, which are by now considered as 'extremely likely to have been the dominant cause of global warming'.[486] The UNFCCC was drafted to prevent that these gases 'caused further warming and long-lasting changes in all components of the climate system, increasing the likelihood

---

484. There are more theories to, basically, the same effect as the two theories discussed here (i.e., they are characterised by the same three elements). For example, H.H. Koh (1997) argues that compliance should not only be sought at the international level but also at the domestic level. Hence his 'transnational legal process' explanation for compliance: states obey international law, he argues, because they 'internalize' international norms. This process can be viewed as having three phases: 'One or more transnational actors provokes an *interaction* (or series of interactions) with another, which forces an *interpretation* or enunciation of the global norm applicable to the situation. By so doing, the moving party seeks not simply to coerce the other party, but to *internalize* the new interpretation of the international norm into the other party's internal normative system. The aim is to "bind" that other party to obey the interpretation as part of its internal value set. Such a transnational legal process is normative, dynamic, and constitutive. The transaction generates a legal rule which will guide future transnational interactions between the parties; future transactions will further internalise those norms; and eventually, repeated participation in the process will help to reconstitute the interests and even the identities of the participants in the process.' (at p. 2646)
485. United Nations Framework Convention on Climate Change; *Kyoto Protocol to the United Nations Framework Convention on Climate Change* (adopted 11 Dec. 1997), 2303 UNTS 162. A lot has been written on the problem of climate change. A good starting point is J.S. Dryzek, R.B. Norgaard and D. Schlosberg eds, *The Oxford Handbook of Climate Change and Society* (OUP 2011).
486. IPCC, *Climate Change 2014 Synthesis Report: Summary for Policymakers*, available through: https://www.ipcc.ch/pdf/assessment-report/ar5/syr/AR5_SYR_FINAL_SPM.pdf, p. 4.

of severe, pervasive and irreversible impacts for people and ecosystems'.[487] To do so, the UNFCCC itself does not contain concrete reduction targets of greenhouse gases, but rather provides a forum in which, in the light of established aims, principles, institutions and procedures, negotiations can take place.[488]

6.4.2 The Problem Structure of Addressing Climate Change Is Comparable to that of Addressing BEPS

What makes the UNFCCC very interesting for comparative purposes here is that the underlying problem structure of addressing climate change can be compared, at least to a certain degree, to the problem structure underlying the curbing of BEPS.[489] Both problem structures are collective action problems and require a global, multilateral solution. But more fundamentally, both issues are characterised by distributive conflict and uncertainties about the effect of alternative policy options.

First, like in tackling BEPS, different policy options as regards climate change have immense distributive consequences, as greenhouse gas production 'goes to the heart of energy, transport, agricultural, and industrial policy in all developed states and increasingly in developing ones too'.[490] Indeed, tackling climate change is characterised by the sharing of a 'carbon pie' amongst nations, which makes up the remaining greenhouse gases that humanity can safely exhaust without causing severe damage to

---

487. Id., p. 8. The widespread success of earlier environmental framework accords (in particular the Vienna Convention for the Protection of the Ozone Layer (adopted 22 Mar. 1985), 1513 UNTS 324 and its Montreal Protocol on Substances that Deplete the Ozone Layer (adopted 16 Sept. 1987), 1522 UNTS 3) led the international community to build a climate change convention on the basis of the framework convention-protocol design. See T. Bernauer, Climate Change Politics, 16 The Annual Review of Political Science 421, 423 (2013).

488. G. Blum (2008) p. 345.

489. In selecting a regime for this section's comparative purposes, the author has primarily looked for a regime with a comparable problem structure to tackling BEPS, and in which political processes and outcomes are transparent and distinct. For instance, the author dismissed a comparison with the trade regime and investment law regime for the following reasons.

    The regime on trade is similar to the regime on the avoidance of double taxation (the aim of both regimes is to reduce trade barriers). Unsurprisingly, bargaining within the trade regime is ultimately bilateral, and the WTO is most of all a negotiating forum. See, e.g., J.L. Goldsmith and E.A. Posner (2005) Ch. 5. However, in comparison to tackling BEPS, trade liberalisation rules have more the aspects of a private good issue than a public good issue (i.e., countries can be excluded from the liberalisation of trade, and this does not necessarily affect the effectiveness of the institution's rules between its members). See WTO, World Trade Report 2007: Six Decades of Multilateral Trade Cooperation: What Have We Learnt? (WTO Publications) pp. 126–127.

    Investment law's problem structure is different too: in contradiction to combating BEPS, the free rider problem is not as dominant. Although host countries use investment treaties to compete to attract investors, it is not clear whether all participating countries face a collective action problem in this regard. A collective action problem may be identified within groups of (developed) countries (i.e., competition pressurises states into signing a BIT, yet each individual state is better off not signing a BIT). But this problem may also be solved by regional agreements. See Z. Elkins, A.T. Guzman and B. Simmons (2006).

490. P.W. Birnie, A.E. Boyle and C. Redgwell, International Law and the Environment (OUP 2009) p. 356.

the environment.[491] One facet of this distribution conflict is that the North and the South have fundamentally different interests in solving the issue. Restrictions on emissions can severely harm the development of developing states' economies, something Western countries were not faced with at the time their economies were developing.[492] Another facet of distributive conflict is the split between major energy producers and others. States without domestic fossil fuel reserves are more likely to accept having to reduce emissions than states whose economies heavily depend on energy exports. It is therefore no wonder that the negotiations on climate change have been named 'the greatest challenge the UN has ever faced'.[493]

Second, like in tackling BEPS, uncertainties exist regarding different policy options of reducing greenhouse gas emissions, in both economic as well as scientific terms. Indeed, uncertainties have persisted in relation to almost every aspect of the climate change problem.[494] As Thompson points out, three kinds of uncertainty have hampered cooperation in the area of climate change. First, 'there is uncertainty about the severity of the global warming problem'.[495] Predictions and models of, for example, temperature change and sea-level rise are incomplete; atmospheric processes are very complex. Second, 'there is uncertainty regarding the regional and local impacts of climate change', because of an incomplete grasp of the regional details. Part of this problem is the difficulty of predicting how well firms and people will adapt to change as well as to what extent technological innovations will ease adaptation.[496] Third, 'there is uncertainty regarding the costs and benefits of different policy options' in tackling climate change. An important factor in this respect is that it is very hard to predict the future effect of policy options, both internationally as well as domestically. Simply said: policy makers do not have the capabilities to make accurate predictions so as to make a cost-benefit analysis of different policy options possible.[497] Now, a quick recall of the uncertainties related to addressing BEPS (see section 5.4.1), shows the relevance of comparing the issue of BEPS with the climate change problem. In both areas, uncertainties are related to: (1) the severity of the problem; (2) the regional/national impact of the problem; and (3) the national economic (cost-benefit) implications of different policy responses related to addressing the problem.

The distributive aspects of the climate change negotiation, in combination with the role played by uncertainty, have particularly surfaced during the negotiations on the Kyoto protocol, that bindingly establishes the baselines for and allocation of

---

491. A. Thompson, *Management under Anarchy: The International Politics of Climate Change*, 78 Climatic Change 7, 10–11 (2006).
492. Hence, the relative importance of historical emissions has played an important role in the North-South discussion. Moreover, as developing states have a more limited access to technology, they expect the wealthier states to take on a higher burden of emission reduction. *See, e.g.*, M. Paterson and M. Grubb, *The International Politics of Climate Change*, 68 International Affairs 293, 295–297 (1992).
493. P.W. Birnie, A.E. Boyle and C. Redgwell (2009) p. 378.
494. D. Bodansky, *The Emerging Climate Change Regime*, 20 Annual Review of Energy and the Environment 425, 426 (1995).
495. A. Thompson (2010) pp. 277–278.
496. *Id.*, at pp. 278–279.
497. *Id.*, at p. 279.

emission reduction targets of 'the carbon pie'.[498] In particular, establishing the size and shares of the 'carbon pie' proved very difficult. The choice of, and the proportioning between, the criteria used to assign emissions quotas, such as per capita, GNP, land area, etc., have created 'obvious winners and losers' in this distributive conflict, making agreement hard if not impossible to achieve.[499] Particularly striking for purposes of the comparison is Kyoto's introduction of the emissions trade mechanism, an innovative 'rule of the road' that allowed states to reach agreement on emission reduction targets. As the future demand for permits was – given the uncertainties related to the climate change problem – uncertain at the time of their allocation,[500] the rule operates 'fairly' in the sense spoken of in Chapter 5. Indeed, states can buy or sell permits as circumstances change, insuring them against uncertainty.[501]

So, in some respects, curbing climate change can be compared to addressing BEPS. Both areas are characterised by stark distributive conflict (i.e., 'sharing a pie') and high levels of uncertainty about both the impact of the problem as well as about the implications of alternative policy options.

6.4.3 Managing the Climate Change Problem by Multilateral Agreement

The climate change regime has been criticised for lacking effectiveness. Indeed, it can be questioned how effective the climate change regime is in reducing CO_2 emissions. Even after the big negotiation achievement of Paris 2015 there is still a lack of agreement on 'real' reduction targets.[502] Moreover, critics say the regime has had little impact on the reduction of global warming.[503]

Yet, the fact is that some form of agreement on curbing climate change is in place. As Bodansky, for instance, notes, 'like politics generally, building a climate change

---

498. Kyoto Protocol to the United Nations Framework Convention on Climate Change, Art. 3. *See also* S. Schiele, *Evolution of International Environmental Regimes* (Cambridge University Press 2014) p. 67.

499. A. Thompson (2006) p. 10.

500. *Id.*, at p. 10. The time frame is a decade: the Kyoto protocol has sought to set targets for 2008–2012 in 1997. *See also* D.G. Victor, *International Agreements and the Struggle to Tame Carbon*, in: Global Climate Change: The Science, Economics and Politics (J.M. Griffin ed., Edward Elgar 2003) pp. 215–216.

501. A. Thompson (2010).

502. *See, e.g.,* P. Friedlingstein and others, *Persistent Growth of CO^2 Emissions and Implications for Reaching Climate Targets*, 7 Nature Geoscience 709 (2014). For an overview and discussion of literature in which the effectiveness of environmental regimes is measured, *see* O.R. Young, *Effectiveness of International Environmental Regimes: Existing Knowledge, Cutting-Edge Themes, and Research Strategies*, 108 Proceedings of the National Academy of Sciencs of the USA 19853 (2011).

503. From 1970 to 2010 the total emissions of anthropogenic greenhouse gasses have only continued to increase, leading to potential detrimental consequences to the environment such as warming oceans and melting glaciers. IPCC, *Climate Change 2014 Synthesis Report: Summary for Policymakers*, available through: https://www.ipcc.ch/pdf/assessment-report/ar5/syr/AR5_SYR_FINAL_SPM.pdf, pp. 3–6. Because it has not met its objectives, it can be argued that the regime must be considered as ineffective. *See, e.g.,* L.E. Susskind, *Environmental Diplomacy: Negotiating More Effective Global Agreements* (OUP 1994) pp. 30–42.

regime is the art of the possible'.[504] The climate change regime has set forces in motion by means of which the climate change problem is managed, and under which, albeit slowly, states converge on common ideals over time. From this viewpoint, some authors have questioned whether critics who aim to expose the lack of effectiveness of the international climate change regime have not overstated the expectations of what treaties really can do. Is it, they suggest, not better to measure the regime's effectiveness by looking at 'its robustness to evolve, better reflect domestic norms, and strengthen itself towards achieving its objectives'?[505]

The 'management' of the climate change problem takes place within the framework of the UNFCCC, which is characterised by the three 'managerial' elements spoken of above: it installs continuous interaction, it is characterised by the use of primarily procedural and some substantive legal norms, and it builds on explicit and implicit shared understandings. Moreover, the regime makes use of flexibility mechanisms to accommodate the high levels of distributive conflict and uncertainty spoken of above.

Because its initial commitments were relatively weak, the UNFCCC enjoys near universal membership. Almost all states were willing from the outset to accept a framework convention.[506] What the UNFCCC's design as a framework convention most importantly has achieved, is that it has created a setting in which states repeatedly interact by coming together at the same place and at the same time, under accepted legal procedures. Indeed: it has international summits held every year.[507] Moreover, the regime establishes legal procedural requirements, for instance, on information exchange and reporting, treaty bodies, and decision-making and amendment rules. For example, the regime's yearly meetings are governed by the regime's supreme body, called Conference of the Parties (COP), which has the authority to review the implementation of the Convention, examine the obligations of the parties in light of the objective of the Convention and develop amendments and protocols.[508] Moreover, there are reporting standards that require states to submit national reports and inventories, for example, on anthropogenic emissions and on the national policies and measures to implement the Convention.[509] Such requirements put pressure on states, as states know their behaviour will be exposed to an international review, and builds trust among them, as free riders can be singled out.[510] Hence, a main aim of the

---

504. D. Bodansky (1995) p. 432.
505. For example, W.B. Chambers, *Towards an Improved Understanding of Legal Effectiveness of International Environmental Treaties*, 16 Georgetown International Environmental Law Review 501, 526 (2003). Also: T. Gehring, *International Environmental Regimes: Dynamic Sectoral Legal Systems*, 1 Yearbook of International Environmental Law 35 (1990); S. Schiele (2014), Ch. 2.
506. *See*, the website of the UN Framework Convention on Climate Change, http://unfccc.int/essential_background/convention/items/2627.php. D. Bodansky (1995) p. 430.
507. M. Bothe (2003) pp. 245–249. The 2015 was the twenty-first yearly session of the COP to the UNFCCC.
508. United Nations Framework Convention on Climate Change Art. 7.
509. *Id.*, at Art. 4. The Kyoto Protocol to the UNFCCC contains information standards too, *see, e.g.*, Art. 7.
510. D. Bodansky, *The United Nations Framework Convention on Climate Change: A Commentary*, 18 Yale Journal of International Law 451, 444–445 (1993).

Convention's procedural functions is to provide a permanent forum for discussion and negotiation and to create a sense of community.

The climate change regime builds on implicit and explicit shared understandings. First of all, the need for a global climate change regime is widely accepted,[511] not only by states but also by an army of NGOs and nongovernmental observers. Moreover, the framework convention sets out the regime's general principles and institutions, which may be seen as the explicitly shared understandings upon which the regime rests. The framework convention's general objective is to achieve 'stabilization of greenhouse gas concentrations in the atmosphere at a level that would prevent serious anthropogenic interference with the climate system'.[512] But some other principles also inform the negotiations, such as the 'common but differentiated responsibility' principle, which comes down to the initial compromise that the North should take the lead in combating climate change and its adverse effects,[513] and the 'precautionary principle', which holds that parties should not use the lack of full scientific certainty as a reason for postponing action.[514]

Finally, the climate change regime makes use of flexibility mechanisms. First of all, the Kyoto protocol introduced the emissions trade mechanism: a clear 'rule of the road' for the climate change problem (see above). But the climate change regime also makes use of a transformative flexibility mechanism: the framework convention/ protocol design. The framework convention/protocol design has enabled treaty negotiators to insulate the regime's core commitments from the risk of negotiation breakdown under successive negotiation rounds. Indeed, the quantified reduction targets and emission trading mechanism of the Kyoto protocol were only committed to by the so-called Annex I parties, which are mostly developed countries, whilst the general obligations of the convention[515] continued to apply to all states.

Ultimately, the point of these elements is to slowly advance and develop cooperation on the climate change problem.[516] As regards the regime's substantive legal rules, this has indeed been a matter of process and gradual development. For instance, after the framework convention's establishment in 1992, the Kyoto protocol was added in 1997, and refinements to the protocol and its procedures have been made since.[517] The flexibility of the market allocation mechanism has provided states with a

511. J. Brunnée and S.J. Toope (2010) p. 142.
512. United Nations Framework Convention on Climate Change Art. 2.
513. Id., at Art. 3(1).
514. Id., at Art. 3(3).
515. These are set out in Art. 4(1) of the convention.
516. See, e.g., T. Gehring (1990); T. Gehring, Treaty-Making and Treaty Evolution, in: The Oxford Handbook of International Environmental Law (D. Bodansky, J. Brunnée and E. Hey eds, OUP 2008).
517. In 1995, a start was made to achieve stricter emission stabilisation obligations by the negotiations on the UNFCCC's Kyoto Protocol. In the Kyoto protocol, the Annex I parties, which mostly are developed countries, committed to quantified reduction targets. To achieve cost-effective results, the Protocol allows the trading of emission permits. However, Parties were not directly able to agree on the implementation and further development of the Kyoto Protocol. See S. Schiele (2014) p. 68. This, in turn, required more detailed rules on the calculation of assigned amounts and on the functioning of the flexibility mechanism, of which the finalisation took place in 2001 (the 'Marrakech Accords'). M. Bothe (2003) p. 241. Further

way to work towards meeting the regime's core aims. It provides, hence, the perfect example of how innovation can lead to states to agree, over time, to a multilateral rule in an area characterised by stark distributive concerns. And more recently, the robustness of the regime has again paid off: the 2015 round was particularly successful, 'charting a fundamental new course in the two-decade-old global climate effort', in which states have agreed to limit global temperature increase below 2°C and to report regularly on emissions and implementation efforts.[518] The hopes are high that the dynamic and sustainable approach to combating climate change will lead to deeper agreement and to the convergence of states' interests in the future.

6.5 CONCLUSIONS

Negotiations in the field of international taxation need to accommodate divergent state interests, and are likely to be and continue to be confined by egocentric and self-interested states. But state interests may change and evolve over time. After all, international cooperation is not static. Indeed, the coming into existence of the BEPS Project is a clear example of how cooperation in the area of international tax is a dynamic rather than a static undertaking, which may be driven by normative forces (e.g., 'fair share').

A multilateral agreement for international taxation that seeks to facilitate progressive, collective international tax lawmaking is characterised by two features. First of all, it must ensure that states engage in solving collective action problems. The point is that the international tax regime should be able to continuously respond to the needs of society. In this regard, treaty designers perceive *ex ante* a management risk *ex post*. The key lies in mechanisms of persuasion, rather than of coercion. The argument against coercive mechanisms is, generally speaking, that the delegation of authority to legislative and adjudicative and institutional bodies is not feasible, and perhaps not even necessary, for the area of international taxation (section 6.2.1). Second, a multilateral treaty may streamline the renegotiation or amendment of bilateral tax treaties. Obviously, would states come to agree to a substantive multilateral norm ('substantive multilateralism'), for example, a 'rule of the road', bilateral tax treaties could be amended *in one go*. This would quicken the tax treaty amendment process, provided that the negotiation of the norm would not take longer than eighteen years (*see* Chapter 3). But even if a 'substantive' multilateral obligation proves unfeasible to negotiate (*see* Chapter 5), a multilateral agreement may be beneficial as it provides a setting that encourages bilateral interaction. Indeed, a 'formal' multilateral agreement may reduce the transaction costs traditionally associated with bilateral tax treaty negotiations. The argument follows from the two-step logic of a multilateral

---

agreements were reached in 2009 in Copenhagen (which contains the aspiration to reduce emissions so that global warming does not exceed two degrees Celsius).

518. Centre for Climate and Energy Solutions, *Outcomes of the U.N. Climate Change Conference in Paris: 21st Session of the Conference of the Parties to the United Nations Framework Convention on Climate Change (COP 21)*, December 2015, http://www.c2es.org/docUploads/cop-21-paris -summary-12-2015-final.pdf.

negotiation: transaction costs of bilateral tax treaty negotiations can be reduced by bringing states together at one central place and time. Moreover, transaction costs can be further reduced by institutionalising bargaining (i.e., by centralising knowledge building and the exchange of information), and by the identification of common value-maximising terms in 'step one', so that states can converge on these terms when entering into deeper forms of cooperation in 'step two' (section 6.2.2).

These two features point at the use of the 'managerial' design strategy for a multilateral agreement for international taxation. The point of the managerial view is that it smoothens collective interplay and facilitates states to progressively deepen their commitments by installing continuous interaction, by enabling them to build on shared understandings (for which transparency and inclusivity are indispensable), and by using legal norms such as 'rules of the road' to act as focal points for further discussions. The point of the combination of the three elements of the 'managerial' strategy is to facilitate 'learning'. Flexibility mechanisms (*see* Chapter 5) can be used to dynamically adjust and readjust commitment levels, so that mutual expectations and actions can be altered as the cooperative effort goes along. After all, from the previous chapter follows that such mechanisms are needed to accommodate diverging state interests.

A managerial treaty improves the exercise of regulatory influence by means of the OECD MTC and Commentaries (i.e., *see* Chapter 3), for two important reasons. First of all, it makes international tax lawmaking fairer (i.e., more inclusive and transparent) and therefore also more likely to develop and respond to deal with the collective action problems that international tax law faces or may come to face. Second, the managerial treaty design allows parties to structurally 'streamline' the tax treaty amendment process. A substantive multilateral deal would of course allow parties to amend their bilateral tax relationships *in one go*. But even if this proves unfeasible, it provides a setting in which transaction costs of bilateral interaction are reduced, as it brings parties together at one time and place and under established principles and procedure.

As in many other areas of international cooperation, such as in the area of climate change, progress towards certain solutions for collective action problems may be slow or indecisive. Rome was not built in a day. But a structural, dynamic legal solution to cooperation in the international tax area may provide a solid basis for fruitful cooperation in the future. 'Fair procedure' is at the heart of this approach. Inclusive, continuous and transparent deliberation provides a setting in which knowledge may be build, interests may shift, and hence norms may change. A multilateral agreement for international taxation should provide, in other words, the correct process and infrastructure for international tax law to advance towards substantive solutions over time.

CHAPTER 7

The Design of a Multilateral Agreement for International Taxation

7.1 INTRODUCTION

The last three chapters were concerned with the construction of a design strategy for a multilateral agreement for international taxation. First of all, we have learned that the agreement must emphasise procedural fairness: achieving procedural fairness is not only the 'right thing to do' (Chapter 4), but also indispensable to enable the international tax system to continuously adapt to and evolve in line with developments (Chapter 6). Continuous interaction, legal norms and building on shared understandings are vital for this. Second, we have seen the importance of flexibility for a multilateral agreement for international taxation. To avoid distributional conflict, interpretative flexibility is needed to accommodate divergent state interests, for example, by reservations and 'rules of the road' (Chapter 5). Also, the multilateral agreement for international taxation itself must be flexible, so that states can easily respond as circumstances change (*see* Chapter 6).

With these understandings in mind, the question remains what legal tools of public international law best fit these outcomes. How should, looking at public international law, the agreement for international taxation be designed?[519]

Part 7A sets forth the central elements that a multilateral agreement for international taxation must possess. The design strategy, that proposes that the multilateral agreement is used to 'manage' international tax matters over time, points in the direction of using a robust forum that facilitates inclusive and transparent discussions. A robust forum leads to continuous interaction (discussed in section 6.3.2). Transparent and inclusive deliberation enables actors to build on shared understandings (*see*

---

519. The discussions below are informed by the toolbox set out in the 2015 – Final Report on Action 15: OECD, *Developing a Multilateral Instrument to Modify Bilateral Tax Treaties, Action 15: 2015 Final Report* (2015).

section 6.3.3). Understandings that have become common can, through interaction in the forum, be hardened into law (*see* section 6.3.4). At the same time, the institutionalisation of such a forum provides for the mundane reduction of transaction costs of bilateral tax treaty negotiations (*see* section 6.2.2).

After having established the core elements of a multilateral agreement for international taxation, two types of agreement are discussed that meet the flexibility requirements set forth by the previous chapters: the framework convention-protocol design and the 'agreement to scope'.

Part 7B discusses the framework convention-protocol design. In the framework convention-protocol design, inspired by the regime on climate change (*see* section 6.4), states initially focus on the negotiation of broad, standard-setting commitments. Once consensus has built up, detailed commitments are fleshed out in protocols. Such broad standards set directions for further negotiation, whilst the institutional setup of the regime facilitates the gathering of further information on the problem and builds trust among participants. This prevents negotiation breakdown. Once parties start negotiating detailed commitments in protocols, the design allows for the inclusion of certain parties only, so that states wishing to engage in deeper cooperation are included in further deliberations, whilst states that do not wish to do so remain bound to the regime's core commitments. Interpretative flexibility mechanisms such as reservations, menu options and 'rules of the road' may be used to tailor-make obligations to the taste of the individual state.

Part 7C deals with the design of an 'agreement to scope'. Under such an agreement, states commit to bilaterally (re)negotiating their (*inter se*) tax treaties on certain multilaterally agreed objectives or (soft-law) norms,[520] similar to a directive as used within the EU, which requires Member States to achieve a certain result without dictating the means of doing so. This type of multilateral agreement thereby 'limits the scope' of further bilateral tax treaty negotiations, as parties agree to (re)negotiate solely on the objectives multilaterally set. To ensure the expeditious amendment of the bilateral conventions, the multilateral regime can provide for a monitoring and reporting mechanism.

In practice, the line separating the framework convention-protocol design and the 'agreement to scope' may be thin. The framework convention-protocol design embodies the idea of *substantive* multilateralism; the 'agreement to scope' represents the idea of *formal* multilateralism (*see* section 6.2.2). As they see fit, states may mix and match the characteristics of either approach. Indeed, on the one hand, when the point of departure is to establish *substantive* multilateral agreement, a framework convention-protocol design may be used. But when a strong need for the use of reservations and 'menu options' exists, the effect of the resulting treaty may not be very different from a formal multilateral agreement. After all, reservations and 'menu options' lead to *inter*

---

520. Such an instrument is called a *pactum de negotiando* in public international law, in which parties agree to subsequently agree on further legal acts. *See, e.g.,* H. Owada, *Pactum de Contrahendo, Pactum de Negotiando,* in: Max Planck Encyclopedia of Public International Law (R. Wolfrum ed., OUP 2010). Also: A. Miaja De La Muela, *Pacta de Contrahendo en Derecho Internacional Publico,* 21 Revista Española de Derecho Internacional 392 (1968).

se agreements between parties. If the depth and number of reservations filed by states are extensive enough, such *inter se* obligations may very well end up as *bilateral inter se* agreements anyway. On the other hand, even though states may agree to flesh out vague norms in bilateral deals under an 'agreement to scope' (i.e., formal multilateralism), the negotiation of these bilateral deals takes place at one central place and time and under common value-maximising terms. So as to further save transaction costs, negotiations under the 'agreement to scope' may take place between groups of countries with converging interests. In this view, the 'agreement to scope' is the piece of rope that ties together bundles of bilateral, and where possible, trilateral or mini-multilateral relationships. Hence, the distinction between the 'agreement to scope' and the framework convention-protocol design, i.e., between formal and substantive multilateralism, should not be perceived as strict, but only serves to guide the discussions. Either option (or a combination thereof) is suitable to embody the design strategy formulated in the previous chapters as shown in Figure 4.

Figure 4   Substantive and Formal Multilateralism in International Tax Law

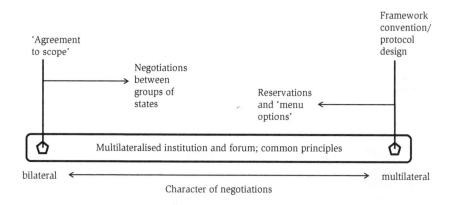

A few remarks beforehand. First, it is conceivable that a wealth of literature will most likely develop on the effect and practical implementation of multilateral tax rules (such as the BEPS Convention) on/in bilateral tax treaties (think of language differences between treaties, the precise drafting of the multilateral texts, etc.).[521] However, for such an analysis, a more thorough understanding of the contents of substantive multilateral rules is required. The sole aim of the chapter is, in other words, to consummate the outcomes of the previous chapters. Second, the inventory of tools discussed is by no means exhaustive. An attempt has been made to select, in the light of the conclusions of the previous chapters, the most demonstrative examples. Third, the word 'amendment' is understood to include changes to a treaty agreed upon by *all*

---

521. *See*, for a first exploration on such matters, N. Bravo, *The Proposal for a Multilateral Tax Instrument for Updating Tax Treaties*, in: Base Erosion and Profit Shifting (M. Lang et al., eds, Linde Verlag 2016) secs V and VI.

treaty parties (which is termed an 'amendment' in international public law doctrine) as well as an amendment between specific particular parties only (which is named a 'modification' in international public law discourse). From the perspective of international public law, the distinction is purely terminological and does not lead to the application of different residual treaty rules set forth in the VCLT.[522] Finally, the interested reader may miss an explicit discussion and systematic consideration of dispute resolution and arbitration mechanisms. The reason this was left out is that it would introduce a more complicated political problem, that exceeds the ambit of Chapter 5's analytical tools.[523]

A model framework convention-protocol treaty as well as a model 'agreement to scope' are included in the Annex and referred to in the text.

PART 7A: THE CORE ELEMENTS OF THE MULTILATERAL AGREEMENT FOR INTERNATIONAL TAXATION

7.2 INTRODUCTION TO PART 7A

What the multilateral agreement should do, is solve the issues related to the implementation of new norms in the network of bilateral tax treaties identified in Chapter 3, and create a level playing field, so that cooperation between states can converge on the necessary solutions for collective action problems. As argued, this can be achieved by the 'managerial' design strategy. The 'core' elements of an agreement based in this strategy, whether ultimately drafted on the basis of a framework convention-protocol design (Part 7B) or an 'agreement to scope' (Part 7C), or a combination of thereof, are discussed in this section.

The multilateral agreement requires a flexible institution or forum that does not function like a traditional IO (section 7.3), and legal principles that guide or inform negotiations and act as focal points for further coordination (section 7.4). Moreover, the question arises what the effect or influence of the multilateral treaty is on third (non-participating) states (section 7.5). From international law follows that a multilateral treaty may be able to influence treaties between participating and non-participating states, i.e., that it may have 'network' effects. This deserves further examination. We have seen that the number of states participating in the decision-

---

522. J. Brunnée, *Treaty Amendments*, in: The Oxford Guide to Treaties (D.B. Hollis ed., OUP 2012) p. 347.

523. First of all, the problem of dispute resolution does not resonate well with the analysis in secs 5.3.2 and 5.3.3, which is about the 'horizontal' distribution of gains in international tax law. Rules for dispute resolution mechanisms do not distribute gains themselves. Rather, the issue is one of agency/delegation (very briefly discussed in secs 6.2.1 and 7.10.3). Second, for dispute resolution in international tax law, individuals can request states to initiate proceedings, even if domestic remedies are exhausted. Hence, a different dynamic may be in play: dispute resolution is not purely a state-to-state affair but seeks to provide legal remedies for groups within the state. Such changes may not be fully comprehended without a domestic politics perspective. *See, e.g.*, R. Keohane, A. Moravcsik and A. Slaughter, *Legalized Dispute Resolution: Interstate and Transnational*, 54 International Organization 457 (2000).

making processes should be gradually increased so as to increase the regime's fairness. But it is likely that some states, for whatever reason, will choose not to sign a multilateral agreement. This brings up the question what the relationship is between the multilateral agreement on the one hand and bilateral tax treaties concluded between treaty members and third states on the other. From a legal perspective, it is not unlikely that the multilateral agreement may influence the interpretation of such bilateral tax treaties, or that treaty parties agree to bring their bilateral tax treaties with non-signatory states in line with the obligations of the multilateral agreement. Such 'network effects' may further enhance the 'managerial' character of international tax cooperation, as it may evolve and influence the identities and interests of those outside the regime.

7.3 THE ORGANISATION MANAGING THE MULTILATERAL REGIME

7.3.1 The Need for Institutional Flexibility

The organisation that has traditionally developed international tax law is the OECD. The previous chapters, however, raise the question whether the OECD is suited as the leading organisation for tax matters. The OECD is a 'club'-like organisation that restricts its membership to a few (rather homogeneous) developed nations. As this causes some legitimacy issues (*see* Chapter 4), lawmaking must be opened up to a more diverse groups of participants, so that 'other' states get an equal opportunity to influence law and decision-making taking place. Only this can ensure that substantive international tax law ultimately developed is 'fair'.

In Chapter 5, this direction was then somewhat watered down: the group of participants may be broadened to a more diverse group of states and other actors, but increasing the influence of 'others' on international tax lawmaking process is not without limits. Extending the influence of 'others' must be a gradual, rather than an abrupt, process. Moreover, it cannot be denied that, in terms of effectiveness, the experience and expertise of the OECD in international tax matters is very important for the progress of international tax law. International tax is a technically difficult area of the law, and the OECD harbours a strong international network of practitioners and lot of expertise. The risk of quickly expanding participation is that this may cause the cooperative effort to implode or end up nowhere.

Be that as it may, the managerial design strategy requires a somewhat formal institutional arrangement. It must instal robustness so that cooperation is continuous and repeated over time, and allows the amount of participating states to be slowly increased. But, if on the one hand, the OECD is unsuited to function as the locus of decision-making in international tax, and if, on the other hand, an abrupt shift of tax policy making to an established forum like the UN seems impossible and the OECD, with its network and expertise, cannot be fully kept out of the equation, what would be a suitable way forward? The solution lies on the spectrum somewhere in between, and again, we can learn from international environmental law with its quasi-formal 'treaty bodies'.

7.3.2 Treaty Bodies in International Environmental Law

In international environmental law, regimes have been built with bodies that are neither IOs nor international courts in the traditional sense. These 'organisations', which are tasked with adopting treaty texts and the organisation of the annual conferences, are called treaty bodies.[524]

Treaty bodies provide the regime with flexibility, because they neither have a fixed membership nor are managed from a fixed location, as traditional IOs have and are.[525] Therefore, by the use of such treaty bodies, the costs and bureaucracies associated with traditional IOs are avoided. Hence, as Alvarez notes, the use of treaty bodies may be explained by the widespread dissatisfaction of states with existing IO bureaucracies and politics.[526] Quasi-formal treaty bodies do not compete with formal IOs, but can rather be used to establish mutually reinforcing networks and coalitions.[527] Indeed, treaty bodies can make use of institutional linkages with other IOs, for instance, by taking into consideration exogenous standards created by other, formal IOs.

Yet, treaty bodies are not IOs in the traditional sense. Of the three elements used to define IOs (founded on international agreement; having at least one organ with a will of its own; established under international law),[528] treaty bodies lack a will of their own. A treaty body is, in the words of Schermers and Blokker, no more than the sum of its members.[529] It hence does not have legal personality: it acts on behalf of its parties.[530]

The COP, the body's central plenary organ, meets annually, if necessary in different locations. It is supported by a secretariat that facilitates the plenary body sessions, conducts studies, prepares draft decisions and circulates reports. Such administrative bodies are often located within existing IOs. For instance, secretariats to global treaties on human rights and on the law of the sea are positioned within the framework of the UN.[531]

The competences of treaty bodies typically comprise internal as well as external ('decision-making') powers. Internal powers are, for instance, the power to adopt rules

---

524. G. Ulfstein, *Treaty Bodies*, in: The Oxford Handbook of International Environmental Law (D. Bodansky, J. Brunnée and E. Hey eds, OUP 2008) and G. Ulfstein, *Treaty Bodies and Regimes*, in: The Oxford Guide to Treaties (D.B. Hollis ed., OUP 2012). Schermers and Blokker also refer to these organisations: H.G. Schermers and N.M. Blokker (2011) para. 44, and in P. Sands and P. Klein, *Bowett's Law of International Institutions* (Sweet & Maxwell sixth ed., 2009) they are referred to in Ch. 4 as 'other autonomous organisations'. Likewise: R.R. Churchill and G. Ulfstein, *Autonomous Institutional Arrangements in Multilateral Environmental Agreements: A Little-Noticed Phenomenon in International Law*, 94 American Journal of International Law 623–659 (2000).
525. G. Ulfstein (2012) p. 430.
526. J.E. Alvarez, *International Organizations as Law-Makers* (OUP 2005) p. 320.
527. *Id.*, at p. 320 at footnote 134.
528. H.G. Schermers and N.M. Blokker (2011) para. 33.
529. *Id.*, at para. 44.
530. V. Röben, *Conference (Meeting) of States Parties*, in: The Max Planck Encyclopedia of Public International Law (R. Wolfrum ed., OUP Online ed., 2010).
531. G. Ulfstein (2012) pp. 431–432.

of procedure, financial regulations and the budget. Decision-making powers, on the other hand, are often related to developing the substantive commitments of the parties, and must be provided for in the treaty (*see, e.g.*, Article 7(2) below: 'The Conference of the Parties, as the supreme body of this Convention (...)'). Treaty bodies therefore contribute to the dynamic character of the regime and are used to overcome the cumbersome treaty-making process.[532] For instance, treaty bodies, by the COP, adopt amendments to the relevant treaty texts or adopt protocols or annexes (sometimes by opt out, *see* section 7.10),[533] facilitate the exchange of information, constitute subsidiary bodies, and seek cooperation with other international governmental and nongovernmental organisations.

In example, the treaty body of the UNFCCC is constituted and organised by the following procedural rules:[534]

Article 2 Objective

The ultimate objective of this Convention and any related legal instruments that the Conference of the Parties may adopt (...)

Article 7 Conference of the Parties
1. A Conference of the Parties is hereby established.
2. The Conference of the Parties, as the supreme body of this Convention, shall keep under regular review the implementation of the Convention and any related legal instruments that the Conference of the Parties may adopt, and shall make, within its mandate, the decisions necessary to promote the effective implementation of the Convention. To this end, it shall:
    (a) Periodically examine the obligations of the Parties and the institutional arrangements under the Convention, in the light of the objective of the Convention, the experience gained in its implementation and the evolution of scientific and technological knowledge;
    (b) Promote and facilitate the exchange of information on measures adopted by the Parties to address climate change (...);
    (c) Facilitate, at the request of two or more Parties, the coordination of measures adopted by them to address climate change and its effects, (...);
    (d) Promote and guide, in accordance with the objective and provisions of the Convention, the development and periodic refinement of comparable methodologies, to be agreed on by the Conference of the Parties, (...);
    (e) Assess, on the basis of all information made available to it in accordance with the provisions of the Convention, the implementation of the Convention by the Parties, the overall effects of the measures taken pursuant to the Convention, (...);
    (f) Consider and adopt regular reports on the implementation of the Convention and ensure their publication;
    (g) Make recommendations on any matters necessary for the implementation of the Convention;

---

532. *Id.*, at p. 435.
533. V. Röben (2010) sec. 2.
534. *See*, for a discussion, G. Loibl, *Conferences of Parties and the Modification of Obligations: The Example of International Environmental Agreements*, in: Interrogating the Treaty: Essays in the Contemporary Law of Treaties (M. Craven and M. Fitzmaurice eds, Wolf Legal Publishers 2005); UN Climate Change Secretariat, *United Nations Framework Convention on Climate Change: Handbook* (UNFCCC 2006).

(h) Seek to mobilise financial resources in accordance with Article 4, paragraphs 3, 4 and 5, and Article 11;

(i) Establish such subsidiary bodies as are deemed necessary for the implementation of the Convention;

(j) Review reports submitted by its subsidiary bodies and provide guidance to them;

(k) Agree upon and adopt, by consensus, rules of procedure and financial rules for itself and for any subsidiary bodies;

(l) Seek and utilise, where appropriate, the services and cooperation of, and information provided by, competent international organizations and inter-governmental and non-governmental bodies; and

(m) Exercise such other functions as are required for the achievement of the objective of the Convention as well as all other functions assigned to it under the Convention.

3. The Conference of the Parties shall, at its first session, adopt its own rules of procedure as well as those of the subsidiary bodies established by the Convention, which shall include decision-making procedures for matters not already covered by decision-making procedures stipulated in the Convention. Such procedures may include specified majorities required for the adoption of particular decisions.

4. The first session of the Conference of the Parties shall be convened by the interim secretariat referred to in Article 21 and shall take place not later than one year after the date of entry into force of the Convention. Thereafter, ordinary sessions of the Conference of the Parties shall be held every year unless otherwise decided by the Conference of the Parties.

5. Extraordinary sessions of the Conference of the Parties shall be held at such other times as may be deemed necessary by the Conference, or at the written request of any Party, (...).

6. The United Nations, its specialized agencies and the International Atomic Energy Agency, as well as any State member thereof or observers thereto not Party to the Convention, may be represented at sessions of the Conference of the Parties as observers. (...)

Article 15 Amendments to the Convention

1. Any party may propose amendments to the convention.

Amendments to the Convention shall be adopted at an ordinary session of the Conference of the Parties. The text of any proposed amendment to the Convention shall be communicated to the Parties by the secretariat at least six months before the meeting at which it is proposed for adoption. The secretariat shall also communicate proposed amendments to the signatories to the Convention and, for information, to the Depositary. (...) [535]

It is not uncommon for treaty bodies, as do 'normal' IOs, to coordinate with other institutions by means of formal or informal coordination mechanisms. In this way, treaty bodies make use of the experience of other organisations in developing policy directions and solutions. In other words, interaction and interplay between treaty bodies and IOs takes place.

As regards to formal cooperation: exogenous standards may be incorporated in the terms of a treaty. There are many examples of soft standards and guidelines that

---

535. United Nations Framework Convention on Climate Change.

have been 'hardened' in this way.[536] In international conventions on, for instance, nuclear safety,[537] the terms of the conventions themselves cross-refer to non-binding legislative standards, as updated from time to time. For instance, the Joint Convention on the Safety Spent Fuel Management and on the Safety of Radioactive Waste Management[538] recalls certain international non-binding standards in its preamble[539] and refers to these standards in some of its articles.[540] Moreover, it is not uncommon for the staff of one IO to be able to act as observer in the work of another IO. As Schermers and Blokker note, many agreements between specialised agencies of the UN provide for reciprocal representation at meetings when interests are shared.[541]

But cooperation need not be formal. The informal consideration of external materials in treaty negotiations may influence the results achieved. For instance, guidelines developed by the International Atomic Energy Agency (IAEA) formed the basis for the swiftly adopted 1986 Convention on Early Notification of a Nuclear Accident.[542] And Article 7(2)(l) of the UNFCCC, cited above, allows the COP to seek and utilise cooperation with another IO (e.g., by providing and exchanging information, etc.). Hence, cooperation may also exist on the basis of 'loosely structured, peer-to-peer ties developed through frequent interaction rather than formal negotiation'.[543] The bottom line is that ideas and knowledge built in one institutional environment impacts decision-making in another through networks among government officials.[544]

---

536. *See,* for such examples, A.E. Boyle, *Soft Law in International Law-Making,* in: International Law (M.D. Evans ed., OUP 3d ed., 2010) p. 904.
537. *See,* for further examples, B.H. Oxman, *The Duty to Respect Generally Accepted International Standards,* 24 New York University Journal of International Law and Politics 109, 122 (1991); F. Kirgis Jr, *Specialized Law-Making Processes,* in: United Nations Legal Order (O. Schachter and C. Joyner eds, Cambridge University Press 1995); G. Handl, *The IAEA Nuclear Safety Conventions: An Example of Successful 'Treaty Management'?,* 72 Nuclear Law Bulletin 7 (2004); D. French, *Treaty Interpretation and the Incorporation of Extraneous Legal Rules,* 55 International and Comparative Law Quarterly 281 (2006).
538. *Joint Convention on the Safety of Spent Fuel Management and on the Safety of Radioactive Waste Management* (adopted 5 Sept. 1997), 2153 UNTS 357.
539. Paragraph XIV of the preamble holds that the contracting parties: 'keeping in mind the principles contained in the interagency "International Basic Safety Standards for Protection against Ionizing Radiation and for the Safety of Radiation Sources" (1996), in the IAEA Safety Fundamentals entitled "The Principles of Radioactive Waste Management" (1995), and in the existing international standards relating to the safety of the transport of radioactive materials; (…) have agreed as follows: (…).'
540. In Arts 4, 11 and 24. For example, Art. 4: 'each Contracting Party shall take the appropriate steps to (…) (iv) provide for effective protection of individuals, society and the environment, by applying at the national level suitable protective methods (…) in the framework of its national legislation which has *due regard to internationally endorsed criteria and standards*' (emphasis added). *See* further, G. Handl (2004) sec. 2.
541. H.G. Schermers and N.M. Blokker (2011) paras 186–187.
542. *1986 Convention on Early Notification of a Nuclear Accident* (26 Sept. 1986), 1457 UNTS 133.
543. K. Raustiala, *The Architecture of International Cooperation: Transgovernmental Networks and the Future of International Law,* 43 Virginia Journal of International Law 2, 5 (2002).
544. A. Slaughter, *A New World Order* (Princeton University Press 2004); K. Raustiala (2002). That the OECD already operates in networks in the international tax field is shown by A. Christians (2010a). She provides a word of caution, however: the way such transnational networks work is poorly understood and such networks are uneasy to access.

7.3.3 Can Treaty Bodies Be Used for the Multilateral Agreement for International Taxation?

A treaty body such as a 'COP' may well work for an agreement for international taxation. Its membership can be slowly expanded and deliberations on international tax norms can take place on 'neutral' grounds (i.e., neither in the OECD nor in the UN). Nevertheless, it may be wise to start with a limited group of homogeneous states, with the aim of slowly increasing the level of participation in the COP.

What would be required? At a minimum, states would need to agree to meet regularly in the future within the 'neutral' COP, and identify some 'guiding principles' to act as common value-maximising terms. In this regard, it should be noted that the first steps in the direction of institutionalising such a treaty body have already been taken. The OECD seems to be slowly expanding participation, by having built on the BEPS Project with its own experts as well as with the G20[545] and other, non-western, countries.[546] Talks about the multilateral instrument for implementing the BEPS Project are organised under the auspices of the 'ad hoc group', which consists of states interested in participating in the BEPS Project. The same can be said of the 'inclusive framework' that the OECD has constituted to involve non-OECD member countries on a more equal level in implementing and further developing the BEPS Project.[547] Finally, the BEPS Convention evidences that a COP may in fact be constituted within the area of international taxation (*see* Chapter 8).

Nevertheless, the design strategy formulated in the previous chapter requires that states will come to have a real and tangible opportunity to influence the debates and negotiations when developing and adopting international tax norms. On this point, current efforts still fall short. The participants of the ad-hoc group have not necessarily been part of the lawmaking processes that generated the BEPS Reports and hence the BEPS Convention. Instead, standard setting has taken place within the environment of expertise of the OECD. The non-binding outcomes of this process (i.e., the BEPS reports) have been proposed as *fait accompli* to the ad hoc group's participants (which includes OECD Members as well as non-Members). And paradoxically, the more equal 'inclusive framework' calls non-OECD Members 'BEPS Associates' (i.e., not 'Members' or 'Participants').

It may be true that, in the short run, linkages with the OECD are unavoidable. A new (quasi-) formal institutional arrangement does not have the tax expertise necessary to develop international tax law and must therefore use or 'borrow' from the

---

545. The final package on BEPS measures has been endorsed by the G20 finance ministers on 15 and 16 Nov. 2016. Still, the involvement of the G20 may enhance the effort's effectiveness but not its legitimacy. As Christians argues, the G20 does not enhance the participation of non-member countries in developing tax policy, so long as the 'framing, discussion, and consensus building takes place within an established order that continues to be dominated by the world's wealthiest economies'. A. Christians (2010b) pp. 35–39.

546. The participation of non-members developing countries in establishing tax norms has been considered 'unprecedented' by the OECD. OECD, *Developing a Multilateral Instrument to Modify Bilateral Tax Treaties, Action 15: 2015 Final Report* (2015) p. 5.

547. OECD, 'Implementing the BEPS Package: Building an Inclusive Framework', http://www.oecd .org/tax/flyer-implementing-the-beps-package-building-an-inclusive-framework.pdf.

OECD's expertise. And there is another issue: the output of the OECD is non-binding. One might wonder whether non-binding influence on multilateral treaty-making could be completely restricted or prevented. Even if the vital process of idea development and negotiation would fully take place at the level of the COP, where states have the ultimate vote in agreeing to international obligations, discussions may be heavily influenced by output generated within the OECD.

How to proceed? First of all, it may be best to formalise the COP's cooperation with the OECD (*see, e.g.,* Articles 5 and 6(6) of the draft conventions taken up in Annex A and B), so that the OECD's input may be balanced against input from other sources. Moreover, as lawmaking should ultimately take place in an inclusive manner, a first step would be to, over time, move the COP's secretariat to the broader membership forum of the UN. This step should remove the 'membership bias' that characterises the development and negotiation of ideas and norms in current international tax lawmaking. Finally, it might be wise to start drafting neutral 'commentaries' and 'model provisions' within the ambit of the COP. Whereas the OECD's model provisions may serve as an inspiration, they should be openly discussed and seen as relevant ideas, and not as texts to be endorsed without any further discussion by participants.

For example, those new model tax provisions and commentaries could be used in the 'agreement to scope' scenario (Part 7C), in which states agree to flesh out common terms in further bilateral interactions. The new model provisions and commentaries might help to guide those bilateral negotiations. In this regard, in line with what De Goede argues, it may be advisable to move to a type of model convention that contains a set of universally accepted framework provisions (i.e., multilateral norms in the 'strong' sense) with commentaries, and a set of 'technically sound alternative provisions', with clearly stated pros and cons.[548] Alternatively, for the purposes of the *substantive* multilateralism effectuated by a framework convention-protocol design (Part 7B), commentaries on adopted norms may provide participants with further interpretative guidance. Where norms need to be amended, states can (re)enter into discourse.

7.4 GUIDING PRINCIPLES

7.4.1 Objectives and Guiding Principles in International Legal Instruments

Managerial treaties often contain guiding principles under which substantive norms may further develop.[549] Such principles indicate a general direction to inform process,

---

548. J.J.P. De Goede, *The BRICS Countries in the Context of the Work on the UN Model*, in: BRICS and the Emergence of International Tax Coordination (Y. Brauner and P. Pistone eds, IBFD 2015) p. 444.
549. Examples of such principles can be primarily found in Framework Conventions/Protocol Designs. *See*, for instance, the United Nations Framework Convention on Climate Change; the *1979 Convention on Long-Range Transboundary Air Pollution* (adopted 15 Nov. 1979), 1302 UNTS 217 (containing the principle of reducing and preventing air pollution); the *WHO Framework Convention on Tobacco Control* (adopted 21 May 2003), 2302 UNTS 166 (containing the objective of protecting present and future generations from the devastating health, social,

treaty interpretation and future negotiations.[550] Although such principles come across as 'rules of the road' (*see* further section 7.10.3), the principles are not meant to generate substantive treaty commitments, but rather to guide the development of the regime. In fact, as they codify shared understandings, they provide parties with directions to 'learn', i.e., redefine and explore their interest.

Under the framework convention for climate change (*see* section 6.4), for instance, the main objective that guides the further development of the regime[551] is to achieve the 'stabilization of greenhouse gas concentrations in the atmosphere at a level that would prevent serious anthropogenic interference with the climate system'. Moreover, the climate change convention states that 'the parties shall be guided, inter alia,'[552] by the principle of the common but differentiated responsibility between developing and developed states, the precautionary principle, the principle that all parties have the right to sustainable development, and the principle that 'a supportive and open international economic system' is promoted. As Birnie notes, these principles have the:

> important merit of providing some predictability regarding the parameters within which the parties are required to work towards the objective of the convention. In particular, they are not faced with a completely blank sheet of paper when entering subsequent protocol negotiations or when the Conference of the Parties takes decisions under the various articles empowering it to do so.[553]

Because the climate change convention explicitly states that these principles are to guide the parties, these principles are not necessarily binding rules that must be complied with. Yet, they are not void of legal effects either. They are relevant to the interpretation and implementation of the convention and 'create expectations concerning matters which must be taken into account in good faith in negotiations of further instruments'.[554] This, as Bodansky notes, may be achieved by placing the objective and guiding principles in separate articles, giving them greater legal status than placing

---

environmental and economic consequences of tobacco consumption, under, for example, the principle of informing every person of the adverse consequences of tobacco consumption and the need to take measures against tobacco consumption, *see* Arts 3 and 4).

    Another interesting set of negotiation-influencing rules are the Draft Articles on a Law of Transboundary Aquifers, in *Official Records of the General Assembly, Sixty-third Session, Supplement No. 10* (A/63/10). Although these rules have never become binding, they were meant by the ILC to serve as binding guidance for further bilateral negotiations on shared groundwater resources, The Law on Transboundary Aquifers would formulate some minimal legal standards to this effect. *See* N. Matz-Lück, *Framework Conventions as a Regulatory Tool*, 1 Goettingen Journal of International Law 439, 449–450 (2009). These draft articles, in other words, have the characteristics of an 'agreement to scope'.

550. A. Chayes and A.H. Chayes (1995) p. 11.
551. P.W. Birnie, A.E. Boyle and C. Redgwell (2009) p. 357.
552. United Nations Framework Convention on Climate Change, Art. 3.
553. P.W. Birnie, A.E. Boyle and C. Redgwell (2009) pp. 358–359.
554. *Id.*, at p. 359.

them in the convention's preamble would.[555] Also, it is possible that the formulation of principles in the manner above causes these principles to arise to become customary international law.[556]

So, in sum, including principles in the articles of the convention guides the conscious development of the commitments under regime.

7.4.2 The Use of Objectives and Guiding Principles in the Multilateral Agreement for International Taxation

As for international tax law, the managerial approach requires the conscious development of the multilateral agreement towards commonly identified ideals. Once guiding principles have been identified, further negotiations can take place under the 'agreement to scope' or framework convention-protocol designs.

Let us examine several examples of guiding principles and objectives for a managerial multilateral treaty below.

Objectives

The development and modernisation of the international tax treaty network. It is clear that international tax law needs a mechanism to more quickly respond to developments in, for example, society, technology and business. As argued in this book, the multilateral agreement for international taxation is key in this regard.

Transparent, continuous and inclusive tax lawmaking. A general type of objective of a managerial multilateral treaty could be one that progressively aims to achieve the procedural requirements set forth in Chapter 4.

Principles

The negotiations can be further influenced and guided by several principles. This section does not aim to make any normative claims as regards their contents, as this would require a separate study into the contents of 'better' substantive international tax rules for the future. Besides, as argued in Chapter 4.1, views on substantive international tax law are likely to be heavily contested. For instance, it is likely that alternative accounts on what constitutes 'fair' corporate income taxation may arise. But in a normative desert, actors can enter into a norm-generating discourse, emphasising the need for structural, procedural managerial underpinnings to international

---

555. D. Bodansky (1993) p. 502.
556. This has, for instance, been argued as regards the precautionary principle: O. Mcintyre and T. Mosedale, *The Precautionary Principle as a Norm of Customary International Law*, 9 Journal of Environmental Law 221 (1997). In fact, to *prevent* such an effect, Bodansky notes, the United States pressed for several changes in the text of the climate change convention: the words 'to guide' was added, the term 'states' was replaced by 'Parties' to signify the limited scope of the principles, and the term '*inter alia*' was added to indicate that other principles than those listed in the article could be taken into account in implementing the convention. D. Bodansky (1993) pp. 501–502.

taxation.[557] Nevertheless, as a way of illustrating an understanding of 'guiding principles' in a managerial tax treaty, some suggestions are provided here. These suggestions are based on the underlying ideas related to the BEPS Project.

For instance, states could agree on an equality principle, in which they agree to treat, for tax purposes, income derived from the cross-border business activities of firms equal to income derived from the non-cross-border (i.e., domestic) business activities of firms.[558] Another suggestion is that parties adhere to the principle of single taxation of corporate income. The single tax principle prevents undertaxation as well as overtaxation, and as Avi-Yonah notes, its normative basis is thus:

> if income derived from cross-border transactions is taxed more heavily than domestic income, the added tax burden creates an inefficient incentive to invest domestically (...) if income from cross-border transactions is taxed less heavily than domestic income, this creates an inefficient incentive to invest internationally rather than at home.[559]

The nexus principle (taxation at the location where economic substance is situated) might be another candidate, as it represents a conception that lies at the heart of the OECD's BEPS Project. Adherence to the nexus principle in guiding the development of international tax might propel evolution towards destination-based corporate tax systems, in which transactions rather than production factors determine a country's corporate tax claims.[560] Finally, treaty negotiators could agree on a principle that allows for the explicit consideration of the source taxation rights of selected developing countries in future negotiations. Part of the outrage caused by MNE BEPS activities relates to the position of developing nations. Developing countries have limited means to assess and collect taxes. Moreover, as Lang and Owens point out, a lack of transparency and the fear of losing foreign investment lead to weak domestic rules, making it hard for developing countries to counter tax avoidance.[561] This could, for instance, lead negotiators to consider tax treaties to function as development aid,[562] for

---

557. T. Risse (2000) shows that when international actors are faced with a 'normative desert', they argue, i.e., they engage in deliberative processes. For this, he refers to the work of Habermas.
558. M.F. De Wilde (2015a) p. 90.
559. R.S. Avi-Yonah (2007) p. 9. *See also* M.F. De Wilde (2015a) p. 49 who holds that 'it is unfair to tax economic rents more than once or less than once'.
560. *See, e.g.,* A. Auerbach and M.P. Devereux (2013); A. Auerbach and M.P. Devereux (2015) and M.F. De Wilde (2015a) Ch. 6.3. As Ault says, some (non-BEPS related) developments in international tax can be interpreted as a general move in the direction of recognising more taxing rights in the 'source' jurisdiction in the economic sense, away from the fixed base and physical presence tests as prerequisites for claiming taxing rights. Such developments include proposals for allocating taxing rights on the basis of the utilisation of services in a country and the ultimate consumption of goods. H.J. Ault, *Some Reflections on the OECD and the Sources of International Tax Principles*, 70 Tax Notes International 1195 (2013).
561. M. Lang and J.P. Owens, *The Role of Tax Treaties in Facilitating Development and Protecting the Tax Base*, WU International Taxation Research Paper Series No. 2014-03 (2014), available at SSRN: http://ssrn.com/abstract = 2398438.
562. *See, e.g.,* on tax treaties as development aid: K. Brooks, *Tax Treaty Treatment of Royalty Payments from Low-Income Countries: A Comparison of Canada and Australia's Policies,* 5 eJournal of Tax Research 169 (2007); P. Pistone, *Tax Treaties with Developing Countries: A Plea for New Allocation Rules and a Combined Legal and Economic Approach,* in: Tax Treaties: Building Bridges between Law and Economics (M. Lang et al., eds, IBFD 2010).

instance, by providing an exemption of foreign income instead of a credit as relief for double taxation.[563]

7.5 THE MULTILATERAL AGREEMENT'S NETWORK EFFECTS

7.5.1 Introduction

It is questionable whether the multilateral agreement for international taxation will be universally accepted, and, as argued, the amount of participating states involved in the nuts and bolts of international tax lawmaking should be incrementally rather than drastically increased. Consequently, some states will – initially or permanently – not participate. It may also be likely that not all of a state's treaties will be covered by the agreement. Nevertheless, the multilateral agreement's 'network effects' may be of importance in the light of the design strategy. They may lead to a more widespread use, development and acceptance of the multilateral agreement's norms.

Treaties can however not be binding on third states due to the *pacta tertiis* rule of international public law. As Article 34 VCLT holds:[564] 'a treaty does not create rights or obligations for a third state without its consent'. Sinclair summarises: 'in so far as the treaty may bear the attributes of a contract, third states are clearly strangers to that contract'.[565] However, a multilateral convention, albeit non-binding on them, may *affect* third states. And indeed, the principle of Article 34 can best be seen as establishing a general presumption that allows some exceptions.[566] After all, the multilateral agreement, once concluded, 'is there'.[567] In other words, any treaty that is in force is a reality for third parties as well.

Let us single out three potential exceptions to the *pacta tertiis* rule in public international law (section 7.5.2), to see whether the multilateral agreement can influence the tax treaties of third states, either 'automatically' (i.e., on the basis of the

---

563. Pistone, for instance, argues for a simplified allocation framework such as the one applied within the ILADT Latin American Model Convention. This Model provides for relief on the basis of an exemption method for almost all types of income it allocates, and favours taxation at source: P. Pistone, *Geographical Boundaries of Tax Jurisdiction, Exclusive Allocation of Taxing Powers in Tax Treaties and Good Tax Governance in Relations with Developing Countries*, in: Tax, Law and Development (Y. Brauner and M. Stewart eds, Elgar Publishing 2013). For a comparison of the ILADT MTC with the OECD MTC: P. Schoueri, *Comparison of the OECD and ILADT Model Conventions*, 68 Bulletin for International Fiscal Documentation (2014).

564. The *pacta tertiis* rule also follows from, for example, Art. 26 and Art. 2(1)(g) VCLT. Art. 26 holds that: 'Every treaty is binding upon the parties to it and must be performed by them in good faith.' A 'party' is defined in Art. 2 as 'a State which has consented to be bound by the treaty and for which the treaty is in force'.

565. I. Sinclair, *The Vienna Convention on the Law of Treaties* (Manchester University Press 2nd ed., 1984) pp. 98–99.

566. *Id.*, at p. 101.

567. B. Vukas, *Treaties, Third-Party Effect*, in: The Max Planck Encyclopedia of Public International Law (R. Wolfrum ed., OUP Online ed., 2011).

existing rules of public international law) or by design. Section 7.5.3, subsequently, considers the relevance of these three exceptions from the perspective of the design strategy.

First of all, there is a possible although remote chance that the institutionalisation of fiscal norms by means of a multilateral agreement could lead to a situation where its norms become a binding obligation on third states through state practice (action) or acquiescence or estoppel (inaction) (see section 7.5.2.1). Second, the multilateral tax agreement could influence the interpretation of bilateral tax treaties with non-signatory states. The institutionalisation of binding fiscal norms could require the treaty interpreter of a non-related tax treaty to take the norms of the multilateral agreement into account on the basis of Article 31(3)(c) VCLT when interpreting that tax treaty (see section 7.5.2.2). Finally, it is possible for signatory states to agree to bring their bilateral tax treaties in conformity with the rules of the multilateral agreement as it is updated from time to time (a *pactum de agendo, see* section 7.5.2.3).

7.5.2 Network Effects in International Public Law

7.5.2.1 Can the Norms of a Multilateral Agreement Become a Binding Obligation on Third States Through Estoppel or Acquiescence?

There is evidence from international public law that suggests that the law of treaties permits some normative influence on treaties in which a third state is a party. Indeed, it can be argued that state practice can lead to the formation of such a normative influence. It is generally accepted that 'positive' state practice of the non-signatory state can indeed influence the interpretation of a treaty[568] and can even modify or amend it.[569] State practice in this regard could, for instance, relate to a third state's exercise of influence on the creation of norms adopted under the framework convention. A state could file a formal statement as regards its position on a norm. Also, state practice can be formed if a third state has not accepted the norm on a multilateral level, but nevertheless uses the norm in its subsequent bilateral tax treaties.

More interestingly, however, is the question whether the construction of state practice in a 'negative' way,[570] i.e., on the basis of *inaction*, can influence the treaty

---

568. *See* Art. 31(3)(b) VCLT.
569. *See,* the advisory opinion of the ICJ in ICJ, *Legal Consequences for States of the Continued Presence of South Africa in Namibia (South West Africa) Notwithstanding Security Council Resolution 276 (1970),* (Advisory Opinion), [1971] IJC Reports 16, para. 22, where the ICJ interpreted the voting practice of abstaining members of the UN Security Council as to not constituting a bar to the adoption of resolutions. Also, *see* the ILC, which held that 'A consistent practice, establishing the common consent of the parties to the application of the treaty in a manner different from that laid down in certain of its provisions, may have the effect *of modifying the treaty'*, ILC, *Draft Articles on the Law of Treaties with Commentaries* (Yearbook of the International Law Commission, 1966, vol. II 1966) p. 236 (emphasis added).
570. For this distinction, *see* I.C. Macgibbon, *The Scope of Acquiescence in International Law,* 31 British Year Book of International Law 143 (1954); ICJ, *Case Concerning the Temple of Preah Vihear (Cambodia v. Thailand),* (Separate Opinion of Sir Gerald Fitzmaurice, Judgement of 15 Jun. 1962), (1962) IJC Reports 3 p. 55.

relationship between a member and a non-signatory state. Legal constructs that endow legal effects to inaction are called acquiescence and estoppel. Could it be argued that if one of the parties to a tax convention has accepted certain norms under the multilateral agreement, and a third party has not, the third state has acquiesced in, or is estopped from, denying to apply and interpret the norms of a bilateral tax treaty concluded after the date of adoption of the multilateral agreement in line with the norms created under the multilateral agreement, if that party has remained silent as regards the effects and functioning of these norms?[571] An example: could it be, in the situation described above, that the third state has acquiesced in the use of a PPT (such as set forth in Action 6)?[572] If such a tacit agreement exists, this agreement could operate as 'any subsequent agreement between the parties regarding the interpretation of the treaty or the application of its provisions', which has to be taken into account together with the context, in the process of treaty interpretation, on the basis of Article 31(3)(a) VCLT.

A clue that the multilateral agreement can indeed have this effect on bilateral tax treaties with third states is Article 103 of the Charter of the UN. This provision holds:

> In the event of a conflict between the obligations of the Members of the United Nations under the present Charter and their obligations under any other international agreement, their obligations under the present Charter shall prevail.

In simple terms, the provision holds that the Charter shall prevail over other agreements, also in relation to agreements concluded between UN Member States and non-UN Member States. Although the issue is of limited relevance in practice considering the UN's almost universal membership,[573] authors writing at a time when the UN did not have such an extended membership questioned whether non-members were formally bound to the Charter by Article 103.[574] One argument that surfaced was that third states were bound on the basis of good faith or estoppel in respect to treaties

---

571. This argument is based on F.A. Engelen (2004) pp. 469–472. Engelen's argument runs as follows: 'It is submitted that the parties to a tax treaty concluded between OECD Member countries cannot assert in good faith that the provisions of the treaty must be given a different meaning than the one established in the Commentaries on the identical provisions of the OECD Model Tax Convention in so far as: (a) both parties have voted in favour of the recommendations concerning the Model made by the OECD Council pursuant to Article 5(b) of the OECD Convention; (b) neither party has entered a reservation on the provisions of the Model nor made an observation on the interpretation of those provisions as set out in the Commentaries thereon; (c) the treaty follows the pattern and the main provisions of the Model; and (d) neither party has indicated in the course of the actual negotiations that it understood the provisions of the treaty differently than as set out in the Commentaries on the identical provisions of the Model. In these circumstances, the presumption must be that the parties have acquiesced in the interpretation set out in the Commentaries. The acquiescence of both parties amounts to a tacit agreement to interpret and apply the provisions of the treaty that are identical to those of the OECD Model Tax Convention in accordance with the Commentaries thereon, and the context for the purpose of the interpretation of the treaty comprises such an agreement on the grounds of Article 31(2)(a) VCLT. In addition, the acquiescence of both parties can also operate as estoppel in cases where one of the parties would later assert that a different interpretation was in fact intended.'
572. OECD, *Preventing the Granting of Treaty Benefits in Inappropriate Circumstances, Action 6: 2015 Final Report* (2015).
573. A. Aust (2013) p. 195.
574. A. Paulus and J.R. Leiss, *Article 103*, in: The Charter of the United Nations: A Commentary (B. Simma et al., eds, OUP 3d ed., 2012) p. 2130.

concluded after the accession of a Member State.[575] Could the knowledge of the non-Member State that UN members had limited their competence under the UN Charter estop the non-Member State from denying the obligations under the Charter when applying a treaty concluded between it and a UN Member State?[576] It seems clear that even though non-Member States are not bound to the primacy of the UN Charter, they must *recognise* that *their treaty parties*, as Member States of the UN, *are* bound to the Charter through Article 103.[577]

For acquiescence and estoppel to arise, however, the circumstances that an inaction or silence can be interpreted as consent or as estoppel need to be clear and convincing. 'Acquiescence is not lightly to be presumed.'[578] As the ICJ expressed in the *North Sea Continental Shelf* case:

> [O]nly a *very definite, very consistent course of conduct* on the part of a State (...) could justify the Court in upholding [the contention that the rule for the delimitation of the continental shelf had become binding in another way].[579]

And in the *Case Concerning the Land and Maritime Boundary between Cameroon and Nigeria:*

> An estoppel would only arise if by its acts or declarations Cameroon had consistently made it fully clear that it had agreed to settle the boundary dispute submitted to the Court (...).[580]

The *Temple of Preah Vihear* case is particularly noteworthy in relation to the concept of acquiescence and also estoppel.[581] The case concerned a boundary dispute between Cambodia and Thailand (then called Siam).

In 1904, the two governments signed a bilateral boundary treaty that held that the boundary would follow a watershed line that placed the Temple on (then) Siamese

---

575. *Id.*, at p. 2130. It was also claimed that this was the case due to the special character of the UN as a peace keeping organisation and due to its extensive membership. *See, e.g.*, W. Czaplinski and G. Danilenko, *Conflicts of Norms in International Law*, 21 Netherlands Yearbook of International Law 3, 15–17 (1990).

576. R.S.J. Macdonald, *Fundamental Norms in Contemporary International Law*, 25 Canandian Yearbook of International Law 115, 122–123 (1987).

577. R. Liivoja, *The Scope of the Supremacy Clause of the United Nations Charter*, 57 International and Comparative Law Quarterly 583, 596 (2008). This idea seems to stem from E. Sciso, *On Article 103 of the Charter of the United Nations in the Light of the Vienna Convention on the Law of Treaties*, 38 Österreichische Zeitschrift für Öffentliches Recht und Völkerrecht 161 (1987), who relates the argument to the operation of Art. 30 VCLT. Since Art. 30 VCLT explicitly exempts Art. 103 of the UN Charter from the working of the *lex posterior* rule, it could be argued that the Charter's priority over treaties of non-members can be found in a general rule of international law, as codified in Art. 30 VCLT. *See* pp. 167–168 and in particular footnote 19.

578. *See* K.H. Kaikobad, *Some Observations on the Doctrine of Continuity and Finality of Boundaries*, 54 British Yearbook of International Law 119, 126 (1984); *Case Concerning the Temple of Preah Vihear (Cambodia v. Thailand)*.

579. ICJ, *North Sea Continental Shelf (Federal Republic of Germany v. Denmark; Federal Republic of Germany v. the Netherlands)*, (Judgement), [1969] IJC Reports 3, at para. 30.

580. ICJ, *Case Concerning the Land and Maritime Boundary Between Cameroon and Nigeria (Cameroon v. Nigeria)*, Preliminary Objections (Judgement), [1998] ICJ Reports 275 para. 57.

581. ICJ, *Case Concerning the Temple of Preah Vihear (Cambodia v. Thailand)*, (Merits, Judgement of 15 Jun. 1962), [1962] IJC Reports 3. In the case, like in the Namibia opinion, the line between treaty amendment and treaty interpretation by subsequent conduct is blurred, *see* above.

territory. Also, the treaty stipulated that a Joint Commission should delimitate the boundary between Siam and Cambodia. However, no records could be found of the Commission's decision on which side of the boundary the Temple of Preah Vihear lay, a beautiful and important religious monument for the peoples of both states. The Siamese representatives of the Commission requested the French authorities to map the border region. The resulting map, which placed the temple on Cambodian territory, was communicated to the Siamese government.

Fifty years later, this map was presented to the ICJ by the Cambodian government, to show that the Temple was located on Cambodian and not on Siamese territory.[582] As regards this map, the Court held that, because the Siamese government had failed to react, it must have tacitly agreed with the boundary set out therein:

> In fact, as will be seen presently, an acknowledgment by conduct was undoubtedly made in a very definite way; but even if it were otherwise, it is clear that the circumstances were such as called for some reaction, within a reasonable period, on the part of the Siamese authorities, if they wished to disagree with the map or had any serious question to raise in regard to it. They did not do so, either then or for many years, and thereby must be held to have acquiesced. *Qui tacet consentire videtur si loqui debuisset ac potuisset.*[583]

There were two circumstances that called for some action on the part of Siam, leading the Court to consider that the Siamese government had acquiesced in the use of the map's boundary. First of all, the government of Siam *itself* requested French topographical officers to prepare the maps of the border regions. The map produced and subsequently communicated to the Siamese government and made public by the French was thus a product of this request. It could therefore be argued that the Siamese government accepted the risk of any mistakes in the map, and it was up to them to verify the results.[584]

Second, the practice of the Siamese government 'on the ground' pointed in the direction of acquiescence.[585] Prince Damrong of Siam, formerly Minister of the Interior of Siam, had visited the premises of the Temple. At the time of his visit, he was president of the Royal Institute of Siam, charged with duties related to archaeological monuments:

> When the prince arrived at Preah Vihear, he was officially received by the French Resident for the Adjoining Cambodian Province (...) with the French flag flying. On the return [of the Prince] to Bangkok, [he] sent the French Resident some photographs of the occasion [and] he used language which seems to admit that France, through her Resident, had acted as the host country.[586]

The circumstances in the Temple case thus clearly *provoked* a reaction on the part the authorities of the Siamese government. The French flag was flying, on disputed

---

582. *See also*, for a discussion of the case, F.A. Engelen (2008) pp. 53–55.
583. *Case Concerning the Temple of Preah Vihear (Cambodia v. Thailand)* p. 23.
584. *Case Concerning the Temple of Preah Vihear (Cambodia v. Thailand)* p. 58.
585. *Case Concerning the Temple of Preah Vihear (Cambodia v. Thailand)* p. 29.
586. *Id.*, at p. 30 (emphasis added).

grounds. Yet, the Siamese representative did not say anything. On the contrary: the minister even sent his French host some photographs of the occasion!

The *Gulf of Maine* and the *Fisheries* cases provide further evidence that provocative circumstances must be present in order to interpret silence as consent. The *Gulf of Maine* case involved a boundary dispute between the US and Canada. Canada had issued permits, on its own side of what it regarded as the median line dividing the fish-rich Georges Bank, for the exclusive exploitation of hydrocarbons. According to Canada, the issue of these permits led to a circumstance under which the US had acquiesced in the idea to adopt a median line as the boundary between the two jurisdictions.[587] These permits were published in the *Monthly Oil and Gas Report*. The Court, however, considered:

> The facts being as described, the Chamber does not feel able to draw the conclusion that the United States acquiesced in delimitation of the Georges Bank continental shelf by a median line.[588]

Clearly, the fact that Canada had issued the exploitation permits did not generate such circumstances as to provoke a reaction from the US. Canada had never issued an official proclamation or other publication for the purpose of advertising its claims internationally.[589] They concerned technical and an internal matter.

In the *Fisheries case*,[590] on the other hand, the circumstances were much more 'consistent' and 'clear'. Norway had drawn straight baselines to delimit a maritime area despite a very irregular and tormented coastline. The dispute concerned the validity of the use of these baselines, as by using these lines, the waters under Norwegian sovereignty were extended.[591] The Court reasoned that the system was consistently applied and enforced by Norway for more than sixty years. More importantly, the Court had encountered no opposition on the part of other states.[592] Particularly, as to the United Kingdom, the Court considered:

> [A]s a coastal state on the North Sea, greatly interested in the fisheries in this area, as a maritime Power traditionally concerned with the law of the sea and concerned particularly to defend the freedom of the seas, the United Kingdom could not have been ignorant of the [delimitation] Decree of 1869, which had at once provoked a request for explanations (...).[593]

---

587. ICJ, *Delimitation of the Maritime Boundary in the Gulf of Maine Area (Canada v. United States of America)*, (Judgement), [1984] IJC Reports 246 pp. 305–306. *See also* H. Thirlway, *The Law and Procedure of the International Court of Justice 1960–1989: Part One*, 60 British Yearbook of International Law 1, 35 (1990).
588. *Delimitation of the Maritime Boundary in the Gulf of Maine Area (Canada v. United States of America)* para. 137.
589. This was in fact an argument used by the US. *See, id.*, at p. 306.
590. ICJ, *Fisheries Case (United Kingdom v. Norway)*, (Judgement), [1951] ICJ Reports 116.
591. R. Kolb, *Principles as Sources of International Law (With Special Reference to Good Faith)*, 53 Netherlands International Law Review 1, 21 (2006).
592. *Fisheries Case (United Kingdom v. Norway)* pp. 136–137.
593. *Id.*, at p. 139.

As a result, the court held that the United Kingdom must have acquiesced in the use of the lines,[594] as:

> The notoriety of the facts, the general toleration of the international community, Great Britain's position in the North Sea, her own interest in the question, and her prolonged abstention would in any case warrant Norway's enforcement of her system against the United Kingdom.[595]

So, for a successful claim on acquiescence or estoppel,[596] circumstances must be present so as to clearly provoke a party to act. Such a provocation may occur when one party triggers another party to respond, for instance, by claiming that it applies or interprets a bilateral treaty with a non-signatory state in line with the multilateral agreement, as this statement would run contrary to the *pacta tertiis* rule.

7.5.2.2 The Influence of a Multilateral Agreement on the Interpretation of Treaties with Third States[597]

A second, more likely, but indirect influence is that of treaty interpretation: it is possible that the Vienna Convention requires the taking into account of rules established in the multilateral agreement in the process of interpreting tax treaties between third states and signatory states. Even if the multilateral agreement lacks binding force in relation to third states in the manner described above, that does not prevent it from having an impact on tax treaty interpretation. Indeed, a treaty does not exist in a legal vacuum. A treaty has a normative environment, or 'system', that cannot be ignored in the process of interpretation. This is in accordance with the principle of systemic integration, which is embodied in Article 31(3)(c) of the Vienna Convention.[598] The principle requires 'the integration into the process of legal reasoning – including reasoning by courts and tribunals – of a sense of coherence and meaningfulness'.[599]

---

594. *See* R. Kolb (2006) pp. 21–22; I. Sinclair, *Estoppel and Acquiescence*, in: Fifty Years of the International Court of Justice: Essays in Honour of Sir Robert Jennings (V. Lowe and R. Jennings eds, Cambridge University Press 1996) pp. 112–113.
595. *Fisheries Case (United Kingdom v. Norway)* p. 139.
596. For an estoppel to arise, the same circumstances are required as for a claim on acquiescence, except as regards the requirement of detriment on the part of the claimant, which is unique to the concept of estoppel. This clearly follows from the case law of the ICJ: 'Since the same facts are relevant to both acquiescence and estoppel, except as regards the existence of detriment, [the Court] is able to take the two concepts into consideration as different aspects of one and the same institution.' *Delimitation of the Maritime Boundary in the Gulf of Maine Area (Canada v. United States of America)*, para. 130.
597. This section is partly based on D.M. Broekhuijsen (2013a), an article the author previously wrote on Art. 31(3)(c) VCLT and the status of the OECD Commentaries. The conclusion of the article is that, considering case law of the ECtHR, the ICJ's *Oil Platforms* case and the ILC's fragmentation report, it is possible to justify recourse to the OECD Commentaries on the basis of Art. 31(3)(c) VCLT when interpreting tax treaties.
598. ILC, *Fragmentation of International Law: Difficulties Arising From the Diversification and Expansion of International Law* (2006) Report of the Study Group of the International Law Commission, para. 419.
599. *Id.*, at para. 419.

Article 31(3)(c) VCLT holds that:

> There shall be taken into account, together with the context (...) (c) any relevant
> rules of international law applicable in the relations between the parties.

Considering the backdrop of the principle of systemic integration, Article 31(3)(c) VCLT must be placed within the general rule of interpretation of Article 31, which also includes the context, object and purpose and the ordinary meaning of a treaty phrase. It cannot be seen to act on a stand-alone basis.[600] Consequently, if the other elements of Article 31, such as the treaty's text, context and object and purpose, cannot provide the interpreter with an argument to take into account the normative environment of a treaty which lies beyond its close proximity,[601] recourse to Article 31(3)(c) may be made in order to proceed in a reasoned way.[602]

The article poses three basic requirements. It requires that the extraneous material is a (1) relevant (2) rule of international law that (3) is applicable in the relations between parties. It is argued that each of these elements must be read as an integrated whole 'to ensure some degree of coherence in international law'.[603]

Still, it is necessary to determine to what types of 'rules of international law' that are 'applicable in the relations between parties' Article 31(3)(c) VCLT refers. Scholars agree that 'any relevant rules of international law' refers to any formal source of international public law such as a treaty, a rule of customary international law and a general principle of international law, if applicable in the relation between parties.[604] The ICJ referred, for instance, to the UN Charter and to customary international law in the *Oil Platforms* Case,[605] when interpreting the 1955 Treaty of Amity, Economic Relations and Consular Rights between Iran and the United States. It considered:

> [I]nterpretation must take into account 'any relevant rules of international law
> applicable in the relations between the parties' (Art. 31, para 3 (c)). The Court
> cannot accept that Article XX, paragraph 1(d) of the 1955 Treaty was intended to
> operate wholly independently of the relevant rules of international law on the use

---

600. Article 31 is headed 'general rule of interpretation', not 'general *rules* of interpretation'. Indeed, as the ILC expressed it in the Commentaries on the VCLT: 'Thus, article 27 is entitled "General rule of interpretation" in the singular, not "General rules" in the plural, because the Commission desired to emphasise that the process of interpretation is a unity and that the provisions of the article form a single, closely integrated rule.' *See Draft Articles on Responsibility of States for Internationally Wrongful Acts with Commentaries* (2001), UN Doc A/56/109, May 2011. *See also* D.M. Broekhuijsen (2013) sec. 3.1.
601. ILC, *Fragmentation of International Law* (2006) para. 423.
602. *See*, for this argument, D.M. Broekhuijsen (2013a) sec. 3.1.
603. Concurring Opinion of Judge Wojtyczek, ECtHR, *Case of the National Union of Rail, Maritime and Transport Workers v. The United Kingdom*, No. 31045/10 (judgement), 8 Apr. 2014, pp. 44–45.
604. M.E. Villiger, *Commentary on the 1969 Vienna Convention on the Law of Treaties* (Nijhoff 2009) p. 433; R. Gardiner, *Treaty Interpretation* (OUP paperback ed., 2008) pp. 267–268; C. Mclachlan, *The Principle of Systemic Integration and Article 31 (3)(c) of the Vienna Convention*, 54 International and Comparative Law Quarterly 279, 290–291 (2005); ILC, *Fragmentation of International Law* (2006) para. 425–426.
605. DE: Bundesfinanzhof *Re Article 11(6) of the UK-Germany DTC – the 'Theatrical Producer' Case*, (1997) 1 ITLR 860; IR 51/96, para. 31.

of force (...) The application of the relevant rules of international law relating to this question thus forms an integral part of the task of interpretation.[606]

And in the *Mutual Assistance in Criminal Matters* case, the ICJ considered that the 1977 Treaty of Friendship and Cooperation between France and Djibouti could bear on the obligations of another treaty in force between the same parties: the 1986 Convention on Mutual Assistance in Criminal Matters.[607]

Thus, as a matter of international public law, there seems no doubt that when interpreting the obligations of a treaty, *another* treaty in force between the *same* parties has to be taken into account on the basis of Article 31(3)(c) VCLT. The question therefore is: can the phrase 'applicable in the relations between the parties' also refer to treaties which one of the parties accepted, but the other did not? The matter can be discussed on two of the provision's elements.

First of all, what does 'the parties' mean? An important argument in this regard is Article 2(2)(g) VCLT, which holds that:

> For the purposes of the present convention: (...) (g) 'Party' means a State which has consented to be bound by the treaty and for which the treaty is in force.

Thus, when considering this provision, a correct interpretation is one in which the term 'the parties' is held to mean 'all the parties to the interpreted treaty'.[608] However, it can be argued that this provision only applies to the parties *to the instrument interpreted*. When considering 'the parties' to *the instrument relied upon*, it can be argued that Article 31(3)(c) VCLT leaves more room for interpretation.[609]

So, it is necessary to consider the provision's second element: what does 'applicable' in the relations between the parties mean? Article 31(3)(c) VCLT refers to *applicable* rules in the relations between the parties. When analysed textually, the term 'applicable' allows for more flexibility than 'in force' or 'binding' would.[610] Indeed, as Pauwelyn notes, a textual analysis lends support to the view that a rule can be considered as within the scope of Article 31(3)(c) if this rule is at least implicitly accepted or tolerated by the parties to the treaty being interpreted; the rule should reasonably express the common intentions or understandings of all treaty parties as to

---

606. *See, id.,* at para. 31.
607. M. Fitzmaurice, *Dynamic Intermigration of Treaties,* 21 Hague Yearbook of International Law 101, 112–113 (2009).
608. *See* U. Linderfalk, *Who are 'The Parties'? Article 31 Paragraph 3(c) of the 1969 Vienna Convention and the 'Principle of Systemic Integration' Revisited,* 55 Netherlands International Law Review 343 (2008). Similarly: M. Samson, *High Hopes, Scant Resources: A Word of Scepticism about the Anti-Fragmentation Function of Article 31(3)(c) of the Vienna Convention on the Law of Treaties,* 24 Leiden Journal of International Law 701 (2011) sec. 3. However, it can also be argued that if *all* the parties to the treaty being interpreted must also be parties to the treaty relied upon, it would be unlikely that any reference to other conventional international law could be made in the interpretation of widely accepted multilateral treaties. Consequently, it has been suggested that 'the parties' means 'the parties to the dispute', *see* ILC, *Fragmentation of International Law* (2006) para. 472.
609. J. Pauwelyn, *Conflict of Norms in Public International Law: How WTO Law Relates to other Rules of International Law* (Cambridge University Press 2003) p. 261.
610. *See* B. Simma and T. Kill, *Harmonizing Investment Protection and International Human Rights: First Steps Towards a Methodology?,* in: International Investment Law for the 21st Century: Essays in Honour of Christoph Schreuer (C. Binder et al., eds, OUP 2009) pp. 696–697.

what the particular term means.[611] Does, in other words, 'applicable' mean 'binding' or 'in force', or can it also refer to standards or treaties that are not binding on the treaty parties to a bilateral tax treaty?

Authors are cautious in extending Article 31(3)(c) VCLT to soft law or to treaties that are not ratified or signed by all states to the treaty under consideration.[612] Nevertheless, in practice, Article 31(3)(c) is used to justify recourse to soft law materials,[613] as well as to other treaties not signed or ratified by (all) the parties to the agreement under consideration.[614] For instance, in the *Saadi v. The United Kingdom* judgment, the European Court of Human Rights (ECtHR) held that 'the European Convention on Human Rights does not apply in a vacuum',[615] and by using Article 31(3)(c) VCLT,[616] referred to materials such as the guidelines of the UN High Commissioner for Refugees (UNHCR), Council of Europe recommendations and a recommendation of the UN Working Group on Arbitrary Detention.[617] Likewise, in *Demir and Baykara v. Turkey*, the ECtHR explicitly considered, by reference to its previous case law, whether it could rely on the European Social Charter, an instrument that Turkey had not ratified, on the basis of Article 31(3)(c) VCLT.[618] Turkey argued that an international treaty to which it had not acceded could not be relied upon against it.[619] The Court however, considered:

> 76. Being made up of a set of rules and principles that are accepted by the vast majority of States, *the common international or domestic law standards of*

611. J. Pauwelyn (2003a) p. 261. *See* similarly, B. Simma and T. Kill (2009) pp. 697–698.
612. *See*, in particular, M.E. Villiger (2009) p. 433, who holds that 'the term "applicable" leaves no room for doubt: non-binding rules cannot be relied upon'. And *see*, Orakhelashvili, who says that Art. 31(3)(c) VCLT: 'covers only established rules of international law, to the exclusion of principles of uncertain or doubtful legal status, so-called evolving legal standards, policy factors or more generally related notions'. A. Orakhelashvili, *The Interpretation of Acts and Rules in Public International Law* (OUP 2008) p. 366. Linderfalk holds: 'each and every one of those states bound by the interpreted treaty at the time of interpretation must also be bound by the relevant rule of law.' U. Linderfalk, *Doing the Right Thing for the Right Reason – Why Dynamic or Static Approaches Should be Taken in the Interpretation of Treaties*, 10 International Community Law Review 109, 112 (2008).
613. *See*, for instance, the case: ECtHR, *Demir and Baykara v. Turkey*, No. 34503/97 (judgement), 12 Nov. 2008, paras 45–51 and 103–105. Other cases in which the ECtHR referred to non-binding standards by reference to Art. 31(3)(c) VCLT were, for example, the *Case of the National Union of Rail, Maritime and Transport Workers v. The United Kingdom* and ECtHR, *Al-Adsani v. United Kingdom*, No. 35763/97 (judgement), 21 Nov. 2001. For a discussion, *see* T. Barkhuysen and M.L. Van Emmerik, *Ongebonden binding: Verwijzing naar soft law-standaarden in uitspraken van het EHRM*, 35 NJCM-Bulletin 827 (2010) A. Mowbray, *The Creativity of the European Court of Human Rights*, 5 Human Rights Law Review 57 (2005). When looking at how the article is applied in practice, it seems to allow recourse to soft law and thus also to the OECD Commentary, *see* D.M. Broekhuijsen (2013a).
614. *See*, in particular, *Demir and Baykara v. Turkey*, but also, for example, cases the ECtHR referred to: ECtHR, *Marckx v. Belgium*, No. 6833/74 (judgement), 13 Jun. 1979. For a discussion, *see* H.C.K. Senden, *Interpretation of Fundamental Rights in a Multilevel Legal System* (Intersentia 2011) Ch. 10.
615. ECtHR, *Saadi v. The United Kingdom*, No. 13229/03 (judgement), 29 Jan. 2008, para. 79.
616. H. Gribnau and A.O. Lubbers, *The Temporal Effect of Dutch Tax Court Decisions*, in: The Effect of Judicial Decisions in Time (P. Popelier et al., eds, Intersentia 2014) paras 62 and 65.
617. *Id.*, at paras 29–37.
618. *Demir and Baykara v. Turkey*, paras 60 and 85–86.
619. *Id.*, at para. 61.

European States reflect a reality that the Court cannot disregard when it is called upon to clarify the scope of a Convention provision that more conventional means of interpretation have not enabled it to establish with a sufficient degree of certainty. (...) 78. *The Court observes in this connection that in searching for common ground* among the norms of international law *it has never distinguished between sources of law according to whether or not they have been signed or ratified* by the respondent State.[620]

Other courts have also referred to the normative environment of a treaty when giving meaning to that treaty's terms. To define the term 'exhaustible natural resources' as in Article XX(g) General Agreement on Tariffs and Trade (GATT) 1994,[621] the WTO's Appellate Body referred to the UN Law of the Sea Convention and to the Convention on Biological Diversity, which were not agreed to by Thailand and the US,[622] even though both states were parties to the dispute. The Court explicitly referred to Article 31(3)(c) VCLT when holding that 'our task here is to interpret the language of the chapeau [of article XX GATT 1994], seeking additional interpretive guidance, as appropriate, from the general principles of international law'.[623]

Given the above, Article 31(3)(c) VCLT can provide an interpretative argument when interpreting a tax treaty with reference to the multilateral agreement, even if one of the parties has not signed this multilateral agreement. However, a few reflections are in order. First of all, caution is warranted when generalising the application of Article 31(3)(c) VCLT on the basis of the case law above.[624] The European Convention on Human Rights (ECHR) has the character of a constitution, which gives effect to universal moral standards. In order to protect these standards under varying and evolving circumstances, a more flexible approach to interpretation is required than under tax treaties, which are reciprocal exchanges of commitments.[625] Second, it follows from ECtHR case law that the point of using extraneous legal sources is to establish the common understandings of the parties to the treaty in dispute. It is submitted that the multilateral agreement for international taxation expresses such understanding only when a third state enters into a tax treaty with a signatory state *after* the multilateral instrument has been concluded.[626]

---

620. *Id.*, at paras 76–78 (emphasis added).
621. WTO Appellate Body *United States – Import Prohibition of Certain Shrimp and Shrimp Products*, Appelate Body Report, 1998 (WT/DS58/AB/R) and the reference to the ICJ's *Legal Consequences for States of the Continued Presence of South Africa in Namibia (South West Africa) Notwithstanding Security Council Resolution 276 (1970)*, opinion, p. 301.
622. *United States – Import Prohibition of Certain Shrimp and Shrimp Products*, para. 130 and footnotes 110–111.
623. *Id.*, at para. 158 and footnote 157. *See also* C. Mclachlan (2005) p. 303. Van Damme holds however that the reference to these materials was based on the principle of effectiveness, not on Art. 31(3)(c) VCLT. *See* I. Van Damme, *Treaty Interpretation by the WTO Appellate Body* (OUP 2009) p. 370.
624. R. Gardiner (2008) p. XXV.
625. M. Fitzmaurice, *Dynamic (Evolutive) Interpretation of Treaties: Part II*, 21 Hague Yearbook of International Law 3, 15–16 (2009); T. Barkhuysen and M.L. Van Emmerik (2010) pp. 834–845.
626. This is one of the presumptions of the principle of systemic integration. *See* C. Mclachlan (2005) p. 311. However, Art. 31(3)(c) is not explicit on whether it applies to the applicable rules of international law determined at the date on which the treaty was concluded (static

7.5.2.3 A Pactum de Agendo: *Harmonising Existing and Future Incompatible Bilateral Treaties with Third States*

A third option to influence the tax treaties between participating and third states is a *pactum de agendo*, which is, unlike the earlier two exceptions to the *pacta tertiis* rule, a conscious design option. A *pactum de agendo*[627] is a clause which establishes the commitment of states to amend their existing incompatible treaties in line with the obligations or 'guiding principles' of the multilateral treaty, and not to enter into incompatible agreements in the future. Such a clause will primarily apply to tax agreements with third states, as these are not included in the direct ambit of both types of multilateral agreement discussed in this chapter due to the *pacta tertiis* rule. A well-drafted *pactum de agendo* can cause the multilateral convention to generate network effects after its conclusion.

A clause that influences the conclusion of *future* agreements is, for instance, used in the North Atlantic Treaty (the NATO Treaty). In this clause, states commit to making an effort not to conclude incompatible agreements in the future:

> Each Party (...) undertakes not to enter into an international engagement in conflict with this Treaty.[628]

Clauses related to future agreements can be abrogated from by later mutual agreement between all the parties. Therefore, such clauses have a limited effect. Nevertheless, the contractual freedom of states seems to be slightly more limited by a *pactum de agendo*. Non-compliance with such a provision might cause the termination or suspension of the treaty into which it is incorporated. This might put states off concluding an incompatible agreement with a third state, as the breach of the *pactum* can cause other parties to the multilateral treaty to terminate it or suspend its operation.[629] Nevertheless, the norms of incompatible future agreements prevail over the rules set out in the multilateral convention, as the treaty applies that governs the parties' mutual relations.[630]

Consequently, the language used in the clause should not leave room for doubt. For instance, the word 'undertake' as in the NATO Treaty leaves states some room to argue against a treaty breach. A stronger obligation to this effect follows from the Chicago Convention on International Civil Aviation:

---

interpretation) or to the applicable rules determined at the date on which the dispute arises (dynamic interpretation). ILC, *Fragmentation of International Law* (2006) para. 426. *See,* for a discussion, U. Linderfalk (2008).

627. *See,* for this term, P. Manzini, *The Priority of Pre-Existing Treaties of EC Member States within the Framework of International Law*, 12 European Journal of International Law 781, 782 (2001).

628. *North Atlantic Treaty* (adopted 4 Apr. 1949), 34 UNTS 243, Art. 8. For more examples: OECD, *Developing a Multilateral Instrument to Modify Bilateral Tax Treaties* (2014) pp. 39–40.

629. If the 'independent' or *inter se* agreement infringes the rights of the other parties to the treaty in which the commitment clause is included, the normal consequences of a treaty breach follow. *See* ILC (1966) pp. 216–217. This could, for instance, lead to the termination of the earlier agreement under Art. 60 VCLT. *See* Art. 30(5) and Art. 41 VCLT.

630. *See* Art. 30(4)(b) VCLT.

Subject to the provisions of the preceding Article, any contracting State may make arrangements not inconsistent with the provisions of this Convention.[631]

A *pactum de agendo* can also relate to *existing* agreements with third states. A good example of such an obligation is Article 351 of the Treaty on the Functioning of the EU, which is, as will be shown, strictly interpreted and applied by the ECJ, even in exceptional circumstances. The provision holds:

The rights and obligations arising from agreements concluded before 1 January 1958 or, for acceding States, before the date of their accession, between one or more Member States on the one hand, and one or more third countries on the other, shall not be affected by the provisions of the Treaties.

To the extent that such agreements are not compatible with the Treaties, the Member State or States concerned shall take all appropriate steps to eliminate the incompatibilities established. Member States shall, where necessary, assist each other to this end and shall, where appropriate, adopt a common attitude.[632]

The above rule is a consequence of the supremacy of EU law: it aims to strike a balance between the *pacta tertiis* rule on the one hand and European integration on the other.[633] To ensure the supremacy of the EU, the Member States are under the obligation to 'take all appropriate steps' to get rid of the inconsistencies existing in their pre-accession treaties with third states. Case law suggests that such 'appropriate steps' could involve the denunciation of a pre-Community agreement if efforts to adjust that agreement failed and the pre-Community treaty expressly provides for its termination or denunciation.[634]

Technically, the distinction between a *pactum de agendo* and a *pactum de negotiando* (*see* section 7.14) may be thin.[635] Both are, after all, procedural obligations under which parties agree to bring – in good faith – other existing and future treaty obligations in line with the treaty obligations of the multilateral treaty. The main difference between a *pactum de agendo* and a *pactum de negotiando* is that the expression of the intention to negotiate under a *pactum de agendo* is made by only one of the two contracting states to, for example, a bilateral convention. Certainly, this

---

631. *Convention on International Civil Aviation* (adopted 12 Jul. 1944), 15 UNTS 295, Art. 83.
632. Treaty on the Functioning of the European Union, Art. 351 (emphasis added). The provision was similarly worded in the older treaties: Art. 234 of the EEC Treaty and Art. 307 of the EC Treaty.
633. Treaty on the Functioning of the European Union, Arts 2 and 3(2). *See also* J. Klabbers, *Treaty Conflict and the European Union* (Cambridge University Press 2009) p. 118.
634. ECJ, *Commission v. Portugal*, 4 Juli 2000, C-62/98 and C-84/98. The Court considered that 'if a Member State encounters difficulties which make adjustment of an agreement impossible, an obligation to denounce the agreement cannot be excluded', *see* paras 46–49. Later case law on the paragraph has followed the Court's analysis. *See* J. Klabbers (2009) p. 139. For further analysis, *see also* P. Manzini (2001).
635. C. Hutchison, *The Duty to Negotiate International Environmental Disputes in Good Faith*, 2 McGill International Journal of Sustainable Development Law and Policy 117 (2006) sec. 4.4 says that as regards the law of watercourses and fish stocks, the obligation to negotiate in good faith resulting from international watercourse law and high seas fisheries law, as established by several court decisions on the matter, requires parties to take into account the interests of third states as well.

means that the obligation of a *pactum de agendo* is less extensive, as the obligation needs only to be performed in good faith by the party that has expressed that intention.

7.5.3 The Multilateral Agreement's Potential Network Effects

From section 7.5.2.1 follows that, generally speaking, the rules of a multilateral agreement can only become binding on third states by means of acquiescence or estoppel, for which a reaction of another state must be *provoked*. This may be the case when one party to a tax treaty with a non-signatory state claims that it interprets or applies the tax treaty in line with the multilateral instrument. A second possibility, set out in section 7.5.2.2, is that of treaty interpretation: Article 31(3)(c) of the Vienna Convention compels treaty interpreters to 'take into account any relevant rules of international law applicable in the relations between the parties'. It, in simple terms, requires that treaties are not interpreted in a vacuum. As a consequence, the operation of the article may mean that the multilateral instrument may bear on tax treaties with third states concluded after the adoption of the multilateral agreement.

These arguments are, however, somewhat remote. For estoppel or acquiescence to arise under a bilateral tax convention, signatory parties must interact somewhat artificially by claiming to interpret the tax convention in line with the multilateral instrument. Likewise, Article 31(3)(c) VCLT may prove of relevance in solving specific interpretative issues, but seems only able to bear on obligations entered into after the conclusion of the multilateral agreement.

For a stronger grip on agreements entered into by states that fall outside of the ambit of the multilateral convention due to the *pacta tertiis* rule, states could choose to include a *pactum de agendo* (section 7.5.2.3), in which they agree not to conclude a treaty incompatible with the convention and to bring their applicable tax conventions with third states in line with its norms.

Such a clause might prevent signatory states to agree to future incompatible tax agreements with third states. Moreover, it would create an obligation to make an effort to amend or revise existing incompatible bilateral tax treaties with third states. The multilateral fiscal treaty should not go as far so as to require signatory states to denounce an incompatible tax treaty. But, as follows from the experience within the EU of the use of the provision, requiring signatory states to take appropriate steps to bring a preexisting bilateral tax treaty in line with the obligations under the multilateral convention is tenable from the perspective of public international law. Disregarding the *pactum* could result in breaching the commitment clause and thus the multilateral treaty.

Would transformative flexibility devices be used in the convention, or would the convention's obligations be adapted over time, issues could arise as to the application of a *pactum de agendo* over time (*see* in particular the use of the dynamic amendment devices discussed in section 7.11). The *pactum* could be dynamically interpreted, i.e., relate to the latest obligations of the multilateral convention. Alternatively, it could also operate in a static fashion, i.e., that it only refers to the norms of the multilateral convention that exist at the time of the conclusion of a bilateral tax treaty. For legal certainty reasons, the solution should be explicitly taken up in the clause. Considering the 'managerial' approach to international tax law, it makes sense that states make an effort to keep their tax treaties in line with the norms of the multilateral convention, as it evolves from time to time. An example clause is taken up in Article 8(2) of the draft framework convention and 8(3) of the draft 'agreement to scope', set forth in the Annex.

7.6 CONCLUSION OF PART 7A: THE CORE ELEMENTS OF THE MULTILATERAL AGREEMENT FOR INTERNATIONAL TAXATION

The design strategy requires some core infrastructure: a forum for repeated discussions between parties, a flexible organisation that manages the regime and to function as a place where states take legal decisions, and some guiding principles around which parties' negotiations (whether bilateral or multilateral in nature, *see* subsequent Parts 7B and C) can gravitate. The multilateral agreement would thereby constitute a level playing field and create a forum enabling international tax law to transform towards being more procedurally (i.e., more inclusive and transparent) and substantively fair over time. Also, by bringing states together at the same time and place, it would reduce the transaction costs of bilateral tax treaty negotiations, potentially enabling states to more swiftly amend their bilateral tax treaty networks on common value-maximising terms.

At the heart of such a structure is the 'COP': a flexible, quasi-formal treaty body that has neither fixed members nor a fixed location for its meetings. A treaty body sets and supervises the periodical sessions of its conference, and usually 'borrows' a Secretariat from a formal IO, such as the OECD or UN. Where it may reap the benefits of cooperating with the OECD on tax technicalities (i.e., the OECD provides the relevant information such as model tax treaties, commentaries and reports), a treaty body is independent from the OECD and not limited by OECD membership restrictions, nor does it carry the costs involved with running an IO. Rather, a treaty body may establish formal and informal links with other IOs such as the OECD, and provide for transnational collaboration and an intergovernmental network on international tax matters. At the same time, a treaty body is far from being as politically diffused as, for example, the forum of the UN. Hence, the forum of a treaty body may prove a suitable in-between alternative.

The potential of a treaty body, then, is that its membership may be slowly expanded, and that the transparent development of and decision-making on (soft) international tax law may be gradually moved from the OECD to the level of its meetings. This may be achieved by 'borrowing' a secretariat from the UN and by the development of independent model treaties and commentaries. What needs to be worked towards, from the design strategy formulated in the previous chapter, is that non-OECD member countries will slowly come to exercise their influence in the vital phase of discussion and deliberation on international tax norms (from 'norm-takers' to 'norm-makers'). A treaty body would, in other words, provide a first step in the direction of making international tax law 'procedurally fair', and, in doing so, propel states into deeper cooperation on substantive norms of international tax law.

To illustrate the approach, the core elements of the multilateral agreement have been taken up in Articles 4–7 of the draft conventions of set out in the Annex.

PART 7B: THE FRAMEWORK CONVENTION-PROTOCOL DESIGN

7.7   INTRODUCTION TO PART 7B

Part 7B discusses the framework convention-protocol design. This design is characterised by 'layering', i.e., the norms concluded under the multilateral convention are 'layered' on top of the bilateral tax treaty network. Unlike the 'agreement to scope', discussed in Part 7C, the framework convention-protocol design aims to establish *substantive* multilateralism, and its core purpose is that it provides the regime with transformative flexibility (i.e., it allows the substantive commitments of the regime to change over time).

Under a treaty characterised by 'layering', some additional issues arise. Therefore, after a brief discussion of the basic elements of the framework convention-protocol design in section 7.8, several additional legal characteristics of the treaty form are discussed.

First of all, the norms generated under the multilateral treaty must somehow relate to the rules set out in bilateral tax conventions. So, the question arises what the relationship is between the framework convention-protocol design and the network of bilateral tax treaties. This means that the rules on the conflict of norms, such as set out in the VCLT, must be considered, as the multilateral convention's rules may clash or supplement rules set out in bilateral tax treaties. As the residual rules of the VCLT on the conflict of norms may cause legal uncertainty, it may be wise to draft a conflict provision that explicitly regulates the relationship (section 7.9). A second issue relates to the findings of Chapter 5: *substantive* multilateralism requires flexibility so as to accommodate diverging states' interests. 'Rules of the road' may relax distributional conflict, or where these prove unsuitable, multilateral rules may be tailored to states' needs by means of reservations and 'menu options' (section 7.10). The third issue that arises is how the rules of the multilateral convention *themselves* can be changed. Changing multilateral norms may be hard, as this requires the same level of consensus as is required for accepting them: unanimity. For this reason, the decision-making processes under a framework convention-protocol design may be relaxed by dynamic treaty amendment procedures. These types of procedures have in common that states *ex ante* agree to consent to norms adopted *ex post*, so that parliamentary approval for an amendment, once adopted, can be skipped. The most relevant example is the opt-out procedure, under which states agree to have consented to an amendment unless they voice their disagreement with the amendment of the text of (a protocol to) a treaty. The use of the opt-out procedure and similar devices is discussed in section

7.11. Although the benefit of such procedures is that they allow the treaty regime to quickly adapt to changing circumstances, they are paired with legitimacy and sovereignty costs.

7.8 THE FRAMEWORK CONVENTION-PROTOCOL DESIGN

7.8.1 The Use of the Framework Convention-Protocol Design in International Law

Treaty drafters have attempted to increase a treaty's transformative flexibility over time by using the multilateral framework convention-protocol design. The use of such a design enables the enactment of new international standards in a dynamic, gradual and continuous way: it requires, by definition, continuous interaction. The most striking example can be found in international environmental law, particularly in the regime on climate change, discussed in section 6.4.

Although a framework convention *as such* is not much different from a 'normal' treaty because the same rules with regard to adopting and ratifying amendments apply,[636] its design can facilitate said adoption and ratification. Indeed, a multilateral framework convention can be used to focus initial negotiations on broad standards and postpone more difficult discussions on detailed rules.[637] Five advantages in this regard are mentioned below. However, like negotiations on a 'normal' treaty, the relative open-endedness of the international legislative process can cause parties to (infinitely) defer negotiations on key issues to a later date,[638] an inherent risk to the 'managerial' design strategy advanced in the previous chapters.

First, the ability to postpone the negotiation of certain specific issues has the political advantage that a general form of consensus can be reached whilst in the meantime more awareness or consensus on an issue can arise.[639] Indeed, a relatively weak framework convention upon which all parties can agree sets the stage for discussion and creates room for further negotiation.[640] Second, as the convention does not attempt to solve all issues in one single instrument, negotiation breakdown is prevented.[641] And protocols provide states with flexibility: not all parties to the convention necessarily have to consent to a protocol. Third, the institutionalised

---

636. These rules are set out in the VCLT, Arts 11 and 39. *See* N. Matz-Lück (2009) p. 453. For instance, amendments to the UNFCCC are adopted by the Conference of the Parties by consensus or by three-fourths majority. These amendments, like in 'normal' multilateral conventions, only come into force for those states that have ratified these amendments: 'The amendment shall enter into force for any other Party on the ninetieth day after the date on which that Party deposits with the Depositary its instrument of acceptance of the said amendment.' *See* United Nations Framework Convention on Climate Change, Art. 15.
637. G. Blum (2008) p. 345.
638. G. Handl, *Environmental Security and Global Change: The Challenge to International Law*, 1 Yearbook of International Environmental Law 3, 6 (1990).
639. A.L. Taylor, *An International Regulatory Strategy for Global Tobacco Control*, 21 Yale Journal of International Law 257, 294 (1996).
640. N. Matz-Lück (2009).
641. A.L. Taylor (1996) p. 294.

environment of a framework convention can provide a basis for further research and information building on an issue, for example, on scientific evidence or on possible solutions. This might benefit the negotiation process in relation to difficult questions. Fourth, political momentum may develop as a consequence of discussions and lawmaking activities within the purview of a framework convention.[642] Finally, to ensure the timely and effective conclusion of new standards, a framework convention can set specific (timed) targets such as the periodic review and update of certain standards as well as timetables.[643]

7.8.2 The Use of the Framework Convention-Protocol Design for the Multilateral Agreement for International Taxation

A step-by-step solution to multilateral international taxation would provide the regime to transform over time. This enables incorporating changing global economic circumstances in decision-making, it means that consensus has the time to develop and that the search for solutions to difficult problems or questions can be pooled internationally. The framework convention-protocol design therefore perfectly fits the design strategy formulated in the previous chapters, as well as the broader objective set by the OECD to structurally address the method by which tax treaties are amended.

However, agreement on difficult political issues cannot be forced. Certainly, the framework convention-protocol design provides a platform for the evolution of the regime towards its objectives, but it does not *guarantee* such progress (*see also* Chapter 5).[644] Consequently, what a framework treaty can and should reasonably be able to achieve should not be overestimated.

7.9 THE RELATIONSHIP BETWEEN THE MULTILATERAL AGREEMENT AND THE BILATERAL TAX TREATY NETWORK

7.9.1 Introduction

One of the most important questions related to the framework convention-protocol design, is: how to 'implement' its substantive multilateral norms in the bilateral tax treaty network? The starting point of the analysis is that substantive multilateral norms, established in a (protocol to the) multilateral framework convention, are a bindingly legal obligation of their own. The Vienna Convention, after all, stipulates that 'a treaty may be amended by agreement between the parties'.[645] This 'agreement' is, in turn, constituted in the same way as any other treaty, as the VCLT's rules on the conclusion

---

642. On experience in environmental law in this regard, *see* T. Gehring (1990).
643. N. Matz-Lück, *Framework Agreements*, in: Max Planck Encyclopedia of Public International Law (R. Wolfrum ed., OUP 2011) paras 14–15.
644. S. Schiele (2014) p. 101.
645. Article 39 VCLT.

and entry into force of treaties, set out in the VCLT's Part II, apply to it.[646] The issue is hence not one of 'implementation', but one related to the interpretation and conflict of two sets of equally applicable norms, i.e., when a norm of a tax agreement and a norm of the multilateral agreement for international taxation apply simultaneously in the same circumstances to the same treaty party.[647]

First, let us look at the operation of the residual rules on the conflict of norms, as set out in the Vienna Convention. As it turns out, leaving the issue open can cause legal uncertainty, as the residual rules of the VCLT are ambiguous in their application (section 7.9.2). It therefore makes sense to draft a conflict clause (section 7.9.3).

7.9.2   The Residual Rules on Conflict Resolution

The starting point in solving any conflict of norms is treaty interpretation. For any residual conflict rule, such as the *lex posterior* or *lex specialis* rules, to apply, a conflict must exist. Indeed, a prima facie conflict should in the first place be solved by treaty interpretation: for instance, by choosing an interpretation that harmonises the two norms.[648] This interpretative exercise is called the 'presumption against conflict', which presupposes that the parties to the treaty did not intend to create conflicting obligations.[649] A harmonised outcome can, for instance, be achieved by restricting a norm's scope or its temporal effects.[650] The presumption against conflict does however not have an overriding character: it cannot go against clear language.[651]

Only after a 'real' conflict has been recognised through the act of treaty interpretation, do the conflict rules such as the *lex posterior* and *lex specialis* rules apply. The *lex posterior* rule is set out in the Vienna Convention's provision on treaty succession (Article 30 VCLT).[652] The third paragraph holds that in the case two treaties relate to the same subject matter: 'the earlier treaty applies only to the extent that its

---

646. *See* Art. 39 VCLT: 'A treaty may be amended by agreement between the parties. The rules laid down in part II apply to such an agreement.'
647. N. Bravo, *The Multilateral Tax Instrument and Its Relationship with Tax Treaties*, 8 World Tax Journal (2016) sec. 2.1.
648. This is called 'the presumption against conflict'. *See, e.g.*, J. Pauwelyn (2003a) pp. 240–241. *See also* S.A. Sadat-Akhavi, *Methods of Resolving Conflicts between Treaties* (Martinus Nijhoff Publishers 2003) pp. 34–42.
649. A. Orakhelashvili, *Article 30: Application of Successive Treaties Relating to the Same Subject Matter*, in: The Vienna Conventions on the Law of Treaties: a Commentary (O. Corten and P. Klein eds, OUP 2011) p. 776.
650. W. Czaplinski and G. Danilenko (1990) p. 13.
651. C.W. Jenks, *The Conflict of Law-Making Treaties*, 30 British Year Book of International Law 401, 459 (1953).
652. Article 30 holds:

   Application of successive treaties relating to the same subject-matter.
   1. Subject to Article 103 of the Charter of the United Nations, the rights and obligations of States parties to successive treaties relating to the same subject-matter shall be determined in accordance with the following paragraphs.
   2. When a treaty specifies that it is subject to, or that it is not to be considered as incompatible with, an earlier or later treaty, the provisions of that other treaty prevail.

provisions are compatible with those of the later treaty'.[653] What the rule does, in effect, is protect the parties' new legislative intent.[654]

However, the Vienna Convention's provision on treaty conflict is ambiguous.[655] Most interestingly, it does not codify the *lex specialis* rule, which is widely supported in doctrine as relevant to treaty conflict.[656] Sinclair, for instance, notes that:

> the principle of the lex specialis is not expressed as such in Article 30, but is widely supported in doctrine; the concept that a specific norm of conventional international law may prevail over a more general norm can of course be seen as raising primarily a question of interpretation.[657]

In the *Case Concerning the Gabcikovo-Nagymaros Project (Hungary v. Slovakia)*, the ICJ explicitly referred to the *lex specialis* rule when it held that:

> (...) the Court has found that the 1977 Treaty is still in force and consequently governs the relationship between the Parties. That relationship is also determined by the rules of other relevant conventions to which the two States are party (...) but it is governed above all, by the applicable rules of the 1977 Treaty as a *lex specialis*.[658]

In fact, two opposing arguments characterise the application and hierarchy of the rule of *lex specialis* and *lex posterior*.[659] The main argument in favour of the *lex posterior* rule is that it is codified in Article 30 VCLT, whereas the rule of *lex specialis* is not. Aust, in his treatise on modern treaty law, for instance, does not discuss the *lex specialis* rule when addressing Article 30 VCLT.[660] The main argument in favour of the *lex specialis* rule, on the other hand, is that based on the drafting history of the Vienna Convention, the *lex posterior* rule should only be used if the process of treaty interpretation, which

---

3. When all the parties to the earlier treaty are parties also to the later treaty but the earlier treaty is not terminated or suspended in operation under article 59, the earlier treaty applies only to the extent that its provisions are compatible with those of the later treaty.

4. When the parties to the later treaty do not include all the parties to the earlier one:
   (a) As between States parties to both treaties the same rule applies as in paragraph 3;
   (b) As between a State party to both treaties and a State party to only one of the treaties, the treaty to which both States are parties governs their mutual rights and obligations.

5. Paragraph 4 is without prejudice to article 41, or to any question of the termination or suspension of the operation of a treaty under article 60 or to any question of responsibility which may arise for a State from the conclusion or application of a treaty the provisions of which are incompatible with its obligations towards another State under another treaty.

653. Article 30(3) VCLT.
654. I. Sinclair (1984) p. 98.
655. *Id.*, at p. 98. *See*, for a discussion, J. Klabbers (2009) Ch. 5.
656. ILC, *Fragmentation of International Law* (2006) paras 58–65.
657. *See* I. Sinclair (1984) p. 96.
658. ICJ, *Gabčikovo-Nagymaros Project (Hungary v. Slovakia)*, (Judgement), [1997] IJC Reports 7, para. 132.
659. N. Matz-Lück, *Conflict Clauses*, in: The Max Planck Encyclopedia of Public International Law (R. Wolfrum ed., OUP Online ed., 2010) para. 3.
660. A. Aust (2013) pp. 202–204.

includes the *lex specialis* rule, has failed to determine priority between two norms.[661] Hence, the *lex specialis* rule should be applied first. Consequently, as Czaplinsky and Danilenko point out: the *lex posterior* rule's codification in Article 30(2) of the Vienna Convention suggests its priority in case of conflict, but judicial practice tends to favour the *lex specialis* rule.[662] A complicating factor is that Article 30 VCLT stipulates that the subsequent treaty has to deal with 'the same subject matter' for the *lex posterior* rule to apply.[663] Consequently, it can be questioned what 'the same subject matter' means,[664] (e.g., does this encompass an application of the *lex specialis* rule?) and what happens if a subsequent treaty is *not* of the same subject matter.[665] As a result, the residual rules on treaty succession cause legal uncertainty not only as to how a treaty *should* be interpreted, but also how a treaty would *in fact* be interpreted, thereby reducing the value (or predictability) of that treaty in practice.[666]

Be that as it may, the standard rules on treaty conflict can be derogated from by an express provision regulating priority.[667] It is, as Aust notes, better to prevent than to cure.[668] It helps when treaty interpreters, in advance, know, which provisions are to are to be considered as modified.[669] Nothing prevents states from drafting a clause that stipulates that the multilateral treaty has priority over bilateral tax treaty obligations.

7.9.3 A Conflict Clause Governing the Relationship Between the Multilateral Agreement and the Bilateral Treaty Network

7.9.3.1 *Introduction*

Conflicts can thus to some extent be prevented *ex ante* by a treaty clause. The purpose of a conflict clause is to determine the relationship between two treaties when these two treaties overlap.[670] Although such a rule will not solve all conflicts because it is still a general rule at best,[671] the careful drafting of a conflict clause might prevent unpredictable outcomes as it gives the one seeking to apply the terms of the two

---

661. J.B. Mus, *Conflicts Between Treaties in International Law*, 45 Netherlands International Law Review 208, 217–219 (1998). *See also* N. Matz-Lück (2010) para. 13.
662. W. Czaplinski and G. Danilenko (1990) pp. 20–21. Article 30(2) reads: 'When a treaty specifies that it is subject to, or that it is not to be considered as incompatible with, an earlier or later treaty, the provisions of that other treaty prevail.'
663. *See* Art. 30 of the VCLT.
664. N. Matz-Lück (2010) para. 13.
665. R. Wolfrum and N. Matz-Lück, *Conflicts in International Environmental Law* (Springer 2003) pp. 148–150.
666. C.J. Borgen, *Resolving Treaty Conflicts*, 37 George Washington International Law Review 573, 590 (2005).
667. The second paragraph of Art. 30 holds that 'When a treaty specifies that it is subject to, or that it is not to be considered as incompatible with, an earlier or later treaty, the provisions of that other treaty prevail.' Further: I. Sinclair (1984) p. 97.
668. A. Aust (2013) p. 194.
669. N. Bravo (2016a) sec. 2.2.
670. S.A. Sadat-Akhavi (2003) p. 85.
671. J. Klabbers (2009) pp. 101–103.

instruments more guidance than the residual rules of the VCLT.[672] This is also recognised by the OECD in the 2014 report on the development of a multilateral instrument.[673] The Vienna Convention leaves room to treaty negotiators to draft a specific conflict clause. Article 30(2) stipulates:

> When a treaty specifies that it is subject to, or that it is not to be considered as incompatible with, an earlier or later treaty, the provisions of that other treaty prevail.[674]

Practice in relation to the use of a conflict clause can be examined on three different elements. First, conflict clauses set out the relationship between two types of instruments. In the case of the multilateral agreement, the clause should determine that both instruments co-exist (section 7.9.3.2).[675] Second, conflict clauses address the consequences of conflict. In the case of the multilateral agreement: the clause should give the multilateral agreement priority over both existing and future tax treaties concluded between signatory states (and not the other way around), *see* section 7.9.3.3. Lastly, conflict clauses should not be read to influence tax treaties with non-signatory states. This runs against the *pacta tertiis* rule set out in Article 34 VCLT (*see* section 7.5). To prevent misunderstandings, conflict clauses therefore usually include a phrase that explicitly codifies the *pacta tertiis* rule (section 7.9.3.4).

7.9.3.2 The Relationship Between the Multilateral Agreement and the Bilateral Tax Treaty Network

The multilateral agreement and the network of bilateral tax treaties it covers should both be applicable simultaneously. This relationship can be regulated by a complex conflict clause that sets the relationship between specific rules of both instruments. The clause may refer to both existing as well as future treaties.[676]

For, instance, the conflict clause of the Agreement on Extradition between the EU and the United States of America holds:[677]

> (1) The European Union, pursuant to the Treaty on the European Union, and the United States of America shall ensure that the provisions of this

---

672. Klabbers however argues that conflict clauses are of a limited value, since 'they merely reproduce the uncertainties that are associated with treaty conflict'. *Id.*, at p. 103.
673. OECD, *Developing a Multilateral Instrument to Modify Bilateral Tax Treaties* (2014) p. 32.
674. See Art. 30(2) VCLT.
675. That is, the clause should not determine that the multilateral instrument *replaces* or *supersedes* the existing bilateral tax treaties; the point is that both types of instrument remain in force.
676. For instance, the conflict clause of the UN Charter, Art. 103, which at applies to any other agreement, in force now or in the future: 'In the event of a conflict between the obligations of the Members of the United Nations under the present Charter and their obligations under any other international agreement, their obligations under the present Charter shall prevail.' Charter of the United Nations (adopted 26 Jun. 1945), 1 UNTS XVI (emphasis added). For more examples: OECD, *Developing a Multilateral Instrument to Modify Bilateral Tax Treaties* (2014) para. A.1.2.
677. *Agreement on Extradition between the United States of America and the European Union (EU)* (adopted 25 Jun. 2003), OJ L 181, 19.7.2003, p. 27, Art. 3.

Agreement *are applied in relation to bilateral extradition treaties* between the Member States and the United States of America (...) on the following terms:

(a) Article 4 shall be applied *in place of* bilateral treaty provisions that authorise extradition exclusively with respect to a list of specified criminal offences; (...)

(b) Article 4 shall be applied *in place of* bilateral treaty provisions governing transmission, certification (...)

(c) Article 6 shall be applied *in the absence of* bilateral treaty provisions authorising direct transmission of provisional arrest requests (...)

(d) Article 7 shall be applied *in addition to* bilateral treaty provisions governing transmission of extradition requests;

(e) Article 8 shall be applied *in the absence of* bilateral treaty provisions (...)

(...), etc.[678]

The clause includes information on the provisions to be modified and provides what could be called 'connection language', i.e., language that sets the detailed circumstances under which the provisions of the convention apply to the texts that are to be amended ('in addition to'; 'are not listed', etc.).[679]

The 'connection language' of the above complex conflict clauses is expressed at the level of the conflict clause, and not at the level of the texts of the specific amendments. But there are also examples of mechanisms that include such 'connection language' in the text of the amendment *itself*. The *Agreement relating to the Implementation of Part XI of the UN Convention on the Law of the Sea* (herinafter: Implementation Agreement) provides such an example.[680]

First, Article 2 of that agreement provides a general interpretation rule, i.e., that both sets of rules are to be interpreted as one instrument (in complex conflict clauses like the one above, this instruction follows from the clause by implication). It says that:

> The provisions of this agreement [the implementation agreement] and part XI shall be interpreted and applied together as a single instrument. In the event of any inconsistency between this Agreement and Part XI, the provisions of this Agreement shall prevail.[681]

Using a rule to this effect in the multilateral agreement for international taxation would imply that the agreement's norms would become an integral part of bilateral tax treaties it covers. This would also have the advantage that norms of the multilateral agreement, by implication, explicitly are meant to influence the interpretation of bilateral tax treaties.

But the instruction to interpret both treaties as one instrument can function in combination with the 'connection language' set out in the text of the substantive

---

678. *Id.*, at Art. 3(1).
679. *See also* OECD, *Developing a Multilateral Instrument to Modify Bilateral Tax Treaties* (2014) p. 37.
680. *Agreement relating to the Implementation of Part XI of the UN Convention on the Law of the Sea of 10 December 1982* (Adopted 28 Jul. 1994, entered into force 28 Jul. 1996), 1836 UNTS 3. This instrument is also discussed in D.M. Broekhuijsen, *Naar een multilateraal fiscaal raamwerkverdrag*, WFR 2013/1443, para. 3.2.
681. *Id.*, at Art. 2.

amendments. In the example of the Implementation Agreement, the amendments themselves are set out in an annex. They include specific language that sets the relationship between the amendments set out in the Implementation Agreement and the provision or part of a provision of the Law of the Sea Convention which it sought to modify.[682] For instance, such amendments hold:

> 'Notwithstanding the provisions of article 153, paragraph 3, and Annex III, article 3, paragraph 5, of the Convention [on the Law of the Sea], a plan of work for the enterprise upon its approval shall be in the form of a contract (...)'.[683]
>
> (...)
>
> 'the provisions of article 161, paragraph 8 (b) and (c), of the Convention [on the Law of the Sea] shall not apply.'[684]

The advantage of using 'connection language' at the level of the norms of the envisaged amendments is that this enables negotiators to regulate the relationship between two instruments in detail. Separating the text of the relevant articles from their desirable effects would make the conflict clause overly complex,[685] particularly considering that the multilateral agreement would potentially only alter parts of a provision or even only parts of a sentence of a bilateral tax treaty. Moreover, bilateral tax treaties are rarely precisely similar in wording. Consequently, the approach of adding detailed connection language in the amendment itself seems more convenient. In example, the text of a substantive multilateral tax rule could, for instance, stipulate that it applies *in place of* a certain sentence in a bilateral tax convention, or *in the absence* or *in addition to* a certain provision.[686] Other possible language options are: '*articles x and y of the bilateral tax convention apply, provided that (...)*', '*except as otherwise provided in (...)*', '*where provision x or y of the bilateral tax treaty does not specify*', etc. More specifically, as Bravo shows, a compatibility clause that implements the minimum standard in the sense of the Action 6 Final Report[687] could read:

> The following LOB clause should be applied to existing tax treaties that do not contain an analogous provision or to existing tax treaties that, while containing an analogous provision, do not reflect the minimum standard ....[688]

---

682. The Implementation Agreement was needed because part XI of the Convention of the Law of the Sea (UNCLOS) was problematic for a number of industrial states, which consequently refused to sign the Convention. The Implementation Agreement removed the obstacles, paving the way for broad support of the Law of the Sea Convention.

683. Paragraph 4 of sec. 2 of the Annex of the Implementation Agreement (emphasis added).

684. Paragraph 8 of sec. 3 of the Annex of the Agreement (emphasis added). The Annex forms an integral part of the Implementation Agreement. *See*, for more concrete examples, L.D.M. Nelson, *The New Deep Sea-Bed Mining Regime*, 10 International Journal of Marine and Coastal Law 189, 192 (1995) and B.H. Oxman, *The 1994 Agreement and the Convention*, 88 The American Journal of International Law 687 (1994).

685. *See also* N. Bravo (2016b) p. 336.

686. Similar language is used in the Agreement on Extradition between the United States of America and the European Union (EU), Art. 3(1).

687. OECD, *Preventing the Granting of Treaty Benefits in Inappropriate Circumstances, Action 6: 2015 Final Report* (2015).

688. N. Bravo (2016a) sec. 3.3.

The clause could then include, in detail, the standard that must be met in each of the bilateral tax treaties to which it applies. For instance, it could stipulate that as to the tax treaty between states A and B, the LOB clause makes an exception for pension funds. This, of course, dilutes the distinction between the framework convention-protocol design and the 'agreement to scope' set forth in Part 7C. But in this way, the relationship between a bilateral tax treaty and a multilateral agreement can be set in detail. As the precise wording of a particular bilateral tax treaty provision may differ from one bilateral tax treaty to another, the 'correct' design of such connection language is, as Bravo notes, indispensable for making the multilateral agreement for international taxation a success.[689]

To what treaties should the clause refer? A practical suggestion is that the clause captures both bilateral as well as multilateral tax conventions. Otherwise, the multilateral agreement would not be able to influence regional multilateral tax conventions such as the Nordic Tax Convention. Moreover, the clause could capture both existing and future tax treaties of the multilateral treaty's signatory states ('it could look forward').[690] However, a clause claiming priority over future treaties has a limited effect. It is limited by an application of the *pacta tertiis* rule, and the parties can always change their minds in the future by mutual consent: *pacta sunt servanda*.[691] This was also set out by the International Law Commission (ILC) in the Commentary to the VCLT:

> As is pointed out in the commentary to article 56 [on the termination of the operation of a treaty implied from entering a subsequent treaty], the parties to the earlier treaty are always competent to abrogate it, whether in whole or in part, by concluding another treaty with that object. That being so, when they conclude a second treaty incompatible with the first, they are to be presumed to have intended to terminate the first treaty or to modify it to the extent of the incompatibility, unless there is evidence of a contrary intention.[692]

7.9.3.3   The Consequences of Conflict

The second element of the provision should stipulate what happens, after both instruments have been interpreted in an integrative manner (*see* the previous section), in the case of conflict or inconsistency between the two sets of norms: the multilateral agreement should be given priority. A rule to that effect, when applied to prior agreements, can be considered to be a restatement of the *lex posterior* rule codified in the VCLT.[693]

An explicit codification of the *lex posterior* rule of Article 30 of the VCLT enhances legal certainty, as it explicates the priority of the *lex posterior* rule over the *lex specialis*

---

689. *Id.*, at sec. 4.
690. OECD, *Developing a Multilateral Instrument to Modify Bilateral Tax Treaties* (2014) p. 39.
691. *See* ILC (1966) p. 216; J. Pauwelyn (2003a) p. 335.
692. ILC (1966) p. 215.
693. G. Plant, *The Convention for the Suppression of Unlawful Acts against the Safety of Maritime Navigation*, 39 International and Comparative Law Quarterly 27, 50 (1990). Article 30(3) VCLT reads: 'When all the parties to the earlier treaty are parties also to the later treaty but the earlier

rule. Including it seems harmless. For this reason, it makes sense to use similar language as used in the VCLT so as to set the clause's threshold, as set by the word '(in)compatibility'.[694]

There are a number of treaty clauses that stipulate that a treaty prevails in case of conflict. For instance, the Implementation Agreement's second sentence holds that in the case of inconsistency, the Implementation Agreement *prevails*:

> In the event of any inconsistency between this Agreement and Part XI, the provisions of this Agreement shall *prevail*.[695]

And Article 39 of the Convention Concerning the International Administration of the Estates of Deceased Persons, which amended bilateral treaties between states, for instance, holds:

> The provisions of this Convention shall prevail over the terms of any bilateral Convention to which Contracting States are or may in the future become Parties and which contains provisions relating to the same subject-matter, unless it is otherwise agreed between the Parties to such Convention.[696]

Article 103(2) of the North American Free Trade Agreement (NAFTA) reads:

> In the event of any inconsistency between this Agreement and such other agreements, *this Agreement shall prevail to the extent of the inconsistency*, except as otherwise provided in this Agreement.[697]

Conflict clauses to the same effect may give priority to the treaty in which they are included by using other language. A conflict rule that holds that the multilateral treaty 'modifies' existing bilateral treaties has the same effect. For instance, the 1988 Convention for the Suppression of Unlawful Acts of Violence Against the Safety of Maritime Navigation (the SUA Convention) makes use of the verb 'to modify':

---

treaty is not terminated or suspended in operation under article 59, *the earlier treaty applies only to the extent that its provisions are compatible with those of the later treaty*' (emphasis added).

694. As an alternative, the word 'conflict' could be used. In the discussions on the VCLT's Art. 30 (then Art. 65), the words 'in the event of conflict' were dropped and replaced by 'in the event of incompatibility'. The point was that no 'conflict' can occur between two successive treaties concluded by the same parties. UN, *Yearbook of the International Law Commission 1964: Summary Records of the Sixteenth Session* (1964) pp. 124–125. It follows from literature that the word 'conflict' can have a very technical definition in the sense that a conflict only exists if two terms are *mutually exclusive*. Jenks, for instance, considered that 'a conflict in the strict sense of direct incompatibility arises only where a party to the two treaties cannot simultaneously comply with its obligations under both treaties'. C.W. Jenks (1953) p. 426. The term 'incompatible' is not prone to such a narrow interpretation. *See*, for a discussion on the construction of 'conflict', J. Pauwelyn (2003a) p. 164.

695. *Id.*, Art. 2.

696. *Convention Concerning the International Administration of the Estates of Deceased Persons* (adopted 2 Oct. 1973), 11 ILM 1277, www.hcch.net.

697. *North American Free Trade Agreement* (17 Dec. 1992), 2 ILM 289, 605.

> With respect to the offences as defined in this Convention, the provisions of all extradition treaties and arrangements applicable between States Parties *are modified* as between States Parties to the extent that they are incompatible with this Convention.[698]

Provisions with a similar wording are included in, for example, the European Convention on the Suppression of Terrorism[699] and in the International Convention for the Suppression of the Financing of Terrorism.[700] As these counterterrorism treaties were to be applied 'on top of' existing bilateral extradition treaties, the verb 'to modify' was used instead of 'prevail' in order to emphasise that extradition should not be rendered impossible in case the former extradition treaty excluded the new treaty's offences.[701] Indeed, as Aust explains: as there would not seem to be any conflict between, on the one hand, extradition treaties, and counterterrorism treaties on the other hand, the provision has been included in counterterrorism conventions 'perhaps more for the avoidance of doubt'.[702]

On the basis of these observations, the clause in the multilateral agreement could include a *lex posterior* rule, which could be based on either the wording used in the Implementation Agreement or the NAFTA. These provisions set out that those conventions *prevail*, signifying the agreement's priority. Alternatively, the multilateral agreement could stipulate that it 'modifies' the bilateral tax treaties it covers.

7.9.3.4 *The Relationship Between the Multilateral Agreement and Treaties with Third States*

Regardless of the wording of a conflict clause, the multilateral agreement cannot influence treaties with non-signatory states due to the *pacta tertiis* rule. This rule applies on the basis of the VCLT, regardless of the wording of a treaty. Indeed, the ILC considered:

> When on the other hand, the parties to a treaty containing a clause purporting to override an earlier treaty do not include all the parties to the earlier one, the rule

---

698. *Convention for the Suppression of Unlawful Acts against the Safety of Maritime Navigation* (adopted 10 Mar. 1988), 1678 UNTS 397, Art. 11(7) (emphasis added).
699. Article 8(3), which holds: 'The provisions of all treaties and arrangements concerning mutual assistance in criminal matters applicable between Contracting States, including the European Convention on Mutual Assistance in Criminal Matters, are modified as between Contracting States to the extent that they are incompatible with this Convention', *European Convention on the Suppression of Terrorism* (adopted 27 Jan. 1977), 113 UNTS 93.
700. Article 11(5), which holds: 'The provisions of all extradition treaties and arrangements between States Parties with regard to offences set forth in article 2 shall be deemed to be modified as between States Parties to the extent that they are incompatible with this convention.' *See International Convention for the Suppression of the Financing of Terrorism* (adopted 9 Dec. 1999), 2178 UNTS 197.
701. This argument is based on S.A. Sadat-Akhavi (2003) p. 150.
702. For instance, the provision of the SUA Convention incorporates the offences of the convention in the existing extradition treaties between states. *See* A. Aust (2013) p. 195.

pacta tertiis non nocent automatically restricts the legal effect of the clause. The later treaty, clause or no clause, cannot deprive a State which is not a party thereto of its rights under the earlier treaty.[703]

Nevertheless, for reasons of legal certainty and to prevent unwanted (and unintended) effects, parties can codify the *pacta tertiis* rule in the conflict clause of their treaty. Article XIV of the 1962 Convention on the Liability of Operators of Nuclear Ships provides an example in this regard, and holds:

> This Convention shall supersede any international conventions in force or open for signature (...) however, nothing in this Article shall affect the obligations of contracting States to non-Contracting States arising under such international conventions.[704]

7.9.3.5 Conclusion

In conclusion, a conflict clause may be included in a framework convention-protocol design type of multilateral treaty, as it serves legal certainty. The practice in relation to the use of such clauses, suggests that these clauses are generally made up out of three elements. The first element guides the interpretation phase by using connection language on the level of the treaty amendment, taking into account that bilateral tax treaties may vary in wording. The second element may set out what happens if an inconsistency nevertheless arises. Since this second element imports the *lex posterior* of the Vienna Convention on conflicts, taking up the clause seems harmless. The same holds for the third element, which may express the *pacta tertiis* rule. An example clause to this end, on the basis of the discussion above, has been set forth in Article 6 of the draft framework convention in Annex A.

7.10 THE USE OF INTERPRETATIVE FLEXIBILITY MECHANISMS

7.10.1 Introduction

To mitigate the effects of distributional conflict underlying multilateral negotiations in international tax law (*see* Chapter 5), countries can make use of reservations, 'menu options',[705] and 'rules of the road'. As for reservations, these enable states to depart from certain 'default' multilateral rules accepted by others. 'Menu options' give states the flexibility to choose between alternatives when deciding on common policy options. 'Rules of the road' are norms that lead to a 'fair' treatment of all actors signing up to the rule, as the rule's operation is dependent on the circumstances at hand.

---

703. ILC (1966), Commentary on Art. 26, p. 215.
704. The *Convention on the Liability of Operators of Nuclear Ships* (Concluded 25 May 1962), not in force. The text of the convention can be found in 57 (1963) American Journal of International Law 268 (emphasis added).
705. There are other treaty flexibility mechanisms, such as escape clauses and the provisional application of a treaty. *See* L.R. Helfer (2012).

Obviously, there is a need for coherent and uniform multilateral norms (i.e., 'internal coherence'). Reservations and 'menu options' lead to rule fragmentation, and create *inter se* agreements between the reserving and non-reserving states. This increases the complexity and incoherence of the regime. But we have seen that there is a stark need for interpretative flexibility in international tax negotiations. Without interpretative flexibly devices, states may decide against participating in the agreement in the first place. And perhaps the complexity resulting from the use of interpretative flexibility devices can be somewhat softened by some smart editing of the *Materials on International Tax Law*.[706] After all, it does not lead to a more fragmented rule system than the bilateral one currently in place.

It goes without saying that the interpretative flexibility devices considered in this section are primarily of relevance in relation to the framework convention-protocol design. After all, the 'agreement to scope' already starts from the presumption that negotiations are ultimately bilateral in nature.

7.10.2   Reservations and Menu Options

7.10.2.1   *Reservations and 'Menu Options' in International Law*

7.10.2.1.1   *Reservations*

By means of reservations, states can tailor the obligations of a treaty to their individual preferences. Reservations create *inter se* obligations between states.[707] And indeed, there are 'modifying reservations', which do not 'dissolve altogether the obligation (or right) that is expressed in a treaty provision, but permit it to prevail under modified forms',[708] and 'excluding reservations', which limit the multilateral obligations established and hence create a norm of the opposite effect.[709]

According to the VCLT, a 'reservation' is defined as a 'unilateral statement, however phrased or named, made by a state, when signing, ratifying, accepting, approving or acceding to a treaty, whereby it purports to exclude or to modify the legal effect of certain provisions of the treaty in their application to that State'.[710] States may formulate reservations, unless reservations are (partly) prohibited by the treaty or the reservation is incompatible with the object and purpose of the treaty.[711]

---

706. As selected and edited annually by C. van Raad, ITC Leiden.
707. A. Pellet, *Article 19: Formulation of Reservations*, in: The Vienna Convention on the Law of Treaties: A Commentary (O. Corten and P. Klein eds, OUP 2011).
708. F. Horn, *Reservations and Interpretative Declarations to Multilateral Treaties* (Uppsala: Uppsala University, Swedish Institute of International Law 1988) p. 80.
709. *Id.*, at p. 84.
710. VCLT Art. 2(1)(d).
711. *Id.*, at Art. 19.

Most interesting for the purpose of international tax law is the effect of reservations.[712] As Giegerich notes, reservations are aimed at creating bilateral legal relationships. They have their intended legal effects only if another contracting party tacitly or explicitly accepts them.

Under an 'excluding reservation', the party that filed the reservation 'has neither rights nor obligations under those provisions in its relations with the other parties with regard to which reservation is established'.[713] And under a 'modifying reservation', 'the author of that reservation has rights and obligations under those provisions, as modified by the reservation, in its relations with the other parties with regard to which a reservation is established'.[714] The exclusions and modifications apply to the other party in its relations with the reserving state to the same extent.[715] Hence, reservations work both ways, i.e., on the basis of reciprocity.[716] It creates *inter se* reciprocal legal relationships between the reserving party and all the other parties that accepted it, and modifies their obligations in a mutual, reciprocal way.[717] However, reservations do not modify the provisions of the treaty for the other parties to the treaty,[718] and as to states that have objected to a reservation, 'the provisions to which the reservation relates do not apply as between the two states to the extent of the reservation'.[719]

As has been stated, it is also possible that the treaty itself provides for 'negotiated' reservations, i.e., reservations expressly authorised by the treaty. Under such pre-authorised reservations, subsequent acceptance by the other contracting states is not

---

712. As to their entry into force, the VCLT strikes a balance between the need for universality on the one hand and integrity of the treaty on the other hand. The VCLT holds (in Art. 20(5)) that a reservation is considered to have been accepted by a state if it has not raised an objection to the reservation by the end of a period of twelve months after it was notified of reservation or by the date on which it expressed its consent to be bound by the treaty. So, the VCLT's regime on reservations functions on the basis of parties' tacit consent. To object to a reservation, a party must take action.

713. UN, *The Guide to Practice on Reservations to Treaties* (2011) Report of the International Law Commission on the Work of its 63rd session, Official Records, 66th Session, Supplement n° 10, Addendum 1, UN Doc. A/66/10/Add.1, para. 4.2.4.

714. VCLT Art. 21(1) and *id.*, at para. 4.2.4.

715. VCLT Art. 21(1).

716. D. Müller, *Article 21: Legal Effects of Reservations and of Objections to Reservations*, in: The Vienna Convention on the Law of Treaties: A Commentary (O. Corten and P. Klein eds, OUP 2011) p. 548.

717. T. Giegerich, *Multilateral Reservations to Treaties*, in: The Max Planck Encyclopedia of Public International Law (R. Wolfrum ed., OUP Online ed., 2010) para. 2.

718. VCLT Art. 21(2).

719. *Id.*, at Art. 21(3) (emphasis added). An objection by another contracting state to a reservation does not preclude the entry into force of a treaty between the objecting in the reserving state, unless a contrary intention is expressed by the objecting state. *Id.*, at Art. 20(4). Given the similarity of language, the legal effects of an objection that leaves the treaty in force on the one hand, and the legal effects of a 'normal' reservation which 'modifies' the provisions to the same extent for the other party (cf. Art. 21(1) VCLT), on the other hand, might not be so different. Sinclair discusses the issue and notes that most commentators believe that 'even in the case of a "modifying" reservation, the legal effects of an objection to and acceptance of the reservation are identical, when the treaty remains in force between the objecting and reserving States'. I. Sinclair (1984) pp. 76–77.

required, as this is considered superfluous.[720] Treaty provisions to this effect can limit the contents of the reservation itself, as well as which provisions states are authorised to make reservations on.[721]

It is possible that 'authorised reservations' are 'specified', in the sense that only those 'specified' reservations may be made by the parties (*see* Article 19(b) VCLT).[722] All other reservations are null or void, and there is no need for other states to reject or accept a reservation prohibited by a treaty, for they have already expressed their objection in the treaty itself.[723]

7.10.2.1.2 *'Menu Options' (Contracting-In and Optional Clauses)*

'Contracting-in' and 'optional clauses', here referred to as 'menu options' are, in the words of Guideline 1.5.3 of the UN Guide to Practice on Reservations:

> unilateral statement[s] made in accordance with a clause in a treaty permitting the parties to accept an obligation that is not otherwise imposed by the treaty, or permitting them to choose between two or more provisions of the treaty.[724]

Such statements look like reservations, but are not. Although their outcomes are the same as those of reservations, as the ILC notes, 'statements made under such clauses actually have little in common at the technical level with reservations, apart from the (important) fact that they both purport to modify the application of the effects of the treaty'.[725] Indeed, as Spiliopoulou Åkermark notes, contracting-in and optional clauses 'start from a presumption that parties are not bound by anything other than they have explicitly chosen',[726] while reservations, that *exclude* the application of an obligation, start from the opposite assumption.[727]

An example of a contracting-in clause, in which states have to choose *between* alternatives, is Article XIV of the IMF statutes, which holds:

> Section 1. Notification to the Fund
>
> Each member shall notify the Fund whether it intends to avail itself of the transitional arrangements in Section 2 of this Article, or whether it is prepared to accept the obligations of Article VIII, Sections 2, 3, and 4. A member availing itself of the transitional arrangements shall notify the Fund as soon thereafter as it is prepared to accept these obligations.[728]

---

720. *See* Art. 20(1) VCLT.
721. *See* UN, *Report of the ILC on the Practice on Reservations to Treaties* (2011) p. 59, as well as pp. 437–442.
722. *Id.*, at pp. 340–347.
723. *Id.*, at pp. 334–335.
724. *Id.*, at p. 101.
725. *Id.*, at pp. 100–101.
726. S. Spiliopoulou Åkermark, *Reservation Clauses in Treaties Concluded with the Council of Europe*, 48 International & Comparative Law Quarterly 479, 505 (1999).
727. UN, *Report of the ILC on the Practice on Reservations to Treaties* (2011) p. 103.
728. *Articles of Agreement of the International Monetary Fund* (22 Jul. 1944 (as amended through 2008)), 2 UNTS 39.

And an example of an 'optional clause' is set out in Article 4(2)(g) of the UNFCCC. Under such a clause, a state has to *opt in* to increase the obligations[729] that would not be applicable on that state by the mere entry into force of a convention:

> Any Party not included in Annex I may, in its instrument of ratification, acceptance, approval or accession, or at any time thereafter, notify the Depositary that it intends to be bound by subparagraphs (a) and (b) above.

Contracting-in and optional clauses are alternatives to reservations, as they provide treaty parties with the opportunity to tailor the application of a treaty to their individual preferences. Moreover, like reservations, they are expressed by means of unilateral statements made at the time of signature or of expression of consent to be bound. Yet, as to 'contracting-in' clauses, in the absence of a state's selection of a 'dish' from the menu provided by the clause, a state cannot become a party to the treaty.[730] The 'optional' clause, on the other hand, does not prevent a state to become a party to the treaty. It can function as a pre-negotiated alternative to a reservation. It applies 'on top of' the obligations 'normally' applicable when a treaty enters into force. Optional clauses may therefore be particularly useful when negotiators feel that only a limited number of states is willing to accept an obligation.

7.10.2.2 Reservations and 'Menu Options' in the Multilateral Agreement for International Taxation

We have seen that interpretative flexibility is required for parties to agree on multilateral norms. The treaty should therefore not disallow the formulation of reservations (or include clauses to a similar effect), otherwise it risks that states decide not to cooperate.[731]

Yet, in accordance with Article 21(3) VCLT, the consequence of a reservation of a reserving state is that an identical reservation applies *against* the reserving state. Hence, the reciprocity of commitments enshrined in the Vienna Convention regime on reservations departs from the presumption that state relationships are symmetrical.[732] However, in international tax law, relations are often *not* symmetrical. For instance, if a state reserves against the use of a rule that limits treaty benefits for entities with little or no economic significance, the reservation works against the reserving state too. But the non-reserving state, in an asymmetric relationship, may gain little from these

---

729. The 'optional clause' should have been discussed in Part 7C ('the agreement to scope'), as it groups pairs of states with similar interests, rather than allowing states to 'relax' multilateral rules. For the sake of simplicity, however, it is discussed here.
730. UN, *Report of the ILC on the Practice on Reservations to Treaties* (2011) p. 107.
731. *See*, specifically as regards reservations in this regard, E.T. Swaine, *Reserving*, 31 Yale Journal of International Law 306, 329–331 (2006) and in reaction L.R. Helfer, *Not Fully Committed – Reservations, Risk, and Treaty Design Response*, 31 Yale Journal of International Law 367 (2006).
732. F. Parisi and C. Sevcenko, *Treaty Reservations and the Economics of Article 21(1) of the Vienna Convention*, 21 Berkeley Journal of International Law 1 (2003). Also: J. Galbraith, *Treaty Options: Towards a Behavioral Understanding of Treaty Design*, 53 Virginia Journal of International Law 309 (2013).

consequences when its interests lie in protecting its tax base instead. Hence, the residual mechanism on treaty reservations, by working on the basis of symmetry (ignoring the effects of uncertainty for the sake of the argument), may upset the equilibrium under which multilateral tax negotiations are possible.[733] It, in other words, creates asymmetric costs and benefits for participants.

The other states may of course 'remedy' this asymmetry. In the extreme, a non-reserving state may, in accordance with the language of Article 20(4)(b) VCLT, declare that the treaty has not entered into force between itself and the reserving state.[734] But the ILC notes that state practice has developed an intermediate category of objections with effects in between those that modify the provisions to which the reservation relates (Article 21(3) VCLT)[735] and those that prevent the treaty from entering into force (Article 20(4)(b) VCLT). This intermediate category of objections excludes 'the application of certain provisions of the treaty that are not (specifically) addressed by the reservation'.[736] This requires, the ILC notes, that the provisions thus excluded 'have a sufficient link with the provisions to which the reservation relates'.[737] Hence, formulating objections with this effect (called 'intermediate' effect by the ILC) safeguards the balance of rights and obligations that result from a state's consent to the treaty as a whole. Nevertheless, the uncontrolled exclusion of the application of provisions not addressed by a reservation may upset the overall treaty balance between all parties and may be harmful to the treaty's integrity, as it further complicates relations through reservations and subsequent objections. Unsurprisingly, the ILC hopes that such objections continue to form exceptions to the practice of reservations.[738]

This is where the advantage of negotiated reservations and 'menu options' (i.e., contracting-in and optional clauses) comes in. Their difference is that of applicable system: a reservation prohibited by the treaty (a 'specified reservation'), is null or void. Hence, on the condition that a reservation is authorised by the treaty, negotiated reservations work on the basis of 'opting out' from the 'normal' obligations applicable at the time a treaty enters into force. 'Menu options', on the other hand, function on the basis of 'opt in'. Under an optional clause, a state's reaction is not required: it may still become a party to the treaty. Under a contracting-in clause, a reaction is required for a state to become a party.

Technicalities aside, these types of provisions are explicitly coordinated by the negotiators. This means they can be used to create 'package deals', i.e., bundles of rights and obligations that go beyond the rights and obligations of one single treaty clause. If a state decides not to agree to a contracting-in clause set by the negotiators, it can, unlike under a 'normal' reservation, not become a party to the treaty. Similarly,

---

733. *See*, for this argument, F. Parisi and C. Sevcenko (2003) p. 16.
734. *See* Art. 20(4)(b) VCLT and the UN, *Report of the ILC on the Practice on Reservations to Treaties* (2011) p. 255.
735. The effects of 21(3) may be similar to those of Art. 21(1) VCLT.
736. UN, *Report of the ILC on the Practice on Reservations to Treaties* (2011) p. 482.
737. *Id.*, at pp. 492 and 493.
738. *Id.*, at p. 495.

if a state wants to reserve on a provision but that reservation is prohibited, that reservation is void. The reserving state may hence have no other option but to completely quit the treaty.

The negotiation of 'package deals' may hence be generalised to the level of the treaty negotiation as a whole, and may therefore be used to 'steer' the need of parties to tailor the convention to their needs without causing the commitments under the treaty to disintegrate. Indeed, 'by indicating which treaty clauses are reservable, by specifying the types of reservations that are permitted (....) negotiators can make treaties politically palatable to a larger number of countries'.[739]

7.10.3 'Rules of the Road'

A core argument of Chapter 5 is that to increase the chances of multilateral cooperation in the international tax field, the focus must be placed on what have been termed 'rules of the road'. These are rules that create substantive tax treaty obligations for parties, but under which distributive effects are absent or uncertain. Remember the example of the two cars crossing an intersection (one south-northbound; the other west-eastbound, *see* section 5.3.4). To avoid car drivers having to bilaterally negotiate who yields the right-of-way to whom at each crossing, a coordination rule can be used that operates 'fairly', i.e., under which all actors get their preferred outcome half the time (section 5.4.3). From this perspective, the feasibility of several tax policy options that are currently on the negotiation table were discussed in section 5.4.4.

Let us first of all formalise this result by providing some suggestions for 'rules of the road' under a multilateral agreement for international taxation. Again, no normative claims as regards these rules shall be made, as they would require a study of their own. The point is rather to refine the argument and single out potential difficulties. As has been briefly discussed in section 5.4.6, a 'rule of the road' may cause uncertainty about the behaviour of others under the rule. This type of uncertainty (called 'Uncertainty about Behaviour' by Koremenos)[740] emphasises the need for centralised information and informal dispute resolution safeguards.[741] Incomplete contracts require tools, so to speak, to uphold the rule's application in specific cases. A centralised adjudicative body falls outside the scope of a 'managerial' approach to international tax law. But political and mediative ways of resolving disputes, in combination with facilitating the access to information, may also do the trick. The example treaty clauses in Articles 2 and 3 of the Protocol to the draft treaty set out in Annex A were drafted based on what is discussed below:

---

739. L.R. Helfer (2006) p. 378.
740. *See* B. Koremenos (2016) Ch. 7. 'Uncertainty about Behaviour' is different from the types of uncertainty discussed in Ch. 5. This latter type of uncertainty related to the uncertainty in respect of the state of the world (e.g., the consequences of different policy options, impacts of BEPS behaviour on revenue and welfare, etc).
741. *Id.*, at Ch. 7, also: B. Koremenos (2007); J. Mccall Smith (2000). In B. Koremenos (2016), Koremenos shows from her dataset that informal dispute resolution mechanisms may help actors to solve 'Uncertainty about Behaviour' problems.

(1) *Treaty GAARs*. We have seen that the open-endedness of GAARs, of which the PPT is the most relevant example, makes them dependent on context. It will be up to judges to further consolidate their operation, weighing the circumstances related to the case at hand, thus causing the rule to operate 'fairly'. However, the open-endedness of GAARs creates an incentive for countries to unilaterally expand their tax jurisdiction (and interpret the provision in a way that best serves their interests). But, as Bender and Engelen note, such uncertainty about the behaviour of other states may be relaxed by further 'consultation agreements' or a 'senior level approval process' between treaty parties.[742] Moreover, under a centrally agreed upon and implemented GAAR, it is not unlikely that judges will take into account the decisions of their foreign colleagues, strengthening a uniform interpretation of the clause.[743]

(2) *A non-discrimination clause that captures cases of 'indirect discrimination'*. This is a bit of a stretch, but to embody the idea that taxpayers engaged in internal or cross-border economic activities should be treated equally for tax purposes if all other circumstances are equal (*see* section 7.4), a non-discrimination clause analogous to that underlying the articles on free movement of the Treaty on the Functioning of the European Union (TFEU) could be used.[744]

Of course, tax treaties based on the OECD MTC do traditionally contain a non-discrimination clause that prevents discrimination on the basis of nationality. But Article 24 MTC does not apply to the tax treatment of non-residents (i.e., it does not cover forms of 'indirect discrimination').[745] As Van Raad notes, Article 24(1) does not prohibit a state from differentiating in its taxation on the basis of residence,[746] and the other provisions of Article 24 prohibit residence-based discrimination in certain specific circumstances only. Article 24 is, in other words, cast on the basis that 'corporate residence' is still a relevant criterion for treating cross-border and domestic economic activities differently.

But as Bammens notes, when Article 24 MTC is compared to the non-discrimination analysis applied under fundamental freedoms of EU law, the latter is broader.[747] EU law requires that cross-border economic activities are taxed in the same way as domestic economic activities and, if state aid rules

---

742. T. Bender and F.A. Engelen, *BEPS-Actie 6: De maatregelen tegen treaty shopping – bedreiging en kans*, WFR 2016/51 sec. 7.
743. Decisions of foreign judges may be used for tax treaty interpretation. *See* D.M. Broekhuijsen, *Verschillen tussen wets- en verdragsinterpretatie*, in: Kwaliteit van belastingrechtspraak belicht (J.P. Boer ed., SDU 2013) and D.A. Ward, *The Use of Foreign Court Decisions in Interpreting Tax Treaties*, in: Courts and tax treaty law (G. Maisto ed., IBFD 2007).
744. This follows of course from M.F. De Wilde (2015a), for example, p. 75.
745. *See also* the 2014 OECD Commentary to Art. 24, para. 1.
746. K. Van Raad, *Non-discrimination in International Tax Law* (Kluwer 1986).
747. N. Bammens, *The Principle of Non-Discrimination in International and European Tax Law* (IBFD 2012) pp. 1013–1014.

were also considered, vice versa. Hence, the underlying right protected under these freedoms is the prohibition of indirect discrimination on grounds of nationality or origin.[748]

Would the EU's non-discrimination rule be agreed upon in a multilateral agreement, the rule could function on the basis of the decision model that Douma proposes.[749] This approach balances the two competing principles in play, i.e.: the principle of state (tax) sovereignty and the principle of equality. If a rule is recognised as (dis)advantageous,[750] the task is then to identify a rule's respectful aim. Given the rule's respectful aim, a suitability test is applied (examining whether the rule at issue is 'apt to attain the objectives pursued'),[751] and then a proportionality test, to weigh the rule's over- and underinclusiveness, its subsidiarity and finally its proportionality *sensu stricto*.[752]

Such a non-discrimination rule, following the decision model that Douma proposes, is clearly a 'rule of the road'. It operates 'fairly' for all actors, and its effects are so uncertain that states might be willing to agree to such a rule. After all, parties to the EU were able to agree to a rule to this effect within the aim of realising the internal market. Nevertheless, the introduction of a non-discrimination clause might be an example of a 'rule of the road' that creates substantial uncertainty about the behaviour of others under the operation of the rule. Where under GAARS these problems may be relaxed by further bilateral consultations, the extent of uncertainty about the behaviour of others introduced by a non-discrimination clause is more substantial, making it likely that further centralisation, for example, a review mechanism, is required. After all, a non-discrimination clause inspired by the rules on the EU's fundamental freedoms requires states to cancel (or even reverse/review) the effects of discriminatory tax rules, and its impact is hence far more severe than that of a GAAR, under which states may protect their tax bases. It is therefore no wonder that as regards the EU, state behaviour under the fundamental freedoms is reviewed by the EU Commission and the ECJ. And also in other areas of international law where tax incentives are regulated,

---

748. B.J.M. Terra and P.J. Wattel, *European Tax Law* (Kluwer 4th ed., 2005) p. 38.
749. S.C.W. Douma, *Optimization of Tax Sovereignty and Free Movement* (IBFD 2011).
750. Douma's model is arguably also applicable as a decision model for EU state aid rules. These address the 'other' side of the discrimination coin: are cross-border economic activities treated more favourably than domestic (internal) economic activities? Following AG Kokott in *Sardegna:* 'the same questions arise with regard to the law of State aid as with regard to the fundamental freedoms, and there is no reason why the reply in relation to the latter should differ from the reply regarding the former. Rather, to avoid conflicting assessments as between the law of State aid and the law of fundamental freedoms, the same criteria must be applied in both cases.' ECJ, *Opinion of Advocate General Kokott, Presidente del Consiglio dei ministri v. Regione Sardegna,* 7 Feb. 2009, C-169/08, paras 133–134.
751. S.C.W. Douma (2011) p. 59.
752. *Id.,* at Ch. 7.

such as under the WTO, dispute resolution systems are used to review the obligations and behaviour of parties.[753]

So, a non-discrimination clause is toothless if not backed up by some form of dispute settlement mechanisms. Of course, the ideal solution would be a review by a centralised and independent adjudicative body. But the design strategy formulated in the previous chapter suggests that informal mechanisms are more feasible for international tax:[754] for example, information exchange to facilitate interaction in the forum, the use of bodies that are able to issue authoritative interpretations so that domestic judges can be informed, or the use of mandatory non-binding mediative procedures similar to the MAP now proposed under BEPS Action 14.[755] If this proves insufficient, the real reason for non-compliance is likely to be related to the fundamental lack of state commitment to the application of the rule, making an extended non-discrimination clause, although 'rule of the road', an unfeasible option.

(3) *Source or residence state priority in regulating certain categories of income.* For the purposes of agreeing on multilateral standards, an attempt to negotiate on a 'rule the road' that prioritises the tax treatment of either the source or residence state for a particular issue is appealing. Such a rule would obviate the need for detailed reservations. Indeed, in the cumulative totality of their treaty relations, 'asymmetric interests', i.e., each state is predominantly a source state in one bilateral relationship, and a residence state in another, may hide a clear distributive conflict, as one treaty relationship cancels out the other. So, a 'rule of the road' that prioritises the source or residence state jurisdiction may work in relation to 'new', tax treaty problems in relation to which the distribution of potential gains has not yet been fully realised or for which the operation of the current tax treaty regime remains ambiguous.

The tax treaty treatment of partnerships and transparent entities provides the obvious example of a priority rule: the main rule proposed by the partnership report is that the source state follows the resident state's classification of a transparent entity for tax purposes.[756] In extending the partnership's conclusions to transparent entities, a rule to this effect, insofar as the residence state actually taxes the income of the entity,[757] has been proposed in Article 3 of the BEPS Convention. And perhaps, the idea of a 'rule of the road' that prioritises

---

753. C. Micheau, *State Aid, Subsidy and Tax Incentives under EU and WTO Law* (Wolters Kluwer Law & Business 2014) pp. 325–333.

754. G.W. Downs, K.W. Danish and P.N. Barsoom (2000) say at p. 484 that advocates of the managerial approach find that dispute resolution mechanisms are 'too formal, overly cumbersome and difficult to initiate'. *See also* J. Brunnée and S.J. Toope (1997) p. 47, who note that states 'are most reluctant to cede any control when a decision may prove to be legally binding. It is noteworthy that despite the numerous dispute settlement provisions included in international environmental treaties, these mechanisms are not widely employed.'

755. A. Chayes and A.H. Chayes (1995) pp. 207–225.

756. OECD, *The Application of the OECD Model Tax Convention to Partnerships* (1999).

757. *See also* OECD, *Neutralising the Effects of Hybrid Mismatch Arrangements, Action 2: Final Report* (2015) OECD/G20 Base Erosion and Profit Shifting Project, OECD Publishing, Paris. http://dx.doi.org/10.1787/9789264241138-en, p. 139.

the residence or source state may be extend to other issues too. Although the BEPS Convention does not include it (*see* Chapter 8), a priority rule might work for Action 6's clauses too (for instance, in the selection of states between a PTT and extended LOB rule, preference could be given to the selection made by the state of source).

7.11 DYNAMIC DECISION-MAKING PROCEDURES

7.11.1 The Need for Dynamic Decision-Making Procedures under the Framework Convention-Protocol Design

Multilateral treaties are rigid tools. Once in place, they are notoriously hard to change, as an amendment to a rule requires the same level of consensus as its adoption. Hence, to facilitate the framework convention's decision-making processes, the convention's decision-making processes can be 'legally engineered'[758] so as to relax the consent requirement traditionally needed to adopt international law.[759]

In short, the 'traditional' method to amend a multilateral treaty functions as follows. First, the text of an amendment needs to be adopted within the organisation tasked with adopting texts: an IO or a treaty body. Then, the text has to be consented to or ratified by participating states, an act by means of which the text becomes binding on them. This process is regulated by Article 11 of the Vienna Convention. That convention holds that to be bound by a treaty (amendment),[760] a state must have consented to that treaty:

> The consent of a State to be bound by a treaty may be expressed by signature, exchange of instruments constituting a treaty, ratification, acceptance, approval or accession, or by any other means if so agreed.

In other words, the amendment of a multilateral treaty requires the renegotiation of the text (the 'adoption requirement') and the subsequent consent of the participating states (the 'consent requirement') before the amendment becomes binding on a participating state. Consequently, one of the main disadvantages of multilateralism – in the form of a binding multilateral convention – is that once a multilateral treaty is in place, changing the convention requires an amendment's acceptance on two levels. This makes the multilateral treaty amendment process cumbersome, particularly when, for instance, quick amendments are required to protocols or annexes.

And indeed, requiring the explicit consent of all participating states before a text has binding force has been considered a serious problem for the international

---

758. R. Lefeber, *Creative Legal Engineering*, 13 Leiden Journal of International Law 1 (2000).

759. *See*, for a first exploration of these issues, D.M. Broekhuijsen (2013b); J. Luts, *Een 'multilateraal instrument' (BEPS actiepunt 15): Denkpistes en verhouding tot de Belgische interne rechtsorde*, Algemeen Fiscaal Tijdschrift 28 (2014).

760. Article 11 VCLT also applies to treaty amendment. *See* Art. 39 of the VCLT and F.A. Engelen, *Fiscaal Verdragsbeleid en het OESO-Modelverdrag*, WFR 2011/548.

system.[761] An inflexible arrangement may prevent the effective operation of the treaty in the long run, as the agreement, once adopted, does not enable the incorporation of further political, economic and scientific developments either in the situation of a particular state or in more global changes affecting all states. This could then cause states to take unilateral action instead, thereby undermining the multilateral cooperative effort.[762] As a result, the current system to amend treaties emphasises the interests of the individual state and not that of the collective.[763] The consent requirement creates the possibility of strategic 'holding out' or 'opportunistic' behaviour,[764] and the 'lack of flexibility and fear of non-compliance in the face of unanticipated events might drive parties to MLTs to accept only shallower obligations'.[765]

7.11.2 Dynamic Decision-Making Procedures in International Law

In international law, the consent requirement has been relaxed by mechanisms in which texts are adopted by a majority vote, and by a softer variant, the so-called the *opt-out* method (which should be distinguished from the optional clauses discussed in section 7.10.2).[766] It is important to point out that both procedures do not affect the ability of states to influence the adoption of the text within the institution or COP. Indeed, a state can exercise its influence in the institutional decision-making process, for instance, within a consensus or a (qualified) majority vote voting system.

The primary example of a system in which texts are adopted by majority vote is Article 2(9) of the Montreal Protocol on Substances that Deplete the Ozone Layer (hereinafter: Montreal Protocol), which is a protocol to the Vienna Convention to the Ozone Layer.[767] This article provides for adjustments to the ozone depleting potentials already specified in the protocol's annexes.[768] These adjustments are, as a last resort,

---

761. *See, e.g.*, A.T. Guzman, *Against Consent*, 52 Virginia Journal of International Law 747 (2012); B. Simma, *Consent: Strains in the Treaty System*, in: The Structure and Process of International Law: Essays in Legal Philosophy, Doctrine and Theory (R.S.J. MacDonald and D.M. Johnston eds, Martinus Nijhoff 1983).
762. Palmer calls the conventional international environmental lawmaking methods 'slow, cumbersome, expensive, uncoordinated and uncertain'. *See* G. Palmer, *New Ways to make International Environmental Law*, 86 American Journal of International Law 259, 259 (1992).
763. E. Pan, *Authoritative Interpretation of Agreements: Developing More Responsive International Administrative Regimes*, 38 Harvard International Law Journal 503, 507 (1997).
764. A.T. Guzman (2012) p. 751.
765. G. Blum (2008) p. 353.
766. For example, P. Széll, *Decision Making under Multilateral Environmental Agreements*, 26 Environmental Policy and Law 210 (1996); R. Lefeber (2000); J. Brunnée, *COPing with Consent: Law-Making Under Multilateral Environmental Agreements*, 15 Leiden Journal of International Law 1 (2002); J. Brunnée, *Reweaving the Fabric of International Law? Patterns of Consent in Environmental Framework Agreements*, in: Developments of International Law in Treaty Making (R. Wolfrum and V. Röben eds, Springer 2005) and G. Ulfstein, *Reweaving the Fabric of International Law? Patterns of Consent in Environmental Framework Agreements, Comment*, in: Developments of International Law in Treaty Making (R. Wolfrum and V. Röben eds, Springer 2005); M. Fitzmaurice, *Consent to Be Bound – Anything New under the Sun?*, 74 Nordic Journal of International Law 483 (2005); G. Loibl (2005).
767. Montreal Protocol on Substances that Deplete the Ozone Layer.
768. *Id.*, at Art. 2(9)(a). To add new substances to the annex, the application of the 'normal' amendment rule is required where all States express their consent.

adopted by a two-third majority vote and are binding on all parties.[769] The only way 'out' of adjustments a party does not agree with is to withdraw from the convention, which a party can do after four years from the date the convention entered into force.[770] So, the Montreal Protocol's amendment system is quite rigorous. It implies that, at the moments of adoption and ratification of the amendment system *itself*, states acquiesced in the complete elimination of the use of harmful chemicals, leaving for further discussion and decision the timing of measures to that end.[771]

The opt-out rule is a softer, less legitimacy and sovereignty-intrusive variant of a dynamic amendment procedure. The idea of an opt-out rule is that, instead of requiring the explicit consent of a treaty state to a certain text (i.e., an *opt-in*), states are 'automatically' bound to a certain treaty amendment *unless a state voices its disagreement*, mostly within a certain time period.[772] This is supposed to make objections to proposed changes politically unattractive, whilst the principle of state sovereignty is not abandoned.[773] In doing so, the opt-out procedure covers the middle ground between the necessity to change a treaty regime and the need to protect state sovereignty through the expression of a state's consent. It leaves states free to withdraw their consent if necessary.[774]

Opt-out methods are not uncommon: they are, for instance, used in treaties regulating the environment,[775] aviation[776] and public health.[777] For example, the Constitution of the World Health Organization (WHO) is a multilateral treaty in which such an opt-out procedure exists. The *Health Assembly* can adopt regulations by a qualified majority.[778] As regards these regulations, Article 22 of the Constitution holds:

> Regulations adopted pursuant to Article 21 shall come into force for all Members after due notice has been given of their adoption by the Health Assembly except for such Members as may notify the Director-General of rejection or reservations within the period stated in the notice.

Perhaps unsurprisingly, experience learns that the opt-out procedure is particularly efficient in relation to amendments to treaty annexes of a technical, procedural or scientific nature.[779] For instance, the UNFCCC has an opt-out procedure to amend its annexes, which cover material of a descriptive nature and with a technical, procedural or administrative character:

---

769. *Id.*, at Art. 2(9)(c) and 2(9)(d).
770. *Id.*, at Art. 19.
771. P. Széll (1996) p. 213.
772. The main difference between an opt-out rule and a reservation is that a reservation is filed at the time of concluding, accepting, or ratifying a treaty text that is known to them; and opt-out rule applies to all *future* treaty texts adopted by the institution.
773. M. Fitzmaurice (2005) pp. 488–489.
774. *Id.*, at pp. 488–489.
775. *See*, for instance, the *Convention on Future Multilateral Co-operation in Northwest Atlantic Fisheries* (adopted 24 Oct. 1978), 1135 UNTS 369 (1978 NAFO Convention).
776. *See, e.g.*, the ICAO Convention.
777. *Constitution of the World Health Organization* (adopted 22 Jul. 1946), 14 UNTS 185.
778. *Id.*, at Art. 21.
779. J. Brunnée (2012) p. 359.

Article 16 Adoption and Amendment of Annexes to the Convention

Annexes to the Convention shall form an integral part thereof and, unless otherwise expressly provided, a reference to the Convention constitutes at the same time a reference to any annexes thereto. Without prejudice to the provisions of Article 14, paragraphs 2(b) and 7, such annexes shall be restricted to lists, forms and any other material of a descriptive nature that is of a scientific, technical, procedural or administrative character.

2. Annexes to the Convention shall be proposed and adopted in accordance with the procedure set forth in Article 15, paragraphs 2, 3 and 4.

3. An annex that has been adopted in accordance with paragraph 2 above shall enter into force for all Parties to the Convention six months after the date of the communication by the Depositary to such Parties of the adoption of the annex, except for those Parties that have notified the Depositary, in writing, within that period of their non-acceptance of the annex. The annex shall enter into force for Parties which withdraw their notification of non-acceptance on the ninetieth day after the date on which withdrawal of such notification has been received by the Depositary.

4. The proposal, adoption and entry into force of amendments to annexes to the Convention shall be subject to the same procedure as that for the proposal, adoption and entry into force of annexes to the Convention in accordance with paragraphs 2 and 3 above.[780]

As these annexes are of a technical nature (i.e., they do not touch upon a regime's 'core' obligations), they are not fraught with political difficulties, and as a result, 'the potential shift of domestic authority over international commitments seems unproblematic'.[781]

The ability to quickly adapt a multilateral treaty to new scientific and technical circumstances greatly enhances the effectiveness and responsiveness of a regime. The introduction of an opt-out procedure at the forum of the International Maritime Organization (IMO, formerly IMCO) is an example of this. The success of the IMO is to some extent attributed to this provision, as the procedure has enabled the IMO 'to keep abreast of the evolving technology in the maritime field and to respond promptly to urgent matters'.[782] In example, in relation to the IMO's International Convention for the Safety of Life at Sea (the 1974 SOLAS Convention),[783] an opt-out procedure enabled the

---

780. United Nations Framework Convention on Climate Change Art. 16. The adoption or amendment of an annex is adopted by the Conference of the Parties by consensus, or if no agreement is reached, by a three-fourths majority votes of the parties present and voting. *See* Art. 15(2).
781. J. Brunnée (2002) p. 20.
782. L. Shi, *Successful Use of the Tacit Acceptance Procedure to Effectuate Progress in International Maritime Law*, 11 University of San Francisco Maritime Law Journal 299, 331 (1998). *See also* A.O. Adede, *Amendment Procedures for Conventions with Technical Annexes: The IMCO Experience*, 17 Virginia Journal of International Law 201 (1976); L. Shi (1998) p. 303.
783. *1974 International Convention for the Safety of Life at Sea* (adopted 1 Nov. 1974), 1184 UNTS 2.

regime to incorporate technical[784] changes in a quicker fashion,[785] preventing unilateral action to disrupt the international shipping industry.[786]

The success of the tacit amendment procedure in the IMO Conventions is shown by the fact that in practice, objections to amendments adopted under the procedure are rare.[787] Also, it turned out that the industry can prepare for upcoming amendments, as the committee adopting amendments may provide an indication of the date on which the amendment is deemed to be accepted and expected to enter into force.[788]

As regards opt-out procedures in relation to non-technical annexes, particularly in relation to environmental regimes with clear and obvious underlying distributive conflicts,[789] the procedure does not add any dynamic or problem solving value. Exemplary in this regard are regimes regulating biodiversity, such as those on fisheries. Setting fish quotas and moratoria has obvious distributive consequences for the participating states (preventing states to fish in waters directly harms its fishery

---

784. The annex comprises standards on for instance the construction of ships, life-saving equipment and radio communications.

785. The amendment provision of the SOLAS 1974 Convention, Art. VIII, reads: (emphasis added):

> (b) Amendments after consideration within the Organization: (...)
> (vi) (2) An amendment to the Annex other than Chapter I shall be *deemed to have been accepted:*
> *(aa) at the end of two years from the date on which it is communicated to Contracting Governments for acceptance*; (...) However, if within the specified period either more than one-third of Contracting Governments, or Contracting Governments the combined merchant fleets of which constitute not less than fifty per cent of the gross tonnage of the world's merchant fleet, notify the Secretary-General of the Organization that they object to the amendment, it shall be deemed not to have been accepted.
> (vii) (...) (2) An amendment to the Annex other than Chapter I *shall enter into force with respect to all Contracting Governments, except those which have objected to the amendment under sub-paragraph (vi)(2) of this paragraph and which have not withdrawn such objections, six months after the date on which it is deemed to have been accepted.* (...).

786. L. Juda, *Imco and the Regulation of Ocean Pollution from Ships*, 26 International & Comparative Law Quarterly 558, 574 (1977). *See also* the resolution by the IMCO Assembly: *Amendment Procedures in Conventions of which IMCO is Depositary*, Resolution A. 249(VII) (1971). Under the old *explicit* amendment procedure used by the IMO, it became clear that it was impossible to secure the timely entry into force of amendments. The 1960 Convention on the Safety of Life at Sea was amended in 1966, 1967, 1968, 1969, 1971 and 1973, but none of these amendments has ever entered into force. *See* M.J. Bowman, *The Multilateral Treaty Amendment Process – A Case Study*, 44 International and Comparative Law Quarterly 540, 551 (1995).

787. If states do object, it is only to allow for additional time to implement the amendment in domestic laws. *See* J. Harrison, *Making the Law of the Sea: A Study in the Development of International Law* (Cambridge University Press 2011) p. 162.

788. *Id.*, at p. 163.

789. O.R. Young (1989) also adds a 'veil of uncertainty' to distributive bargaining to explain why states have come to reach agreement in some environmental regimes, but not in others, emphasising the role of equity in bargaining solutions. Particularly fishery regimes are a good example of how, lacking a clear 'veil of uncertainty', actors may end up in an international deadlock under distributive issues. Indeed, '[the veil of uncertainty] also helps us understand the difficulties that plague efforts to devise mutually acceptable arrangements dealing with acid precipitation, biological diversity, or the global warming trend. To put it simply, the key players find it easier to see through the veil of uncertainty in these cases than in a number of other areas referred to in this discussion', *id.*, at p. 362.

industries, but fish stocks are mobile and hence not bound to states' rights over water). And opt-out procedures have helped little in mitigating or softening such distributive stalemates. A demonstrative example is the management of fishing stocks by the fisheries commission of the Northwest Atlantic Fisheries Organization (NAFO), which can issue proposals on the total allowable catch.[790] Under the 1978 NAFO Convention,[791] proposals on fish quotas by the fisheries commission become binding on all contracting states after a certain time period, unless a party objects.[792] The possibility to object to these quotas has been used by members who were not satisfied with quotas, which then enabled those states to set their own (higher) quotas, leaving the door open for over-fishing. This, in turn, influenced the 'fish pie' (i.e., the total of fish stock that can be caught without endangering the area's biodiversity).[793] The alleged overfishing by Spain and the EU in NAFO waters[794] led to a conflict between the EU, in particular Spain, and Canada known as the Turbot War, that ultimately resulted in the renovation of the NAFO Convention in 2007.[795] Another example in this regard is the conflict regulated by the International Convention for the Regulation of Whaling (ICRW).[796] One of the most important objections filed by states in the history of the International Whaling Commission (IWC) was the one lodged by in particular Norway and Japan against the moratorium on commercial whaling that prohibited all whaling activities from the 1985/1986 season onwards.[797] And clearly, the moratorium has obvious consequences for Norway and Japan. Although the ban was supposed to be temporary, it has been extended year after year, causing a deadlock in the discussions within the IWC between the pro and anti-whaling members of the Commission.[798] Article V(3), the convention's dynamic amendment procedure regarding the amendment of whale conservation rules and catch limits,[799] has helped little to prevent such deadlock.

---

790. Although these proposals have the character of a (binding) decision of a treaty body rather than a proposed amendment to the text or annex of a treaty, they are worth mentioning here because the method by means of which states can opt out to become bound by these proposals is analogous to the method used to amend a treaty's texts or annexes described above.
791. 1978 NAFO Convention (1978 NAFO Convention).
792. The NAFO is established by the 1978 NAFO Convention. The procedure is regulated in Art. XII.
793. A. Rey Aneiros, *Spain, The European Union, and Canada: A New Phase in the Unstable Balance in the Northwest Atlantic Fisheries*, 42 Ocean Development & International Law 155, 164 (2011).
794. House of Commons, *Foreign Overfishing: Its Impacts and Solutions. Conservation on the Nose and Tail of the Grand Banks and the Flemish Cap* (2002) Standing Committee on Fisheries and Oceans, Tenth Report 8 (June 2002).
795. These amendments have been ratified by the EU and Canada. *See* http://www.nafo.int/about/frames/convention.html, last accessed January 2016.
796. *International Convention for the Regulation of Whaling* (adopted 2 December 1946), 161 UNTS 72.
797. The so-called moratorium on commercial whaling of 1982 is still in effect today. *See*: ICRW, *Schedule to the Convention* (July 2012), http://iwc.int/convention last accessed June 2016. For a discussion, *see* H.S. Schiffman, *Marine Conservation Agreements: The Law and Policy of Reservations and Vetoes* (Martinus Nijhoff Publishers 2008) pp. 80–86.
798. *See*, for the discussion in the IWC, D. Goodman, *The 'Future of the IWC': Why the Initiative to Save the International Whaling Commission Failed*, 14 Journal of International Wildlife Law and Policy 63 (2011).
799. ICRW, Art. V(1) and V(2).

7.11.3 The Use of Dynamic Decision-Making Procedures in the Multilateral Agreement for International Taxation

From the above, it can be generally concluded that dynamic decision-making procedures can be used to quickly change annexes of a technical nature. They are however no help in streamlining the decision-making process of issues characterised by clear distributive conflicts.

In combination with the outcomes of the previous chapters, it may hence be suggested that, prima facie, dynamic decision-making procedures can be successfully used for international tax law in relation to certain technical aspects, such as, for example, transfer pricing regulation or the attribution of profits to PEs, or measures of administrative concern.

Nevertheless, tax literature has raised the question whether dynamic decision-making procedures erode the legitimacy of international tax lawmaking. What is the basis for the rule-making authority of these institutions? Does this authority follow from the 'general consent' of states to the lawmaking procedure,[800] which involves a much more significant surrender of authority than a state's specific consent to a specific rule? After all, under the majority vote mechanism, states can be bound against their will to commitments they do not yet know.[801] And by agreeing to the opt-out procedure, states give their 'general consent' to amendments in the future.[802]

Under high degrees of 'generativity',[803] the erosion of the legitimacy of (and hence also of state sovereignty under) the tax lawmaking process is a thorny issue. After all, taxation is an involuntary fee levied on individuals and corporations, enforced by government. In most jurisdictions, the exercise of the government's power is strictly defined by law. Legitimising this authority is important: illegitimate tax law is nothing but brute force, and this undermines routine forms of voluntary compliance.[804] But as tax lawmaking is becoming more and more removed from its domestic (democratic) basis of legitimation, these democratic underpinnings erode. The wariness of some authors in respect of the use of such procedures for international tax law is therefore completely understandable.[805]

---

800. D. Bodansky, *The Legitimacy of International Governance: A Coming Challenge for International Environmental Law?*, 93 The American Journal of International Law 596–624 (1999).
801. *Id.*, at p. 609.
802. A. Wiersema, *The New International Law-Makers? Conferences of the Parties to Multilateral Environmental Agreements*, 31 Michigan Journal of International Law 231 (2009) questions how, in a typology of international legal obligation, such types of 'treaty activity' can be classified. She evaluates such consensus-based lawmaking activities on the basis of four axes: voting and level of consent; the level to which the treaty delegates authority to such activities; the level of obligation contained in language used; the effect of the resulting rules.
803. This term is used by Raustiala and expresses the ability of international institutions to produce new substantive rules that modify or amend a given legal agreement. K. Raustiala, *Sovereignty and Multilateralism*, 1 Chicago Journal of International Law 401, 412 (2000).
804. H. Gribnau, *Equality, Legal Certainty and Tax Legislation in the Netherlands. Fundamental Legal Principles as Checks on Legislative Power: A Case Study*, 9 Utrecht Law Review 52, 56–57 (2013).
805. C. Peters (2014) pp. 343–344 and J. Luts (2014).

The legitimacy perspective would in any case disqualify the use of a majority voting method. Such a procedure can bind a state to treaty amendments against its will. This implies a significant and unacceptable surrender of democratic legitimacy. But what of the opt-out procedure, when its use is limited to amending rules of a technical nature? After all, states remain in control under such a procedure: they ultimately have the possibility to withdraw the general consent already given.

Luts argues that the use of such procedures is very problematic from the perspective of the Belgian internal legal order.[806] But the Constitution of the Netherlands allows some leeway.[807] Indeed, Article 7(f) of the *Rijkswet goedkeuring en bekendmaking verdragen* (Kingdom Act on the approval and publication of treaties) says that Parliament does not have to consent to amendments to integrated annexes of an 'executive' nature (the term used is '*uitvoerende aard*').[808] With this rule, the Netherlands tries to meet the requirements of a dynamic international legal practice, as the Netherlands might benefit from a quick and efficient government response.[809] What particularly seems to matter in this regard, is whether Parliament can anticipate or foresee the contents of future annex amendments.[810]

Hence, a workable dynamic mechanism for international taxation is one under which states have a real and tangible influence.[811] Such influence is of course best safeguarded by explicit state consent and hence by parliamentary control. But as regards annexes of a technical or 'executive' nature, the consent requirement may be somewhat relaxed by an opt-out procedure, such as the one drafted in Article 5 to the Protocol of the convention of Annex A. In this way, the state retains its influence in international matters that require a dynamic approach to cooperation, without severely violating legitimacy concerns.

---

806. J. Luts (2014).
807. The parliamentary consent requirement is set out in Art. 91 of the Constitution. Decisions of international bodies fall within the ambit of Art. 91 of the Constitution. They can also be considered a 'treaty' in the sense of that article, as they require an act of state consent. *See* H.H.M. Sondaal, *De Nederlandse Verdragspraktijk* (TMC Asser Instituut 1986) pp. 134–135.
808. Article 7(f) of the *Rijkswet goedkeuring en bekendmaking verdragen*. In Dutch, the article holds: 'Tenzij een verdrag bepalingen bevat welke afwijken van de Grondwet of tot zodanig afwijken noodzaken, is de goedkeuring niet vereist (...) (f) indien het verdrag betreft wijziging van een integrerend onderdeel van een goedgekeurd verdrag vormende bijlage waarvan de inhoud van uitvoerende aard is ten opzichte van de bepalingen van het verdrag waar de bijlage onderdeel van vormt, voor zover in de wet tot goedkeuring geen voorbehoud terzake is gemaakt'.
809. *Kamerstukken II* 1992/1993, 21 214, 17, pp. 1–2. Whether the annex is of an 'executive nature' follows from a comparison of that annex with the main body of the convention. The correct interpretation of the provision therefore depends on the contents of the main treaty text.
810. In Dutch parliamentary history, it was argued by the Raad van State that the exception is to be narrowly interpreted. Only annexes of a very technical nature, such as those of the International Convention for Safe Containers and the Customs Convention on the International Transport of Goods under cover of TIR Carnets, are considered admissible under the exception. Nevertheless, the Administration has disagreed with this position, arguing that if Parliament fails to file a reservation as regards the use of the exception when consenting to the main treaty in which the amendment procedure was included, this forms an indication of its wish to follow the exception. At the time of consenting to the main treaty, Parliament knows the purpose of the annexes and can hence anticipate the contents of future amendments to the annexes. *Kamerstukken II* 1992/93, 21 214, 17, pp. 2–3.
811. J. Luts (2014) p. 32.

7.12 CONCLUSIONS OF PART 7B: THE FRAMEWORK CONVENTION-PROTOCOL DESIGN

Under the framework convention-protocol design, exemplified in Annex A, states slowly expand and deepen their commitments over time by agreeing to protocols. It is not necessary for all states to the framework convention to agree to participate in them; only interested parties may agree to deepen commitments. Yet, parties that do not wish to sign a protocol remain included in the deliberations that take place within the regime, potentially propelling them towards deeper cooperation at a later stage.

Because the framework convention-protocol type of treaty is 'layered' on top of the bilateral tax treaty network, a conflict clause is required that regulates the relationship between the two types of treaties. Such a clause has been considered in section 7.9, and an example clause has been drafted in Article 8 of Annex A.

Furthermore, the framework convention-protocol design should be supplemented by interpretative flexibility devices: reservations and 'menu options' provide solutions for states to tailor commitments to their needs. The advantage of using 'menu options' and *negotiated* reservations is that these become part of a package deal, as the different choices have been coordinated on by the negotiators. Under a 'menu option', states can only become a party to the treaty or protocol after having selected one of the options provided for in the 'menu'. And under negotiated reservations, states can only reserve on provisions when this is explicitly authorised by the treaty. Any other reservation, i.e., a reservation not explicitly authorised by the treaty, is void. This means that a state must agree to the list of negotiated reservations, or back out. Uncoordinated reservations, on the other hand, function on the basis of symmetry. The uncoordinated formulation of reservations may therefore upset the consensual balance of reciprocity underlying the agreement, or may lead to further disintegration, as it is possible that non-reserving states file objections to these reservations that modify or exclude provisions not addressed by the reservation. Also, states may agree on 'rules of the road'. 'Rules of the road' increase the chance that states participate in a treaty or a protocol's substantive multilateral commitments. The point is, as shown in Chapter 5, that such a rule 'fairly' accommodates the diverse interests of a group of participants. To set the discussion for debate, three examples of 'rules of the road' were proposed: a non-discrimination clause, a GAAR and a rule that prioritises the taxing right of either the source or residence state for 'new' categories of income or for categories of income in relation to which tax treaties currently operate ambiguously (*see* e.g., Article 3(1) of the BEPS Convention).

Finally, to increase its resilience as a managerial regime, the drafters of the framework convention may consider the use of dynamic decision-making devices such as the opt-out procedure. Article 5 of the Protocol to the draft treaty of Annex A is an example of such a clause. However, using such forms of legal engineering may erode the democratic legitimacy underpinning tax rules thus made (*see* section 7.11). Hence, the use of these procedures, with the aim to increase the regime's dynamic operation, must be balanced against the need to protect the legitimacy of tax lawmaking. Limiting the use of such devices to tax rules of a 'technical' rather than distributive nature (e.g., certain refinements to transfer pricing reporting requirements) may soften the legitimacy concerns somewhat.

PART 7C: THE 'AGREEMENT TO SCOPE'

7.13 INTRODUCTION TO PART 7C

In many respects, the 'agreement to scope' is easier to develop and envisage than a treaty based on the framework convention-protocol design, as it does not require that its norms are 'layered' on top of bilateral tax treaties.

The commitments of an 'agreement to scope' can be added to the multilateral treaty's 'constitutional' elements (*see* Part 7A). The purpose of the 'agreement to scope' is to further facilitate bilateral bargaining in the forum by means of some procedural obligations. These additional procedural obligations involve states' commitment to 'limit the scope' of the general principles or (soft law) model treaties in their bilateral tax treaty relationships by means of a *pactum de negotiando* or a *pactum de contrahendo*. The behaviour of states as regards this commitment may be monitored and reviewed. This ensures that a level playing field is upheld and that states' legal commitment to flesh out value-maximising terms in their bilateral tax conventions is put in practice.

Section 7.14.1 will first discuss the background of the procedural characteristics of an 'agreement to scope' in international public law. Section 7.14.2 considers its use for the purposes of international tax law.

7.14 THE 'AGREEMENT TO SCOPE'

7.14.1 The 'Agreement to Scope' in International Public Law

Obviously, states do not necessarily have to bindingly agree on a rule that establishes the performance or omission of a certain act (an 'obligation of conduct'), such as is required by a framework convention-protocol design. States can also agree on a procedural obligation to implement norms, within a certain broad legal purview, in a treaty or in domestic law in the future (an 'obligation of *result*'),[812] *see* section 7.14.1.1. Soft-law model treaties may guide or inform the practical facets of such a future negotiation. An open norm is thereby 'made precise' by means of a future legal act. In this view, an 'agreement to scope' functions much like an EU directive does: it sets out a certain legal purview that states have to implement in future legal acts. By

---

812. *See*, for a discussion, R. Wolfrum, *Obligation of Result Versus Obligation of Conduct: Some Thoughts About the Implementation of International Obligations*, in: Looking to the Future: Essays on International Law in Honor of W. Michael Reisman (M.H. Arsanjani et al., eds, Martinus Nijhoff Publishers 2011).

implication, and like the framework convention-protocol design, the 'agreement to scope' is iterative in nature, as it requires subsequent (centralised) bilateral negotiations. If necessary, the obligation of result can be backed up by monitoring and reporting mechanisms (section 7.14.1.2).

7.14.1.1 Pactum de Contrahendo *and* Pactum de Negotiando

An obligation of result can be designed in two ways: it can either require the conclusion of a future agreement (a *pactum de contrahendo*) or the (re)negotiation of a (later) treaty (a *pactum de negotiando*). Although the distinction between the two forms is considered hardly necessary or practical,[813] the latter obligation is less extensive as it does not require states to actually *arrive* at an agreement.[814] Nevertheless, both types of obligation are to be performed in good faith, which is a concept that lies at heart of such *pacta*.[815] Consequently, a *pactum de negotiando* is not without legal consequences, as it means that 'both sides have to make an effort, in good faith, to bring about a mutually satisfactory solution by way of a compromise, even if that meant the relinquishment of strongly held positions earlier taken'.[816] Thus, the negotiation takes place 'with a view to concluding agreements'.[817] Keeping the requirements of good faith in mind, a refusal of one of the parties to negotiate or conclude an agreement is considered a breach of international law.[818] Likewise, breaking off discussions without justification, disregard of procedure, causing delays, etc., may be against the rule of good faith.[819]

Generally speaking, *pacta de negotiando* and *pacta de contrahendo* contain a procedural as well as a substantive element. The procedural element has the nature of looking ahead: what is to be done in future negotiations? The substantive element of *pacta*, on the other hand, cabins the object of future negotiations. Sometimes, the object of future negotiations is made explicit; sometimes, the substance of such negotiations follows from agreements already in place (this particularly occurs in *pacta* related to international dispute resolution).

---

813. U. Beyerlin, *Pactum de contrahendo und pactum denegotiando im Völkerrecht?*, 36 Zeitschrift für ausländisches öffentliches Recht und Völkerrecht 407 (1976); also: L. Marion, *La notion de 'pactum de contrahendo' dans la jurisprudence internationale*, 78 Revue General de Droit International Public 351, 386–389 (1974).
814. H. Owada (2010) M.A. Rogoff, *The Obligation to Negotiate in International Law: Rules and Realities*, 16 Michigan Journal of International Law 141, 148 (1994).
815. H. Owada (2010) para. 43; S.L. Kass, *Obligatory Negotiations in International Organizations*, 3 Canadian Yearbook of International Law 36 (1965).
816. *See* the Arbitral Tribunal in *Claims Arising out of Decisions of the Mixed Graeco-German Arbitral Tribunal set up under Article 304 in Part X of the Treaty of Versailles (Greece v The Federal Republic of Germany)*, 19 RIAA 27, p. 56.
817. According to the Permanent Court of International Justice in PCIJ, *Railway Traffic between Lithuania and Poland (Railway Sector Landwarów-Kaisiadorys) (Judgements, Orders and Advisory Opinions)*, PCIJ Rep Series A/B No. 42, and later in: *North Sea Continental Shelf (Federal Republic of Germany v. Denmark; Federal Republic of Germany v. the Netherlands)*, p. 47.
818. H. Owada (2010) paras 34–45.
819. C. Hutchison (2006) p. 142.

Examples of *pacta de negotiando* and *pacta de contrahendo* are related to: (1) the settlement of international disputes; (2) the initiation of a subsequent agreement on open questions; and (3) the elaboration of further details at a later stage.[820] A *pactum* in the first category requires parties to negotiate their difference of views. For instance, Article 286 of the UN Convention on the Law of the Sea holds:

> Subject to section 3, any dispute concerning the interpretation or application of this Convention shall, where no settlement has been reached by recourse to section 1, be submitted at the request of any party to the dispute to the court or tribunal having jurisdiction under this section.[821]

Another, perhaps more familiar, example of such a clause can be found in Article 25 of the OECD MTC:

> 2. The competent authority shall endeavour, if the objection appears to it to be justified and if it is not itself able to arrive at a satisfactory solution, to resolve the case by mutual agreement with the competent authority of the other Contracting State, with a view to the avoidance of taxation which is not in accordance with the Convention. Any agreement reached shall be implemented notwithstanding any time limits in the domestic law of the Contracting States.

A *pactum* in the second category obliges parties to continue or open negotiations on a certain issue, possibly under a time schedule. Consider, for instance, Article 18 of the Treaty on Conventional Armed Forces in Europe, which held:

> 1. The States Parties, after signature of this Treaty, shall continue the negotiations on conventional armed forces with the same Mandate and with the goal of building on this Treaty.
>
> 2. The objective for these negotiations shall be to conclude an agreement on additional measures aimed at further strengthening security and stability in Europe, and pursuant to the Mandate, including measures to limit the personnel strength of their conventional armed forces within the area of application.
>
> 3. The States Parties shall seek to conclude these negotiations no later than the follow-up meeting of the Conference on Security and Cooperation in Europe to be held in Helsinki in 1992.[822]

Pacta of the third category can usually be found in framework agreements, which set the scene for further technical or practical agreement at the implementation stage.[823] An example is article VII of the 1993 Declaration of Principles on Interim Self-Government Arrangements between the Palestine Liberation Organisation and Israel (the Oslo Agreement):

> 1. The Israeli and Palestinian delegations will negotiate an agreement on the interim period (the 'Interim Agreement').[824]

---

820. U. Beyerlin (1976) pp. 417–421.
821. *United Nations Convention on the Law of the Sea* (adopted 10 Dec. 1982), 1833 UNTS 3.
822. *Treaty on Conventional Armed Forces in Europe* (adopted 19 Nov. 1990), 30 ILM 6.
823. U. Beyerlin (1976) pp. 420–421.
824. *Declaration of Principles on Interim Self-Government Arrangements ('Oslo Agreement')* (adopted 13 Sept. 1993), 32 ILM 1525.

This Interim Agreement had to include the following specifications:

2. The Interim Agreement shall specify, among other things, the structure of the Council, the number of its members, and the transfer of powers and responsibilities from the Israeli military government and its Civil Administration to the Council. The interim Agreement shall also specify the Council's executive authority, legislative authority in accordance with Article IX below, and the independent Palestinian judicial organs.[825]

Similarly, in the 1997 UN Convention on the Law of Non-Navigational uses of International Watercourses (hereinafter: International Watercourse Convention) it has been agreed that:

2. parties to agreements referred to in paragraph 1 [that is: watercourse agreements in force] may, where necessary, consider harmonizing such agreements with the basic principles of the present convention.

3. Watercourse States may enter into one or more agreements, hereinafter referred to as 'watercourse agreements', which apply and adjust the provisions of the present Convention to the characteristics and uses of a particular international watercourse or part thereof.[826]

Hence, the International Watercourse Convention functions as an 'agreement to scope' in that it may influence negotiations of watercourse agreements (predominantly: regional and bilateral) that already exist as well as those that are to be developed and concluded in the future. The principles that the International Watercourse Convention sets forth are the equitable and reasonable utilisation and participation of watercourses (Article 5) and the obligation to prevent harm to other riparian states (Article 7). For the aims of Article 5, the Watercourse Convention sets forth relevant factors that states have to take into account to achieve the principle, such as the social and economic needs of the watercourse state concerned, and the conservation, protection, development and economy of the use of water resources of a watercourse.[827] Hence, the main function of the International Watercourse Convention is to influence *inter se* negotiations on specific shared watercourses. And as McCafferey notes, states have started to converge on these principles in their *inter se* conventions since 1997,[828] even though the Convention has only recently (in 2014) come into force.

So, in sum, *pacta de negotiando* and *pacta de contrahendo* cabin the outcomes of future negotiations (for instance, by means of certain principles or by other forms of predetermined legal confines such as the terms of an existing treaty) and contain look-ahead provisions in which states procedurally agree on the result that is to be achieved in good faith.[829]

---

825. *Id.*, at Art. VII.
826. *UN Convention on the Law of the Non-Navigational Uses of International Watercourses* (adopted 21 May 1997), 36 ILM 700 Art. 3(2).
827. *See* further, S.C. Mccaffrey, *The Law of International Watercourses* (OUP 2nd ed., 2007).
828. *Id.*, at p. 361.
829. Another excellent example of a *pacta* of the second/third category is a series of treaties between the United States and the Soviet Union governing strategic nuclear weaponry. These treaties are: *Interim Agreement on Certain Measures with respect to the Limitation of Strategic Offensive Arms* (26 May 1972), 94 UNTS 3 (also: SALT I); *Treaty Between the United States of America*

7.14.1.2 Monitoring and Reporting Mechanisms under the 'Agreement to Scope'

To oversee that states actually do negotiate their treaties in line with a *pactum de negotiando* or *contrahendo*, treaty drafters may make use of review and reporting mechanisms, commonly referred to as 'compliance control'.[830] Whereas such mechanisms are non-coercive, 'they exert strong pressure parties to comply with their obligations'.[831] Indeed, they rely on persuasion rather than coercion.

In a comparative study on treaty mechanisms that induce compliance in three areas of international law (human rights, environment and arms control), the authors note that compliance control is anchored in reporting requirements.[832] These reporting requirements relate to the implementation of measures as well as to indicators of performance toward specified outcomes, such as emission data of harmful substances in international environmental law.[833] Generally, reporting plays two important roles in a treaty regime. Reporting enhances transparency as to the performance of parties, particularly when such reports are released to the general public. But reporting also provides the foundation for compliance assessment processes within regimes. Usually, such an assessment is made by a specific neutral or expert body that reviews the reports submitted.

For instance, the Convention on International Trade in Endangered Species of Wild Fauna and Flora (hereinafter: CITES) requires in Article VIII(7)(b) that parties shall transmit to the convention Secretariat 'a biannual report on legislative, regulatory and administrative measures taken to enforce the provisions of the present convention'. [834] The secretariat can then study these reports, request more information, and prepare annual reports on implementation.[835] For instance, the secretary to the convention has reviewed the implementation of domestic legislation. Parties that did not meet all of the requirements were required to provide national legislation plans and enact legislation within specified deadlines.[836] Likewise, the UNFCCC requires parties to communicate to the COP 'a general description of steps taken or envisaged by the Part to implement the Convention'.[837] The Conference of Parties is able to:

---

and *The Union of Soviet Socialist Republics on the Limitation of Strategic Offensive Arms, Together With Agreed Statements and Common Understandings Regarding the Treaty (signed but not entered into force)* (1979), S. Exec. Dox, Y, 96th Cong., 1st Session (also: SALT II). They are further discussed by J.K. Setear (1996) pp. 224–227. SALT stands for 'strategic arms limitation talks'.

830. J. Brunnée, *Compliance Control*, in: Making Treaties Work: Human Rights, Environment and Arms Control (G. Ulfstein ed., Cambridge University Press 2007) p. 374.
831. A. Chayes and A.H. Chayes (1995) p. 230.
832. J. Brunnée (2007) p. 374.
833. *See, e.g.,* LTRAP Art. 8; United Nations Framework Convention on Climate Change Art. 12 and its Kyoto Protocol to the United Nations Framework Convention on Climate Change Art. 7.
834. *Convention on International Trade in Endangered Species of Wild Fauna and Flora* (adopted 3 Mar. 1973), 993 UNTS 243.
835. *Id.*, at Art. XII. *See also* R. Reeve, *The Convention on International Trade in Endangered Species of Wild Fauna and Flora (CITES)*, in: Making Treaties Work: Human Rights, Environment and Arms Control (G. Ulfstein ed., Cambridge University Press 2007).
836. R. Reeve (2007) p. 144.
837. United Nations Framework Convention on Climate Change Art. 12(1)(b).

assess, on the basis of all information made available to it in accordance with the provisions of the convention, the implementation of the convention by the parties, the overall effects of the measures taken pursuant to the convention (...) And the extent to which progress towards the objectives of the convention is being achieved.[838]

And a more innovative way of ensuring the implementation of treaty commitments is the 'peer review' practiced by the OECD, a method in which one State examines another State's performance on a particular area in the form of an open dialogue. In this way, countries exchange information, attitudes and views, which encourage compliance.[839]

All in all, such reporting and compliance control mechanisms are designed to use parties' interconnectedness as a way to apply pressure. States that work against prevailing norms are treated as outsiders of the system.[840] Being an 'outsider' hurts, as in the end, as the authors Chayes and Chayes note, sovereignty is status: 'the vindication of the state's existence as a member of the international system. (...) Isolation from the pervasive and rich international context means that the state's potential for economic growth and political influence will not be realized.'[841]

7.14.2 The Use of the 'Agreement to Scope' Design for the Multilateral Agreement for International Taxation

The 'agreement to scope' adds the infrastructure to the basic 'managerial' requirements set out in part 7A. Its purpose is to entice participating states to enter into bilateral tax treaty negotiations that may converge around periodically held conference sessions of the treaty's main body and may be guided and informed by principles identified at the outset. Hence, the 'agreement to scope' provides the structure for the multilateral agreement for international taxation to operate successfully.

In many ways, the 'agreement to scope' is similar to a proposal on the parallel amendment of bilateral tax treaties proposed by Avery Jones and Baker.[842] Like the agreement to scope, the main idea of the Avery Jones and Baker proposal is that pairs of tax treaty parties bilaterally agree on multilaterally established norms. Their proposal is unique because it preserves the bilateral nature of the avoidance of double taxation to some extent. Indeed, Avery Jones and Baker suggest concluding a multilateral framework agreement with the purpose of amending the bilateral tax treaties:

[T] the OECD would prepare a multilateral agreement, (...) to provide a framework for the amendment. The agreement itself would not make any amendments.

---

838. *Id.*, at Art. 7(2)(e).
839. OECD, *Peer Review: An OECD Tool for Co-operation and Change* (2003) OECD Publishing, Paris. DOI: http://dx.doi.org/10.1787/9789264099210-en-fr.
840. M.P. Cottrell and D.M. Trubek (2012) p. 374.
841. A. Chayes and A.H. Chayes (1995) p. 27.
842. J.F. Avery Jones and P. Baker, *The Multiple Amendment of Bilateral Double Taxation Conventions*, 60 Bulletin for International Taxation 19 (2006).

Instead, it would provide a framework within which individual pairs of states could agree that the amendment in the framework agreement would apply to their existing bilateral DTC.[843]

The Avery Jones and Baker proposal would include the text of the proposed amendment, to which pairs of states would consent on the basis of 'declarations': bilateral agreements which include specific details such as the relevant tax treaty article and paragraph to be amended, the language in which the amendment is to be adopted and the effective date of the amendment. The text of the multilateral treaty and thus the text of the proposed amendment would, in accordance with Article 9 VCLT, be adopted at an international conference by the vote of two-thirds of the States present and voting.[844]

However, in the Avery Jones and Baker proposal, states are not allowed to deviate from the text in bilateral negotiations after this text is adopted at the level of the multilateral agreement. Indeed: 'no further changes would be permitted or necessary'.[845] But exactly in this respect, the 'agreement to scope' differs from the Avery Jones and Baker proposal. Bilateral negotiations should be used to further flesh out commonly identified terms. The OECD MTC may be used to inspire this process.

This means that, as regards the 'agreement to scope', state consent is needed on two levels: once at the level of the multilateral agreement and once at the level of the bilateral tax treaties. But this is not 'unnecessarily burdensome', as Innamorato argues in respect of the Avery Jones and Baker proposal.[846] The point is that the bilateral negotiations in step two add value by allowing states to deepen obligations, and this hence enables the regime to evolve over time. And, in terms of outcome, an 'agreement to scope' is comparable to the framework convention-protocol design, which also requires two rounds of negotiations and ratification (once at the level of the framework treaty, once at the level of the protocols).[847] To the end that parties need inspiration in fleshing out broad, multilaterally set norms, the COP may draft soft law: reports, model provisions and commentaries, etc.

In this regard, the BEPS Convention contains evidence of elements of an 'agreement to scope' (*see* Chapter 8). The choice of a state on implementing the BEPS Project's commitments may depend on the specific relationship with a treaty partner.[848] In this regard, the menu options that Parties may choose from to implement BEPS Action 6's minimum standard may create a difficult matrix: a country may decide

---

843. *Id.*, at p. 21.
844. *Id.*, at p. 21 and the draft convention prepared by the authors in the same work. *See* further, C. Innamorato, *Expeditious Amendments to Double Tax Treaties based on the OECD Model*, 36 Intertax 98, 119 (2008). Innamorato also discusses the framework convention- protocol solution at p. 118. She does away with the solution however on the basis of its infeasibility: 'it is rather improbable that many countries would join the agreement'.
845. J.F. Avery Jones and P. Baker (2006) p. 21.
846. In the Avery Jones and Baker proposal, subsequent rounds of 'declarations' are inflexible. The authors do not allow parties to bilaterally deviate from multilaterally set benchmarks. C. Innamorato (2008) p. 120 critiques this approach as: 'seeking twice for the approval of the Parliament [to ratify the amendments] would indeed ensure the right and lawful level of democratic legitimacy, but at the expenses of streamlining the treaty amendment process'.
847. This is said to make its amendment sluggish. *See*, *e.g.*, A.L. Taylor (1996) p. 295.
848. T. Bender and F.A. Engelen (2016).

to 'supplement' the PPT with an LOB clause with one state and favour just a PPT with another. The choice of menu may depend, in other words, on a state's company at the dining table, necessitating further bilateral fine-tuning.

7.15 CONCLUSIONS OF PART 7C: THE 'AGREEMENT TO SCOPE'

The 'agreement to scope' adds some infrastructure to the 'core' elements (*see* Part 7A) required to make the multilateral agreement for international taxation work. This would involve states' agreement on procedural commitments to further flesh out certain broader norms in their bilateral tax treaties (a *pactum de negotiando* or *pactum de contrahendo*). Reporting and review mechanisms could be used to identify implementation obstacles and to assess whether the implementation and negotiation of common value-maximising norms takes place in a satisfactory way, keeping in mind the need for a level playing field. Although the 'agreement to scope' requires the consent of parliaments in two rounds (once at the level of the agreement itself, and once at the level of the bilateral treaties), this does not make interaction unnecessarily burdensome, as each (additional) bilateral interaction may add depth to parties' obligations. Indeed, it sets the common terms and conditions for negotiation and brings states together at one place and time, where parties agree, in pairs if necessary, to engage in further bilateral fine-tuning or matching.

7.16 CONCLUSIONS: THE CONTOURS OF THE MULTILATERAL AGREEMENT FOR INTERNATIONAL TAXATION

This chapter illustrated the multilateral agreement for international taxation, using some prototypical tools of international public law. At its core, the treaty must contain a robust forum in which parties, time and again, engage to keep up with developments in society. A COP should be at the heart of this approach: a flexible quasi-institution, gathering regularly and at different locations. The COP is backed up by a secretariat that is set up within an existing IO (ideally: the UN). Negotiation takes place on the basis of objectives and some general principles set by the COP.

Depending on the type of policy objective under discussion, parties may then decide to use elements (or a combination) of the 'agreement to scope' or the 'framework convention-protocol' designs. Both are principally agreements of procedure rather than content. Under the agreement to scope, parties agree to further flesh out multilaterally set objectives in a bilateral fashion by means of a *pactum de negotiando* or a *pactum de contrahendo*. Where necessary, bilateral negotiation efforts can be subjected to monitoring and reporting mechanisms. Under the framework convention-protocol, parties agree on substantive multilateral norms, if opportune, in protocols. Such substantive multilateral agreements are layered 'on top of' bilateral tax treaties: a conflict clause prioritises rules of the multilateral treaty over those of bilateral conventions. Reservations and 'rules of the road' can be used to relax distributive problems. Dynamic decision-making procedures will ease subsequent amendments to the multilateral convention.

It is not unthinkable that the locus of decision-making on international tax issues is slowly moved from the OECD to the COP. Whereas the influence of OECD soft law on tax lawmaking within the environment of the COP cannot be prevented or prohibited, the independence of the COP vis-à-vis OECD non-member countries will prove indispensable to solve the (future) collective action problems of international tax law that affect OECD members and non-members alike. In fact, the COP itself may start to draft model tax treaty provisions and commentaries thereon so as to guide or inspire treaty negotiators in fulfilling their procedural obligations under the multilateral convention.

This does not (re)introduce the problems identified in Chapter 3. On the contrary: the multilateral agreement for international taxation fundamentally changes the way that tax treaty relationships are managed. It provides the opportunity to deal with the (future) collective action problems of international tax law, and in a fairer, coordinated and more responsive way.

CHAPTER 8

An Evaluation of the Multilateral Convention to Implement Tax Treaty Related Measures to Prevent Base Erosion and Profit Shifting

8.1 INTRODUCTION

This chapter evaluates the text of the Multilateral Convention to Implement Tax Treaty Related Measures to Prevent Base Erosion and Profit Shifting (hereinafter: BEPS Convention or BC) against the outcomes of the previous chapters. The BEPS Convention was adopted on 24 November 2016,[849] and may be called a remarkable achievement. As much as 100 countries[850] participated in drafting its text. As it will exist alongside the tax treaties brought under the ambit of the BEPS Convention on the basis of Article 2(1) BC (hereinafter: Covered Tax Agreements),[851] the Convention will fundamentally alter the landscape of international tax law.

The evaluation, first of all, serves an *explanatory* purpose: can the theory set out in prior chapters of the book help us understand the BEPS Convention? As to the Convention's substantive obligations (*see* section 8.2.1), particularly Chapter 5 proves of value: it follows that the neoliberal institutionalist perspective on multilateral cooperation functions surprisingly well to explain the scope of the Convention's substantive multilateral commitments. Moreover, the Convention's procedural rules echo the rational design presumptions of section 5.4.5. This, however, inevitably

---

849. The Multilateral Convention to Implement Tax Treaty Related Measures to Prevent Base Erosion and Profit Shifting (2016).
850. In the discussion below, the words 'party', 'state' and 'country' should be read so as to refer to 'contracting jurisdictions', as meant in Art. 2 of the BEPS Convention, too.
851. According to Art. 2(1)(a) BC, 'the term "Covered Tax Agreement" means an agreement for the avoidance of double taxation (…) that is in force between two or more (…) Parties (…) and (…) with respect to which each such Party has made a notification to the Depositary.'

introduces some of the issues discussed in Chapter 7, such as those related to reservations, *pacta de negotiando* and the relationship between bilateral tax treaties and the BEPS Convention (section 8.2.2).

But an evaluation of the Convention can also tell us something about the things it should have done better, which will be dealt with in section 8.3. This second line of enquiry is therefore *normative*. What other steps should have been taken, keeping in mind the idea of the 'multilateral agreement for international taxation', build up in the previous chapters?

As this chapter is most of all an exposition of points earlier made, repetition is avoided; instead, references are made to previous sections of the book. It is neither the point of the discussion below to provide an encyclopaedic analysis of all articles of the Convention nor to add any arguments 'new' to the discussion. Only those articles are discussed that, in the light of the foregoing chapters, are of relevance to the research questions. For this reason, a discussion of the Convention's rules on dispute resolution and arbitration is omitted, as well as an explicit consideration of, for example, issues of treaty interpretation and of those related to the (implementation of) specific substantive obligations (*see also* section 7.1).

8.2 EXPLAINING THE BEPS CONVENTION

8.2.1 Articles 3–15 Avoid Distributive Concerns

8.2.1.1 Introduction

The substantive obligations of the BEPS Convention can generally be explained by making use of the neoliberal institutionalist view on international tax cooperation. To accommodate diverging state interests in relation to its substantive commitments, the Convention applies three methods to relax distributive concerns. First, it makes use of 'rules of the road' (section 8.2.1.2). Second, parties under the Convention have explicitly agreed to engage in further bilateral negotiations (section 8.2.1.3). Finally, some of the obligations entered avoid distributive concerns altogether; these involve commitments in which gains/losses are perceived as small (section 8.2.1.4).[852] The discussion below reflects, in other words, the conclusions of Chapter 5.

8.2.1.2 Multilateral Consensus on 'Rules of the Road'

The Convention contains four provisions that are clear 'rules of the road' (*see* sections 5.4.3 and 7.10.3): Articles 3 and 6 BC, the PPT clause of Article 7 BC and Article 10 BC.

---

852. It may further be pointed out that, despite the fact that some issues, such as triangular cases and issues of transparency, are best solved multilaterally, the text BEPS Convention is explicitly written to be applied to *bilateral* tax relations. This is not a drafting mistake: the need for interpretative flexibility (*see* sec. 5.4.6) was prioritised over a comprehensive multilateral approach, increasing the likelihood that the Convention is broadly supported.

The rule on hybrid mismatches (Article 3 BC) is a clear rule of the road. As countries may be residence countries in one treaty relationship but source countries in another, the rule clearly depends on context. Asymmetric tax relationships may hence hide a clear distributive conflict, making the rule feasible to be agreed upon in a multilateral convention. *See* for a further examination of this argument section 7.10.3.

Article 6 BC comprises a 'true' multilateral commitment, as it sets forth a minimum standard from which parties, after signing up to the BEPS Convention, cannot derogate. The preamble it adds to existing tax treaties sets out that tax treaties should eliminate double taxation, but not 'create opportunities for non-taxation or reduced taxation through tax evasion or avoidance' through, for instance, treaty shopping. In this regard, this 'new' purpose of bilateral tax treaties is worded in stronger or 'clearer' language than the purpose formulated in earlier amendments to the Commentary on Article 1 OECD MTC (e.g., those of 2003).[853] In addition to the 2003 Commentary, Article 6 now also introduces the idea that tax avoidance and 'non-taxation or reduced taxation' are closely linked.

Its principle-like language suggests Article 6 is a 'rule of the road'. Nevertheless, as its purpose is to influence the interpretation of tax treaties,[854] it may also be perceived missing distributive effects altogether (it could, in other words, also have been discussed in section 8.2.1.4).

Article 7 BC presents another example to showcase the explanatory power of Chapter 5's neoliberal institutionalist perspective on international tax relations. Indeed, Chapter 5 suggests that avoiding treaty abuse may best be served by a PPT rather than an LOB clause. To the exclusion of Luxemburg and the Netherlands, most countries likely perceive it as a 'rule of the road' (*see* section 5.4.4). And indeed, the PPT embodies the Convention's minimum standard in relation to treaty abuse. It is therefore not surprising that it has come to function as *the* central commitment of Article 7 BC: the text of the article only allows parties to file reservations to the PPT if they commit to concluding a detailed LOB in combination with a rule that addresses conduit financing structures in their tax treaties (*see* Article 7(15)(a) BC) or when parties cannot reach agreement on supplementing the PPT with a simplified LOB (Article 7(16) BC). The simplified LOB provision on its own is not able to fulfil the minimum standard settled upon in the negotiations on the Action 6 BEPS Final Report.

---

853. According to para. 7 of the OECD Commentary on Art. 1, 'the principal purpose of double taxation conventions is to promote, by eliminating international double taxation, exchanges of goods and services, and the movement of capital and persons. It is also a purpose of tax conventions to prevent tax avoidance and evasion.'

854. *See* OECD, *Preventing the Granting of Treaty Benefits in Inappropriate Circumstances, Action 6: 2015 Final Report* (2015) para. 73. The question comes up whether the Hoge Raad, had it faced a preamble of the type set out in Art. 6, would have decided differently in e.g. HR 15 Dec. 1993, nr. 29 296, *BNB* 1994/259 or in HR 28 Jun. 1989, nr. 25 451, *BNB* 1990/45. *See*, *e.g.*, in relation to the 'purpose' of tax treaties introduced by the 2003 Commentaries: J. Vleggeert, *Misbruik van belastingverdragen*, in: Kwaliteit van belastingrechtspraak belicht (J.P. Boer ed., SDU 2013).

Finally, Article 10 of the BEPS Convention allows the source state to disregard the application of Articles 10, 11 and 12 OECD MTC.[855] It is, as a consequence, obviously distributive and would be fraught with difficulties (e.g., parties may disagree on the applicable threshold rate, arbitrarily set at 60%).[856] Nevertheless, a huge escape, in the form of a 'rule of the road', is taken up in Article 10 BC's second paragraph. This exception holds that the first paragraph is not applicable when the income is 'derived in connection with or is incidental to the active conduct of a business carried on through the PE'. Moreover, paragraph 3 of Article 10 provides, as a last resort, at the request of the taxpayer, a 'discretionary relief' procedure in which the authorities of the source state consult the authorities of the residence state, further relaxing the application of Article 10's first paragraph.

8.2.1.3 Agreement Is Facilitated by Coordinated Bilateral Negotiations

From the neoliberal institutionalist perspective on international tax relations follows that detailed, hard-law rules that affect the allocation of passive income, such as the LOB clause or a rule that determines residence status under a tax treaty, emphasise disagreement (*see* section 5.4.4). Principled agreement on such clauses may be possible, provided that procedural agreements allow states to engage in additional bilateral fine-tuning.

The most exemplary provision of the Convention in this regard is that on dual resident entities. Indeed, Article 4 introduces a rule that requires parties to further bilaterally negotiate 'by mutual agreement'. Deferring 'breaking the tie' to later bilateral negotiations is a procedural obligation in the sense of section 7.14, making the rule politically acceptable for all parties concerned. The significant uncertainty it introduces for taxpayers may be seen as a conscious policy direction to deter taxpayers to enter into dual residence structures in the first place, but the rule may turn out to be broadly supported.

Adding a simplified LOB provision to tax treaties by means of a multilateral agreement will also require further bilateral negotiations. And indeed, from the text of the Convention follows that the simplified LOB applies only in addition to the PPT insofar as both parties to a tax treaty choose to apply it (Article 7(6) BC). If parties disagree, the Convention itself, in Article 7(7) BC, provides two standardised bilateral solutions. First, it is possible that, contrary to their initial decisions under paragraph 6, parties agree to apply the simplified LOB symmetrically (Article 7(7)(a) BC). Second, parties can agree to apply the simplified LOB *asymmetrically*. In the bilateral tax treaty

---

855. The article can be invoked when the residence state attributes the income covered in those articles to a lowly-taxed PE situated in a third jurisdiction and subsequently exempts that income. The language of the convention is worded so as to include all forms of income ('any item of income') that can be attributed to a PE and for which the source state would be required to grant treaty benefits.

856. In this regard, the Explanatory Statement notes in paragraph 143 that the reference to the lower tax rate, 'to be determined bilaterally', was scrapped 'to avoid requiring bilateral negotiation of a tax rate'.

relationship between, for example, State A and B, State A would apply the PPT *and* the LOB, whereas State B would apply the PPT only (Article 7(7)(b) BC).

If parties fail to reach agreement on supplementing a PPT with a simplified LOB provision, Article 7(16) BC enables the party that wished to supplement the PPT to completely opt out of Article 7. Nevertheless, Article 7(16) BC places that party under the obligation to 'endeavour to reach a mutually satisfactory solution which meets the minimum standard for preventing treaty abuse'. Similarly, Article 7(15)(a) BC allows parties that seek to satisfy the minimum standard by means of a 'detailed' LOB, to opt out of Article 7 BC altogether. These parties are under an identical obligation to negotiate a future, satisfactory, agreement that meets the minimum standard. By using such *pacta de negotiando* (*see* section 7.14 as well as section 8.2.2.5 below), the BEPS Convention recognises the need for further bilateral fine-tuning.

8.2.1.4 *Provisions that Avoid Distributive Concerns Altogether*

Multilateral norms can, finally, also be agreed upon when distributive concerns are, simply said, (perceived to be) absent. States have no problem agreeing on norms that are free of real consequences or perceived to involve small gains/losses only. We are speaking, in other words, about matters that can be placed in the left two quadrants of the Figure 2 set out in section 5.4.5. This classification does not imply that such norms are 'negotiation failures'. On the contrary, the point is that it should not be overestimated what multilateral agreements can achieve in the area of international taxation.

Article 5 of the BEPS Convention changes the operation of the relief mechanism for hybrid mismatch situations.[857] To address the operation of the relief mechanism in mismatch situations, Options A and B both provide switch-over clauses, triggered on different conditions. Option As switch-over clause is triggered by a rule similar to paragraph 4 of Article 23A of the 2014 OECD MTC. As regards Option B, the switch-over clause is linked to the source state's domestic treatment of the income.

The switch-over clauses of Option A and B mostly avoid distributive concerns. Indeed, these options are clearly not applicable on states that already provide for a credit for passive income in their bilateral tax treaties (*see* Article 5, paragraphs 3 and 5, BC). Moreover, Article 5 BC explicitly covers exemptions provided on the basis of *bilateral tax treaties* only (*see* Article 5, paragraphs 3, 5 and 7, BC). The article hence is, as such, not problematic for states exempting passive income on the basis of domestic corporate tax laws. For the states that *do* provide an exemption for passive

---

857. The broad language of the provision is not particularly helpful in understanding what situations the provision is exactly meant to cover. Reading the Action 2 Final Report, however, it seems that the provision is drafted to address the operation of the relief mechanism in hybrid mismatch situations. Some tax treaties provide for an exemption (instead of a credit) for passive income. The phrase 'income derived or capital owned by a resident' should hence be construed so as to refer to Arts 10 and 11, and perhaps also to Art. 12 OECD MTC. *See* the Explanatory Statement to the BEPS Convention as well as OECD, *Neutralising the Effects of Hybrid Mismatch Arrangements, Action 2: Final Report* (2015) paras 442–444.

income in their treaties (e.g., Germany), Options A and B are more difficult. Such states may be expected not to opt in (it is worth noting here that Article 5 BC is an optional clause in the sense of section 7.10).

Such observations, however, do not hold for Option C, which clearly goes far beyond the more modest Options A and B. Given its broad language, it will potentially deliver a blow to the source-residence balance struck in tax treaties. Under Option C, the exemption method would be simply replaced by the credit method of Article 23B OECD MTC in respect of 'income derived or capital owned by a resident of [a] Contracting Jurisdiction, which, in accordance with the provisions of the Covered Tax Agreement, may be taxed in the other Contracting Jurisdiction' (*see* paragraph 7 to Article 5 of the BEPS Convention). Further bilateral negotiations are likely inevitable, if Option C is opted for.

As to Article 8 BC: there is some evidence that Article 8 BC avoids distributive problems altogether (i.e., perceived gains/losses involved are small). Indeed, the Explanatory Statement to Article 8 BC notes that the purpose of the article is 'not to change the substantive allocation of taxation rights' between the parties to a bilateral tax treaty.[858] What the Explanatory Statement means to say, is that the 365-day period is only a minor alteration to Article 10 OECD MTC. More substantial amendments to Article 10 OECD MTC, such as 'language relating to the specific tax rate and ownership threshold provided by the model provision'[859] were unsurprisingly (*see* sections 5.3.2 and 5.3.3) more problematic. Such types of amendments were, according to the Explanatory Statement, omitted from the text of the Convention.

The same may hold for Article 9 BC, that amends Article 13(4) OECD MTC[860] on a 365-day testing period, as well as on an expansion of the scope of interest covered. However, it can only be said that Article 9 avoids distributive concerns insofar as a tax convention already includes a provision similar to Article 13(4) OECD MTC. If that is not the case (this situation is addressed in Article 9, paragraphs 3 and 4, BC), the article changes a distributive baseline, for which bilateral negotiations will be necessary (this is recognised in Article 9(8) BC).

The saving clause of Article 11 BC does not alter any distributions already agreed upon in bilateral tax treaties either. The saving clause, included in the BEPS Convention at the request of the United States, merely 'confirms the Contracting States' right to tax their residents (and citizens, in the case of the United States) notwithstanding the provision of the tax treaty except those, such as the rules on relief of double taxation, that are clearly intended to apply to residents'.[861]

Finally, as may be expected, Articles 12–15 BC limit or extend the situations in which a PE exists under a tax treaty only to a very moderate degree. Indeed, 'hard-law' changes to the PE threshold will be fraught with political difficulties: perceived

---

858. *See* the Explanatory Statement to the BEPS Convention, para. 120.
859. *See id.*
860. Article 13(4) OECD MTC holds: 'Gains derived by a resident of a Contracting State from the alienation of shares deriving more than 50% of their value directly or indirectly from immovable property situated in the other Contracting State may be taxed in that other State.'
861. OECD, *Preventing the Granting of Treaty Benefits in Inappropriate Circumstances, Action 6: 2015 Final Report* (2015) paras 61–63.

gains/losses involved are large, as the provision involves the allocation of business income. Consequentially, the rules of Articles 12–15 BC have the character of 'clarifications' rather than 'modifications'.

Indeed, Article 12 BC is aimed at achieving a 'better reflection' of the policy behind the commissionaire rule: an enterprise has sufficient taxable nexus in the source state when the activities of an intermediary result in the regular conclusion of contracts, to be performed by the principal in the residence state.[862]

The first three paragraphs of Article 13 BC spell out that the 'specific activity exceptions' to the PE status of Article 5(4) OECD MTC are available only for activities that are of a preparatory or auxiliary nature. Paragraph 4 prevents taxpayers from fragmenting one cohesive business into smaller, 'auxiliary' operations. The overall effect of Article 13 is, therefore, that it 'clarifies' the PE threshold: the exceptions of Article 5(4) OECD MTC do not apply when they are, in fact, not of a 'preparatory or auxiliary character'. This interpretation, however, was already commonly accepted under the 1963 OECD MTC.[863]

Similarly, Article 14 BC 'hardens' the interpretation that the splitting up of contracts runs against the object and purpose of Article 5(3) OECD MTC's twelve-month period.[864] Indeed, such behaviour has been determined 'abusive' by the OECD Commentary on Article 5(3) OECD MTC since 1992.

Finally, Article 15 BC is related to Articles 12–14 BC, as it includes a definition of 'a person closely related to an enterprise'. As Articles 12–14 BC avoid distribute concerns, such concerns are absent in Article 15, too.

8.2.2 The Convention Employs Elements of the Framework Convention/Protocol and the Agreement to Scope Designs

8.2.2.1 Introductory Observations

From the previous section follows that the BEPS Convention avoids distributive concerns by means of interpretative flexibility devices, such as 'rules of the road', coordinated bilateral negotiations, or simply by avoiding such concerns altogether.

---

862. OECD, *Preventing the Artificial Avoidance of Permanent Establishment Status: Action 7 2015 Final Report* (2015) OECD/G20 Base Erosion and Profit Shifting Project, OECD Publishing, Paris. http://dx.doi.org/10.1787/9789264241220-en, pp. 15–16.
863. Paragraph 13 of the OECD Commentary on Art. 5(3) of the 1963 OECD MTC holds: 'In the first place, since it would be unreasonable to seek to claim that the list of examples quoted in paragraph 3 is, or in the nature of things could hope to be exhaustive, the last words of sub-paragraph *e)* ["or for similar activities which have a preparatory or auxiliary character for the enterprise"] are intended to cover any further examples (...) which are not listed among the exceptions in paragraph 3 but are nevertheless within the spirit of them. The words in question are, therefore, intended to make it unnecessary to attempt to produce an exhaustive list of exceptions which, even if it were comprehensive, would inevitably be of inordinate length and undesirable rigidity. (...) To put the matter in another way, the last words of subparagraph *e)* refine the general definition in paragraph 1.'
864. *See* para. 18 of the OECD Commentary on Art. 5(3) OECD MTC, that calls such behaviour 'abusive'.

The Convention's 'procedural' obligations provide it with additional flexibility mechanisms, reflecting the presumptions of section 5.4.5. Indeed, on the one hand, the Convention has some of the elements of the framework convention/protocol design (reflecting substantive multilateralism), set out in Chapter 7B. For instance, once a party has decided that a tax treaty is covered by the obligations of the Convention, only a reservation can prevent such obligations to become applicable. And completely dressed down, the BEPS Convention requires states to adopt the minimum standard only, as all other requirements can be opted out/reserved upon. May future fine-tuning be necessary, the Convention provides for its amendment as well as for the adoption of protocols (*see* Articles 33 and 38 BC). On the other hand, the Convention also has some of the elements of the 'agreement to scope' (reflecting formal multilateralism), set out in Chapter 7C. It explicitly recognises the importance of bilateral negotiations. This follows, most importantly, from Article 2(1)(ii) BC: the Convention is only applicable on a bilateral treaty when 'listed' by a contracting state. This allows pairs of states to form groups (*see* section 7.1), encouraging multilateral convergence where the Convention best serves states' interests, but allowing them to focus on bilateral negotiations when it does not. Similarly, some of the Convention's provisions are 'optional', such as Articles 5 and 13 BC. These permit states to 'opt in' to predetermined options, potentially 'grouping' states with similar interests. Finally, under certain conditions, the notification system under the Convention's compatibility clauses may cause the Convention's obligations to have the characteristics of a protocol to a bilateral tax treaty (*see* section 8.2.2.3 below),[865] further reflecting the importance of bilateral fine-tuning.

As a consequence, some of the characteristics of each design option, discussed in Chapters 7B and 7C, may be identified under the BEPS Convention as well.[866] They are discussed below.

8.2.2.2 *Reservations and Optional Provisions*

As we have seen, reservations, as interpretative flexibility devices, are indispensable for forging agreement on multilateral tax rules. From the outcomes of Chapter 5 (and in particular section 5.4.5) follows that reservations – and the complexity associated with the use of reservations – are an essential feature for the multilateral instrument to be broadly acceptable to states.

Reservations can be 'formulated' or 'made' at the time of signature or ratification (i.e., they are not 'notified', *see* Article 28(5)–28(8) BC and Article 19 VCLT).[867] The

---

865. *See* P.J. Hattingh, *The Multilateral Instrument from a Legal Perspective: What May Be the Challenges?* 71 Bulletin for International Taxation 4.2 (2017) and as suggested by S. Austry et al., (2016): *The Proposed OECD Multilateral Instrument Amending Tax Treaties*, British Tax Review 454 (2016).

866. In more detail: F.P.G. Pötgens and D.M. Broekhuijsen, *Het multilaterale instrument met zijn vele bilaterale schakeringen*, WFR 2017/76 and R.A. Bosman, *Formele aspecten van het multilaterale instrument*, MBB 2017/04.

867. A reservation is not 'notified' but 'formulated' or 'made'. To 'formulate' or 'make' reservations, a (provisional) list or document of reservations has to be submitted to the Depositary. *See* Art.

Convention determines which reservations are authorised and which are not. Indeed, Article 28(1) BC specifies that 'no reservations may be made to this Convention except those expressly permitted'. Why does the BEPS Convention expressly determine which reservations are authorised and which are not? It could have been possible to simply leave the issue of reservations to the practice of states.

In this regard, the system on reservations of the BEPS Convention serves one main purpose: to balance the symmetry of state interests (*see* on this section 7.10.2). In this regard, Article 28(3)(a) of the BEPS Convention holds that a reservation shall 'modify for the reserving Party in its relations with another Party the provision of this Convention to which the reservation relates to the extent of the reservation'. Article 28(3)(b) BC, vice versa, modifies the same provisions to the same extent for the other party in its relations with the reserving party. So, like the regime on reservations of the VCLT, reservations under the Convention function on the basis of reciprocity: they start off from the presumption that state interests are symmetrical. Yet, as clearly follows from section 5.3.2 and as further explained in section 7.10.2, international tax relationships are often *not* symmetrical.

The detailed system of negotiated reservations, set out in each of the specific substantive articles of the BEPS Convention and summarised in Article 28(1) BC, remedies that situation. As a general rule, a reservation apply to all Covered Tax Agreements of the reserving state. A fair number of the reservations authorised by the Convention are 'excluding reservations' (*see* section 7.10.2). Article 8(3)(a) BC, for instance, holds that 'a Party may reserve the right (a) for the entirety of this Article not to apply to its Covered Tax Agreements'. Functioning in combination with 'modifying reservations' (*see* again section 7.10.2), such as Article 8(3)(b) BC, parties to the Convention, by agreeing to allow specific reservations to the Convention only, created 'package deals'. The system of reservations prevents states from choosing *parts* of the obligations set out in the Convention only (i.e., 'cherry-picking'). Article 8(3) BC, for instance, does not authorise a party to choose a period longer or shorter than the 365-day period. It must either bilaterally have negotiated an alternative period (Article 8(3)(b) BC), or opt out of Article 8 BC *for all* its Covered Tax Agreements altogether. Other reservations are null or void.

In this way, reservations are generalised to the negotiation of the text of the provision, which, in turn, is generalised to the negotiation of the BEPS Convention as a whole. Agreeing to the list of 'authorised reservations', summarised in Article 28 BC, is a *condicio sine qua non* of treaty participation. As pointed out in section 7.10.2, such negotiated 'package deals' make it more likely that a larger number of countries is willing to participate.

One interesting type of reservation allowed by the Convention is the reservation that has been termed a 'partial reservation' in recent literature on the BEPS

28(5)–(7) BC. If a state has made 'partial' reservation(s), it should also include a list of Covered Tax Agreements to which these apply. *See* Art. 28(8) BC.

Convention.[868] As reservations generally apply to *all* the Covered Tax Agreements of the reserving state, these reservations are 'partial' in the sense that they apply to one specific Covered Tax Agreement only. As a general rule, such reservations are allowed in cases where the Covered Tax Agreement in question already addresses situations covered by a specific article of the MLI.[869] As reservations apply symmetrically on the basis of Article 28(3) BC, the relations between the parties of a bilateral tax treaty consist of the lowest common denominator.[870] For instance, where state A makes the reservation of Article 4(3)(b) BC (reserving the right for the entirety of Article 4 not to apply to a Covered Tax Agreement that already contains a rule to 'break the tie' by mutual agreement) and state B makes the reservation of Article 4(3)(e) BC (reserving the right to alter the last sentence of Article 4(1) BC), Article 4 BC will not apply to that bilateral relationship.

The Convention also includes some 'optional provisions' (*see also* section 7.10.2). Like reservations, the point of such rules is to provide for interpretative flexibility, increasing the chances that the Convention will be broadly accepted. The choice for an option, for which a party has to 'notify' the Depositary (*see* Article 29 BC), applies to *all* of a party's Covered Tax Agreements. However, optional provisions function on the basis of *opt-in* rather than *opt-out*: the presumption underlying such provisions is, in other words, that no obligation is applicable on a state unless expressly agreed otherwise. Some optional provisions only apply when both parties to a Covered Tax Agreement have chosen to apply the same option; i.e., a 'match' is needed in these cases (cf. Article 13(7) BC). But not all optional clauses need 'matches': the *asymmetrical application* of an option is sometimes allowed. This means that the option is applied to the residents of the state that opted in only. Examples of such clauses are Article 5 BC (as regards the application of methods for the elimination of double taxation) and Article 7(7) BC (as regards the application of the simplified LOB clause).

Listing tax treaties under the Convention can also be seen as an 'optional provision' in this regard, as a signatory party has to *act* (i.e., notify the Depositary) in order to have a tax treaty covered by the Convention (*see* Article 2(1)(a)(ii) BC). Other optional provisions are Articles 5 and 13 BC and Part VI.

8.2.2.3 How Is the Relationship Between the BEPS Convention and the Network of Bilateral Tax Treaties Governed?

As the BEPS Convention has some of the elements of a 'framework convention', discussed in section 7.8, the question arises what the relationship is between the

---

868. R. García Antón, *Untangling the Role of Reservations in the OECD Multilateral Instrument: The OECD Legal Hybrids*, 71 Bulletin for International Taxation 544, 4.3.2 (2017).

869. A good example is Art. 4(3)(b)–(d) BC, that allows reservations for bilateral tax treaties that already contain rules on the place of residence of a person other than an individual.

870. *See* P.J. Hattingh (2017) para. 5.1. Also, R. García Antón (2017) who refers to the compatibility clause's notification clause to untangle the effects of such partial reservations. The notification clause that is related to the compatibility clause should, however, only be consulted for the effect of notifications related to compatibility clauses and not for the effect of reservations. *See* sec. 8.2.2.3.

Convention and the network of bilateral tax treaties it seeks to amend. The Convention, although implicit, includes the three elements of a conflict clause, set out in section 7.9.3. As noted in section 7.9.3, a conflict clause usually contains three elements: (1) it regulates the relationship between the two relevant instruments; (2) it stipulates what happens should a conflict of norms arise; and (3) it regulates/makes explicit the relationship with treaties of third (non-participating) states. Each of these three elements is discussed in a corresponding section below.

8.2.2.3.1   The Relationship Between the BEPS Convention and the Bilateral Tax Treaty Network

The BEPS Convention aims to amend bilateral tax treaties. But it is not 'automatically' applicable on all *inter se* tax treaties of participating states. States have to 'list' their tax treaties under Article 2(1)(a) BC. As it is applicable only on 'listed' tax agreements (cf. Articles 1 and 2(1)(a) BC), it does not automatically 'look forward', as it does not capture future tax conventions of parties. For this, an explicit notification is required in the sense of Article 29(5) (extending Article 2(1)(a)(ii) BC's list of agreements).

But once covered by it, the Convention is, in the words of its Explanatory Statement, to be 'applied alongside existing tax treaties'.[871] This first of all follows from the texts of the substantive amendments themselves, which are specifically designed with the purpose of determining their relationship with bilateral tax treaties. Second, Article 2(2) BC ('interpretation of terms') implies that the Convention is to be applied alongside tax treaties. The article holds that 'as regards the application of this Convention at any time by a Party, any term not defined therein shall, unless the context otherwise requires, have the meaning that it has at that time under the relevant Covered Tax Agreement'.

What follows from these texts, in other words, is that the Convention and a Covered Tax Agreement should be interpreted and applied as a single instrument. In this interpretative exercise, 'connection language' (*see* section 7.9.3.2), set out in each of the Convention's substantive provisions, regulates the relationship between the two sets of rules – i.e., tax treaties and the Convention – in detail. For instance, Article 3(1) holds: 'for the purposes of a Covered Tax Agreement (...) income derived (...) shall be considered income of a resident'; Article 6(1) BC: 'A Covered Tax Agreement shall be modified to include (...)'; Article 7(1) BC: 'Notwithstanding any provisions of a Covered Tax Agreement, a benefit (...) shall not be granted' and Article 8(1) BC: 'provisions of a Covered Tax Agreement (...) shall apply only if (...).'

The process of interpreting both sets of rules as one single instrument is further influenced by the Convention's general rule of interpretation (Article 2(2) BC), which

---

871. *See* para. 13 of the Explanatory Statement.

incorporates the bilateral tax treaty meaning for the Convention's undefined terms, and hence, through provisions similar to Article 3(2) OECD MTC, a domestic law meaning. The BEPS Convention, in other words, explicitly builds on the system of bilateral tax treaties. As prima facie, both sets of rules are equally applicable, it has to be kept in mind that the presumption against conflict applies (*see* section 7.9.2).

By interpreting both instruments as one, the obligations of the BEPS Convention will, in accordance with the Convention's 'connection language', be read in relation to the obligations set out in a bilateral tax treaty.

8.2.2.3.2   *The Consequences of Conflict; 'Compatibility Clauses'*

What to do if the interpretative exercise leads to a conflict between the text of the BEPS Convention and that of a bilateral tax treaty? In this regard, Article 1 of the BEPS Convention, in combination with each of the 'compatibility clauses' set out in the Convention's substantive provisions, comprises the *second* element of a conflict clause, discussed in section 7.9.3.3, that the BEPS Convention implicitly contains.

It is up to the interpreter of both instruments to identify a conflict of norms. Without a conflict of norms, there is no need to turn to the provisions regulating such conflict. The Explanatory Statement notes in this regard that:

> many of the provisions of the Convention overlap with provisions found in Covered Tax Agreements. In some cases, they can be applied without conflict with the provisions of Covered Tax Agreements.[872]

A conflict, for instance, does not arise when the Convention expressly stipulates that its norms are not applicable. An example is the last sentence of Article 4(2) of the BEPS Convention, a 'compatibility clause', which holds that 'paragraph 1 *shall not apply*, to provisions (...) specifically addressing the residence of companies participating in dual-listed company arrangements.'

But more often than not, prima facie conflicts of norms cannot be reconciled by adopting an integrative interpretation. For these situations, the Convention includes a set of detailed conflict rules. A general rule on the conflict of norms is provided in Article 1, which sets out that the 'scope' of the BEPS Convention is to 'modify' all covered tax agreements. Indeed, Article 1 BC suggests that, once leaving the realm of 'interpretation', the norms of the BEPS Convention are to be prioritised over ('modify') those of bilateral tax treaties. Compare, in this regard, Article 1's language to that of conflict clauses used in other multilateral treaties, such as counterterrorism treaties, set out in section 7.9.3.3. But regardless of the operation of Article 1 BC, the BEPS Convention includes detailed 'compatibility clauses', specifically drafted to address conflicts of norms. The Convention leaves, in other words, little room for doubt. In the words of the explanatory statement:

---

872. Paragraph 15 of the Explanatory Statement.

Where the provisions of the Convention may conflict with existing provisions covering the same subject matter, however, this conflict is addressed through one or more compatibility clauses which may, for example, describe the existing provisions which the Convention is intended to supersede, as well as the effect on Covered Tax Agreements that do not contain a provision of the same type.[873]

Compatibility clauses operate in conjunction with notification clauses. The aim of these notification clauses is to provide additional clarity as to the operation of the BEPS Convention in relation to the bilateral tax treaties it covers. They require parties to identify whether provisions of Covered Tax Agreements are 'within the objective scope of the compatibility clause',[874] and notify the Depositary accordingly. The objective scope of a compatibility clause describes the tax treaty provisions the BEPS Convention seeks to amend. For instance, Article 4(2) BC holds that the mutual agreement procedure for dual resident entities replaces provisions of Covered Tax Agreements that:

> provide rules for determining whether a person other than an individual shall be treated as a resident of one of the Contracting Jurisdictions in cases in which that person would otherwise be treated as a resident of more than one Contracting Jurisdiction.

The legal effects produced by the system of compatibility clauses depend on two elements: (1) have both states made a matching notification on whether the relevant provision of their Covered Tax Agreement 'is within the objective scope of the compatibility clause'?; and (2) the category of indicator used in the compatibility clause. As to (1), the lack of a matching notification would imply that the parties to a Covered Tax Agreement interpret the obligations therein differently, disagreeing on the Covered Tax Agreement's compatibility with the relevant provision of the BEPS Convention. As to (2), four categories of indicators exist: (1) 'in place of'; (2) 'applies to' or 'modifies'; (3) 'in the absence of'; and (4) 'in place or in the absence of'. Each indicator has distinct legal effects, set out on p. 6 of the Explanatory Statement. The legal effects of the system of compatibility clauses and related notifications are summarised in the following table.[875]

---

873. Explanatory Statement, p. 5.
874. Explanatory Statement, p. 5. The exercise to identify the tax treaty provisions that are within the 'objective scope' of a compatibility clause is, therefore, preceded by the process of interpretation described in the previous paragraph.
875. This table is reproduced from F.P.G. Pötgens and D.M. Broekhuijsen (2017) p. 477. *See also* OECD, *Applying the Multilateral Instrument Step-by-Step*, available at http://www.oecd.org/tax/treaties/step-by-step-tool-on-the-application-of-the-MLI.pdf, and R.A. Bosman, *General Aspects of the Multilateral Instrument*, 45 Intertax 642, 655 (2017).

Table 3   The Consequences of Notifications Related to Compatibility Clauses

	(1) 'In Place of'	(2) 'Applies to'/'Modifies'	(3) 'In the Absence of'	(4) 'In Place of or in the Absence of'
Matching Notification	The provision of the BC replaces, in its entirety, the relevant provision of the specific Covered Tax Agreement.	The provision of the BC modifies or changes the application of the relevant provision of the specific Covered Tax Agreement.	The provision of the BC is, in its entirety, added to the specific Covered Tax Agreement.	The provision of the BC replaces, in its entirety, the relevant provision of the specific Covered Tax Agreement.
No Matching Notification	The provision of the BC does not apply to the relevant Covered Tax Agreement.	The provision of the BC does not apply to the relevant Covered Tax Agreement.	The provision of the BC does not apply to the relevant Covered Tax Agreement.	The provision of the BC and the provision of the Covered Tax Agreement are equally applicable. The provision of the BC supersedes the provision of the BC 'to the extent that it is incompatible with the relevant provisions of the Convention'.

For instance, if a compatibility clause holds that an obligation of the BEPS Convention applies 'in place of' a provision of a Covered Tax Agreement, it applies, much like a protocol to a bilateral tax treaty, *entirely* 'in place of' that provision, provided that both parties identified the provision to be within the objective scope of the compatibility clause and notified the Depositary accordingly. If the two parties did not make a matching notification, the provision does *not* apply within the ambit of that specific Covered Tax Agreement.[876] Likewise, where a provision applies 'in place of' in the absence of' a provision in a Covered Tax Agreement, a matching notification would *entirely* replace the provision of a Covered Tax Agreement (if it exists) by the text of the provision of the BEPS Convention. In the absence of a matching notification, the text of the relevant provision of the BEPS Convention would come to exist alongside that of the relevant provision of the Covered Tax Agreement, 'superseding it to the extent that it is incompatible with the relevant provision of the Convention'.[877] In this case, the compatibility clause leaves it to the interpreter to determine to what extent the BEPS Convention prevails.

---

876. Paragraph 15 of the Explanatory Statement.
877. Paragraph 15 of the Explanatory Statement.

By means of the notification procedure related to compatibility clauses, the drafters of the Convention have, therefore, smartly circumvented some of the implementation problems associated with applying multilateral rules on different bilateral tax treaties. After all, tax treaties may be worded differently from the OECD MTC, or in a language different from English or French (the BEPS Convention's authentic languages). For instance, Article 4(2) BC, the compatibility clause of the BEPS Convention's rule on dual resident entities, uses indicator (4). A matching notification under Article 4(4) BC would have the result that a Covered Tax Agreement's corporate tie-breaker (formulated e.g., in Dutch), would be completely replaced by the text of the mutual agreement procedure of Article 4(1) BC (formulated in English and French). Absent such a notification, the English/French texts of Article 4(1) BC would come to exist alongside the Dutch text of the corporate tie-breaker. As the provision of the BEPS Convention supersedes the corporate tie-breaker rule to the extent that it is incompatible,[878] it is left to the interpreter to read the two texts as one and apply this rule on conflict. The Explanatory Statement further notes that, would disagreements between parties arise as to whether 'existing provisions are within the scope of a compatibility clause',[879] parties can resort to the mutual agreement procedure, or refer the matter to the COP.[880]

From the above follows that the system of conflict clauses can, just like reservations, influence the rules applicable in the relations between the parties to a bilateral tax treaty (*see* the effects of mismatches under indicators (1)–(3) in Table 3). However, unlike reservations, the notification procedures under compatibility clauses are not *meant* to influence the rules applicable in the relations between the parties. Instead, their purpose is to provide clarity and transparency about the relationship between the BEPS Convention and a specific Covered Tax Agreement. A matching notification reflects the common understandings of the tax treaty parties about this relationship.

As reservations apply to all Covered Tax Agreements of the reserving state, and as no reservations may be made to the Convention except those expressly permitted,[881] the notification procedure under a compatibility clause should not be used by states wishing to exclude the application of a particular provision of the BEPS Convention from a specific Covered Tax Agreement. In the light of the Convention's closed system of reservations, notifying under a compatibility clause is an obligation to be performed by the parties in good faith. And indeed, the Explanatory Statement notes that 'it is expected that Parties would *use their best efforts* to identify all provisions that are within the objective scope of the compatibility clause'.[882]

878. *See*, in this regard, Art. 4(4) BC.
879. Paragraph 18 of the Explanatory Statement.
880. Such disagreements may materialise by means of the notification procedure, i.e., when one of the parties notifies the Depositary a compatible tax treaty provision exists, and the other party does not. The notification procedure, therefore, exposes the situations in which further bilateral fine-tuning is necessary.
881. *See* Art. 28(1) BC.
882. Paragraph 15 of the Explanatory Statement (emphasis added).

To read the BEPS Convention's complex notification clauses correctly, it is important to distinguish notifications related to compatibility clauses from: (1) the notifications reflecting choices of optional provisions; and (2) the system of reservations.[883]

As regards (1), optional provisions are also 'notified' by the participating states, but the purpose and legal effects of optional clauses are distinct (*see* section 8.2.2.2 above). For instance, the first sentence of Article 5(10) BC compels states to notify their choice of option. It reads: 'Each Party that chooses to apply an Option under paragraph 1 shall notify the Depositary of its choice of option.' In its second sentence, Article 5(10) BC also requests states to make a notification, but this notification relates to the operation of the compatibility clause. It reads:

> Such notification shall also include: a) in the case of a Party that chooses to apply Option A, the list of its Covered Tax Agreements which contain a provision described in paragraph 3 [the compatibility clause of Option A], as well as the article and paragraph number of each such provision.

Similar language is used for the notification procedure under the compatibility clauses of Options B and C.[884] Distinguishing between the two types of notifications may hence help to read such more complex notification clauses (*see also, e.g.,* Article 9(10) BC).[885]

As regards (2), it should be remarked here that reservations are not 'notified', but 'formulated' or 'made' by the participating states.[886] Notification clauses have, in other words, nothing to say about (the effects of) reservations (which are dealt with in Article 28 BC). The references to reservations in notification clauses merely serve to set the conditions under which a party must make a notification under a compatibility clause. Consider, for instance, Article 3(6) BC. This article requires a state to produce a notification under the condition that it has not made the reservation set out in Article 5(a) and (b) BC. Its first sentence reads:

> Each party that has not made a reservation described in subparagraph a) or b) of paragraph 5 shall notify the Depositary of whether each of its Covered Tax Agreements contains a provision described in paragraph 4 that is not subject to a reservation under subparagraphs c) through e) of paragraph 5, and if so, the article and paragraph number of each such provision.

In the notification thus produced, states should identify whether their Covered Tax Agreements contain the provision described in Article 3(4) that is not subject to a reservation as expressed under Article 3(5)(c)–(f).

---

883. *See* Arts 28 and 29 BC as well as p. 5 of the Explanatory Statement.
884. This is expressed in Arts 5(10)b and 5(10)c BC. The compatibility clause of Option B is set out in Art. 5(5) BC; the compatibility clause of Option C is set out in Art. 5(7) BC.
885. To get a rough grip on Art. 9(8) BC's operation, the first three sentences of Art. 9(8) BC relate to the notification to opt in to Art. 9(4). The notification related to the compatibility clause seems to start with the article's fourth sentence. Unfortunately, the Explanatory Statement provides little insight in how Art. 9(8) operates in conjunction with Arts 9(1), 9(4), 9(5) and 9(7) BC.
886. *See* sec. 8.2.2.2 above.

The consequences of a matching compatibility clause notification under Article 3(6) BC are set out in that article's third and fourth sentences. These sentences read:

> Where all Contracting Jurisdictions have made such a notification with respect to a provision of a Covered Tax Agreement, that provision shall be replaced by the provisions of paragraph 1 (as it may be modified by paragraph 3) to the extent provided in paragraph 4. In other cases, paragraph 1 (as it may be modified by paragraph 3) shall supersede the provisions of the Covered Tax Agreement only to the extent that those provisions are incompatible with paragraph 1 (as it may be modified by paragraph 3).

The consequences of a matching notification are, in other words, those related to indicator (4) (compare Table 3 above).[887] Hence, they should be distinguished from the legal effects of *reserving* on Article 3 BC.[888]

Finally, there is one, less obvious, conflict clause in the treaty, relating to future abrogation by mutual consent: Article 30 BC. It holds: 'the provisions in this Convention are without prejudice to subsequent modifications to a Covered Tax Agreement which may be agreed between the Contracting Jurisdictions of the Covered Tax Agreement'. This is, as noted in section 7.9.3.2, in accordance with consensual system of international obligation set out in Article 30(2) VCLT: parties can always change their minds in the future by mutual consent. The same result would have been achieved without an explicit clause to that effect.[889]

8.2.2.3.3 The Relationship Between the BEPS Convention and Treaties with Third States

As noted in section 7.9.3.4, conflict clauses sometimes include an explicit statement of the VCLT's *pacta tertiis* rule: a multilateral treaty cannot influence treaties with non-signatory states. Article 2(1)(a) of the BEPS Convention defines the term 'Covered Tax Agreement'. Any agreement it covers has to be in force between two or more parties. As Article 1 BC determines that the Convention modifies Covered Tax Agreements only, the Convention includes a pacta tertiis rule. The BEPS Convention, in sum, includes the three elements of a conflict clause, as identified in section 7.9.3.

8.2.2.4 The BEPS Convention's COP

8.2.2.4.1 General Aspects

The BEPS Convention includes a clause that enables the Parties to convene a COP (*see* on COPs section 7.3). Article 31 BC sets out only the most basic rules of procedure in this regard. Parties may convene a COP for the purposes of taking any decisions or exercising any functions as may be required or appropriate under the Convention's

---

887. Article 3(4) BC, that article's compatibility clause, speaks of 'in place or in the absence of'.
888. In accordance with Art. 28(3) BC, reservations apply symmetrically; it is not necessary for states to make a 'matching' reservation to opt out of Art. 3 BC.
889. Article 30(3) VCLT. Also: A. Orakhelashvili (2011) p. 786.

provisions. A COP may be convened, at the request of any Party, provided that a third of all Parties support that request within a time period of six months. Once convened, the COP 'shall be served' by the Depositary (i.e., the secretary-general of the OECD).[890]

The 'functions' and 'decisions' of the COP, mentioned in Article 31 BC, are in any case those set out in Article 32 BC (interpretation and implementation of provisions of the Convention) and Article 33 BC (on amendments to the Convention). Moreover, although Article 38 BC does not include an explicit reference to Article 31 BC, the COP may also adopt protocols.

Apart from these rules, Article 31 BC does not include any more detailed rules of procedure, powers and duties of the COP (e.g., as is common in other areas of international law, on financial and organisational aspects, subsidiary bodies, etc.).

8.2.2.4.2 Interpretation and Implementation of Provisions of the Convention

Article 32(1) BC explicitly stipulates that the COP does not have the ability to discuss the interpretation or implementation of provisions of Covered Tax Agreements, as modified by the BEPS Convention. Such issues (i.e., those related to the texts of Covered Tax Agreements) are left to the discretion of the two parties to that Covered Tax Agreement. But the COP may address any question arising as to the interpretation or implementation of the Convention itself, as set out in Article 32(2) BC. According to the Explanatory Statement, questions addressed to the COP are, for instance, those related to disagreements on the operation of compatibility clauses.[891] Following the distinction between substantive and formal multilateralism (*see* section 6.2.2), Article 32(2) BC seems to apply to disagreements on rules of the BEPS Convention that may be called 'substantively multilateral'; in any case, it seems to comprise disagreements about the Convention's complex procedural obligations.[892]

Again, it is clear that the Convention strikes a balance between using elements of the framework convention – protocol design and the 'agreement to scope'.

Although the BEPS Convention does not stipulate an explicit voting rule, Lang argues that the matters covered by Article 31(2) BC are to be agreed upon by two-thirds of the parties present and voting.[893] This suggestion makes a lot of sense, considering Article 9 VCLT's default voting rule, that requires two-thirds of the parties present and voting when adopting texts at international conferences.

8.2.2.4.3 Amendments to the BEPS Convention

Article 33(1) of the BEPS Convention stipulates that 'any Party may propose an amendment to this Convention by submitting the proposed amendment to the

---

890. *See* Art. 39(1) BC.
891. *See* paras 18 and 315 of the Explanatory Statement and also: M. Lang, *Die Auslegung des mulitlateralen Instruments,* Steuer & Wirtschaft International 2017/11.
892. *See* sec. 6.2.2. Distinguishing the 'multilateral' obligations of the BEPS Convention from its 'bilateral' obligations is an area that needs further research attention.
893. M. Lang (2017).

Depositary'. To 'consider' the amendment, a COP may be convened (Article 33(2) BC). Any proposed amendment will require acceptance on two levels. First, at the level of the COP, for which the votes of two-thirds of the States present and voting are required.[894] Second, acceptance is required at the level of each participating state (i.e., ratification), so that the text of the Convention becomes binding on them. This has the drawback that the multilateral convention will prove notoriously hard to change. *See* for further comments section 7.11.1.

8.2.2.4.4   *Adoption of Protocols*

Article 38 holds that the Convention may be supplemented by one or more protocols. Parties to the Convention can join a protocol if they wish (Article 38(3) BC). However, in order to join a protocol, parties have to join the Convention (Article 38(2) BC). It seems likely that proposals for protocols are discussed by the COP, although the BEPS Convention does not include explicit rules of procedure in this regard. Again, the VCLT's default rules on voting apply.[895]

The ability of a COP to adopt protocols is a central element of the idea underlying the framework convention-protocol design. Usually, framework conventions are general, procedural type of commitments, in which substantive commitments are further fleshed out in protocols. In this way, Conventions may built momentum, trust and generate knowledge. Moreover, under the framework convention-protocol design, new rules can be dynamically and gradually agreed upon by parties (*see* section 7.8.1).

And indeed, when completely dressed down, the BEPS Convention has the *aspects* of a framework convention. However, its efficacy *as* a framework convention can be questioned (*see* section 8.3).

8.2.2.5   *Obligations to Reach Agreement:* **Pacta de Negotiando**

Article 7(15)(a) BC and Article 7(16) BC contain clauses that may be termed *pacta de negotiando*: parties agree to 'endeavour to reach a mutually satisfactory solution which meets the minimum standard'. As pointed out in section 7.14.1, such clauses are part of an 'agreement to scope', as it requests parties to engage in further bilateral coordination.

As noted in section 8.2.1.3, 'pacta' are used to forge agreement on the minimum standard agreed upon during the negotiations on the BEPS Project. The texts of the 'pacta' of the BEPS Convention require states to 'endeavour to reach a mutually satisfactory solution which meets the minimum standard [for preventing treaty abuse]'.[896] States are not obliged to actually *arrive* at such an agreement. A *pactum* requires states to *negotiate, in good faith*, a measure that meets the minimum standard.

---

894. *See* Art. 9(2) VCLT.
895. *See* Art. 9 VCLT.
896. *See* Art. 7(15)(a) and 7(16) BC. The part quoted between brackets appears in Art. 7(16) BC only.

The notification procedure required by compatibility clauses is based on a similar type of legal obligation. Compatibility clauses require states to notify the Depositary whether the provisions of their bilateral tax treaties are compatible with the Convention (*see* pp. 6 and 7 of the Explanatory Statement). Implicit in this notification procedure lies a requirement of good faith:

> Parties are generally required to make a notification (...). It is expected that Parties would use their best efforts to identify all provisions that are within the objective scope of the compatibility clause. It is therefore not intended that Parties would choose to omit some relevant provisions while listing others. (...)

> (...) It is expected that Parties would use their best efforts to identify all provisions that are within the objective scope of each compatibility clause. This should reduce to a minimum situations in which a relevant existing provision is not identified by the Contracting Jurisdictions to a Covered Tax Agreement. Such situations are not impossible, however, either because the Contracting Jurisdictions to a Covered Tax Agreement disagree about whether a particular provision is within the scope of a compatibility clause; or because both Contracting Jurisdictions agree that there is a relevant provision, but disagree about which provision it is. (...) To the extent that [such disagreements] nevertheless arise, [they] could be settled through the mutual agreement procedure provided for in the Covered Tax Agreement.[897]

8.3 THE BEPS CONVENTION: A STRUCTURAL SOLUTION TO MODERNISING INTERNATIONAL TAX LAW?

The BEPS Project has been sceptically evaluated in academic literature. It may indeed safely be assumed that the BEPS Convention will not completely solve the problem tax avoidance.[898] Nevertheless, from the analysis above follows that the obligations of the BEPS Convention are in conformity with what, in accordance with the neoliberal institutionalist perspective of Chapter 5, may be expected of multilateral tax cooperation. Also, in line with the presumptions of section 5.4.5, the Convention employs elements of both the framework convention-protocol design as well as the 'agreement to scope' (*see* Chapter 7). Clearly, given the restrictions to multilateral negotiation posed by states protecting/pursuing their self-interests, it should not be overestimated what a multilateral agreement can do.

This conclusion underscores the relevance of the central argument of this book: a multilateral agreement for international taxation should function as a robust 'managerial' framework that facilitates interaction, enabling the system to progressively transform and develop *over time*. Certainly, the purpose of the BEPS Convention is different from that of the 'multilateral agreement for international taxation' of Chapter 7.[899] The BEPS Convention's purpose: 'implementing the BEPS Project', is more limited

---

897. The first-mentioned quote is from para. 15; the second from para. 18 of the Explanatory Statement.
898. *See* the text and footnotes of sec. 5.4.4.
899. The BEPS Convention is, according to its preamble, aimed at the 'swift, coordinated and consistent implementation of the treaty related BEPS measures'.

and 'instrumental' than that of the multilateral agreement for international taxation. Nevertheless, the question: 'does the BEPS Convention satisfy the central claims of the book?' is relevant. To what extent have tax policy makers, knowing that the rules of the BEPS Project might not be sufficient to completely put an end to the issues of tax avoidance and tax competition, been able to forge agreement on a more structural multilateral solution for international taxation?

Where the previous discussion was *explanatory*, the discussion here, consequently, takes a normative turn. What are, in the light of the arguments set out in this book, the Convention's problems and promises?

(1) *A robust institutional framework* (*see* section 6.3.2 and Chapter 7A). The BEPS Convention does not instal a structural framework for continuous discussion.

Article 31 provides for parties to call an international conference, in which they can discuss the obligations and operation of the Convention. This allows them, for instance, to discuss questions of interpretation.[900] It is, for instance, not unthinkable that questions as to the correct interpretation of compatibility clauses may arise.[901] Also, the Conference may be called to discuss the amendment of the Convention (Article 33 BC) as well as to supplement the Convention by one or more protocols, for which participation by all parties to the Convention is not deemed necessary (Article 38 BC). The fact that the Convention mentions the possibility to call an international COP, which can adopt protocols and enact amendments to the Convention, should be applauded, and is a step in the right direction of further integrative cooperation in international taxation.

However, Articles 31, 33 and 38 BC are hollow promises: parties have not agreed to organise any *recurring* or *continuous* forms of interaction. Continuous deliberation, first of all, is necessary for the norms of today to remain in line with social criteria of the future. Without it, there is no way to ensure that outcomes reached will be considered 'fair' (*see*, in particular, section 4.2.3). In addition, ad-hoc conferences can be called on all types of issues, if this serves states' interests. For 'tit-for-tat' to occur, however, a forum in which the cooperative game can be played indefinitely is needed (*see*, in particular, sections 6.3.2 and 6.3.5). Without a forum in which parties agree to repeatedly reciprocate, interaction will continue on an ad-hoc basis. This, in turn, may mean that parties will not be able to forgo short-term interests and opportunism over long-term goals. As has been repeatedly argued (*see* e.g., section 3.4), much is at stake: neither a chaos of overlapping unilateral anti-abuse rules nor the complete redundancy of income tax systems is, due to increased tax competition a more welcome alternative to recurring and continuous multilateral cooperation.

---

900. *See* Art. 32 of the BEPS Convention.
901. *See* para. 18 of the Explanatory Statement.

The Convention, moreover, does not mention any organisational structure needed to deal with issues on a more holistic basis, such as a secretariat. It also fails to mention any explicit powers and duties (e.g., financial, organisational, etc.) or rules of procedure of the COP (*see* the discussion in sections 7.3.2, 7.3.3 and section 8.2.2.4 as well as Articles 6 and 7 of the Draft Conventions of the Annex. Although the Convention mentions the Secretary-General of the OECD as 'Depositary', which is usually a function performed by secretariats,[902] functions exercised by depositaries relate to the formalities involved with singing a treaty and keeping custody of the treaty's text.[903]

The issue of the absence of structural institutional rules, however, might be a minor one, given the important role of the OECD in forging international tax policy. This does, however, lead us to the matter discussed next.

(2) *Transparent, open and equal discussions* (*see* sections 4.2.3, 5.4.7, 6.3.3 and 7.3). The BEPS Convention does not deal with the question of how future rules of international tax law are adopted. Lacking any institutional framework (*see* above), it may be expected that the OECD will take the lead in forging new tax rules, whether in relation to the BEPS Convention (i.e., amendments or protocols),[904] or to any future international tax policy affair. Negotiators have, perhaps, deemed this issue irrelevant, as the outcomes of the BEPS Project were already produced.

Transparency, openness and equality are, however, at a fundamental level, absent from lawmaking processes within the OECD (*see* section 4.2.3). Fair procedure, however, is not only necessary for 'fair' international tax rules in the future (Chapter 4), but is also indispensable for parties to build shared understandings and/or 'learn' (*see* section 6.3.3).[905] As argued, such elements are crucial for dealing with collective action problems over time.

---

902. *See* H.G. Schermers and N.M. Blokker (2011) para. 457.
903. *See* Arts 76–77 of the VCLT.
904. But *see* the discussion under point 1.
905. The Explanatory Statement includes the 'agreed understanding of the negotiators with respect to the Convention' (*see* para. 11 of the Explanatory Statement), and could, consequently, be seen to reflect the understandings of *all* parties to the Convention. In this regard, the Explanatory Statement may be said to be an 'agreement' or 'instrument' made in connection with the conclusion of the treaty in the sense of Art. 31(2) VCLT. Of particular importance is that the Explanatory Statement is 'agreed' between *all* the Parties. *See*, for a discussion, F.A. Engelen (2004) secs 6.7.3 and 6.7.4. The BEPS Final Reports and OECD Commentaries related to the measures of the BEPS Convention, however, have all been crafted within the closed-door environment of the OECD. It may therefore be questioned whether these documents can be said to express the intentions of parties to the Convention, if these parties have not had a real and tangible influence in preparing and creating these rules within the OECD. For interpreting the multilateral obligations of such parties, international law suggests that the BEPS Final Reports may not be used as preparatory work or *travaux préparatoires* within the ambit of Art. 32 VCLT. *See* PCIJ *Case Concerning the Jurisdiction of the International Commission of the River Oder (Order of 20 August 1929)*, PCIJ Rep, Series A, No. 16, in which the Court held at p. 42: 'Whereas three of the Parties concerned in the present case did not take part in the work of the Conference which prepared the Treaty of Versailles; as, accordingly, the record of this work cannot be used to determine, in so far as they are concerned, the import of the Treaty.' *See also* S. Rosenne, *Travaux Préparatoires*, 12 International & Comparative Law Quarterly 1378 (1963).

(3) *Guiding principles* (*see* sections 6.3.4 and 7.4). The BEPS Convention is, first and foremost, an instrument to modify bilateral tax treaties on the BEPS Project's outcomes. As a result, it does not expressly and consciously define or determine ideals to which international tax law can develop in the future. But the BEPS Convention is not completely free of commonly identified ideals and/or 'new' shared beliefs on international tax law either. It contains some evidence that not only interests, but values matter too in international tax law.

Indeed, from the perspective of section 6.3.4, the BEPS Convention can be seen as a (first) step forward in the direction of addressing tax avoidance and tax competition. Its publicised legal commitments, once implemented and ratified, may come to function as focal points around which future discussion and hence progression can gravitate. This may, in turn, mean that the BEPS Convention, once successfully implemented and entered into effect, will in fact turn out to be an important step in the direction of solving the issues of tax avoidance and tax arbitration.

In terms of focal points, particular Article 6 could prove of relevance. Surely, the article could turn out to reflect nothing more but the result of 'simple' reciprocal bartering of interests, reflecting a negotiation outcome that suits countries seeking to protect their source interests (*see* sections 5.3.2 and 5.3.3). But given its general language, and the fact that it is a 'minimum standard', agreed to by the negotiators of around 100 jurisdictions: may it also be said that Article 6 is a substantive, principle-like multilateral commitment of a multilateral convention?

It may indeed be argued that Article 6 BC's codification was driven by normative rather than 'material' concerns (*see* section 5.2 on the distinction between constructivism and neoliberal institutionalism). If this argument is accepted, then one may also accept that Article 6's wording ('intending to eliminate double taxation with respect to the taxes covered by this agreement *without creating opportunities for non-taxation or reduced taxation through tax evasion or avoidance*')[906] codifies the idea of the single tax principle as a principle of international tax law, much like Avi-Yonah has argued.[907] This may then – taking the argument a step further – imply that the article encompasses an implicit, shared understanding between the Convention's parties of what international tax law *is about*. If this is true, then, over time, Article 6 BC may come to inform future negotiations in the area of international tax law, directing the way in which substantive norms of international tax law should further develop. The BEPS Convention, by presenting a widely supported idea that international tax law is not only about preventing double taxation, but also about preventing double non-taxation, may hence influence

---

But *see*, U. Linderfalk, *On the Interpretation of Treaties: the Modern International Law as Expressed in the 1969 Vienna Convention on the Law of Treaties* (Springer 2007) pp. 241–242.

906. Article 6(1) of the BEPS Convention (emphasis added).
907. *See*, in particular, R.S. Avi-Yonah (2007) pp. 8–10, also: sec. 7.4.2.

negotiations in international tax law. The BEPS Convention may, in other words, turn out to be evidence of, and of relevance to, gradually changing views on the interests at stake in international taxation.

(4) *Network effects* (*see* section 7.5). From the perspective of the design strategy presented in Chapter 6, 'network effects' are of importance, as these may lead to a more widespread use, development, and acceptance of the agreement's norms in tax treaties not covered by the Convention.

The Convention, however, is clearly not applicable on agreements of non-participatory states or jurisdictions (*see* Article 2(1)(a)(i) BC). It neither contains the *pactum de agendo* of section 7.5.2.3; a conscious design option to influence treaties with non-participatory states. Moreover, as the Convention explicitly applies to 'covered' bilateral tax treaties only, which need to be 'listed' by states, it seems unlikely that the Convention may bear on tax treaties by becoming a binding obligation through estoppel or acquiescence (*see* section 7.5.2.1). Indeed, for estoppel or acquiescence to arise, a clear and provocative statement of one of the two parties to a tax agreement is required. But even if a party to a tax agreement, participating in the BEPS Convention, makes a statement that it interprets or applies a bilateral tax agreement in line with the Convention, the Convention clearly holds that, for it to become applicable, *each* party to a tax agreement 'has made a notification to the Depositary listing the agreement'.[908] Consequently, it seems difficult to maintain that if one party makes a statement to the effect that it interprets and applies a tax agreement in line with the obligations of the Convention, and the other party to that tax agreement fails to react to this statement, the first-mentioned party may interpret such inaction, against a clear rule to the contrary set out in the same Convention the first-mentioned party itself seeks to apply, as consent.

The most likely scenario in which the Convention may bear on tax treaties with third states is through Article 31(3)(c) VCLT. In particular, the article on the interpretation of treaties requires the interpreter to take into account the normative environment of a tax treaty when interpreting and applying it. Indeed, as argued in section 7.5.2.2, the Convention, by 'being there', can influence the interpretation of tax treaties with non-participatory states. Again, particularly Article 6 of the Convention could prove of relevance in providing the normative environment of international tax law, also for treaties with non-participatory states.[909]

---

908. *See* Art. 2(1)(a)(ii) of the BEPS Convention.
909. *See*, in this regard, also the outcomes under circumstance 3 ("One of the parties is not a member of the OECD") of Table 2 ("The relevance of the OECD Commentary under varying circumstances in courts of OECD member countries") of sec. 3.3.5.

8.4 SUMMARY AND CONCLUSIONS

The obligations set out in the BEPS Convention generally follow the neoliberal institutionalist perspective on multilateral tax cooperation of Chapter 5. Indeed, the substantive obligations of the BEPS Convention avoid distributive concerns: they are 'rules of the road', they encourage further bilateral negotiations, or they avoid departing from existing distributive baselines altogether (section 8.2.1). Moreover, the Convention employs some of the aspects of the 'agreement to scope' as well as the 'framework convention-protocol design' as set out in Chapter 7 and the Annex, underscoring the need for flexibility mechanisms in international tax law (section 8.2.2). As was pointed out in section 7.1, the distinction between both design options should not be perceived as strict. But the need for flexibility (in the sense of sections 5.4.5 and 5.4.6) introduces questions related to, for example, reservations, conflict clauses and 'pacta', discussed throughout Chapters 7B and 7C.

In 8.3, the evaluation then turned to the question to what extent the BEPS Convention mirrors the 'multilateral agreement for international taxation' argued for in this book. This question is relevant: assuming that the BEPS Convention will not 'solve' the issues of tax avoidance and tax arbitration, the focus must turn to the future, and hence, to the Convention's institutional aspects. Classifying the Convention's substance as 'flawed' is, as follows from earlier chapters, fruitless. What may be expected of a multilateral treaty for the area of international taxation should not be overestimated.

The main point resulting from section 8.3's evaluation of the Convention's 'institutional' aspects is that the BEPS Convention is not suitable to modernise international tax law. It lacks a fair and robust forum for continuous discussions. Also, it misses explicit guiding principles to guide and inform future negotiation efforts. By focusing on the short term, it is, in other words, above all an 'instrument' to implement the outcomes of the BEPS Project.

Nevertheless, the Convention has some aspects to be excited about. It is, after all, a multilateral convention. And as a multilateral convention, it will undoubtedly set new focal points and horizons to guide the development of the international tax regime as a whole. In particular, there is some evidence that the Convention contains changing views on what international taxation *is about*. This may, in turn, influence tax treaty interpretation, practice and negotiations in the years to come.

CHAPTER 9
Conclusions

Answering the research questions related to the multilateral agreement for international taxation has proven a continuous balancing test between bilateralism and multilateralism. And indeed, if full-fledged multilateralism would be perceived as white, and bilateralism as black, then certainly, a multilateral agreement for international taxation is painted in shades of grey. Ideas on a multilateral agreement should, by implication, be modest.

From their start, the rules for the avoidance of double taxation have never been purely bi- or multilateral. Although the rules to avoid double taxation have always been based on bilateral treaties, the OECD MTC and its Commentaries provided for a multilateral template around which bilateral tax treaty negotiations could be coordinated. In fact, the current system is the second-best result of a failed effort for a comprehensive multilateral tax treaty. Where states could not agree on the distribution of taxing rights over mobile capital, a bilateral tax treaty system slowly evolved. And in the light of this expanding network of bilateral tax treaties, a comprehensive multilateral tax treaty proved less and less practicable. Yet, a 'weak' form of multilateralism could be introduced in the form of the flexible OECD MTC and its Commentaries. And the system has been particularly resilient in relation to its core concepts: 'PE'; 'arm's length', and also 'residence' and 'dividends': these are concepts that practitioners all over the world recognise, perhaps even making these terms 'multilateral' in the strong sense. The OECD MTC and Commentaries, although a second-best outcome, have hence provided the international tax system with a great deal of uniformity and solidity.

Yet, the use of this loose type form of regulatory influence on bilateral tax treaties is not without limits. Despite its immense influence on tax treaties, OECD soft tax law falls short on dynamic grounds. Indeed, the loose type of tax coordination by means of soft law norms has not been able to prevent the international tax system to become outdated and unresponsive. As has been shown in Chapter 3, states rarely amend their bilateral tax treaties. Of the 397 tax treaties in force before 1977, 41% were not amended between 1977 (the year of the first update to the OECD MTC) and 2013. And the figures related to later OECD MTC updates provide an even bleaker view on reality. Would the results of Chapter 3 be applied to the BEPS outcomes for which the OECD proposes OECD MTC amendments, these would be not be fully implemented in bilateral tax treaties before the year 2035 (in approximately eighteen years from the time of writing). But that is not all: amendments to the OECD Commentary, introduced by the OECD so as to influence the contents of tax treaties, are regularly ignored by courts of OECD Member countries, who have, after all, 'the last word' on tax treaty interpretation, and hence on the contents of tax treaties.

Moreover, as states are free to modify on and postpone the implementation of soft OECD standards in their bilateral tax treaty relationships, the current system is characterised by the absence of a level playing field, necessary to arrive at common solutions for current and future collective action problems of international taxation, such as tax arbitrage and tax competition. What is at stake? Establishing a level playing field is essential because inaction may lead, at least in the long term, to either the redundancy of corporate income taxation due to increased tax competition, or to an incoherent chaos of unilateral anti-abuse rules, caused by public outrage. An indication of the relevance of this observation is that tax avoidance is estimated to lead to a reduction of global corporate income tax revenues of about 4–10%. A level playing field, established by multilateral agreement, provides a more suitable and appealing alternative.

So, a fundamental reconsideration of the way tax treaties are amended is necessary. What can and should the multilateral agreement then look like? Re-enter the balancing test between bilateralism and multilateralism, first identified in Chapter 2. In between the normative, comprehensive model on multilateral tax cooperation, aimed at restoring the 'fairness' of international taxation by means of 'correct' procedure (Chapter 4), and a model on cooperation that reflects the political realities of collaboration in the field of international tax (Chapter 5), lies the concept of the multilateral agreement for international taxation (Chapter 6). This multilateral agreement is of a procedural rather than regulatory character. It provides a level playing field in the form of a forum for discussions (section 6.2). Where agreement on true multilateral norms ('substantive multilateralism') proves slow or unfeasible, a multilateral agreement may at least reduce the transaction costs traditionally associated with bilateral tax treaty negotiations by bringing states together at one central place and time, and by providing for an institutional structure ('formal multilateralism'), *see* section 6.2.2.

Ideally, what a multilateral agreement should do (*see* Chapter 4.3) is create a level playing field that includes in its deliberations all states that are interested in participating, in a transparent manner. This would enable states to, over time, reach 'fair' multilateral solutions to collective action problems such as tax competition and tax arbitrage, as the law thus created would come to include all relevant social, moral and political perspectives.

Achieving 'procedural fairness' seems politically feasible in the long run: transparent and inclusive deliberations may be gradually achieved and further institutionalisation seems not so far off. In fact, the OECD recognises the importance of equal and inclusive negotiations, hence the 'ad hoc group' and the 'inclusive framework' that have recently been formed. But political realities restrict the type of substantive rules that states can agree on, as is argued in Chapter 5. In the considerations to enter into a multilateral or bilateral agreement on international tax rules, countries are likely to be led by the motive of maximising or protecting their national interests. Multilateral agreement is unlikely when the distributive consequences of cooperation are relatively certain, but likely when the distributional aspect is uncertain or absent. Indeed, states that are faced with uncertainty as regards their own positions in the future will tend to agree on 'centralised' or 'fair' multilateral arrangements, i.e., arrangements that may be expected to generate acceptable outcomes for all. Vice versa, Chapter 5s perspective suggests that multilateral agreement on rules that generate *certain* distributive outcomes, such as those necessary to fundamentally counter BEPS (e.g., replacing the arm's length standard with formulary apportionment to tackle certain difficult issues such as 'hard-to-measure intangibles'), will prove politically unfeasible, or at least highly unlikely. The selection of and ratio between any of the baselines of a formula or CCCTB ('sales', 'assets' or 'labour') create obvious winners and losers. A state that foresees losing gains under a new baseline to divide the 'tax pie' (which includes states' source as well as residence interests, *see* sections 5.3.2 and 5.3.3) will only accept such a baseline when placed under high internal or external political pressure. Likewise, proposals for a switch to a destination-based corporate income tax, which embody the economist's solution to most current issues of tax competition and tax arbitrage, are pie in the sky, as they emphasise conflict between consumption and producing states. But this does not necessarily mean that multilateral agreement will be impossible in international taxation. Diverging state interests may be accommodated in a multilateral deal by 'rules of the road' (i.e., rules that operate 'fairly' for all participants) and distributional conflict may be relaxed by reservations or *inter se* bilateral negotiations. Nevertheless, this does compel tax policy makers to take on a modest view on what is possible in a multilateral agreement.

A level playing field in which collective action problems are 'managed' over time seems the only fruitful step forward (*see* Chapter 6). But does this also imply that the implementation of new norms in bilateral tax treaties will take place in a quicker and 'more streamlined' fashion? This is hard to predict. A complex multilateral negotiation may take just as long as many bilateral ones. But provided that the negotiation on a 'substantive' multilateral norm (i.e., a 'rule of the road') does not exceed the eighteen years identified in Chapter 3, multilateral agreement may indeed be the quicker option, as it amends the network of bilateral tax treaties *in one fell swoop*. And for those issues for which 'substantive multilateralism' proves unnegotiable, the two-step logic of multilateral negotiations suggests that a mere 'formal' multilateral arrangement may also be able to do the trick. The mundane reduction of transaction costs of the 'first step' of a multilateral negotiation, i.e., agreeing on where and when states will meet and identifying the objectives of the negotiations (termed 'speed dating' by the OECD), may prove sufficient to quicken the bilateral negotiations that take place in 'step two'. An institutional arrangement may further reduce transaction costs by facilitating the exchange and generation of information. 'Formal multilateralism' hence provides states with economies of scale that the current 'system' by means of which bilateral tax treaties are (re)negotiated lacks.

A central theme in the discussions of Chapter 6 is the coordinative role of legal rules. In providing the infrastructure to reach tax policy goals over time, legal rules form the multilateral agreement's pivotal element: by agreeing on 'rules of the road' and some guiding principles, states do not need to re-enter into discussions already entered into before. Agreement on a 'rule of the road' prevents states from engaging in bilateral discussions each time they run into each other at the figurative intersection. But 'rules of the road' will also function as shared background assumptions in ongoing, evolving discussions on norms. Similarly, as there are several answers to each issue, procedure and guiding principles can be used to inform and guide the selection and identification of feasible solutions. Indeed, as argued in Chapter 6.3, provided that states repeatedly interact, and provided that legal rules are used to pin down the understandings that have become common, international norms may be changed modestly when states come to share new understandings about issues and possible solutions. This means that requirements of 'fair' procedure, as discussed in Chapter 4, are indispensable: 'learning' cannot be fully realised when deliberations within the regime are non-transparent and under-inclusive. Hence, the coordinative function of legal rules propels states into deeper commitments, provided that the other conditions for 'managing' the international tax regime (building on shared understandings, repetition of interaction) are present. This means that, even if understandings about optimal solutions for collective action problems may be heavily debated or unclear in practice, 'fair procedure' is, in any case, a prerequisite for driving states into substantive multilateral solutions over time.

So, binding multilateralism in the area of international tax law has to be seen as a system to 'manage' the evolution and modernisation of international tax law by influencing bilateral tax treaties from 'the top down' rather than marginally from 'the bottom up'. This is illustrated using some legal tools of international public law in Chapter 7 and the Annex. The bottom line is that the multilateral agreement for international taxation should, at the least, constitute a quasi-formal IO (a 'COP') that organises recurring meetings, and under which common value-maximising terms are established towards which the regime can build. The regime hence created should facilitate 'learning' by providing or working towards transparent and inclusive deliberations and by facilitating the exchange of relevant information. Connections with other IOs, such as the OECD, can be used to generate knowledge and inform the discussions (e.g., by means of model conventions, reports, commentaries, etc.). But the point of establishing a treaty body is its independence: states participating in the forum, OECD Member and non-member alike, should get a real influence on the vital phase of discussions and norm generation.

On top of this 'constitutional' basis, states can then mix-and-match some relevant tools of international public law. Where *substantive* multilateralism, such as 'rules of the road' proves feasible, it makes sense to use elements of the framework convention-protocol design, so that the regime may be developed towards common ideals. Where, on the other hand, substantive multilateralism proves unfeasible, *formal* multilateralism may be employed, in which states merely agree on the procedure in 'step one' to flesh out the common value-maximising terms in their bilateral tax treaties in 'step two'. It is important to note that the distinction between both design types should not be perceived as strict. Formal multilateralism may have substantive characteristics when groups of states further agree to common terms; substantive multilateralism may have formal characteristics when states use reservations and 'menu options' to further tailor a multilateral norm to their needs. And indeed, as shown in Chapter 8, the BEPS Convention contains a mix of both institutional forms.

The overall picture is that, regrettably, a multilateral agreement for international tax law will not provide a quick fix for most modern collective action problems of international tax law. Multilateral agreement on the 'big' solutions to tax arbitrage and tax competition may never be possible. The BEPS Convention, in this respect, does not 'solve' the issues of international tax competition and tax arbitrage. But the prospect of a multilateral agreement is indeed a quicker tax treaty amendment process. Moreover, it may provide the prelude towards more integrative and 'fair' cooperation in the international tax field in the future. This however requires a shift in thinking on the part of policy makers. Discussions on international tax law have mostly resulted in texts and proposals of a dominantly technical and 'ad hoc' nature. The BEPS Project and its Convention, for instance, are presented as the final stop on the line against tax avoidance. But they must rather be perceived as the beginning of a longer process of integrative cooperation in the international tax field. Without the facilitation of 'correct' procedure, endurance, the generation and exchange of ideas, 'learning', vision and innovation, the international tax regime may remain stuck in its adolescence of the 1960s. The multilateral agreement for international taxation may provide the breakthrough for the international tax regime to come of age.

Draft Clauses to the Framework Convention-Protocol Design and the 'Agreement to Scope'

This Annex includes draft clauses of the framework convention-protocol design and the 'agreement to scope' so as to illustrate the points made in Chapter 7 (*see* the table below). The reader may notice that the drafts below include clauses that have not been discussed in the book. The author felt that a detailed explanation of every single treaty clause taken up below was unnecessary: the aim here and of Chapter 7 is to illustrate, by means of some example clauses, the book's core arguments. It is not the aim of this Annex to provide a handbook for treaty drafters of a multilateral convention, such as the UN (2012): *Treaty Handbook* (United Nations Revised ed. 2012); the UN (2003): *Final Clauses of Multilateral Treaties: Handbook* (United Nations 2003) and, applicable by analogy, the handbook on the UNFCCC: UN Climate Change Secretariat, United Nations Framework Convention on Climate Change: Handbook (UNFCCC 2006). The author has been careful in expressing thoughts on substantive tax treaty principles or rules, as they are not at the heart of this study.

For inspiration in drafting the clauses of the framework convention-protocol design, the author has made use of the UN Framework Convention on Climate Change and the WHO Framework Convention on Tobacco Control.[910] Similarly, for the 'agreement to scope', he has looked at the UN Convention on the Law of the Non-Navigational Uses of International Watercourses and the Draft articles on the Law of Transboundary Aquifers.[911] Moreover, the author consulted the BEPS Action Plan and BEPS Final Reports for some of the language used.

---

910. *United Nations Framework Convention on Climate Change* (adopted 9 May 1992), 1771 UNTS 107; *WHO Framework Convention on Tobacco Control* (adopted 21 May 2003), 2302 UNTS 166.
911. *UN Convention on the Law of the Non-Navigational Uses of International Watercourses* (adopted 21 May 1997), 36 ILM 700; Draft Articles on a Law of Transboundary Aquifers, in Official Records of the General Assembly, Sixty-third Session, Supplement No. 10 (A/63/10).

Table A1   Overview of Draft Articles and Related Sections of Chapter 7

Section	Draft Articles
7.3 (The organisation managing the multilateral regime)	Annex A and B: Articles 5, 6 and 7
7.4 (Guiding principles)	Annex A and B: Articles 3 and 4; Preambles
7.5 (Network effects: pactum de agendo)	Annex A: Article 8(2); Annex B: Article 8(3)
7.8 (Framework convention-protocol design)	Annex A, particularly Articles 3, 4 and 10
7.9 (Conflict clause)	Annex A: Article 6
7.10.2 (Interpretative flexibility: 'menu options' and reservations)	None (the residual rules of the VCLT apply)
7.10.3 (Interpretative flexibility: 'rules of the road')	Protocol to Annex A: Articles 2, 3 and 4
7.11 (Dynamic decision-making procedures)	Protocol to Annex A: Article 5
7.14.1.1 (Agreement to scope: Pactum de contrahendo)	Annex B: Article 8
7.14.1.2 (Agreement to scope: Monitoring and reporting requirements)	Annex B: Article 9
Other treaty provisions, e.g., right to vote; depositary; ratification (not discussed in Ch. 7)	Annex A and B: Articles 11-18. Protocol to Annex A: Articles 6-11

A. THE FRAMEWORK CONVENTION-PROTOCOL DESIGN

The Framework Convention on International Taxation
The Parties to the present Convention,
Recognising that globalisation has impacted countries' income tax systems;
Recognising that the tax treaty network is outdated, as it is for instance unable to effectively address opportunities for multinational companies to greatly minimise their tax burdens and/or issues related to the increased relevance of the digital economy;
Desiring to conclude a multilateral agreement to swiftly implement or incorporate in their bilateral tax treaty relationships new developments in society, business and technology;
Recognising that this requires a fair level playing field that ensures that all countries and jurisdictions implement their commitments equally and on an equal footing;
Recognising that this requires continuous interaction in the future;
Have agreed as follows:

Article 1. Scope of the present Convention

The present Convention applies to tax treaties in force or to be concluded in relation to provisions that the Conference of the Parties may adopt.

Article 2. Terminology

For the purposes of the present Convention:

1. 'Tax treaty' means any agreement for the avoidance of double taxation and the prevention of fiscal evasion applicable in the relations between Signatory States or between Signatory States and third states.
   (etc.)

Article 3. Objective

The ultimate objective of this Convention and any related instruments that the Conference of the Parties may adopt is to achieve, in accordance with the relevant provisions of the Convention, that the international tax treaty network is modernised and updated in accordance with the latest developments in society, business and technology. In doing so, the Parties will promote an open and transparent negotiating environment in which they cooperate on an equal footing.

Article 4. Principles

As determined by the Conference of the Parties, in their actions to achieve the objective of this Convention and to implement its provisions, the Parties shall be guided, *inter alia*, by the following:
[Possible principles that the Conference of the Parties could adopt, could be, for example:]

1. The Parties shall ensure that profits are taxed where value is created and economic activities take place.
2. The Parties shall endeavour to ensure that the domestic tax burdens on profits derived from cross-border business activities equals the domestic tax burden on profits derived from non-cross-border business activities, given that all other circumstances taxpayers are the same.
3. The Parties shall aim to prevent double non-taxation as well as double taxation. In seeking to achieve this aim, the Parties shall strike a fair balance between the need to eliminate obstacles to international trade on the one hand and preventing practices in which taxable income are artificially segregated from activities that generate it on the other hand.
4. The needs of designated developing countries in taxing corporate income at source shall be given full consideration.

Article 5. Development of international tax rules and exchange of information

1. The Parties shall undertake to develop and promote research and research programmes at the regional and international levels in the field of international taxation with the aim of pursuing the objective of this Convention. Toward this end, Parties shall:
    a. Initiate and cooperate, either directly or through international and regional international organisations such as the Organisation for Economic Co-operation and Development, the United Nations and the International Monetary Fund, the conduct of research and development of rules of international tax law that are identified by the Conference of the Parties.
    b. Support and strengthen, with the support of competent international and regional international organisations such as the Organisation for Economic Co-operation and Development, the United Nations and International Monetary Fund, the training and support of tax officers or others engaged in government activities related to international tax law, including tax assessment, transfer pricing, tax treaty law and business accounting.
2. The Parties shall promote and facilitate the exchange of available information on international tax law, including model tax conventions and tax laws, commentaries to the model tax conventions, and other legal and economic materials where appropriate.
3. The Parties shall make publicly available, after a reasonable period of time to be decided on by the Conference of the Parties, the records and minutes of the discussions regarding the development of model tax laws, model tax treaties and commentaries thereon, as these may be amended from time to time.

Article 6. Conference of the Parties

1. A Conference of the Parties is hereby established.
2. The first session of the Conference of the Parties shall be convened by the Organisation for Economic Co-operation and Development no later than one year after the entry into force of this Convention. The Conference will determine the venue and timing of subsequent regular sessions at its first session.
3. Extraordinary sessions of the Conference of the Parties shall be held at such other times as may be deemed necessary by the Conference, or at the written request of any Party, provided that, within six months of the request being communicated to them by the Secretariat of the Convention, it is supported by at least one third of the Parties.

4. The Conference of the Parties shall adopt by consensus its rules of procedure at its first session.

5. The Conference of the Parties shall by consensus adopt financial rules for itself as well as governing the funding of any subsidiary bodies it may establish as well as financial provisions governing the functioning of the Secretariat. At each ordinary session, it shall adopt a budget for the financial period until the next ordinary session.

6. The Conference of the Parties shall keep under regular review the operation of the Convention. To achieve the objective of the Convention, it may adopt protocols and amendments to the Convention, in accordance with Article 9. Towards this end, it shall:

   a. promote and facilitate the exchange of information between Parties;
   b. promote and adopt, as appropriate, the development and evaluation of rules, strategies, plans, policies, model treaties, commentaries to model treaties, model legislation and other measures;
   c. consider reports submitted by the Organisation for Economic Co-operation and Development, United Nations and International Monetary Fund in achieving the objective of the Convention;
   d. request, where appropriate, the services and cooperation of, and information provided by, the Organisation for Economic Co-operation and Development, the United Nations and International Monetary Fund and other international and regional intergovernmental organisations as a means of achieving the objective of this Convention.
   e. establish subsidiary bodies as are necessary to achieve the objective of the Convention;
   f. consider other action, as appropriate, for the achievement of the objective of the Convention in the light of experience gained in its operation.

7. The Conference of the Parties shall establish the criteria for the participation of observers at its proceedings.

Article 7. Secretariat

1. The Conference of the Parties shall designate a permanent secretariat and make arrangements for its functioning. The Conference of the Parties shall endeavour to do so at its first session.

2. Until such time as a permanent secretariat is designated and established, secretariat functions under this Convention shall be provided by the Organisation for Economic Co-operation and Development in the first year of this Convention's entry into force, and by the United Nations thereafter.

3. Secretariat functions shall be:

   a. to make arrangements for sessions of the Conference of the Parties and any subsidiary bodies and to provide them with services as required;

b. to transmit reports received by it pursuant to the Convention;

c. to provide support to the Parties, particularly developing country Parties and Parties with economies in transition, on request, in the compilation and communication of information required;

d. to prepare reports on its activities under the Convention under the guidance of the Conference of the Parties and submit them to the Conference of the Parties;

e. to ensure, under the guidance of the Conference of the Parties, the necessary coordination with the competent international and regional intergovernmental organisations and other bodies;

f. to enter, under the guidance of the Conference of the Parties, into such administrative or contractual arrangements as may be required for the effective discharge of its functions; and

g. to perform other secretariat functions specified by the Convention and by any of its protocols and such other functions as may be determined by the Conference of the Parties.

Article 8. The relationship between this Convention and tax treaties

1. The provisions of this Convention and any related instruments that the Conference of the Parties may adopt, and of any tax treaty of a Party to this Convention, shall be interpreted and applied together as a single instrument. In the event of any incompatibility between this Convention and any tax treaty, the provisions set out in this Convention shall prevail. However, nothing in this article shall affect the rights and obligations of the Parties to non-Contracting states arising under a tax treaty.

2. The Parties shall endeavour not to conclude tax treaties with non-signatory states inconsistent with the provisions of the present Convention, as it is amended from time to time. To the extent that such tax treaties are not compatible with the obligations of the present Convention, as amended from time to time, the Parties shall try to make the necessary steps to eliminate the incompatibilities established.

Article 9. Amendments to this Convention

1. Any Party may propose amendments to this Convention. Such amendments will be considered by the Conference of the Parties.

2. Amendments to the Convention shall be adopted by the Conference of the Parties. The text of any proposed amendment to the Convention shall be communicated to the Parties by the Secretariat at least six months before the

session at which it is proposed for adoption. The Secretariat shall also communicate proposed amendments to the signatories of the Convention and, for information, to the Depositary.

3. The Parties shall make every effort to reach agreement by consensus on any proposed amendment to the Convention. If all efforts at consensus have been exhausted, and no agreement reached, the amendment shall as a last resort be adopted by a three-quarters majority vote of the Parties present and voting at the session. For purposes of this Article, Parties present and voting means Parties present and casting an affirmative or negative vote. Any adopted amendment shall be communicated by the Secretariat to the Depositary, who shall circulate it to all Parties for acceptance.

4. Instruments of acceptance in respect of an amendment shall be deposited with the Depositary. An amendment adopted in accordance with paragraph 3 of this Article shall enter into force for those Parties having accepted it on the ninetieth day after the date of receipt by the Depositary of an instrument of acceptance by at least two-thirds of the Parties to the Convention.

5. The amendment shall enter into force for any other Party on the ninetieth day after the date on which that Party deposits with the Depositary its instrument of acceptance of the said amendment.

Article 10. Protocols

1. The Conference of the Parties may, at any ordinary session, adopt protocols to the Convention.

2. The text of any proposed protocol shall be communicated to the Parties by the secretariat at least six months before such a session.

3. The requirements for the entry into force of any protocol as well as of its amendment shall be established by that instrument.

4. Only Parties to the Convention may be Parties to a Protocol.

5. Decisions under any protocol shall be taken only by the Parties to the protocol concerned.

Article 11. Right to vote

Each Party to the Convention shall have one vote.

Article 12. Settlement of disputes

1. In the event of a dispute between any two or more Parties concerning the interpretation or application of the Convention, the Parties concerned shall seek a settlement of the dispute through negotiation or any other peaceful

means of their own choice, including good offices, mediation, or conciliation. Failure to reach agreement by good offices, mediation or conciliation shall not absolve Parties to the dispute from the responsibility of continuing to seek to resolve it.

2. When ratifying, accepting, approving or acceding to the Convention, or at any time thereafter, a Party may declare in a written instrument submitted to the Depositary that, in respect of any dispute concerning the interpretation or application of the Convention, it recognizes as compulsory ipso facto and without special agreement, in relation to any Party accepting the same obligation:
   a. submission of the dispute to the International Court of Justice; and/or
   b. arbitration in accordance with procedures to be adopted by the Conference of the Parties as soon as practicable, in a protocol on arbitration.

Article 13. Depositary

The Secretary-General of the United Nations shall be the Depositary of the Convention and of protocols adopted in accordance with Article 10.

Article 14. Signature

This Convention shall be open for signature for all interested States.

Article 15. Ratification, acceptance, approval or accession

The Convention shall be subject to ratification, acceptance, approval or accession by States and by regional economic integration organisations. It shall be open for accession from the day after the date on which the Convention is closed for signature. Instruments of ratification, acceptance, approval or accession shall be deposited with the Depositary.

Article 16. Withdrawal

1. At any time after three years from the date on which the Convention has entered into force for a Party, that Party may withdraw from the Convention by giving written notification to the Depositary.
2. Any such withdrawal shall take effect upon expiry of one year from the date of receipt by the Depositary of the notification of withdrawal, or on such later date as may be specified in the notification of withdrawal.
3. Any Party that withdraws from the Convention shall be considered as also having withdrawn from any protocol to which it is a Party.

Article 17. Entry into force

1. The Convention shall enter into force on the ninetieth day after the date of deposit of the twentieth instrument of ratification, acceptance, approval or accession.
2. For each State that ratifies, accepts or approves the Convention or accedes thereto after the deposit of the twentieth instrument of ratification, acceptance, approval or accession, the Convention shall enter into force on the ninetieth day after the date of deposit by such State of its instrument of ratification, acceptance, approval or accession.

Article 18. Authentic texts

The original of this Convention, of which the Arabic, English, French, Chinese and Spanish texts are equally authentic, shall be deposited with the Secretary-General of the United Nations.

IN WITNESS WHEREOF the undersigned, being duly authorized to that effect, have signed this Convention.

DONE at XXY this ... day of .... of the year ....

PROTOCOL I

The Parties to this Protocol,

Being Parties to the Framework Convention on International Taxation, hereinafter referred to as 'the Convention',

In pursuit of the ultimate objective of the Convention as stated in its Article 3 under the principles as stated in Article 4,

Recalling the provisions of the Convention,

Have agreed as follows:

Article 1. Terminology

1. 'Party' means, unless the context otherwise requires, a Party to this Protocol.
2. 'Convention' means the Framework Convention on International Taxation
3. 'Source state' means the state in which income arises under a permanent establishment, in which a corporate body paying dividends, interest or royalties is a resident, or from which capital gains derive.
   (...) etc.

Article 2. On preventing the granting of treaty benefits in inappropriate circumstances

1. Each Party, in achieving the objective of the Convention, agrees not to grant tax treaty benefits in respect of an item of income or capital, if it is reasonable

to conclude, having regard to all relevant facts and circumstances, that obtaining that benefit was one of the principal purposes of any arrangement or transaction that resulted directly or indirectly in that benefit, unless it is established that granting that benefit in these circumstances would be in accordance with the object and purpose of the relevant provisions of this Convention.

2. Parties who notify the secretariat of the Convention that they cannot agree on the rule set out in paragraph 1 of this Article as to a specific tax treaty relationship, may also opt for [**provisions that would deny treaty benefits to a resident of a Contracting state who is not a 'qualified person', as defined by this provision**] applicable in that relationship in which that Party acts in the capacity as a source state.

3. In applying paragraphs 1 and 2 of this article on a specific bilateral relationship between two Parties, the rule that a Party has selected acting in its capacity as a source state, applies in that relationship.

Article 3. Non-discrimination

Each Party shall, by means of a domestic tax rule, treat an item of income, in respect of the taxation of a resident of that Party, no less favourable or more burdensome than an item of income of a corporate body that is not a resident of that Party, having regard to all relevant factual circumstances as well as to the suitability, degree of fit, subsidiarity and proportionality of the tax rule in light of its respectful aim.

Article 4. (...) etc.

(...) etc.
[and other commitments in further articles].

Article 5. Amendments to the Protocol

1. Any Party may make proposals for amendments to this Protocol.

2. Amendments to this Protocol shall be adopted at an ordinary session of the Conference of the Parties serving as the meeting of the Parties to this Protocol. The text of any proposed amendment shall be communicated to the Parties by the secretariat at least six months before the meeting at which it is proposed for adoption. The secretariat shall also communicate the text of any proposed annex or amendment to an annex to the Parties and signatories to the Convention and, for information, to the Depositary.

3. The Parties shall make every effort to reach agreement on any proposed amendment to this Protocol by consensus. If all efforts at consensus have been exhausted, and no agreement reached, the amendment to this Protocol shall as a last resort be adopted by a three-fourths majority vote of the Parties present

and voting at the meeting. The adopted amendment to this Protocol shall be communicated by the secretariat to the Depositary, who shall circulate it to all Parties for their acceptance.

4. Any amendment to one of the articles [XY: articles on technicalities and/or 'managerial' issues, if proven feasible, e.g., certain aspects of transfer pricing rules, attribution of profits to PEs, administrative measures, etc.], adopted in accordance with paragraphs 3 and 4 above, shall enter into force for all Parties to this Protocol six months after the date of the communication by the Depositary to such Parties of the adoption of the annex or adoption of the amendment to the Protocol, except for those Parties that have notified the Depositary, in writing, within that period of their non-acceptance of the amendment to this Protocol. The amendment to this Protocol shall enter into force for Parties which withdraw their notification of non-acceptance on the ninetieth day after the date on which withdrawal of such notification has been received by the Depositary.

5. Amendments to [**all other articles than those mentioned in paragraph 4**] to this Protocol shall be adopted and enter into force in accordance with the procedure set out in Article 9 of the Convention.

Article 6. Signature

This Convention shall be open for signature for all interested States.

Article 7. Ratification, acceptance, approval or accession

The Protocol shall be subject to ratification, acceptance, approval or accession by States and by regional economic integration organisations. It shall be open for accession from the day after the date on which the Protocol is closed for signature. Instruments of ratification, acceptance, approval or accession shall be deposited with the Depositary.

Article 8. Withdrawal

1. At any time after three years from the date on which the Protocol has entered into force for a Party, that Party may withdraw from the Protocol by giving written notification to the Depositary.

2. Any such withdrawal shall take effect upon expiry of one year from the date of receipt by the Depositary of the notification of withdrawal, or on such later date as may be specified in the notification of withdrawal.

3. Any Party that withdraws from the Protocol shall be considered as also having withdrawn from any protocol to which it is a Party.

Article 9. Entry into force

1. The Protocol shall enter into force on the ninetieth day after the date of deposit of the tenth instrument of ratification, acceptance, approval or accession.
2. For each State that ratifies, accepts or approves the Protocol or accedes thereto after the deposit of the twentieth instrument of ratification, acceptance, approval or accession, the Protocol shall enter into force on the ninetieth day after the date of deposit by such State of its instrument of ratification, acceptance, approval or accession.

Article 10. Authentic texts

The original of this Protocol, of which the Arabic, English, French, Chinese and Spanish texts are equally authentic, shall be deposited with the Secretary-General of the United Nations.

IN WITNESS WHEREOF the undersigned, being duly authorized to that effect, have signed this Convention.

DONE at XXY this ... day of .... of the year ....

B. THE 'AGREEMENT TO SCOPE'

The Framework Convention on International Taxation

The Parties to the present Convention,

Recognising that globalisation has impacted countries' income tax systems;

Recognising that the tax treaty network is outdated, as it is for instance unable to effectively address opportunities for multinational companies to greatly minimise their tax burdens and/or issues related to the increased relevance of the digital economy;

Desiring to conclude a multilateral agreement to swiftly implement or incorporate in their bilateral tax treaty relationships new developments in society, business and technology;

Recognising that this requires a fair level playing field that ensures that all countries and jurisdictions implement their commitments equally and on an equal footing;

Recognising that this requires continuous interaction in the future;

Have agreed as follows:

Article 1. Scope of the present Convention

The present Convention applies to tax treaties in force or to be concluded in relation to provisions that the Conference of the Parties may adopt.

Article 2. Terminology

For the purposes of the present Convention:

1. 'Tax treaty' means any agreement for the avoidance of double taxation and the prevention of fiscal evasion applicable in the relations between Signatory States or between Signatory States and third states.
   (etc.)

Article 3. Objective

The ultimate objective of this Convention and any related instruments that the Conference of the Parties may adopt is to achieve, in accordance with the relevant provisions of the Convention, that the international tax treaty network is modernised and updated in accordance with the latest developments in society, business and technology. In doing so, the Parties will promote an open and transparent negotiating environment in which they cooperate on an equal footing.

Article 4. Principles

As determined by the Conference of the Parties, in their actions to achieve the objective of this Convention and to implement its provisions, the Parties shall be guided, *inter alia*, by the following:
[Possible principles that the Conference of the Parties could adopt, could be for example:]

1. The Parties shall ensure that profits are taxed where value is created and economic activities take place.
2. The Parties shall endeavour to ensure that the domestic tax burdens on profits derived from cross-border business activities of corporate bodies equals the domestic tax burden on profits derived from non-cross-border business activities of corporate bodies, given that all other circumstances taxpayers are the same.
3. The Parties shall aim to prevent double non-taxation as well as double taxation. In seeking to achieve this aim, the Parties shall strike a fair balance between the need to eliminate obstacles to international trade on the one hand and preventing practices in which taxable income are artificially segregated from activities that generate it on the other hand.
4. The needs of designated developing countries in taxing corporate income at source shall be given full consideration.
5. In cooperating, the Parties will promote an open and transparent negotiating environment in which Parties cooperate on an equal footing, and which aims for the gradual increase of the amount of States Parties to this Convention.

Article 5. Development of international tax rules and exchange of information

1. The Parties shall undertake to develop and promote research and research programmes at the regional and international levels in the field of international taxation with the aim of pursuing the objective of this Convention. Toward this end, Parties shall:
   a. Initiate and cooperate, either directly or through international and regional international organisations such as the Organisation for Economic Co-operation and Development, the United Nations and the International Monetary Fund, the conduct of research and development of rules of international tax law research that are identified by the Conference of the Parties.
   b. Support and strengthen, with the support of competent international and regional international organisations such as the Organisation for Economic Co-operation and Development, the United Nations and International Monetary Fund, the training and support of tax officers or others engaged in government activities related to international tax law, including tax assessment, transfer pricing, tax treaty law and business accounting. The Parties shall promote and facilitate the exchange of available information on international tax law, including model tax conventions and tax laws, commentaries to the model tax conventions, and other legal and economic materials where appropriate.
2. The Parties shall make publicly available, after a reasonable period of time to be decided on by the Conference of the Parties, the records and minutes of the discussions regarding the development of model tax laws, model tax treaties and commentaries thereon, as these may be amended from time to time.

Article 6. Conference of the Parties

1. A Conference of the Parties is hereby established.
2. The first session of the Conference of the Parties shall be convened by the Organisation for Economic Co-operation and Development no later than one year after the entry into force of this Convention. The Conference will determine the venue and timing of subsequent regular sessions at its first session.
3. Extraordinary sessions of the Conference of the Parties shall be held at such other times as may be deemed necessary by the Conference, or at the written request of any Party, provided that, within six months of the request being communicated to them by the Secretariat of the Convention, it is supported by at least one third of the Parties.
4. The Conference of the Parties shall adopt by consensus its rules of procedure at its first session.

5. The Conference of the Parties shall by consensus adopt financial rules for itself as well as governing the funding of any subsidiary bodies it may establish as well as financial provisions governing the functioning of the Secretariat. At each ordinary session, it shall adopt a budget for the financial period until the next ordinary session.

6. The Conference of the Parties shall keep under regular review the operation of the Convention. To achieve the objective of the Convention, it may adopt protocols and amendments to the Convention, in accordance with Article 9. Towards this end, it shall:
   a. promote and facilitate the exchange of information between Parties;
   b. promote, and adopt, as appropriate, the development and evaluation of rules, strategies, plans, policies, model treaties, commentaries to model treaties, model legislation and other measures;
   c. consider reports submitted by the Organisation for Economic Co-operation and Development, United Nations and International Monetary Fund in achieving the objective of the Convention;
   d. request, where appropriate, the services and cooperation of, and information provided by, the Organisation for Economic Co-operation and Development, the United Nations and International Monetary Fund and other international and regional intergovernmental organisations as a means of achieving the objective of this Convention;
   e. establish subsidiary bodies as are necessary to achieve the objective of the Convention;
   f. consider other action, as appropriate, for the achievement of the objective of the Convention in the light of experience gained in its operation.

7. The Conference of the Parties shall establish the criteria for the participation of observers at its proceedings.

Article 7. Secretariat

1. The Conference of the Parties shall designate a permanent secretariat and make arrangements for its functioning. The Conference of the Parties shall endeavour to do so at its first session.

2. Until such time as a permanent secretariat is designated and established, secretariat functions under this Convention shall be provided by the Organisation for Economic Co-operation and Development in the first year of this Convention's entry into force, and by the United Nations thereafter.

3. Secretariat functions shall be:
   h. to make arrangements for sessions of the Conference of the Parties and any subsidiary bodies and to provide them with services as required;
   i. to transmit reports received by it pursuant to the Convention;

j. to provide support to the Parties, particularly developing country Parties and Parties with economies in transition, on request, in the compilation and communication of information required;

k. to prepare reports on its activities under the Convention under the guidance of the Conference of the Parties and submit them to the Conference of the Parties;

l. to ensure, under the guidance of the Conference of the Parties, the necessary coordination with the competent international and regional intergovernmental organisations and other bodies;

m. to collect and transmit reports on the negotiation and implementation within the bilateral tax treaties of the Parties to the Convention of the principles set out in Article 3 and any other model treaty or rule that the Conference of the Parties may establish, so as to achieve the Objective of the present Convention as set out in Article 3

n. to enter, under the guidance of the Conference of the Parties, into such administrative or contractual arrangements as may be required for the effective discharge of its functions; and

o. to perform other secretariat functions specified by the Convention and by any of its protocols and such other functions as may be determined by the Conference of the Parties.

Article 8. The relationship between this Convention and Tax Treaties

1. The Parties to this Convention agree to negotiate their current and future tax treaties with other Parties to this Convention on the principles set out in Article 3 of this Convention, and on any other principle, model treaty or other rule that the Conference of the Parties may establish at its ordinary sessions, so as to achieve the Objective of the present Convention, set out in Article 2.

2. In negotiating their current and future tax treaties with other Parties to this Convention in line with this Convention's objective, the Parties shall take into consideration the basic principles set out in Article 3 of the present Convention, taking into account the specific characteristics of their bilateral relationships.

3. Any Party to this Convention shall endeavour not to conclude arrangements with non-signatory states inconsistent with the provisions of the present Convention, as it is amended from time to time. To the extent that such tax agreements are not compatible with the obligations of the present Convention, Contracting States shall try to make the necessary steps to eliminate the incompatibilities established.

Article 9. Implementation and monitoring requirements

1. In their fulfilment of the requirements set out in Article 6 paragraphs 1 and 2 of this Convention, the Parties shall submit to the Secretariat a report on the efforts made at negotiation and implementation of the principles as set out in Article 3, or of provisions of model tax treaties or any other rule that the Conference of the Parties may establish at its ordinary sessions, in their bilateral tax treaties.
2. The frequency and format of such reports by all Parties shall be determined by the Conference of the Parties. Each Party shall make its initial report within one year of the entry into force of the Convention for that Party. At a minimum, Parties agree to submit such a report before each ordinary session of the Conference of the Parties.
3. Where appropriate, the Conference of the Parties may establish deadlines for the implementation in the bilateral tax treaties of Parties to this Convention, of a principle, model tax provision, or any other rule that it may adopt.
4. After each ordinary session of the Conference of the Parties, the Secretariat shall file a general report on the negotiation and implementation requirements set forth by this Article.

Article 10. Amendments to this Convention

1. Any Party may propose amendments to this Convention. Such amendments will be considered by the Conference of the Parties.
2. Amendments to the Convention shall be adopted by the Conference of the Parties. The text of any proposed amendment to the Convention shall be communicated to the Parties by the Secretariat at least six months before the session at which it is proposed for adoption. The Secretariat shall also communicate proposed amendments to the signatories of the Convention and, for information, to the Depositary.
3. The Parties shall make every effort to reach agreement by consensus on any proposed amendment to the Convention. If all efforts at consensus have been exhausted, and no agreement reached, the amendment shall as a last resort be adopted by a three-quarters majority vote of the Parties present and voting at the session. For purposes of this Article, Parties present and voting means Parties present and casting an affirmative or negative vote. Any adopted amendment shall be communicated by the Secretariat to the Depositary, who shall circulate it to all Parties for acceptance.
4. Instruments of acceptance in respect of an amendment shall be deposited with the Depositary. An amendment adopted in accordance with paragraph 3 of this Article shall enter into force for those Parties having accepted it on the ninetieth day after the date of receipt by the Depositary of an instrument of acceptance by at least two-thirds of the Parties to the Convention.

5. The amendment shall enter into force for any other Party on the ninetieth day after the date on which that Party deposits with the Depositary its instrument of acceptance of the said amendment.

Article 11. Right to vote

Each Party to the Convention shall have one vote.

Article 12. Settlement of disputes

1. In the event of a dispute between any two or more Parties concerning the interpretation or application of the Convention, the Parties concerned shall seek a settlement of the dispute through negotiation or any other peaceful means of their own choice, including good offices, mediation, or conciliation. Failure to reach agreement by good offices, mediation or conciliation shall not absolve Parties to the dispute from the responsibility of continuing to seek to resolve it.
2. When ratifying, accepting, approving or acceding to the Convention, or at any time thereafter, a Party may declare in a written instrument submitted to the Depositary that, in respect of any dispute concerning the interpretation or application of the Convention, it recognizes as compulsory ipso facto and without special agreement, in relation to any Party accepting the same obligation:
   a. submission of the dispute to the International Court of Justice; and/or
   b. arbitration in accordance with procedures to be adopted by the Conference of the Parties as soon as practicable, in a protocol on arbitration.

Article 13. Depositary

The Secretary-General of the United Nations shall be the Depositary of the Convention and of protocols adopted in accordance with Article 10.

Article 14. Signature

This Convention shall be open for signature for all interested States.

Article 15. Ratification, acceptance, approval or accession

The Convention shall be subject to ratification, acceptance, approval or accession by States and by regional economic integration organisations. It shall be open for accession from the day after the date on which the Convention is closed for signature. Instruments of ratification, acceptance, approval or accession shall be deposited with the Depositary.

Article 16. Withdrawal

1. At any time after three years from the date on which the Convention has entered into force for a Party, that Party may withdraw from the Convention by giving written notification to the Depositary.
2. Any such withdrawal shall take effect upon expiry of one year from the date of receipt by the Depositary of the notification of withdrawal, or on such later date as may be specified in the notification of withdrawal.

Article 17. Entry into force

1. The Convention shall enter into force on the ninetieth day after the date of deposit of the twentieth instrument of ratification, acceptance, approval or accession.
2. For each State that ratifies, accepts or approves the Convention or accedes thereto after the deposit of the twentieth instrument of ratification, acceptance, approval or accession, the Convention shall enter into force on the ninetieth day after the date of deposit by such State of its instrument of ratification, acceptance, approval or accession.

Article 18. Authentic texts

The original of this Convention, of which the Arabic, English, French, Chinese and Spanish texts are equally authentic, shall be deposited with the Secretary-General of the United Nations.

IN WITNESS WHEREOF the undersigned, being duly authorized to that effect, have signed this Convention.

DONE at XXY this ... day of .... of the year ....

Bibliography

Literature

Abbott, K.W. and Snidal, D. (1998): *Why States Act Through Formal International Organizations*, 42 The Journal of Conflict Resolution 3.

Abbott, K.W. and Snidal, D. (2000): *Hard and Soft Law in International Governance*, 54 International Organization 421–456.

Abbott, K.W. et al. (2000): *The Concept of Legalization*, 54 International Organization 401.

Adams, T.S. (1929): *International and Interstate Aspects of Double Taxation*, 22 National Tax Association Proceedings 193.

Adede, A.O. (1976): *Amendment Procedures for Conventions with Technical Annexes: The IMCO Experience*, 17 Virginia Journal of International Law 201.

Adler, E. (2013): *Constructivism in International Relations: Sources, Contributions, and Debates*, in: Handbook of International Relations (W. Carlsnaes, T. Risse and B. Simmons eds, SAGE 2nd ed.).

Altshuler, R. and Goodspeed, T.J. (2015): *Follow the Leader? Evidence on European and US Tax Competition*, 43 Public Finance Review 485.

Alvarez, J.E. (2005): *International Organizations as Law-Makers* (Oxford University Press).

Arnold, B.J. and van Weeghel, S. (2006): *The Relationship Between Tax Treaties and Domestic Anti-Abuse Measures*, in: Tax Treaties and Domestic Law (G. Maisto ed., IBFD).

Arnold, B.J., Sasseville, J. and Zolt, E.M. (2002): *Summary of the Proceedings of an Invitational Seminar on Tax Treaties in the 21st Century*, 56 Bulletin for International Taxation 233.

Auerbach, A. and Devereux, M.P. (2013): *Consumption and Cash-flow Taxes in an International Setting*, Oxford University Centre for Business Taxation WP 13/11.

Auerbach, A. and Devereux, M.P. (2015): *Cash Flow Taxes in an International Setting*, Said Business School RP 2015-3.

Ault, H.J. (1993): *The Role of the OECD Commentaries in the Interpretation of Tax Treaties*, in: Essays on International Taxation (H.H. Alpert and K. van Raad eds, Kluwer Law and Taxation).

Ault, H.J. (1994): *The Role of the OECD Commentaries in the Interpretation of Tax Treaties*, 22 Intertax 144.

Ault, H.J. (2008): *Reflections on the Role of the OECD in Developing International Tax Norms*, 34 Brooklyn Journal of International Law 757.

Ault, H.J. (2013): *Some Reflections on the OECD and the Sources of International Tax Principles*, 70 Tax Notes International 1195.

Aust, A. (2013): *Modern Treaty Law and Practice* (Cambridge University Press 3d ed.).

Avery Jones, J.F. (1999): *The David R. Tillinghast Lecture: Are Tax Treaties Necessary?*, 53 Tax Law Review 1.

Avery Jones, J.F. and Baker, P. (2006): *The Multiple Amendment of Bilateral Double Taxation Conventions*, 60 Bulletin for International Taxation 19.

Avi-Yonah, R.S. (2007): *International Tax as International Law: An Analysis of the International Tax Regime* (Cambridge University Press).

Avi-Yonah, R.S. and Benshalom, I. (2011): *Formulary Apportionment: Myths and Prospects*, 3 World Tax Journal 371.

Avi-Yonah, R.S. and Xu, H. (2016): *Global Taxation after the Crisis: Why BEPS and MAATM are Inadequate Responses, and What Can Be Done About It*, University of Michigan Public Law Research Paper No. 494, available at SSRN: http://papers.ssrn.com/sol3/papers.cfm?abstract_id = 2716124.

Axelrod, R. (1984): *The Evolution of Cooperation* (Basic Books Inc.).

Axelrod, R. and Keohane, R.O. (1985): *Achieving Cooperation under Anarchy: Strategies and Institutions*, 38 World Politics 226.

Baker, P. (2001): *Double Taxation Conventions, a Manual on the OECD Model Tax Convention on Income and on Capital* (Sweet and Maxwell 3d ed.).

Bammens, N. (2012): *The Principle of Non-Discrimination in International and European Tax Law* (IBFD).

Barkhuysen, T. and van Emmerik, M.L. (2010): *Ongebonden binding: Verwijzing naar soft law-standaarden in uitspraken van het EHRM*, 35 NJCM-Bulletin 827.

Barkin, S.J. (2015): *When Institutions Can Hurt You: Transparency, Domestic Politics, and International Cooperation*, 52 International Politics 349.

Beach, D. (2012): *Analyzing Foreign Policy* (Palgrave Macmillan).

Bearce, D.H., Eldredge, C.D. and Jolliff, B.J. (2015): *Do Finite Duration Provisions Reduce International Bargaining Delay?*, 69 International Organization 219.

Bender, T. and Engelen, F.A. (2016): *BEPS-Actie 6: De maatregelen tegen treaty shopping – bedreiging en kans*, WFR 2016/51.

Bernauer, T. (2013): *Climate Change Politics*, 16 The Annual Review of Political Science 421.

Beyerlin, U. (1976): *Pactum de contrahendo und pactum denegotiando im Völkerrecht?*, 36 Zeitschrift für ausländisches öffentliches Recht und Völkerrecht 407.

Birnie, P.W., Boyle, A.E. and Redgwell, C. (2009): *International Law and the Environment* (OUP).

Blum, G. (2008): *Bilateralism, Multilateralism, and the Architecture of International Law*, 49 Harvard International Law Journal 323.

Bodansky, D. (1993): *The United Nations Framework Convention on Climate Change: A Commentary*, 18 Yale Journal of International Law 451.

Bodansky, D. (1995): *The Emerging Climate Change Regime*, 20 Annual Review of Energy and the Environment 425.

Bodansky, D. (1999): *The Legitimacy of International Governance: A Coming Challenge for International Environmental Law?*, 93 The American Journal of International Law 596–624.

Bohman, J. (2005): *From Demos to Demoi: Democracy Across Borders*, 18 Ratio Juris 293.

Bohman, J. and Rehg, W. (2014): *Jürgen Habermas*, in: Stanford Encyclopedia of Philosophy (E.N. Zalta ed., Stanford University Fall 2014 ed.).

Borgen, C.J. (2005): *Resolving Treaty Conflicts*, 37 George Washington International Law Review 573.

Bosman, R.A. (2017a): *Formele aspecten van het multilaterale instrument*, MBB 2017/04.

Bosman, R.A. (2017b): *General Aspects of the Multilateral Instrument*, 45 Intertax (2017) 642.

Bothe, M. (2003): *The United Nations Framework Convention on Climate Change: An Unprecedented Multilevel Regulatory Challenge*, 63 Zeitschrift für ausländisches öffentliches Recht und Völkerrecht 239.

Bowman, M.J. (1995): *The Multilateral Treaty Amendment Process – A Case Study*, 44 International and Comparative Law Quarterly 540.

Boyle, A.E. (2010): *Soft Law in International Law-Making*, in: International Law (M.D. Evans ed., OUP 3d ed.).

Boyle, A.E. and Chinkin, C.M. (2007): *The Making of International Law* (OUP).

Boyle, A.E. and McCall Smith, K. (2013): *Transparency in International Law-Making*, in: Transparency in International Law (A. Bianchi and A. Peters eds, Cambridge University Press).

Bradley, C.A. and Kelley, J.G. (2008): *The Concept of International Delegation*, 71 Law and Contemporary Problems 1.

Braithwaite, J. and Drahos, P. (2000): *Global Business Regulation* (Cambridge University Press).

Brauner, Y. (2003): *An International Tax Regime in Crystallization*, 56 Tax Law Review 259.

Brauner, Y. (2014a): *BEPS: An Interim Evaluation*, 6 World Tax Journal 10.

Brauner, Y. (2014b): *What the BEPS*, 16 Florida Tax Review 55.

Brauner, Y. (2016): *Treaties in the Aftermath of BEPS*, University of Floriday Levin College of Law Research Paper Nos 16–18, available at SSRN: https://papers.ssrn.com/sol3/papers.cfm?abstract_id=2744712.

Bravo, N. (2016a): *The Multilateral Tax Instrument and Its Relationship with Tax Treaties*, 8 World Tax Journal.

Bravo, N. (2016b): *The Proposal for a Multilateral Tax Instrument for Updating Tax Treaties*, in: Base Erosion and Profit Shifting (M. Lang et al. eds, Linde Verlag).

Brennan, G. and Buchanan, J.M. (1985): *The Reason of Rules: Constitutional Political Economy*, in: The Collected Works of James M. Buchanan (Liberty Fund).

Brock, G. (2015): *Global Justice*, in: Stanford Encyclopedia of Philosophy (E.N. Zalta ed., Stanford University Spring 2015 ed.).

Broekhuijsen, D.M. (2013): *A Modern Understanding of Article 31(3)(c) of the Vienna Convention (1969): A New Haunt for the Commentaries to the OECD Model?*, 67 Bulletin for International Taxation September.

Broekhuijsen, D.M. (2013): *Naar een multilateraal fiscaal raamwerkverdrag*, WFR 2013/1443.

Broekhuijsen, D.M. (2013): *Verschillen tussen wets- en verdragsinterpretatie*, in: Kwaliteit van belastingrechtspraak belicht (J.P. Boer ed., SDU).

Broekhuijsen, D.M. and Van der Velde, K.M. (2015): *The Retroactive Effects of Changes to the Commentaries on the OECD Model*, 69 Bulletin for International Taxation 623.

Broekhuijsen, D.M. and Vording, H. (2016): *Multilaterale samenwerking ten aanzien van het BEPS-Project: een prognose*, WFR 2016/53.

Broekhuijsen, D.M. and Vording, H. (2016): *The Multilateral Tax Instrument: How to Avoid a Stalemate on Distributional Issues?*, British Tax Review 39 (2016).

Brooks, K. (2007): *Tax Treaty Treatment of Royalty Payments from Low-Income Countries: A Comparison of Canada and Australia's Policies*, 5 Journal of Tax Research 169.

Brooks, K. (2009): *Inter-nation Equity: The Development of an Important but Underappreciated International Tax Policy Objective*, in: Tax Reform in the 21st Century: A Volume in Memory of Richard Musgrave (J.G. Head and R. Krever eds, Kluwer Law International).

Brooks, K. (2010): *The Potential of Multilateral Tax Treaties*, in: Tax Treaties: Building Bridges between Law and Economics (M. Lang et al. eds, IBFD).

Brunnée, J. (2002): *COPing with Consent: Law-Making Under Multilateral Environmental Agreements*, 15 Leiden Journal of International Law 1.

Brunnée, J. (2005): *Reweaving the Fabric of International Law? Patterns of Consent in Environmental Framework Agreements*, in: Developments of International Law in Treaty Making (R. Wolfrum and V. Röben eds, Springer).

Brunnée, J. (2007): *Compliance Control*, in: Making Treaties Work: Human Rights, Environment and Arms Control (G. Ulfstein ed., Cambridge University Press).

Brunnée, J. (2012): *Treaty Amendments*, in: The Oxford Guide to Treaties (D.B. Hollis ed., OUP).

Brunnée, J. and Toope, S.J. (1997): *Environmental Security and Freshwater Resources: Ecosystem Regime Building*, 91 American Journal of International Law 26.

Brunnée, J. and Toope, S.J. (2002): *Persuasion and Enforcement: Explaining Compliance with International Law*, 13 Finnish Yearbook of International Law 273.

Brunnée, J. and Toope, S.J. (2010): *Legitimacy and Legality in International Law: An Interactional Account* (Cambridge University Press).

Brunnée, J. and Toope, S.J. (2011): *Interactional International Law: An Introduction*, 3 International Theory 307.

Buchanan, A. and Keohane, R.O. (2009): *The Legitimacy of Global Governance Institutions*, in: Legitimacy, Justice and Public International Law (L.H. Meyer ed., Cambridge University Press).

Bühler, O. (1964): *Prinzipien des internationalen Steuerrechts IStR: ein systematischer Versuch* (IBFD).

Carroll, M.B. (1968): *International Tax Law*, 2 The International Lawyer 692.

Carroll, M.B. (1939): *Prevention of International Double Taxation and Fiscal Evasion: Two Decades of Progress under the League of Nations* (League of Nations).

Chambers, W.B. (2003): *Towards an Improved Understanding of Legal Effectiveness of International Environmental Treaties*, 16 Georgetown International Environmental Law Review 501.

Charnovitz, S. (2006): *Nongovernmental Organizations and International Law*, 100 American Journal of International Law 348.

Chayes, A. and Chayes, A.H. (1995): *The New Sovereignty: Compliance with International Regulatory Agreements* (Harvard University Press).

Christians, A. (2009): *Sovereignty, Taxation and Social Contract*, 18 Minnesota Journal of International Law 99.

Christians, A. (2010a): *Networks, Norms, and National Tax Policy*, 9 Washington University Global Studies Law Review 1.

Christians, A. (2010b): *Taxation in a Time of Crisis: Policy Leadership from the OECD to the G20*, 5 Northwestern Journal of Law & Social Policy 19.

Christians, A. (2012a): *How Nations Share*, 87 Indiana Law Journal 1407.

Christians, A. (2012b): *Tax Activists and the Global Movement for Development through Transparency*, in: Tax Law and Development (M. Stewart and Y. Brauner eds, Edward Elgar Publishing, available at SSRN: http://ssrn.com/abstract = 19 29055).

Christians, A. et al. (2007): *Taxation as a Global Socio-Legal Phenomenon*, 14 ILSA Journal of International and Comparative Law 304, available at SSRN: http://papers.ssrn.com/sol3/papers.cfm?abstract_id = 1088455.

Churchill, R.R. and Ulfstein, G. (2000): *Autonomous Institutional Arrangements in Multilateral Environmental Agreements: A Little-Noticed Phenomenon in International Law*, 94 American Journal of International Law 623-659.

Comes, R. and Sandler, T. (1986): *The Theory of Externalities, Public Goods, and Club Goods* (Cambridge University Press).

Cottrell, M.P. and Trubek, D.M. (2012): *Law as Problem Solving: Standards, Networks, Experimentation, and Deliberation in Global Space*, 21 Transnational Law and Contemporary Problems 359.

Craven, M. (2000): *Legal Differentiation and the Concept of the Human Rights Treaty in International Law*, 11 European Journal of International Law 489.

Czaplinski, W. and Danilenko, G. (1990): *Conflicts of Norms in International Law*, 21 Netherlands Yearbook of International Law 3.

Dagan, T. (2000): *The Tax Treaties Myth*, 32 New York University Journal of International Law and Politics 939.

Dagan, T. (2015): *BRICS: Theoretical Framework and the Potential of Cooperation*, in: BRICS and the Emergence of International Tax Coordination (Y. Brauner and P. Pistone eds, IBFD).

Dagan, T. (2016): *Community Obligations in International Taxation*, Global Trust Working Paper Series 01/2016, available at SSRN: http://papers.ssrn.com/sol3/papers.cfm?abstract_id = 2736923.

de Goede, J.J.P. (2015): *The BRICS Countries in the Context of the Work on the UN Model*, in: BRICS and the Emergence of International Tax Coordination (Y. Brauner and P. Pistone eds, IBFD).

de Graaf, A.C.G.A.C., de Haan, P. and de Wilde, M.F. (2014): *Fundamental Change in Countries' Corporate Tax Framework Needed to Properly Address BEPS*, 42 Intertax 306.

de Wilde, M.F. (2015a): *'Sharing the Pie': Taxing Multinationals in a Global Market* (Erasmus University Rotterdam).

de Wilde, M.F. (2015b): *'Sharing the Pie': Taxing Multinationals in a Global Market*, 43 Intertax 438.

Devereux, M.P. and de la Feria, R. (2014): *Designing and Implementing a Destination-Based Corporate Tax*, Oxford University Centre for Business Taxation WP 14/07.

Devereux, M.P. and Vella, J. (2014): *Are We Heading Towards a Corporate Tax System Fit for the 21st Century?*, 35 Fiscal Studies 449.

Dharmapala, D. (2014): *What Do We Know About Base Erosion and Profit Shifting? A Review of the Empirical Literature*, 35 Fiscal Studies 421.

Dietsch, P. (2011): *Rethinking Sovereignty in International Fiscal Policy*, 37 Review of International Studies 2107.

Donaldson, M. and Kingsbury, B. (2013): *Power and the Public: The Nature and Effects of Formal Transparency Policies in Global Governance Institutions*, in: Transparency in International Law (A. Bianchi and A. Peters eds, Cambridge University Press).

Douma, S.C.W. (2011): *Optimization of Tax Sovereignty and Free Movement* (IBFD).

Douma, S.C.W. (2014): *Legal Research in International and EU Tax Law* (Kluwer).

Douma, S.C.W. and Engelen, F.A. eds, (2008): *The Legal Status of the OECD Commentaries* (IBFD).

Downs, G.W., Danish, K.W. and Barsoom, P.N. (2000): *The Transformational Model of International Regime Design: Triumph of Hope or Experience?*, 38 Columbia Journal of Transnational Law 465.

Downs, G.W., Rocke, D.M. and Barsoom, P.N. (1996): *Is the Good News About Compliance Good News About Cooperation?*, 50 International Organization 379.

Downs, G.W., Rocke, D.M. and Barsoom, P.N. (1998): *Managing the Evolution of Multilateralism*, 52 International Organization 397.

Dryzek, J.S., Norgaard, R.B. and Schlosberg, D. eds, (2011): *The Oxford Handbook of Climate Change and Society* (OUP).

Easson, A. (2000): *Do We Still Need Tax Treaties*, 54 Bulletin for International Taxation 619.

Edwards-Ker, M. (1994): *Tax Treaty Interpretation* (In-Depth).

Elkins, Z., Guzman, A.T. and Simmons, B. (2006): *Competing for Capital: The Diffusion of Bilateral Investment Treaties, 1960-2000*, 60 International Organization 811.

Engelen, F.A. (2004): *Interpretation of Tax Treaties under International Law: A Study of Articles 31, 32 and 33 of the Vienna Convention on the Law of Treaties and Their Application to Tax Treaties* (IBFD).

Engelen, F.A. (2008): *How Acquiescence and Estoppel Can Operate to the Effect that the States Parties to a Tax Treaty are Legally Bound to Interpret the Treaty in*

Accordance with the Commentaries on the OECD Model Tax Convention, in: The Legal Status of the OECD Commentaries (S. Douma and F.A. Engelen eds, IBFD).

Engelen, F.A. (2011): *Fiscaal Verdragsbeleid en het OESO-Modelverdrag*, WFR 2011/548.

Engelen, F.A. and Gunn, A.F. (2013): *Het BEPS-project: een inleiding*, WFR 2013/1413.

Essers, P. (2014): *International Tax Justice Between Machiavelli and Habermas*, 68 Bulletin for International Taxation 54.

Esty, D.C. (1998): *Non-governmental Organizations at the World Trade Organization: Cooperation, Competition, or Exclusion*, 1 Journal of International Economic Law 123.

Fearon, J.D. (1998): *Bargaining, Enforcement, and International Cooperation*, 52 International Organization 269.

Finel, B. and Lord, K. (1999): *The Surprising Logic of Transparency*, 43 International Studies Quarterly 315.

Finnemore, M. (1996): *Constructing Norms of Humanitarian Intervention*, in: The Culture of National Security: Norms and Identity in World Politics (P.J. Katzenstein ed., Columbia University Press).

Finnemore, M. and Sikkink, K. (1998): *International Norm Dynamics and Political Change*, 52 International Organization 887.

Fitzmaurice, M. (2005): *Consent to Be Bound – Anything New under the Sun?*, 74 Nordic Journal of International Law 483.

Fitzmaurice, M. (2009): *Dynamic (Evolutive) Interpretation of Treaties: Part II*, 21 Hague Yearbook of International Law 3.

Fitzmaurice, M. (2009): *Dynamic Intermigration of Treaties*, 21 Hague Yearbook of International Law 101.

Franck, T.M. (1988): *Legitimacy in the International System*, 82 The American Journal of International Law 705.

Franck, T.M. (1990): *The Power of Legitimacy Among Nations* (OUP).

Franck, T.M. (1995): *Fairness in International Law and Institutions* (Clarendon Press).

French, D. (2006): *Treaty Interpretation and the Incorporation of Extraneous Legal Rules*, 55 International and Comparative Law Quarterly 281.

Frischmann, B. (2004): *A Dynamic Institutional Theory of International Law*, 51 Buffalo Law Review 679.

Fuest, C. et al. (2013): *Profit Shifting and 'Aggressive' Tax Planning by Multinational Firms: Issues and Options for Reform*, 5 World Tax Journal.

Fuller, L.L. (1964): *The Morality of Law* (Yale University Press).

Galbraith, J. (2013): *Treaty Options: Towards a Behavioral Understanding of Treaty Design*, 53 Virginia Journal of International Law 309.

García Antón, R. (2016): *The 21st Century Multilateralism on International Taxation: The Emperor's New Clothes?*, 8 World Tax Journal 147.

Gardiner, R. (2008): *Treaty Interpretation* (OUP paperback ed.).

Garrett, G. and Weingast, B. (1993): *Ideas, Interests, and Institutions: Constructing the EC's Internal Market*, in: Ideas and Foreign Policy (J. Goldstein and R. Keohane eds, Cornell University Press).

Gehring, T. (1990): *International Environmental Regimes: Dynamic Sectoral Legal Systems*, 1 Yearbook of International Environmental Law 35.

Gehring, T. (2008): *Treaty-Making and Treaty Evolution*, in: The Oxford Handbook of International Environmental Law (D. Bodansky, J. Brunnée and E. Hey eds, OUP).

Giegerich, T. (2010): *Multilateral Reservations to Treaties*, in: The Max Planck Encyclopedia of Public International Law (R. Wolfrum ed., OUP Online ed.).

Gilligan, M.J. (2004): *Is There a Broader-Deeper Trade-Off in International Multilateral Agreements?*, 58 International Organization 459.

Goldsmith, J.L. and Posner, E.A. (2003): *International Agreements: A Rational Choice Approach*, 44 Virginia Journal of International Law 113.

Goldsmith, J.L. and Posner, E.A. (2005): *The Limits of International Law* (OUP).

Goldstein, J. and Martin, L.L. (2000): *Legalization, Trade Liberalization, and Domestic Politics: A Cautionary Note*, 54 International Organization 603.

Goodman, D. (2011): *The 'Future of the IWC': Why the Initiative to Save the International Whaling Commission Failed*, 14 Journal of International Wildlife Law and Policy 63.

Goodman, R. and Jinks, D. (2004): *How to Influence States: Socialization and International Human Rights Law*, 54 Duke Law Journal 621.

Gordon, R.H. (1992): *Can Capital Income Taxes Survive in Open Economies?*, 47 The Journal of Finance 1159.

Graetz, M.J. (2001): *The David R. Tillinghast Lecture: Taxing International Income – Inadequate Principles, Outdated Concepts, and Unsatisfactory Policy*, 54 Tax Law Review 261.

Graetz, M.J. and O'Hear, M.M. (1997): *The 'Original Intent' of U.S. International Taxation*, 51 Duke Law Journal 1021.

Gribnau, H. (2008a): *Soevereiniteit en legitimiteit: Grenzen aan (fiscale regelgeving)* (SDU Uitgevers).

Gribnau, H. (2008b): *Soft Law and Taxation: EU and International Aspects*, 2 Legisprudence 67.

Gribnau, H. (2013a): *Belastingen als moreel fenomeen: vertrouwen en legitimiteit in de praktijk* (Boom fiscale uitgevers).

Gribnau, H. (2013b): *Equality, Legal Certainty and Tax Legislation in the Netherlands. Fundamental Legal Principles as Checks on Legislative Power: A Case Study*, 9 Utrecht Law Review 52.

Gribnau, H. (2015): *Tweehonderd jaar belastingwetenschap*, in: Tweehonderd jaar Rijksbelastingen (H. Vording ed., SDU).

Gribnau, H. and Lubbers, A.O. (2014): *The Temporal Effect of Dutch Tax Court Decisions*, in: The Effect of Judicial Decisions in Time (P. Popelier et al. eds, Intersentia).

Grinberg, I. (2016): *The New International Tax Diplomacy*, 104 Georgetown Law Journal 1137.

Guzman, A.T. (2002): *A Compliance-Based Theory of International Law*, 90 California Law Review 1823.

Guzman, A.T. (2008): *How International Law Works: A Rational Choice Theory* (OUP).

Guzman, A.T. (2012): *Against Consent*, 52 Virginia Journal of International Law 747.

Haas, E.B. (1990): *When Knowledge is Power: Three Models of Change in International Organizations* (University of California Press).

Haas, P.M. (1992): *Introduction: Epistemic Communities and International Policy Coordination*, 46 International Organization 1.

Haas, P.M. (2012): *Epistemic Communities*, in: The Oxford Handbook of International Environmental Law (D. Bodansky, J. Brunnée and E. Hey eds, OUP).

Haas, P.M. (2015): *Epistemic Communities, Constructivism, and International Environmental Politics* (Routledge).

Habermas, J. (1987): *The Theory of Communicative Action, Volume 2: Lifeworld and System: A Critique of Functionalist Reason* (Polity Press).

Habermas, J. (1996): *Between Facts and Norms: Contributions to a Discourse Theory of Law and Democracy* (W. Rehg trans. Polity).

Handl, G. (1990): *Environmental Security and Global Change: the Challenge to International Law*, 1 Yearbook of International Environmental Law 3.

Handl, G. (2004): *The IAEA Nuclear Safety Conventions: An Example of Successful 'Treaty Management'?*, 72 Nuclear Law Bulletin 7.

Happé, R.H. (2011): *Belastingethiek: een kwestie van fair share*, in: Belastingen en ethiek, geschriften van de Vereniging voor Belastingwetenschap no. 243 (Kluwer).

Happé, R.H. (2015): *Fiscale ethiek voor multinationals*, WFR 2015/938.

Harrison, J. (2011): *Making the Law of the Sea: A Study in the Development of International Law* (Cambridge University Press).

Hattingh, P.J. (2017): *The Multilateral Instrument from a Legal Perspective: What May Be the Challenges?* 71 Bulletin for International Taxation.

Held, D. (1995): *Democracy and the Global Order: From the Modern State to Cosmopolitan Governance* (Polity).

Helfer, L.R. (2003): *Constitutional Analogies in the International Legal System*, 37 Loyola of Los Angeles Law Review 193.

Helfer, L.R. (2006): *Not Fully Committed – Reservations, Risk, and Treaty Design Response*, 31 Yale Journal of International Law 367.

Helfer, L.R. (2012): *Flexibility in International Agreements*, in: Interdisciplinary Perspectives on International Law and International Relations (J.L. Dunoff and M.A. Pollack eds, Cambridge University Press).

Henkin, L. (1979): *How Nations Behave: Law and Foreign Policy* (Columbia University Press 2nd ed.).

Higgins, R. (1994): *Problems and Process: International Law and How We Use It* (OUP).

Hofstra, H.J. (1979): *Over belastingbeginselen*, WFR 1979/1212.

Horn, F. (1988): *Reservations and Interpretative Declarations to Multilateral Treaties* (Uppsala: Uppsala University, Swedish Institute of International Law).

Hurd, I. (2009): *Constructivism*, in: The Oxford Handbook of International Relations (C. Reus-Smit and D. Snidal eds, OUP).

Hutchison, C. (2006): *The Duty to Negotiate International Environmental Disputes in Good Faith*, 2 McGill International Journal of Sustainable Development Law and Policy 117.

ILC (1966): *Draft Articles on the Law of Treaties with Commentaries* (Yearbook of the International Law Commission, 1966, vol. II).

Innamorato, C. (2008): *Expeditious Amendments to Double Tax Treaties Based on the OECD Model*, 36 Intertax 98.

Jarvis, R. (1999): *Realism, Neoliberalism, and Cooperation: Understanding the Debate*, 24 International Security 42.

Jenks, C.W. (1953): *The Conflict of Law-Making Treaties*, 30 British Year Book of International Law 401.

Juda, L. (1977): *Imco and the Regulation of Ocean Pollution from Ships*, 26 International & Comparative Law Quarterly 558.

Jupille, J., Caporaso, J.A. and Checkel, J.T. (2003): *Integrating Institutions: Rationalism, Constructivism, and the Study of the European Union*, 36 Comparative Political Studies 7.

Kaikobad, K.H. (1984): *Some Observations on the Doctrine of Continuity and Finality of Boundaries*, 54 British Yearbook of International Law 119.

Kass, S.L. (1965): *Obligatory Negotiations in International Organizations*, 3 Canadian Yearbook of International Law 36.

Kaufman, N.H. (1998): *Fairness and the Taxation of International Income*, 29 Law and Policy in International Business 145.

Kelly, C.R. (2005): *Enmeshment as a Theory of Compliance*, 37 New York University Journal of International Law and Politics 303.

Kemmeren, E. (2011): *De rol van het OESO-Commentaar bij de uitleg van belastingverdragen en het Europese recht: Trias politica onder toenemende druk?*, in: Principieel belastingrecht: Liber Amicorum Richard Happé (H. Gribnau ed., Wolf Legal Publishers).

Keohane, R. (1982): *The Demand for International Regimes*, 36 International Organization 325.

Keohane, R., Moravcsik, A. and Slaughter, A. (2000): *Legalized Dispute Resolution: Interstate and Transnational*, 54 International Organization 457.

Keohane, R.O. (1984): *After Hegemony: Cooperation and Discord in the World Political Economy* (Princeton University Press).

Keohane, R.O. (1986): *Reciprocity in International Relations*, 40 International Organization 1.

Keohane, R.O. (2002): *International Relations and International Law: Two Optics*, in: Power and Governance in a Partially Globalized World (R.O. Keohane ed., Routledge).

Keohane, R.O. and Nye, J.S.J. (1989): *Power and Interdependence* (Longman 3d ed.).

Keohane, R.O. and Nye, J.S.J. (2002): *The Club Model of Multilateral Cooperation and Problems of Democratic Legitimacy*, in: Power and Governance in a Partially Globalized World (R.O. Keohane ed., Routledge).

Kirgis Jr, F. (1995): *Specialized Law-Making Processes*, in: United Nations Legal Order (O. Schachter and C. Joyner eds, Cambridge University Press).

Klabbers, J. (2009): *Treaty Conflict and the European Union* (Cambridge University Press).

Kleingeld, P. and Brown, E. (2014): *Cosmopolitanism*, in: Stanford Encyclopedia of Philosophy (E.N. Zalta ed., Stanford University Fall 2014 ed.).

Kobetsky, M. (2008): *The Case for Unitary Taxation of International Enterprises*, 62 Bulletin for International Taxation 201.

Kobetsky, M. (2011): *International Taxation of Permanent Establishments: Principles and Policy* (Cambridge University Press).

Koh, H.H. (1996): *Transnational Legal Process*, 75 Nebraska Law Review 181.

Koh, H.H. (1997): *Why Do Nations Obey International Law?*, 106 Yale Law Journal 2599.

Kolb, R. (2006): *Principles as Sources of International Law (With Special Reference to Good Faith)*, 53 Netherlands International Law Review 1.

Koremenos, B. (2001): *Loosening the Ties That Bind: A Learning Model of Agreement Flexibility*, 55 International Organization 289.

Koremenos, B. (2005): *Contracting Around International Uncertainty*, 99 American Political Science Review 549.

Koremenos, B. (2007): *If Only Half of International Agreements Have Dispute Resolution Provisions, Which Half Needs Explaining?*, 36 Journal of Legal Studies 189.

Koremenos, B. (2008): *When, What, and Why do States Choose to Delegate?*, 71 Law and Contemporary Problems 151.

Koremenos, B. (2016): *The Continent of International Law: Explaining Agreement Design* (Cambridge University Press).

Koskenniemi, M. (2005): *From Apology to Utopia: the Structure of International Legal Argument* (Cambridge University Press Reissued ed.).

Krasner, S.D. (1983): *Structural Causes and Regime Consequences: Regimes as Intervening Variables*, in: International Regimes (S.D. Krasner ed., Cornell University Press).

Krasner, S.D. (1991): *Global Communications and National Power: Life on the Pareto Frontier*, 43 World Politics 336.

Kratochwil, F.V. (1989): *Rules, Norms, and Decisions: On the Conditions of Practical and Legal Reasoning in International Relations and Domestic Affairs* (Cambridge University Press).

Kreveld, N.M.A. (2016): *Consultatie bij fiscale wetgeving* (SDU).

Lang, M. (2017): *Die Auslegung des mulitlateralen Instruments*, Steuer & Wirtschaft International 2017/11.

Lang, M. and Brugger, F. (2008): *The Role of the OECD Commentary in Tax Treaty Interpretation*, 23 Australian Tax Forum 95.

Lang, M. and Owens, J.P. (2014): *The Role of Tax Treaties in Facilitating Development and Protecting the Tax Base*, WU International Taxation Research Paper Series No. 2014-03, available at SSRN: http://ssrn.com/abstract=2398438.

Lang, M. ed., (1998): *Multilateral Tax Treaties: New Developments in International Tax Law* (Kluwer Law International).

Lang, M. et al. eds, (2012): *The Impact of the OECD and UN Model Conventions on Bilateral Tax Treaties* (Cambridge University Press).

Lefeber, R. (2000): *Creative Legal Engineering*, 13 Leiden Journal of International Law 1.

Liivoja, R. (2008): *The Scope of the Supremacy Clause of the United Nations Charter*, 57 International and Comparative Law Quarterly 583.

Linderfalk, U. (2007): *On the Interpretation of Treaties: the Modern International Law as Expressed in the 1969 Vienna Convention on the Law of Treaties* (Springer).

Linderfalk, U. (2008): *Doing the Right Thing for the Right Reason – Why Dynamic or Static Approaches Should be Taken in the Interpretation of Treaties*, 10 International Community Law Review 109.

Linderfalk, U. (2008): *Who are 'The Parties'? Article 31 Paragraph 3(c) of the 1969 Vienna Convention and the 'Principle of Systemic Integration' Revisited*, 55 Netherlands International Law Review 343.

Loibl, G. (2005): *Conferences of Parties and the Modification of Obligations: The Example of International Environmental Agreements*, in: Interrogating the Treaty: Essays in the Contemporary Law of Treaties (M. Craven and M. Fitzmaurice eds, Wolf Legal Publishers).

Loukota, H. (1998): *Multilateral Tax Treaty Versus Bilateral Tax Treaty Network*, in: Multilateral Tax Treaties (M. Lang ed., Kluwer Law International).

Luts, J. (2014): *Een 'multilateraal instrument' (BEPS actiepunt 15): Denkpistes en verhouding tot de Belgische interne rechtsorde*, Algemeen Fiscaal Tijdschrift 28.

MacDonald, R.S.J. (1987): *Fundamental Norms in Contemporary International Law*, 25 Canandian Yearbook of International Law 115.

MacGibbon, I.C. (1954): *The Scope of Acquiescence in International Law*, 31 British Year Book of International Law 143.

Maisto, G. (2005): *The Observations on the OECD Commentaries in the Interpretation of Tax Treaties*, in: A Tax Globalist, Essays in Honour of Maarten J. Ellis (H. Arendonk, F.A. Engelen and S. Jansen eds, IBFD).

Manzini, P. (2001): *The Priority of Pre-Existing Treaties of EC Member States Within the Framework of International Law*, 12 European Journal of International Law 781.

March, J.G. and Olsen, J.P. (1998): *The Institutional Dynamics of International Political Orders*, 52 International Organization 943.

Marcoux, C. (2009): *Institutional Flexibility in the Design of Multilateral Environmental Agreements*, 26 Conflict Management and Peace Science 209.

Marion, L. (1974): *La notion de 'pactum de contrahendo' dans la jurisprudence internationale*, 78 Revue General de Droit International Public 351.

Martin, L.L. (1992): *Interests, Power, and Multilateralism*, 46 International Organization 765.

Martin, L.L. (1999): *The Political Economy of International Cooperation*, in: Global Public Goods: International Cooperation in the 21st Century (I. Kaul, I. Grunberg and M.A. Stern eds, OUP).

Martin, P. (2011): *Interaction Between Tax Treaties and Domestic Law*, 65 Bulletin for International Taxation 205.

Matz-Lück, N. (2009): *Framework Conventions as a Regulatory Tool*, 1 Goettingen Journal of International Law 439.

Matz-Lück, N. (2010): *Conflict Clauses*, in: The Max Planck Encyclopedia of Public International Law (R. Wolfrum ed., OUP Online ed.).

Matz-Lück, N. (2010): *Conflicts Between Treaties*, in: The Max Planck Encyclopedia of Public International Law (R. Wolfrum ed., OUP Online ed.).

Matz-Lück, N. (2011): *Framework Agreements*, in: Max Planck Encyclopedia of Public International Law (R. Wolfrum ed., OUP).

McCaffrey, S.C. (2007): *The Law of International Watercourses* (OUP 2nd ed.).

McCall Smith, J. (2000): *The Politics of Dispute Settlement Design: Explaining Legalism in Regional Trade Pacts*, 54 International Organization 137.

McIntyre, O. and Mosedale, T. (1997): *The Precautionary Principle as a Norm of Customary International Law*, 9 Journal of Environmental Law 221.

McLachlan, C. (2005): *The Principle of Systemic Integration and Article 31 (3)(c) of the Vienna Convention*, 54 International and Comparative Law Quarterly 279.

Mégret, F. (2012): *International Law as Law*, in: The Cambridge Companion to International Law (J. Crawford and M. Koskenniemi eds, Cambridge University Press).

Miaja de la Muela, A. (1968): *Pacta de Contrahendo en Derecho Internacional Publico*, 21 Revista Española de Derecho Internacional 392.

Micheau, C. (2014): *State Aid, Subsidy and Tax Incentives under EU and WTO Law* (Wolters Kluwer Law & Business).

Miller, A. and Kirkpatrick, A. (2013): *The Use of Multilateral Instruments to Achieve the BEPS Action Plan Agenda*, British Tax Review 682 (2013).

Mitchell, R.B. (1997): *International Control of Nuclear Proliferation: Beyond Carrots and Sticks*, 5 The Nonproliferation Review 40.

Mitchell, R.B. (2005): *Flexibility, Compliance and Norm Development in the Climate Regime*, in: Implementing the Climate Regime: International Compliance (O.S. Stokke, J. Hovi and G. Ulfstein eds, Earthscan Press).

Moore, M. (2006): *Globalization and Democratization: Institutional Design for Global Institutions*, 37 Journal of Social Philosophy 21.

Morrow, J.D. (1994): *Modeling the Forms of International Cooperation: Distribution Versus Information*, 48 International Organization 387.

Mosquera Valderrama, I.J. (2015): *Legitimacy and the Making of International Tax Law: The Challenges of Multilateralism*, 7 World Tax Journal.

Mössner, J.M. (2010): *Klaus Vogel Lecture 2009 – Comments*, 64 Bulletin for International Taxation 16.

Mowbray, A. (2005): *The Creativity of the European Court of Human Rights*, 5 Human Rights Law Review 57.

Müller, D. (2011): *Article 21: Legal Effects of Reservations and of Objections to Reservations*, in: The Vienna Convention on the Law of Treaties: A Commentary (O. Corten and P. Klein eds, OUP).

Müller, H. (2004): *Arguing, Bargaining and All That: Communicative Action, Rationalist Theory and the Logic of Appropriateness in International Relations*, 10 European Journal of International Relations 395.

Murphy, L. and Nagel, T. (2002): *The Myth of Ownership: Taxes and Justice* (OUP).

Mus, J.B. (1998): *Conflicts Between Treaties in International Law*, 45 Netherlands International Law Review 208.

Musgrave, P.B. (2000): *Consumption Tax Proposals in an International Setting*, 54 Tax Law Review 77.

Musgrave, R.A. and Musgrave, P.B. (1972): *Inter-nation Equity*, in: Modern Fiscal Issues: Essays in Honor of Carl S. Shoup (R.M. Bird and J.G. Head eds, University of Toronto Press).

Nadelmann, E.A. (1990): *Global Prohibition Regimes: The Evolution of Norms in International Society*, 44 International Organization 479.

Nelson, L.D.M. (1995): *The New Deep Sea-Bed Mining Regime*, 10 International Journal of Marine and Coastal Law 189.

Nussbaum, M.C. (2006): *Frontiers of Justice* (Harvard University Press).

OECD (2014): *Introduction*, in: Model Tax Convention on Income and on Capital: Condensed Version.

Orakhelashvili, A. (2008): *The Interpretation of Acts and Rules in Public International Law* (Oxford University Press).

Orakhelashvili, A. (2011): *Article 30: Application of Successive Treaties Relating to the Same Subject Matter*, in: The Vienna Conventions on the Law of Treaties: A Commentary (O. Corten and P. Klein eds, OUP).

Owada, H. (2010): *Pactum de Contrahendo, Pactum de Negotiando*, in: Max Planck Encyclopedia of Public International Law (R. Wolfrum ed., OUP).

Oxman, B.H. (1991): *The Duty to Respect Generally Accepted International Standards*, 24 New York University Journal of International Law and Politics 109.

Palmer, G. (1992): *New Ways to Make International Environmental Law*, 86 American Journal of International Law 259.

Pan, E. (1997): *Authoritative Interpretation of Agreements: Developing More Responsive International Administrative Regimes*, 38 Harvard International Law Journal 503.

Parisi, F. and Sevcenko, C. (2003): *Treaty Reservations and the Economics of Article 21(1) of the Vienna Convention*, 21 Berkeley Journal of International Law 1.

Paterson, M. and Grubb, M. (1992): *The International Politics of Climate Change*, 68 International Affairs 293.

Paulus, A. and Leiss, J.R. (2012): *Article 103*, in: The Charter of the United Nations: A Commentary (B. Simma et al. eds, OUP 3d edn ed.).

Pauwelyn, J. (2003a): *Conflict of Norms in Public International Law: How WTO Law Relates to other Rules of International Law* (Cambridge University Press).

Pauwelyn, J. (2003b): *A Typology Of Multilateral Treaty Obligations: Are WTO Obligations Bilateral or Collective in Nature?*, 14 European Journal of International Law 907.

Payne, R.A. (2001): *Persuasion, Frames and Norm Construction*, 7 European Journal of International Relations 37.

Pellet, A. (2011): *Article 19: Formulation of Reservations*, in: The Vienna Convention on the Law of Treaties: A Commentary (O. Corten and P. Klein eds, OUP).

Pendergast, W.R. (1990): *Managing the Negotiation Agenda*, 6 Negotiation Journal 135.

Peters, C. (2014): *On the Legitimacy of International Tax Law* (IBFD).

Picciotto, S. (1992): *International Business Taxation: A Study in the Internationalization of Business Regulation* (Cambridge University Press Electronic ed.).

Pickering, A. (2014): *Why Negotiate Tax Treaties*, in: Papers on Selected Topics in Negotiation of Tax Treaties for Developing Countries (A. Trepelkov, H. Tonino and D. Halka eds, UN).

Pijl, H. (2006): *The OECD Commentary as a Source of International Law and the Role of the Judiciary*, 46 European Taxation 216.

Pijl, H. (2011): *Interpretation of Article 7 of the OECD Model, Permanent Establishment Financing and Other Dealings*, 65 Bulletin for International Taxation 294.

Pistone, P. (2010): *Tax Treaties with Developing Countries: A Plea for New Allocation Rules and a Combined Legal and Economic Approach*, in: Tax Treaties: Building Bridges between Law and Economics (M. Lang et al. eds, IBFD).

Pistone, P. (2013): *Geographical Boundaries of Tax Jurisdiction, Exclusive Allocation of Taxing Powers in Tax Treaties and Good Tax Governance in Relations with Developing Countries*, in: Tax, Law and Development (Y. Brauner and M. Stewart eds, Elgar Publishing).

Plant, G. (1990): *The Convention for the Suppression of Unlawful Acts Against the Safety of Maritime Navigation*, 39 International and Comparative Law Quarterly 27.

Pötgens, F.P.G. and Broekhuijsen, D.M. (2017): *Het multilaterale instrument met zijn vele bilaterale schakeringen*, WFR 2017/76.

Putnam, R.D. (1988): *Diplomacy and Domestic Politics: The Logic of Two-Level Games*, 42 International Organization 427.

R. García Antón (2017), *Untangling the Role of Reservations in the OECD Multilateral Instrument: The OECD Legal Hybrids*, 71 Bulletin for International Taxation 544.

Raustiala, K. (2000): *Sovereignty and Multilateralism*, 1 Chicago Journal of International Law 401.

Raustiala, K. (2002): *The Architecture of International Cooperation: Transgovernmental Networks and the Future of International Law*, 43 Virginia Journal of International Law 2.

Raustiala, K. and Slaughter, A. (2002): *International Law, International Relations and Compliance*, in: The Handbook of International Relations (T.R. Carlnaes, T. Risse and B. Simmons eds, Sage Publications).

Rawls, J. (1971): *A Theory of Justice* (Harvard University Press).

Reeve, R. (2007): *The Convention on International Trade in Endangered Species of Wild Fauna and Flora (CITES)*, in: Making Treaties Work: Human Rights, Environment and Arms Control (G. Ulfstein ed., Cambridge University Press).

Reimer, E. (1999): *Interpretation of Tax Treaties*, 39 European Taxation 458.

Rey Aneiros, A. (2011): *Spain, The European Union, and Canada: A New Phase in the Unstable Balance in the Northwest Atlantic Fisheries*, 42 Ocean Development & International Law 155.

Ring, D.M. (2000): *Prospects for a Multilateral Tax Treaty*, 26 Brooklyn Journal of International Law 1699.

Ring, D.M. (2007): *International Tax Relations: Theory and Implications*, 60 Tax Law Review 83.

Ring, D.M. (2008): *What's at Stake in the Sovereignty Debate: International Tax and the Nation-State*, 49 Virginia Journal of International Law 155.

Ring, D.M. (2009): *Democracy, Sovereignty and Tax Competition: The Role of Tax Sovereignty in Shaping Tax Cooperation*, 9 Florida Tax Review 555.

Ring, D.M. (2010): *Who is Making International Tax Policy? International Organizations as Power Players in a High Stakes World*, 33 Fordham International Law Journal 649.

Risse, T. (2000): *Let's Argue!: Communicative Action in World Politics*, 54 International Organization 1.

Risse, T. and Klein, M. (2010): *Deliberation in Negotiations*, 17 Journal of European Public Policy 708.

Rixen, T. (2010): *Bilateralism or Multilateralism? The Political Economy of Avoiding International Double Taxation*, 16 European Journal of International Relations 589.

Röben, V. (2010): *Conference (Meeting) of States Parties*, in: The Max Planck Encyclopedia of Public International Law (R. Wolfrum ed., OUP Online Edition ed.).

Rogoff, M.A. (1994): *The Obligation to Negotiate in International Law: Rules and Realities*, 16 Michigan Journal of International Law 141.

Rosenne, S. (1963): *Travaux Préparatoires*, 12 International & Comparative Law Quarterly 1378.

Rosenzweig, A.H. (2015): *Defining a Country's 'Fair Share' of Taxes*, 42 Florida State University Law Review 373.

Ruggie, J.G. (1992): *Multilateralism: The Anatomy of an Institution*, 46 International Organization 561.

Ruggie, J.G. (1998): *What Makes the World Hang Together? Neo-Utilitarianism and the Social Constructivist Challenge*, 52 International Organization 855.

Sadat-Akhavi, S.A. (2003): *Methods of Resolving Conflicts Between Treaties* (Martinus Nijhoff Publishers).

Samson, M. (2011): *High Hopes, Scant Resources: A Word of Scepticism About the Anti-Fragmentation Function of Article 31(3)(c) of the Vienna Convention on the Law of Treaties*, 24 Leiden Journal of International Law 701.

Sands, P. and Klein, P. (2009): *Bowett's Law of International Institutions* (Sweet & Maxwell sixth ed.).

Scharpf, F.W. (1999): *Governing in Europe: Effective and Democratic?* (OUP).

Schelling, T.C. (1980): *The Strategy of Conflict* (Harvard University Press New ed.).

Schermers, H.G. and Blokker, N.M. (2011): *International Institutional Law: Unity Within Diversity* (Martinus Nijhoff 5th rev edn. ed.).

Schiele, S. (2014): *Evolution of International Environmental Regimes* (Cambridge University Press).

Schiffman, H.S. (2008): *Marine Conservation Agreements: The Law and Policy of Reservations and Vetoes* (Martinus Nijhoff Publishers).

Schön, W. (2009): *International Tax Coordination for a Second-Best World (Part I)*, 1 World Tax Journal 67.

Schön, W. (2010a): *International Tax Coordination for a Second-Best World (Part II)*, 2 World Tax Journal 65.

Schön, W. (2010b): *International Tax Coordination for a Second-Best World (Part III)*, 2 World Tax Journal 227.

Schoueri, P. (2014): *Comparison of the OECD and ILADT Model Conventions*, 68 Bulletin for International Fiscal Documentation.

Sciso, E. (1987): *On Article 103 of the Charter of the United Nations in the Light of the Vienna Convention on the Law of Treaties*, 38 Österreichische Zeitschrift für Öffentliches Recht und Völkerrecht 161.

Sebenius, J.K. (1991): *Designing Negotiations Toward a New Regime: The Case of Global Warming*, 15 International Security 110.

Senden, H.C.K. (2011): *Interpretation of Fundamental Rights in a Multilevel Legal System* (Intersentia).

Setear, J.K. (1996): *An Iterative Perspective on Treaties: A Synthesis of International Relations Theory and International Law*, 37 Harvard International Law Journal 139.

Shi, L. (1998): *Successful Use of the Tacit Acceptance Procedure to Effectuate Progress in International Maritime Law*, 11 University of San Francisco Maritime Law Journal 299.

Sikkink, K. (1993): *The Power of Principled Ideas: Human Rights Policies in the United States and Western Europe*, in: Ideas and Foreign Policy (J. Goldstein and R. Keohane eds, Cornell University Press).

Simma, B. (1983): *Consent: Strains in the Treaty System*, in: The Structure and Process of International Law: Essays in Legal Philosophy, Doctrine and Theory (R.S.J. MacDonald and D.M. Johnston eds, Martinus Nijhoff).

Simma, B. (1995): *From Bilateralism to Community Interest in International Law*, in: Recueil des Cours: Collected Courses of The Hague Academy of International Law 1994 IV (Martinus Nijhoff).

Simma, B. and Kill, T. (2009): *Harmonizing Investment Protection and International Human Rights: First Steps Towards a Methodology?*, in: International Investment Law for the 21st Century: Essays in Honour of Christoph Schreuer (C. Binder et al. eds, OUP).

Simonelli, N.M. (2011): *Bargaining over International Multilateral Agreements: The Duration of Negotiations*, 37 International Interactions: Empirical and Theoretical Research in International Relations 147.

Sinclair, I. (1984): *The Vienna Convention on the Law of Treaties* (Manchester University Press 2nd ed.).

Sinclair, I. (1996): *Estoppel and Acquiescence*, in: Fifty Years of the International Court of Justice: Essays in Honour of Sir Robert Jennings (V. Lowe and R. Jennings eds, Cambridge University Press).

Slaughter, A. (2004): *A New World Order* (Princeton University Press).

Sondaal, H.H.M. (1986): *De Nederlandse Verdragspraktijk* (TMC Asser Instituut).

Spiliopoulou Åkermark, S. (1999): *Reservation Clauses in Treaties Concluded with the Council of Europe*, 48 International & Comparative Law Quarterly 479.

Stasavage, D. (2004): *Open-Door or Closed-Door? Transparency in Domestic and International Bargaining*, 58 International Organization 667.

Stein, A.A. (1990): *Why Nations Cooperate: Circumstance and Choice in International Relations* (Cornell University Press).

Sunstein, C.R. (1996): *Social Norms and Social Roles*, 96 Columbia Law Review 903.

Swaine, E.T. (2006): *Reserving*, 31 Yale Journal of International Law 306.

Széll, P. (1996): *Decision Making under Multilateral Environmental Agreements*, 26 Environmental Policy and Law 210.

Tams, C.J. (2007): *Enforcement*, in: Making Treaties Work: Human Rights, Environment and Arms Control (G. Ulfstein ed., Cambridge University Press).

Taylor, A.L. (1996): *An International Regulatory Strategy for Global Tobacco Control*, 21 Yale Journal of International Law 257.

Terra, B.J.M. and Wattel, P.J. (2005): *European Tax Law* (Kluwer 4th ed.).

Thakur, R. and Weiss, T.G. (2009): *Framing Global Governance, Five Gaps*, in: Thinking about Global Governance: Why People and Ideas Matter (T.G. Weiss ed., Routledge).

Thirlway, H. (1990): *The Law and Procedure of the International Court of Justice 1960–1989: Part One*, 60 British Yearbook of International Law 1.

Thompson, A. (2006): *Management under Anarchy: The International Politics of Climate Change*, 78 Climatic Change 7.

Thompson, A. (2010): *Rational Design in Motion: Uncertainty and Flexibility in the Global Climate Regime*, 16 European Journal of International Relations 269.

Thompson, A. and Verdier, D. (2014): *Multilateralism, Bilateralism, and Regime Design*, 58 International Studies Quarterly 15.

Thuronyi, V. (2000): *International Tax Cooperation and a Multilateral Treaty*, 26 Brooklyn Journal of International Law 1641.

Tomazela, R. (2015): *A Critical Evaluation of the OECD's BEPS Project*, 79 Tax Notes International 239.

Ulfstein, G. (2005): *Reweaving the Fabric of International Law? Patterns of Consent in Environmental Framework Agreements, Comment*, in: Developments of International Law in Treaty Making (R. Wolfrum and V. Röben eds, Springer).

Ulfstein, G. (2008): *Treaty Bodies*, in: The Oxford Handbook of International Environmental Law (D. Bodansky, J. Brunnée and E. Hey eds, OUP).

Ulfstein, G. (2012): *Treaty Bodies and Regimes*, in: The Oxford Guide to Treaties (D.B. Hollis ed., OUP).

UN (1964): *Yearbook of the International Law Commission 1964: Summary Records of the Sixteenth Session*.

UN Climate Change Secretariat (2006): *United Nations Framework Convention on Climate Change: Handbook* (UNFCCC).

van Brunschot, F. (2005): *The Judiciary and the OECD Model Tax Convention and its Commentaries*, 59 Bulletin for International Fiscal Documentation 5.

Van Damme, I. (2009): *Treaty Interpretation by the WTO Appellate Body* (Oxford University Press).

van den Tempel, A.J. (1967): *Relief from Double Taxation: A Comparison of the Work of the League of Nations and of the Organisation for Economic Cooperation and Development* (IBFD).

van der Bruggen, E. (2003): *Unless the Vienna Convention Otherwise Requires: Notes on the Relationship Between Article 3(2) of the OECD Model Tax Convention and Articles 31 and 32 of the Vienna Convention on the Law of Treaties*, 43 European Taxation 142.

van Raad, K. (1986): *Non-discrimination in International Tax Law* (Kluwer).

Vann, R.J. (1991): *A Model Tax Treaty for the Asian-Pacific Region? (Part I)*, 45 Bulletin for International Fiscal Documentation 99.

Vann, R.J. (2014): *Policy Forum: The Policy Underpinnings of the BEPS Project: Preserving the International Corporate Income Tax?*, 62 Canadian Tax Journal 433.

Verloren van Themaat, P. (1946): *Internationaal belastingrecht: Een studie naar aanleiding van literatuur en verdragen over de uitschakeling van dubbele belasting* (H.J. Paris Amsterdam).

Victor, D.G. (2003): *International Agreements and the Struggle to Tame Carbon*, in: Global Climate Change: The Science, Economics and Politics (J.M. Griffin ed., Edward Elgar).

Villiger, M.E. (2009): *Commentary on the 1969 Vienna Convention on the Law of Treaties* (Nijhoff).

Vleggeert, J. (2013): *Misbruik van belastingverdragen*, in: Kwaliteit van belastingrechtspraak belicht (J.P. Boer ed., SDU).

Vleggeert, J. (2016): *De implementatie van de BEPS-acties door Nederland: Kroonjuwelen versus 'aggressive tax planning indicators'*, WFR 2016/47.

Vogel, K. (1986): *Double Tax Treaties and Their Interpretation*, 4 International Tax and Business Lawyer 1.

Vogel, K. (2000): *The Influence of the OECD Commentaries on Treaty Interpretation*, 54 Bulletin for International Fiscal Documentation 612.

Vording, H. (2006): *Vooruitgang in de fiscale rechtswetenschap*, in: Vooruit met het recht (J.H. Nieuwenhuis and C.J.J.M. Stolker eds, Boom Juridische Uitgevers).

Vukas, B. (2011): *Treaties, Third-Party Effect*, in: The Max Planck Encyclopedia of Public International Law (R. Wolfrum ed., OUP Online ed.).

Wagenaar, L. (2015): *The Effect of the OECD Base Erosion and Profit Shifting Action Plan on Developing Countries*, 69 Bulletin for International Taxation 84.

Ward, D.A. (2007): *The Use of Foreign Court Decisions in Interpreting Tax Treaties*, in: Courts and Tax Treaty Law (G. Maisto ed., IBFD).

Ward, D.A. et al. (2005): *The Interpretation of Income Tax Treaties with Particular Reference to the Commentaries on the OECD Model* (International Fiscal Association).

Waters, M. (2005): *The Relevance of the OECD Commentaries in the Interpretation of Tax Treaties*, in: Praxis des Internationalen Steuerrechts, Festschrift für Helmut Loukota zum 65. Geburtstag (M. Lang and H. Jirousek eds, Linde Verlag Wien).

Webb, M. (2004): *Defining the Boundaries of Legitimate State Practice: Norms, Transnational Actors and the OECD's Project on Harmful Tax Competition*, 11 Review of International Political Economy 787.

Wendt, A. (1999): *Social Theory of International Politics* (Cambridge University Press).

West, C. (2017): *References to the OECD Commentaries in Tax Treaties: A Steady March from 'Soft' Law to 'Hard' Law?*, 9 World Tax Journal 117.

Wiersema, A. (2009): *The New International Law-Makers? Conferences of the Parties to Multilateral Environmental Agreements*, 31 Michigan Journal of International Law 231.

Wohlforth, W.C. (2009): *Realism*, in: The Oxford Handbook of International Relations (C. Reus-Smit and D. Snidal eds, OUP).

Wolfrum, R. (2011): *Obligation of Result Versus Obligation of Conduct: Some Thoughts About the Implementation of International Obligations*, in: Looking to the Future: Essays on International Law in Honor of W. Michael Reisman (M.H. Arsanjani et al. eds, Martinus Nijhoff Publishers).

Wolfrum, R. and Matz-Lück, N. (2003): *Conflicts in International Environmental Law* (Springer).

Young, O.R. (1989): *The Politics of International Regime Formation: Managing Natural Resources and the Environment*, 43 International Organization 349–375.

Young, O.R. (1991): *Political Leadership and Regime Formation: On the Development of Institutions in International Society*, 45 International Organization 281.

Young, O.R. (2011): *Effectiveness of International Environmental Regimes: Existing Knowledge, Cutting-Edge Themes, and Research Strategies*, 108 Proceedings of the National Academy of Sciences of the USA 19853.

Cases

DE: Bundesfinanzhof *Re Article 11(6) of the UK-Germany DTC – the 'Theatrical Producer' Case*, (1997) 1 ITLR 860; IR 51/96.

ECJ, *Commission v. Council*, 31 March 1971, C-33/70 (ERTA).

ECJ, *Commission v. Portugal*, 4 Juli 2000, C-62/98 and C-84/98.

ECJ, *Finanzamt Köln-Altstadt v. Schumacker*, 14 February 1995, C-279/93.

ECJ, *Opinion of Advocate General Kokott, Presidente del Consiglio dei ministri v. Regione Sardegna*, 7 February 2009, C-169/08.

ECtHR, *Al-Adsani v. United Kingdom*, no. 35763/97 (Judgment), 21 November 2001.

ECtHR, *Case of the National Union of Rail, Maritime and Transport Workers v. The United Kingdom*, no. 31045/10 (Judgment), 8 April 2014.

ECtHR, *Demir and Baykara v. Turkey*, no. 34503/97 (Judgment), 12 November 2008.

ECtHR, *Marckx v. Belgium*, no. 6833/74 (Judgment), 13 June 1979.

ECtHR, *Saadi v. The United Kingdom*, no. 13229/03 (Judgment), 29 January 2008.

ICJ, *Case Concerning the Land and Maritime Boundary Between Cameroon and Nigeria (Cameroon v. Nigeria)*, Preliminary Objections (Judgment), [1998] ICJ Reports 275.

ICJ, *Case Concerning the Temple of Preah Vihear (Cambodia v. Thailand)*, (Merits, Judgment of 15 June 1962), [1962] IJC Reports 3.

ICJ, *Case Concerning the Temple of Preah Vihear (Cambodia v. Thailand)*, (Separate Opinion of Sir Gerald Fitzmaurice, Judgment of 15 June 1962), [1962] IJC Reports 3.

ICJ, *Delimitation of the Maritime Boundary in the Gulf of Maine Area (Canada v. United States of America)*, (Judgment), [1984] IJC Reports 246.

ICJ, *Fisheries Case (United Kingdom v. Norway)*, (Judgment), [1951] ICJ Reports 116.

ICJ, *Gabčikovo-Nagymaros Project (Hungary v. Slovakia)*, (Judgment), [1997] IJC Reports 7.

ICJ, *Legal Consequences for States of the Continued Presence of South Africa in Namibia (South West Africa) Notwithstanding Security Council Resolution 276 (1970)*, (Advisory Opinion), [1971] IJC Reports 16.

ICJ, *North Sea Continental Shelf (Federal Republic of Germany v. Denmark; Federal Republic of Germany v. the Netherlands)*, (Judgment), [1969] IJC Reports 3.

PCIJ *Case Concerning the Jurisdiction of the International Commission of the River Oder (Order of 20 August 1929)*, PCIJ Rep, Series A, no. 16.

PCIJ, *Railway Traffic between Lithuania and Poland (Railway Sector Landwarów-Kaisiadorys) (Judgments, Orders and Advisory Opinions)*, PCIJ Rep Series A/B no. 42.

RIAA, *Claims Arising out of Decisions of the Mixed Graeco-German Arbitral Tribunal set up under Article 304 in Part X of the Treaty of Versailles (Greece v. The Federal Republic of Germany)*, 19 RIAA 27.

WTO Appellate Body *United States – Import Prohibition of Certain Shrimp and Shrimp Products*, Appelate Body Report, 1998 (WT/DS58/AB/R).

Treaties

1974 International Convention for the Safety of Life at Sea (adopted 1 November 1974), 1184 UNTS 2.

1979 Convention on Long-Range Transboundary Air Pollution (adopted 15 November 1979), 1302 UNTS 217.

1986 Convention on Early Notification of a Nuclear Accident (26 September 1986), 1457 UNTS 133.

Agreement for the Implementation of the Provisions of the United Nations Convention on the Law of the Sea of 10 December 1982 Relating to the Conservation and Management of Straddling Fish Stocks and Highly Migratory Fish Stocks (adopted 4 August 1995), 2167 UNTS 88.

Agreement on Extradition between the United States of America and the European Union (EU) (adopted 25 June 2003), OJ L 181, 19.7.2003, p. 27.

Articles of Agreement of the International Monetary Fund (22 July 1944 (as amended through 2008)), 2 UNTS 39.

Charter of the United Nations (adopted 26 June 1945), 1 UNTS XVI.

Constitution of the World Health Organization (adopted 22 July 1946), 14 UNTS 185.

Convention Concerning the International Administration of the Estates of Deceased Persons (adopted 2 October 1973), 11 ILM 1277, www.hcch.net.

Convention for the Suppression of Unlawful Acts against the Safety of Maritime Navigation (adopted 10 March 1988), 1678 UNTS 397.

Convention on Access to Information, Public Participation in Decision-Making and Access to Justice in Environmental Matters (adopted 25 June 1998), 2161 UNTS 447.

Convention on Future Multilateral Co-operation in Northwest Atlantic Fisheries (adopted 24 October 1978), 1135 UNTS 369.

Convention on International Civil Aviation (adopted 12 July 1944), 15 UNTS 295.

Convention on International Trade in Endangered Species of Wild Fauna and Flora (adopted 3 March 1973), 993 UNTS 243.

Declaration of Principles on Interim Self-Government Arrangements ('Oslo Agreement') (adopted 13 September 1993), 32 ILM 1525.

Draft Articles on Responsibility of States for Internationally Wrongful Acts with Commentaries (2001), UN Doc A/56/109, May 2011.

European Convention on the Suppression of Terrorism (adopted 27 January 1977), 113 UNTS 93.

Interim Agreement on Certain Measures with respect to the Limitation of Strategic Offensive Arms (26 May 1972), 94 UNTS 3.

International Convention for the Regulation of Whaling (adopted 2 December 1946), 161 UNTS 72.

International Convention for the Suppression of the Financing of Terrorism (adopted 9 December 1999), 2178 UNTS 197.

Joint Convention on the Safety of Spent Fuel Management and on the Safety of Radioactive Waste Management (adopted 5 September 1997), 2153 UNTS 357.

Kyoto Protocol to the United Nations Framework Convention on Climate Change (adopted 11 December 1997), 2303 UNTS 162.

Montreal Protocol on Substances that Deplete the Ozone Layer (adopted 16 September 1987), 1522 UNTS 3.

Multilateral Convention to Implement Tax Treaty Related Measures to Prevent Base Erosion and Profit Shifting, OECD, available at http://www.oecd.org/tax/treaties/multilateral-convention-to-implement-tax-treaty-related-measures-to-prevent-BEPS.pdf.

North American Free Trade Agreement (17 December 1992), 2 ILM 289, 605.

North Atlantic Treaty (adopted 4 April 1949), 34 UNTS 243.

OECD Council Recommendation (23 October 1997) C(97)195/FINAL, OECD.

Treaty Between the United States of America and The Union of Soviet Socialist Republics on the Limitation of Strategic Offensive Arms, Together With Agreed Statements and Common Understandings Regarding the Treaty (signed but not entered into force) (1979), S. Exec. Dox, Y, 96th Cong., 1st Session.

Treaty on Conventional Armed Forces in Europe (adopted 19 November 1990), 30 ILM 6.

UN Convention on the Law of the Non-Navigational Uses of International Watercourses (adopted 21 May 1997), 36 ILM 700.

United Nations Convention on the Law of the Sea (adopted 10 December 1982), 1833 UNTS 3.

United Nations Framework Convention on Climate Change (adopted 9 May 1992), 1771 UNTS 107.

Vienna Convention for the Protection of the Ozone Layer (adopted 22 March 1985), 1513 UNTS 324.

Vienna Convention on Diplomatic Relations (18 April 1961), 500 UNTS 95.

The Vienna Convention on the Law of Treaties (adopted 23 May 1969), 1155 UNTS 331.

WHO Framework Convention on Tobacco Control (adopted 21 May 2003), 2302 UNTS 166.

Other

Bodansky, D. (1999): *WHO Technical Briefing Series: The Framework Convention/ Protocol Approach* WHO/NCD/TFI/99.1.

CPB Netherlands for Economic Policy Analysis (2009): *The Economic Effects of EU-Reforms in Corporate Income Tax Systems: Study for the European Commission Directorate General for Taxation and Customs Union* TAXUD/2007/DE/324.

House of Commons (2002): *Foreign Overfishing: Its Impacts and Solutions. Conservation on the Nose and Tail of the Grand Banks and the Flemish Cap* Standing Committee on Fisheries and Oceans, Tenth Report, June 2002.

ILC (2006): *Fragmentation of International Law: Difficulties Arising From the Diversification and Expansion of International Law* Report of the Study Group of the International Law Commission.

IMF (2014): *Spillovers in International Corporate Taxation* IMF Policy Paper, 9 May 2014.

League of Nations (1927): *Double Taxation and Tax Evasion. Report Presented by the Committee of Technical Experts on Double Taxation and Tax Evasion* C. 216. M 85. 1927 II.

League of Nations (1928): *Double Taxation and Tax Evasion: Report by the General Meeting of Governmental Experts on Double Taxation and Fiscal Evasion* C.562.M.178. 1928 II.

League of Nations (1929): *Fiscal Committee: Report to the Council on the Work of the First Session of the Committee* C516.M.175.1929.II.

League of Nations (1930): *Fiscal Committee: Report to the Council on the Work of the Second Session of the Committee* C.340.M.140.1930.II.

League of Nations (1931): *Fiscal Committee: Report to the Council on the Work of the Third Session of the Committee* C.415.M.171.1931.II.A.

League of Nations (1933): *Fiscal Committee: Report to the Council on the Work of the Fourth Session of the Committee* C.399.M.204.1933.II.A.

League of Nations (1935): *Fiscal Committee: Report to the Council on the Fifth Session of the Committee* C.252.M.124.1935.II.A.

League of Nations (1946): *Fiscal Committee: London and Mexico Model Tax Conventions Commentary and Text* C.88.M.88.1946.II.A.

Lejour, A. (2013): *The Foreign Investment Effects of Tax Treaties* CPB Netherlands Bureau for Economic Policy Analysis: CPB Discussion Paper 265.

OECD (1963): *OECD, Report of the Fiscal Committee on the Draft Convention for the Avoidance of Double Taxation with respect to Taxes on Income and Capital Among the Member Countries of the O.E.C.D.* C(63) 87, Part I.

OECD (1999): *The Application of the OECD Model Tax Convention to Partnerships* OECD, Issues ini International Taxation no. 6.

OECD (2003): *Peer Review: An OECD Tool for Co-operation and Change* OECD Publishing, Paris. DOI: http://dx.doi.org/10.1787/9789264099210-en-fr.

OECD (2013): *Action Plan on Base Erosion and Profit Shifting* OECD Publishing, http://www.oecd.org/ctp/BEPSActionPlan.pdf.

OECD (2013): *International Regulatory Co-operation: Case Studies, Vol. 1: Chemicals, Consumer Products, Tax and Competition* OECD Publishing, http://dx.doi.org/1 0.1787/9789264200487-en.

OECD (2013): *Rules of Procedure of the Organisation.*

OECD (2014): *Developing a Multilateral Instrument to Modify Bilateral Tax Treaties* OECD/G20 Base Erosion and Profit Shifting Project, http://dx.doi.org/10.1787/ 9789264219250-en.

OECD (2015): *Action 15: A Mandate for the Development of a Multilateral Instrument on Tax Treaty Measures to Tackle BEPS* OECD/G20 Base Erosion and Profit Shifting Project, http://www.oecd.org/ctp/beps-action-15-mandate-for-develo pment-of-multilateral-instrument.pdf.

OECD (2015): *Developing a Multilateral Instrument to Modify Bilateral Tax Treaties, Action 15: 2015 Final Report* OECD/G20 Base Erosion and Profit Shifting Project, OECD Publishing, Paris. http://dx.doi.org/10.1787/9789264241688-en.

OECD (2015): *Limiting Base Erosion Involving Interest Deductions and Other Financial Payments, Action 4: 2015 Final Report* OECD/G20 Base Erosion and Profit Shifting Project, OECD Publishing, Paris. http://dx.doi.org/10.1787/9789264241176-en.

OECD (2015): *Neutralising the Effects of Hybrid Mismatch Arrangements, Action 2: Final Report* OECD/G20 Base Erosion and Profit Shifting Project, OECD Publishing, Paris. http://dx.doi.org/10.1787/9789264241138-en.

OECD (2015): *Preventing the Artificial Avoidance of Permanent Establishment Status: Action 7 2015 Final Report* OECD/G20 Base Erosion and Profit Shifting Project, OECD Publishing, Paris. http://dx.doi.org/10.1787/9789264241220-en.

OECD (2015): *Preventing the Granting of Treaty Benefits in Inappropriate Circumstances, Action 6: 2015 Final Report* OECD/G20 Base Erosion and Profit Shifting Project, OECD Publishing, Paris. http://dx.doi.org/10.1787/9789264241688-en.

OEEC (1958): *Report by the Fiscal Committee on its Activities* C(58) 118, Part I.

UN (2011): *The Guide to Practice on Reservations to Treaties* Report of the International Law Commission on the Work of its 63rd session, Official Records, 66th Session, Supplement no. 10, Addendum 1, UN Doc. A/66/10/Add.1.

UN General Assembly (2015): *Resolution adopted by the General Assembly on 27 July 2015: Addis Ababa Action Agenda of the Third International Conference on Financing for Development* UN A/RES/69/313.

WTO (2007): *World Trade Report 2007: Six Decades of Multilateral Trade Cooperation: What Have We Learnt?*, WTO Publications.

Index

SERIES ON INTERNATIONAL TAXATION

1. Alberto Xavier, *The Taxation of Foreign Investment in Brazil*, 1980 (ISBN 90-200-0582-0).
2. Hugh J. Ault & Albert J. Rädler, *The German Corporation Tax Law with 1980 Amendments*, 1981 (ISBN 90-200-0642-8).
3. Paul R. McDaniel & Hugh J. Ault, *Introduction to United States International Taxation*, 1981 (ISBN 90-6544-004-6).
4. Albert J. Rädler, *German Transfer Pricing/Prix de Transfer en Allemagne*, 1984 (ISBN 90-6544-143-3).
5. Paul R. McDaniel & Stanley S. Surrey, *International Aspects of Tax Expenditures: A Comparative Study*, 1985 (ISBN 90-654-4163-8).
6. Kees van Raad, *Nondiscrimination in International Tax Law*, 1986 (ISBN 90-6544-266-9).
7. Sijbren Cnossen (ed.), *Tax Coordination in the European Community*, 1987 (ISBN 90-6544-272-3).
8. Ben Terra, *Sales Taxation. The Case of Value Added Tax in the European Community*, 1989 (ISBN 90-6544-381-9).
9. Rutsel S.J. Martha, *The Jurisdiction to Tax in International Law: Theory and Practice of Legislative Fiscal Jurisdiction*, 1989 (ISBN 90-654-4416-5).
10. Paul R. McDaniel & Hugh J. Ault, *Introduction to United States International Taxation* (3rd revised edition), 1989 (ISBN 90-6544-423-8).
11. Manuel Pires, *International Juridicial Double Taxation of Income*, 1989 (ISBN 90-6544-426-2).
12. A.H.M. Daniels, *Issues in International Partnership Taxation*, 1991 (ISBN 90-654-4577-3).
13. Arvid A. Skaar, *Permanent Establishment: Erosion of a Tax Treaty Principle*, 1992 (ISBN 90-6544-594-3).
14. Cyrille David & Geerten M.M. Michielse (eds), *Tax Treatment of Financial Instruments*, 1996 (ISBN 90-654-4666-4).
15. Herbert H. Alpert & Kees van Raad (eds), *Essays on International Taxation*, 1993 (ISBN 90-654-4781-4).
16. Wolfgang Gassner, Michael Lang & Eduard Lechner (eds), *Tax Treaties and EC Law*, 1997 (ISBN 90-411-0680-4).
17. Glória Teixeira, *Taxing Corporate Profits in the EU*, 1997 (ISBN 90-411-0703-7).
18. Michael Lang et al. (eds), *Multilateral Tax Treaties*, 1998 (ISBN 90-411-0704-5).
19. Stef van Weeghel, *The Improper Use of Tax Treaties*, 1998 (ISBN 90-411-0737-1).
20. Klaus Vogel (ed.), *Interpretation of Tax Law and Treaties and Transfer Pricing in Japan and Germany*, 1998 (ISBN 90-411-9655-2).
21. Bertil Wiman (ed.), *International Studies in Taxation: Law and Economics; Liber Amicorum Leif Mutén*, 1999 (ISBN 90-411-9692-7).
22. Alfonso J. Martín Jiménez, *Towards Corporate Tax Harmonization in the European Community*, 1999 (ISBN 90-411-9690-0).

23. Ramon J. Jeffery, *The Impact of State Sovereignty on Global Trade and International Taxation*, 1999 (ISBN 90-411-9703-6).

24. A.J. Easson, *Taxation of Foreign Direct Investment*, 1999 (ISBN 90-411-9741-9).

25. Marjaana Helminen, *The Dividend Concept in International Tax Law: Dividend Payments Between Corporate Entities*, 1999 (ISBN 90-411-9765-6).

26. Paul Kirchhof, Moris Lehner, Kees van Raad, Arndt Raupach & Michael-Rodi (eds), *International and Comparative Taxation: Essays in Honour of Klaus Vogel*, 2002 (ISBN 90-411-9841-5).

27. Krister Andersson, Peter Melz & Christer Silfverberg (eds), *Liber Amicorum Sven-Olof Lodin*, 2001 (ISBN 90-411-9850-4).

28. Juan Martín Jovanovich, *Customs Valuation and Transfer Pricing: Is It Possible to Harmonize Customs and Tax Rules?*, Second Edition, 2018 (ISBN 978-90-411-6134-5).

29. Stefano Simontacchi, *Taxation of Capital Gains under the OECD Model Convention: With Special Regard to Immovable Property*, 2007 (ISBN 978-90-411-2549-1).

30. Michael Lang, Josef Schuch, & Claus Staringer (eds), *Tax Treaty Law and EC Law*, 2007 (ISBN 978-90-411-2629-0).

31. Duncan Bentley, *Taxpayers' Rights: Theory Origin and Implementation*, 2007 (ISBN 978-90-411-2650-4).

32. Sergio André Rocha, *Interpretation of Double Taxation Conventions: General Theory and Brazilian Perspective*, 2008 (ISBN 978-90-411-2822-5).

33. Robert F. van Brederode, *Systems of General Sales Taxation: Theory, Policy and Practice*, 2009 (ISBN 978-90-411-2832-4).

34. John G. Head & Richard Krever (eds), *Tax Reform in the 21st Century: A Volume in Memory of Richard Musgrave*, 2009 (ISBN 978-90-411-2829-4).

35. Jens Wittendorff, *Transfer Pricing and the Arm's Length Principle in International Tax Law*, 2010 (ISBN 978-90-411-3270-3).

36. Marjaana Helminen, *The International Tax Law Concept of Dividend*, Second Edition, 2017 (ISBN 978-90-411-8394-1).

37. Robert F. van Brederode (ed.), *Immovable Property under VAT: A Comparative Global Analysis*, 2011 (ISBN 978-90-411-3126-3).

38. Dennis Weber & Stef van Weeghel, *The 2010 OECD Updates: Model Tax Convention & Transfer Pricing Guidelines - A Critical Review*, 2011 (ISBN 978-90-411-3812-5).

39. Yariv Brauner & Martin James McMahon, Jr. (eds), *The Proper Tax Base: Structural Fairness from an International and Comparative Perspective— Essays in Honour of Paul McDaniel*, 2012 (ISBN 978-90-411-3286-4).

40. Robert F. van Brederode (ed.), *Science, Technology and Taxation*, 2012 (ISBN 978-90-411-3125-6).

41. Oskar Henkow, *The VAT/GST Treatment of Public Bodies*, 2013 (ISBN 978-90-411-4663-2).

42. Jean Schaffner, *How Fixed Is a Permanent Establishment?*, 2013 (ISBN 978-90-411-4662-5).

43. Miguel Correia, *Taxation of Corporate Groups*, 2013 (ISBN 978-90-411-4841-4).
44. Veronika Daurer, *Tax Treaties and Developing Countries*, 2014 (ISBN 978-90-411-4982-4).
45. Claire Micheau, *State Aid, Subsidy and Tax Incentives under EU and WTO Law*, 2014 (ISBN 978-90-411-4555-0).
46. Robert F. van Brederode & Richard Krever (eds), *Legal Interpretation of Tax Law*, 2014 (ISBN 978-90-411-4945-9).
47. Radhakishan Rawal, *Taxation of Cross-border Services*, 2014 (ISBN 978-90-411-4947-3).
48. João Dácio Rolim, *Proportionality and Fair Taxation*, 2014 (ISBN 978-90-411-5838-3).
49. Paulo Rosenblatt, *General Anti-avoidance Rules for Major Developing Countries*, 2015 (ISBN 978-90-411-5839-0).
50. Gaspar Lopes Dias V.S., *Tax Arbitrage through Cross-Border Financial Engineering*, 2015 (ISBN 978-90-411-5875-8).
51. Geerten M.M. Michielse & Victor Thuronyi (eds), *Tax Design Issues Worldwide*, 2015 (ISBN 978-90-411-5610-5).
52. Oktavia Weidmann, *Taxation of Derivatives*, 2015 (ISBN 978-90-411-5977-9).
53. Chris Evans, Richard Krever & Peter Mellor (eds), *Tax Simplification*, 2015 (ISBN 978-90-411-5976-2).
54. Reuven Avi-Yonah & Joel Slemrod (eds), *Taxation and Migration*, 2015 (ISBN 978-90-411-6136-9).
55. Alexander Bosman, *Other Income under Tax Treaties: An Analysis of Article 21 of the OECD Model Convention*, 2015 (ISBN 978-90-411-6610-4).
56. John Abrahamson, *International Taxation of Manufacturing and Distribution*, 2016 (ISBN 978-90-411-6664-7).
57. Frederik Boulogne, *Shortcomings in the EU Merger Directive*, 2016 (ISBN 978-90-411-6713-2).
58. Angelika Meindl-Ringler, *Beneficial Ownership in International Tax Law*, 2016 (ISBN 978-90-411-6833-7).
59. Andreas Waltrich, *Cross-Border Taxation of Permanent Establishments: An International Comparison*, 2016 (ISBN 978-90-411-6832-0).
60. Sergio André Rocha & Allison Christians (eds), *Tax Sovereignty in the BEPS Era*, 2017 (ISBN 978-90-411-6707-1).
61. Peter Antony Wilson, *BRICS and International Tax Law*, 2018 (ISBN 978-90-411-9435-0).
62. Louise Otis, Brigitte Alepin & Blanca Moreno-Dodson (eds), *Winning the Tax Wars: Tax Competition and Cooperation*, 2018 (ISBN 978-90-411-9460-2).
63. Marta Castelon, *International Taxation of Income from Services under Double Taxation Conventions: Development, Practice and Policy*, 2018 (ISBN 978-90-411-9594-4).
64. D.M. Broekhuijsen, *A Multilateral Tax Treaty: Designing an Instrument to Modernise International Tax Law*, 2018 (ISBN 978-90-411-9872-3).